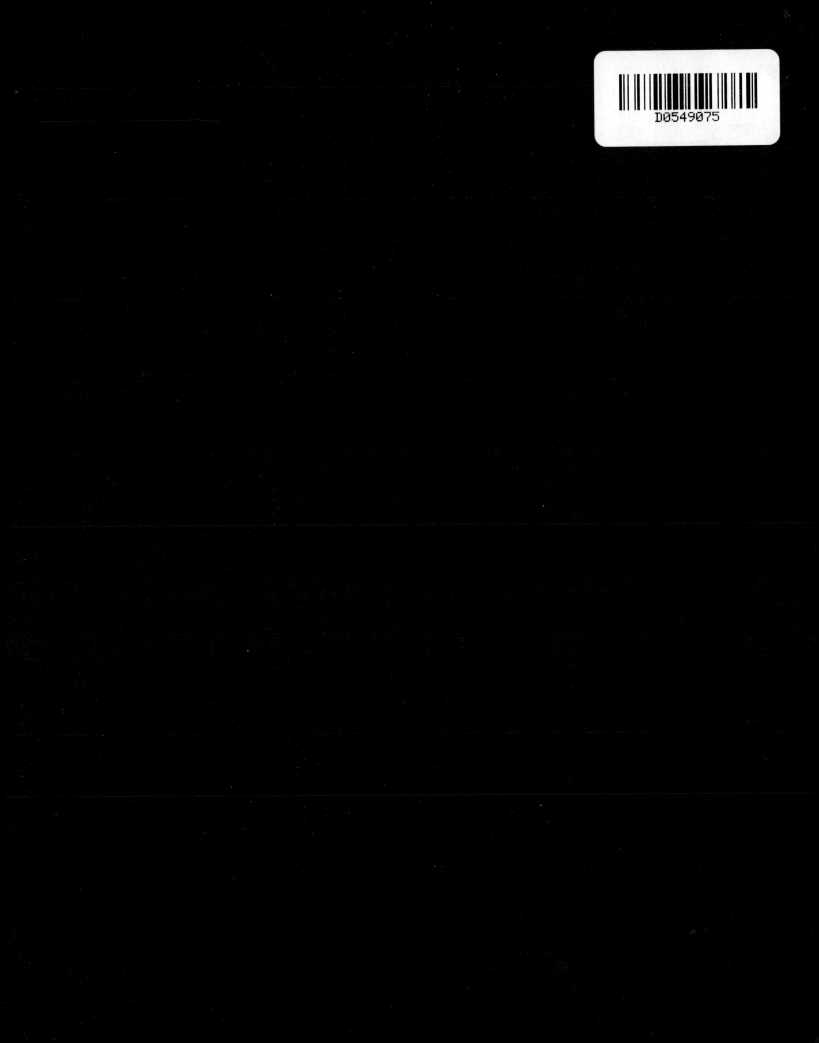

Cuisine Foundations

THE CHEFS OF LE CORDON BLEU

LE CORDON BLEU

Cuisine Foundations

THE CHEFS OF LE CORDON BLEU

DELMAR
CENGAGE Learning

Australia • Brazil • Japan • Korea • Mexico • Singapore • Spain • United Kingdom • United States

Le Cordon Bleu Cuisine Foundations
The Chefs of Le Cordon Bleu

Vice President, Career and
Professional Editorial: Dave Garza

Director of Learning Solutions:
Sandy Clark

Senior Acquisitions Editor: Jim Gish

Managing Editor: Larry Main

Product Manager: Nicole Calisi

Editorial Assistant: Sarah Timm

Vice President Marketing, Career and
Professional: Jennifer Baker

Marketing Director: Wendy Mapstone

Senior Marketing Manager:
Kristin McNary

Associate Marketing Manager:
Jonathan Sheehan

Production Director: Wendy Troeger

Senior Content Project Manager:
Glenn Castle

Senior Art Director:
Casey Kirchmayer

Technology Project Manager:
Chris Catalina

Production Technology Analyst:
Tom Stover

Principle Photography by J. Enrique
Chavarria

Supplemental Photography by Lois
Siegel, Lois Siegel Productions and
Randy Van Dam, ©2008.

For product information and technology assistance, contact us at
Cengage Learning Customer & Sales Support, 1-800-354-9706

For permission to use material from this text or product, submit all requests online at **www.cengage.com/permissions.**

Further permissions questions can be e-mailed to
permissionrequest@cengage.com

Library of Congress Control Number: 2010922489

ISBN-13: 978-1-4354-8137-4

ISBN-10:   1-4354-8137-2

Delmar
5 Maxwell Drive
Clifton Park, NY 12065-2919
USA

Cengage Learning is a leading provider of customized learning solutions with office locations around the globe, including Singapore, the United Kingdom, Australia, Mexico, Brazil, and Japan. Locate your local office at: international.cengage.com/region

Cengage Learning products are represented in Canada by Nelson Education, Ltd.

To learn more about Delmar, visit www.cengage.com/delmar

Purchase any of our products at your local college store or at our preferred online store www.ichapters.com

Notice to the Reader

Publisher does not warrant or guarantee any of the products described herein or perform any independent analysis in connection with any of the product information contained herein. Publisher does not assume, and expressly disclaims, any obligation to obtain and include information other than that provided to it by the manufacturer. The reader is expressly warned to consider and adopt all safety precautions that might be indicated by the activities described herein and to avoid all potential hazards. By following the instructions contained herein, the reader willingly assumes all risks in connection with such instructions. The publisher makes no representations or warranties of any kind, including but not limited to, the warranties of fitness for particular purpose or merchantability, nor are any such representations implied with respect to the material set forth herein, and the publisher takes no responsibility with respect to such material. The publisher shall not be liable for any special, consequential, or exemplary damages resulting, in whole or part, from the readers' use of, or reliance upon, this material.

Printed in the United States of America
2 3 4 5 6 7 X X X 14 13 12 11 10

CONTENTS

Foreword vii
Key Features viii

1. History and Evolution
of French Cuisine 2

2. A Life and Career in
the Kitchen 12

Discipline and the Kitchen Brigade 16
The Kitchen Brigade 20
Hygiene and Sanitation 29
Tools of the Trade 30
Personal Hygiene and Appearance 31
Safe and Hygienic Work Habits 32
Advice on Equipment 33
General Safety Precautions 33
Preparing Your Work Area 34
Menu 36

3. Techniques and Basic
Preparations 38

Classic Vegetable Cuts—Coupe
de Légume Classique 40
Vegetables and Fruits 78
Vegetables 79
Pears and Apples 173

Citrus Fruits 175
Grapes and Berries 182
Melon 187
Stone Fruits 189
Herbs and Spices 194
Exotic Spices and Spice Blends 213
Les Fonds—Basic Stocks 215
Les Sauces—Basic Sauces 222
Eggs 241
Fish and Shellfish 254
Meats 304
Offal 320
Game—Gibier 328
Poultry—Volaille 331
Basic Mixed Preparations—
Les Farces 346
Dairy 355
Basic Doughs—Les Pâtes de Base 364
Les Biscuits—Basic Mixtures 399
Crèmes, Meringues, and Other
Finishings 404

4. Classic Cooking Methods 418

Introduction 420
Les Cuissons 420
The Categories 421
The Seven Classic Cooking Methods 423
Additional Cooking Terms 439
Finishing Techniques 441

5. Technical Fabrication
Sheets for Classic French
Preparations 442

Fonds—Stocks 444

Fonds blanc de volaille—
White Stock (Chicken) 446
Fonds brun de veau—
Brown Stock (Veal) 448
Fumet de poisson—Fish Stock 450
Liaisons—Thickeners 452

Beurre manié 454
Roux 455
Jaunes d'oeufs—Egg Yolks 457
Sauces de base—Basic sauces 458

Mayonnaise and Derivatives 460
Sauce nantaise—Nantaise Sauce 462
Sauce hollandaise 464
Sauce béarnaise 466
Sauce béchamel—Béchamel Sauce 468
Sauce mornay—Mornay Sauce 470
Sauce velouté and Derivatives—
Velouté Sauce 471
Sauce tomate—Tomato Sauce 473
Fondue de Tomate 475
Préparations de base—
Basic preparations 476

Farce à Gratin 478
Farce Simple—Simple Stuffing 480
Farce Mousseline—Fish Mousse 482
Légumes glacés—Glazed Vegetables 483
Riz créole—Creole Rice 485
Riz pilaf—Rice Pilaf 486
La pâtisserie—
kitchen doughs and mixtures 488

Pâte à pâte—Pasta Dough 490
Pâte brisée 491
Pâte feuilletée—Puff Pastry 492
Pâte sucrée—Sweet Dough 494
Pâte sablée 495
Biscuit cuillère—Ladyfinger biscuit 496
Biscuit Dacquoise 498
Biscuit Génoise 499
Les préparations de base
de la pâtisserie—
Basic pastry preparations 500

Crème Anglaise—Custard 502
Crème d'Amandes—Almond Cream 503
Crème Pâtissière—Pastry Cream 504

Conversion Charts 506

Glossary 508

Index 515

FOREWORD

I am proud to present *Le Cordon Bleu's Cuisine Foundations*—a project that was two years in the making. We hope that this book will provide a useful reference as you explore the world of cooking and that it will also serve you well as you embark on your own journey, both personally and professionally. At first glance you might think that this is just "another culinary textbook," but on closer examination you will realize that the focus is on technique. To demonstrate those techniques, we have provided visual step-by-step photographs for most of them. We took our cue from the many students and graduates around the world who were looking for a single reference that would explain and show the techniques that have existed and been respected for more than three centuries. With human ingenuity came progress in the kitchen, but the techniques have remained practically unchanged. The tools have changed from wood-burning stoves to induction ovens to the "anti-griddle," and though they certainly influenced the evolution of cooking, they have not replaced the tried-and-true techniques.

What we wanted to do was reset the counter and refresh everyone's history and knowledge of these techniques before they are lost to us. For this reason, we chose to use the recipes that were created throughout the history of French cuisine that best exemplify the application of these techniques, and if you look at the integrity of each recipe, you will recognize the origins of these recipes on today's menus—all around the globe.

We also wanted to pay homage to the generations of chefs who have upheld and passed on their passion for cooking to each succeeding generation, from Taillevent, who as an apprentice probably stood before hot flames, hand-turning a spit, to Ferran Adrià who has used modern technology to redefine gastronomy. These chefs represent the patrimony of *L'art culinaire*—the art of cooking.

Le Cordon Bleu has served its patrimony for more than a century through its chefs, who have chosen a very important calling—teaching. From the moment Le Cordon Bleu opened its kitchens in 1895 on the rue St.-Honoré in Paris, students of all nationalities and all walks of life have come to join us in continuing to respect what French culinary technique represents. It is not about the recipes, but about how you work in a kitchen, whether you are cooking for loved ones or paying customers.

Even with a worldwide network of schools and programs around the world, we can extend our classroom through books and other mediums. I hope you enjoy *Le Cordon Bleu's Cuisine Foundations*, not only as a guide and reference, but as an inspiration.

Amitiés gourmandes,
André J. Cointreau
President, Le Cordon Bleu International

KEY FEATURES

Key Features

Step-by-Step Procedural Photographs

This beautifully illustrated textbook contains more than 1,600 full-color photographs that illustrate proper technique in detail.

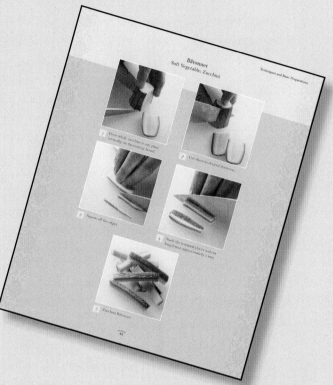

Basic Recipes

Les bases, or basic recipes, highlight the basic preparations of stocks, sauces, thickening agents, and pâtisserie that each aspiring chef must know and master before being able to complete any composed dish.

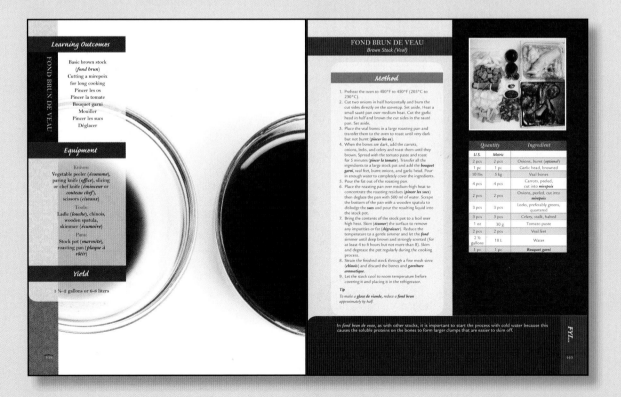

Recipe Photography

Every recipe in this book has been artfully photographed from start to finish. The mise en place planches show all of the ingredients needed to complete the recipe in the quantity called for.

The final shot shows the finished dish immediately after it was prepared by Le Cordon Bleu Chef Patrick Martin.

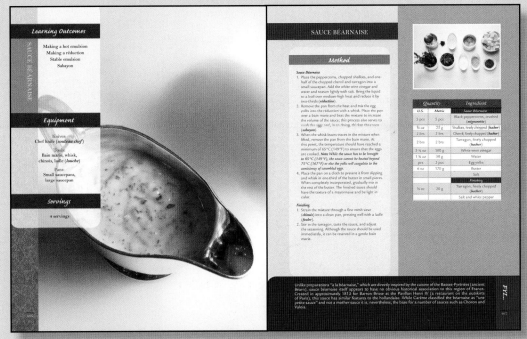

Vegetable Cuts

There are many classic methods of cutting vegetables. You will find vegetable planches throughout the Vegetables section of Chapter 3 that clearly show the various cuts that can be applied to the vegetable being shown. Each cut is labeled with its French name for easy identification.

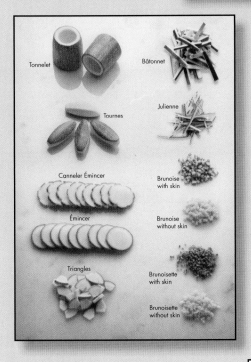

Did You Know?

Did You Know sidebars offer the reader fun and interesting facts on a variety of culinary topics.

Broccoli

Species name: *Brassica oleracea italica*

The cultivation of **broccoli** dates back to ancient Rome and it takes its name from the Latin word *brachium*, which means "branch" or "arm." Broccoli has dark or bright green florets with a compact head; the stem should be cleanly cut. Broccoli contains substances called *indoles*, which are attributed to have some cancer-fighting properties. Both the head and stalk of this plant may be eaten. The most commonly known and consumed broccoli is green, and is known in the United Kingdom as *Calabrese broccoli*.

Did you know?

Broccoli is a very good source of vitamins A and C; is rich in potassium, calcium, phosphorus, and folate; and contains some iron. A 1-cup (250-mL) serving of cooked broccoli contains about 45 kilocalories.

Sidebars and Notes

Sidebars and Notes throughout the text provide additional, valuable information on the topic being presented.

What's in a Word?

What's in a Word features describe in detail uncommon terms used in the book.

Culinary French 101

Culinary French 101 sidebars define commonly used French culinary terminology.

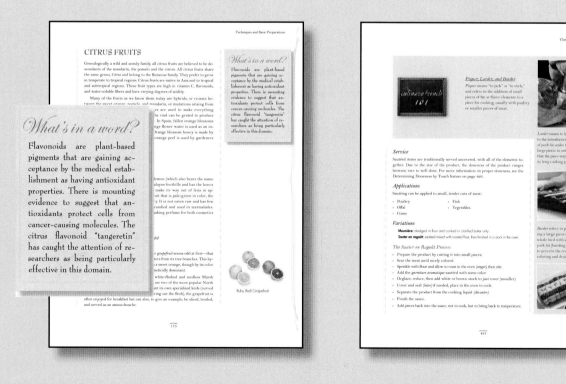

Conversion Charts

Conversion charts located at the end of the book provide a handy reference of all necessary culinary conversions.

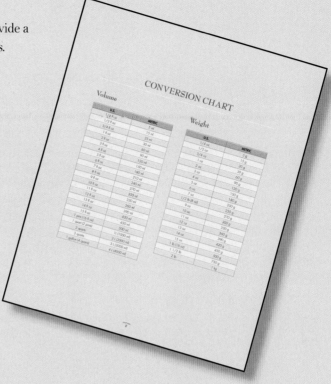

Le Cordon Bleu Classic Recipes

Available separately, *Le Cordon Bleu Classic Recipes* showcases more than 160 classic recipes whose preparation puts the techniques demonstrated to practical use.

ACKNOWLEDGMENTS

Le Cordon Bleu would like to thank the chefs and staff of the Le Cordon Bleu schools:

Le Cordon Bleu Paris, Le Cordon Bleu London, Le Cordon Bleu Ottawa, Le Cordon Bleu Madrid, Le Cordon Bleu Amsterdam, Le Cordon Bleu Japan, Le Cordon Bleu Inc., Le Cordon Bleu Australia, Le Cordon Bleu Peru, Le Cordon Bleu Korea, Le Cordon Bleu Lebanon, Le Cordon Bleu Mexico, Le Cordon Bleu Thailand

Le Cordon Bleu College of Culinary Arts in Atlanta, Le Cordon Bleu College of Culinary Arts in Austin, Le Cordon Bleu College of Culinary Arts Inc., A Private, Two-Year College in Boston, Le Cordon Bleu College of Culinary Arts in Chicago, Le Cordon Bleu College of Culinary Arts in Dallas, Le Cordon Bleu College of Culinary Arts in Las Vegas, Le Cordon Bleu College of Culinary Arts in Los Angeles, Le Cordon Bleu College of Culinary Arts in Miami, Le Cordon Bleu College of Culinary Arts in Minneapolis, Le Cordon Bleu College of Culinary Arts in Orlando, Le Cordon Bleu Institute of Culinary Arts in Pittsburgh, Le Cordon Bleu College of Culinary Arts in Portland, Le Cordon Bleu College of Culinary Arts in Sacramento, Le Cordon Bleu College of Culinary Arts in Saint Louis, California Culinary Academy, Le Cordon Bleu College of Culinary Arts in Scottsdale, Le Cordon Bleu College of Culinary Arts in Seattle.

Special acknowledgement to Chef Patrick Martin, Chef Arnaud Guerpillon, Chef Christian Leroy, Chef Jean-Marc Baqué, Chef Christian Faure, M.O.F., Chef Nicolas Rollet, Chef Hervé Chabert, Katharyn Shaw, Carrie Carter, Charles Gregory. Student assistants: Jing Hao Wong, Adam Goodman, Sylvie Dupuis.

Chapter 1

dark chocolate

CHOCOLAT NOIR

DESSUS

FARINE
BEURRE
JAUNES D'ŒUFS
SUCRE
EXTRAIT DE VANILLE

AMANDES GRILLÉES

ADIRAULT

METTEZ
MÉLANGER
BOUTS DE

PÂTE FEUILLETÉE

TAMISER
FARINE

ROULEAU DE PÂ
BROSSE
FOUET

PÂTON

Walking through the doors on your first day of culinary school can be exciting, but also a little scary. What will the chef-instructors be like? Will I be able to keep up? Although we call it "cooking school," people don't come to learn to cook. Almost everybody can cook to some degree, at least well enough to feed themselves, and some of the students might be people with many years of experience working in a professional kitchen. Cooking schools serve to help you improve and refine your skills, expose you to cooking in a professional setting, and most of all, provide you with the history and an understanding of where it all started.

There is a huge difference between learning a recipe and mastering a technique, and this book is all about technique. Whether you are preparing a French menu or family favorites, with good technique you can do it better, cleaner, and faster. Once you master the techniques, you can use them to make a broad range of preparations, but like the tools a chef uses in the kitchen, if you think that a paring knife is only used for paring, you limit your possibilities and your confidence.

The mention of French cuisine usually invokes images of rich foods covered by heavy sauces, but in reality and in practice, it represents a centuries-old tradition of respecting the ingredients in a dish and preparing them in a way that highlights their quality and flavor. This tradition and respect has been passed down from generation to generation where the sharing of a meal was a respite to be appreciated and savored at the end of a working day. French cuisine is not respected just for its dishes, but for the generations of chefs who have contributed to the recognition and codification of techniques that have become a common language in the kitchen. In France, this tradition was passed on from mothers to daughters, and from chefs to apprentices.

Until the past few decades, people often found themselves working in a kitchen not necessarily out of choice, but out of circumstance. Many of the great chefs are said to have been taken in off the streets to work in kitchens, where their passion and talent helped them rise to "star" status, even in the 18th and 19th centuries. In the 20th century, after completing their requisite public education, the choice for young people usually involved either university or vocational training. Young people apprenticed, learning on the job at a very young age. Unfortunately, this is all changing and the knowledge that was once passed on from the chef to young apprentices is beginning to disappear.

Chef Patrick Martin, the primary contributor to this book, is a product of the apprentice system, and the history and techniques that he learned as a young apprentice working in France he wholeheartedly shares with his students and the young chefs he meets through his travels. A majority of this knowledge was transmitted to him orally by the generation of chefs who still held the legacies of Georges-Auguste Escoffier, Felix Urbain Dubois, and Jules Gouffé fresh in their minds and hands. His chefs also recognized the passion and dedication he had for the art, so they also passed on old books from their own collections, that long preceded and inspired Escoffier's *Le Guide Culinaire*. With the new trends in cooking, Chef Martin passionately believes that without understanding the history

Chef Patrick Martin

and evolution of cooking, one cannot confidently adapt it to the various types of cooking around the world. Very early on in his career with Le Cordon Bleu, Chef Martin established a policy for the chefs invited to participate in festivals and galas around the world. They travel alone, sometimes in pairs, but with only their uniform and knives. So whatever might arrive in the kitchen, the chef must adapt the technique to the ingredient at hand. They work with the local brigade, always leading, always teaching, always mentoring. Chef Martin explains to his students and young chefs, that French chefs and French dishes have been known across the world for decades, even centuries, due to invasions, wars, and the meeting of cultures through travel and intermarriages. Today, modern travel provides new inspiration to chefs of all nationalities introducing them to ingredients and dishes that were once rare and unknown.

Chef Martin has also seen cooking become a social phenomenon. The recent craze for cooking has evolved from television shows that have become popular in all countries, food magazines, newspapers, and other media outlets. As a result, in today's homes, cooking is no longer the domain of women; men are also cooking for their friends and families. Cooking is no longer a chore—everyone is deriving great pleasure from it. The act of cooking has even been incorporated by companies as a team-building exercise. It is an act that most people are familiar with so that the principle of "to learn is to know better" can be easily applied.

In almost any professional kitchen, you can find a dog-eared copy of *Le Guide Culinaire*, a universal reference for French technique and cuisine. For generations of chefs and cooks, most of what they know about French culinary technique began with its author. Auguste Escoffier (1846–1935) is considered to be the grandfather of French cuisine and is best known as the "King of Chefs." Escoffier's celebrated career included cooking for royalty and for celebrities of his generation such as Dame Nellie Melba and Queen Victoria. As was the custom then, dishes were often created for and named after known figures and royalty such as Pêches Melba, and Cherries Jubilee (prepared for the Jubilee celebration for Queen Victoria). He worked during the era of the Grand Hotel where he partnered with César Ritz, and his wartime experience led him to create the kitchen brigade system, which is still used today.

Antonin Carême

But who inspired Escoffier? We know that he was an admirer of Antonin Carême (1784–1833), but who were his peers and to whom did he turn to for advice and inspiration? There was no one person responsible for the creation of French cuisine, but who were the teachers and mentors of Escoffier's generation? What inspired them? The greatest service the French did for the culinary world was to codify and formalize what had been done for centuries—the French have the most extensive terminology, giving a name to a technique versus a description. The process of thinly slicing a vegetable then cutting it into fine threads is called a *julienne,* and the process of adding flour to meat and roasting it is called *singer*. It is a common language and understanding that still exists in professional kitchens around the world.

Walk into any bookstore and you will find an extensive selection of cookbooks. The popularity of cookbooks isn't new. The first known cookbook is attributed to a Roman gourmand, not a chef. It appeared between the fourth and fifth century BC and the author is commonly known as Apicius. The *Re de Coquinaria* is attributed to Marcus Gavius Apicius who was known for his excesses and love of entertaining. He is famous for a comment expressing his preference for flamingo tongues. The recipes of Apicius's time relied heavily on spices and fermented seasonings such as garam (fermented fish, similar to the Vietnamese *nuoc mam*) and verjus (sour grape juice).

The beginning of French cuisine can be marked by *Le Viandier*, a recipe collection by Guillaume Tirel, better known as Taillevent (c.1310–1395). The manuscript of *Le Viandier* is said to have been created 10 years before his birth (around 1300), but Taillevent is acknowledged to have edited it during his career. Four versions have survived, and a reading of all four reveals the advancement of the recipes as they evolved over time. As the title suggests, *Le Viandier* focuses on the preparation and cooking of meats (*viande* being the French word for meat). Unlike the cookbooks of today, the recipes do not provide accurate quantities of ingredients nor explanations of the cooking methods, because it was assumed that the reader was already well acquainted with this information.

When Catherine de' Medici married Henri II in 1533, food in France fell under the influence of the Italians until the 17th century when in 1651, François Pierre de La Varenne (1618–1678), who had trained in the kitchens of Marie de' Medici, published *Le Cuisinier François*, followed by *Le Pâtissier François* (1653). *Le Cuisinier François* was the first book to break away from the Italian dependence on spices, advocating in their stead that cooking should emphasize the flavor and quality of the ingredient instead of covering it up. It is also one of the first books to include recipes for vegetables. While in the service of the Marquis d'Uxelles, La Varenne is attributed with naming *duxelles*, the now classic mixture of chopped mushrooms. Later editions show the first references to the terms bisque, béchamel, roux (replacing stale bread as a thickener), and butter (replacing lard). We also see for the first time, bouquet garni, fonds de cuisine, and the use of egg whites to clarify a stock. There is also an early form of what we now know as hollandaise sauce. More than 30 editions of *Le Cuisinier François* were printed over a period of 75 years.

François Massialot (1660–1733) followed suit in 1691 with his book *Le Nouveau Cuisinier Royal et Bourgeois*. A working chef, the "royal" refers to the fact that some of the recipes within his book had been prepared for royal functions. In it, one finds the first recipe for crème brûlée. Massialot's book was presented in the format of a dictionary, arranging the recipes in alphabetical order. As with all cookbooks of this era, recipes were still incomplete, not always providing quantities or clear instructions. One also sees certain terms such as *braise* already in use.

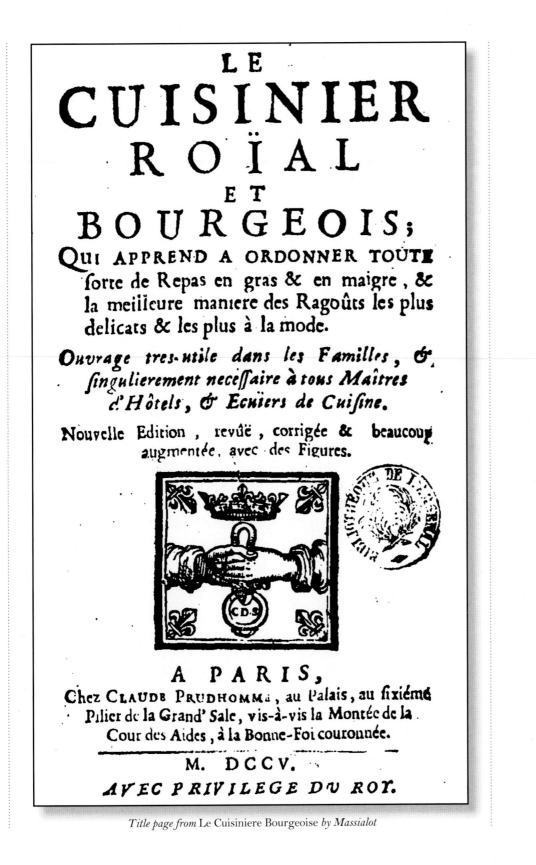

LE CUISINIER ROÏAL

ET

BOURGEOIS;

QUI APPREND A ORDONNER TOUTE
forte de Repas en gras & en maigre, &
la meilleure maniere des Ragoûts les plus
delicats & les plus à la mode.

*Ouvrage tres-utile dans les Familles, &
singulierement necessaire à tous Maîtres
d'Hôtels, & Ecuiers de Cuisine.*

Nouvelle Edition, revûë, corrigée & beaucoup
augmentée, avec des Figures.

A PARIS,

Chez CLAUDE PRUDHOMME, au Palais, au sixiéme
Pilier de la Grand' Sale, vis-à-vis la Montée de la
Cour des Aides, à la Bonne-Foi couronnée.

M. DCCV.

AVEC PRIVILEGE DU ROY.

Title page from Le Cuisiniere Bourgeoise *by Massialot*

Crème brûlée.

Il faut prendre quatre ou cinq jaunes d'œufs, selon la grandeur de votre plat ou assiette. Vous les délaïerez bien dans une casserole, avec une bonne pincée de farine; & peu à peu vous y verserez du lait, environ une chopine. Il y faut mettre un peu de canelle en bâton, & de l'écorce de citron verd haché, & d'autre confit. On y peut aussi hacher de l'écorce d'orange comme celle de citron; & alors on l'appelle *Crème brûlé à l'Orange.* Pour la faire plus délicate, on y peut mêler des pistaches pilées, ou des amandes, avec une goute d'eau de fleur d'orange. Il faut aller sur le fourneau allumé, & la toûjours remuer, prenant garde que vôtre Crême ne s'attache au fond. Quand elle sera bien cuite, mettez un plat ou une assiette sur un fourneau allumé; & aïant versé la crème dedans, faites-la cuire encore, jusqu'à ce que vous voïez qu'elle s'attache au bord du plat. Alors, il la faut tirer en arriere & la bien sucrer par-dessus, outre le sucre que l'on y met dedans: on prend la pêle du feu, bien rouge; & du même tems on en brûle la Crême, afin qu'elle prenne une belle couleur d'or. Pour garniture, servez-vous de feüillantine, de petits fleurons ou meringues, ou autres découpûres de pâte croquante. Glacez votre Crême, si vous voulez; sinon servez sans cela, toûjours pour Entremets.

Crème Brûlée

Take 4 or 5 egg yolks based on the size of your dish or plate. Mix it well in a pan with a good pinch of flour, and then gradually add a chopine of milk. Add a little cinnamon stick and chopped lime zest and other candied fruit. One can also add orange zest as well as lemon, which then would be Orange crème brûlée. To make it more delicate, one can mix in ground pistachios or almonds with a drop of orange flower water. Place it on a heated stovetop and stir constantly making sure the cream does not stick to the bottom. When it is cooked, place the dish or plate on the stovetop and pour the cream in and cook it again until it begins to stick to the edges. Move it to the back of the stove and coat well with sugar. Once it has been sugared, take a fire shovel, nice and red and burn the cream until a nice golden color. For a garnish, serve with feuillantines, small fleurons or meringues, or other crisp pastry trimmings. Glaze your cream if you want, if not, serve without doing so, always served as an entremets.

Note: a chopine is an old measure that is equivalent to about ½ pint or 250 mL.

In 1742, François Marin, chef to Madame de Pompadour, came out with *Les Dons de Comus.* Some attribute him with being the first to have really begun the codification of French cuisine. His introductions are very philosophical, addressing the practice of eating meat and the social responsibility of the chef for the health and welfare of his clients.

LA
CUISINIERE
BOURGEOISE,
SUIVIE
DE L'OFFICE,
A l'usage de tous ceux qui se mélent de
la dépense des maisons ;

Contenant la manière de disséquer, connoître
et servir toutes sortes de viandes.

NOUVELLE ÉDITION,

Augmentée de plusieurs ragoûts des plus nouveaux ;
de différentes recettes pour les liqueurs.

A PARIS,
Chez Louis Libraire, rue Saint-Severin,
Nº. 29.

1794.

Title page from La Cuisiniere Bourgeoise *by Menon*

Jules Gouffé

The book that bridges these two titles was *La Cuisinière Bourgeoise* by Menon in 1746. Menon is a pen name and to this day, the identity of the original author is unknown. However, this book was written specifically for the female cook (*cuisinière* being the feminine of *cuisinier*). In this book, Menon simplifies recipes so they can be performed by a domestic or home cook. These books all predated Antonin Carême's *L'Art de la Cuisine Française (1832–1833),* by which time, French cuisine had completely broken away from the Italian style and had established itself in its own right.

The 1800s saw an explosion of cookbooks in addition to Carême's, including Antoine Beauvilliers' *L'Art de Cuisinier* (1814), which could be considered the first restaurant cookbook. Beauvilliers was the former chef for the Prince de Condé and officier de bouche for Louis XVIII. Tired of working as a "servant" he opened La Grande Taverne de Londres in Paris.

Most of the books at this time were written for the home and domestic cook, but it wasn't until 1867 that Jules Gouffé, a protégé of Antonin Carême, addressed home cooking, la cuisine bourgeoise, and la grande cuisine both in the same book, *Le Livre de Cuisine.* In his introduction, he states:

A majority of cookbooks published so far are useless because they are copies of other people's recipes and always the same recipes, often vague or incorrect as they copy the same routines and errors. They are not precise in their quantities, measurements or cooking times thus providing absolutely no help, even for those with some experience, or those who wish to learn, neither for the average person nor a professional.

Can I do better? All I can say is that I have done something different to what has been done to date.

Antonin Carême had been abandoned to the streets by his destitute parents and rose to be one of the first "star" chefs. Known as the "Architect of Cuisine" he felt that food should be presented as art, on display in all its glory upon the table awaiting its guests. The drawback to this method was that by the time the food was ready to be presented and served—it was cold. Furthermore, all of the food was served at once on an enormous table, so guests were limited to only those dishes within arm's reach—it was considered rude to pass food around the table.

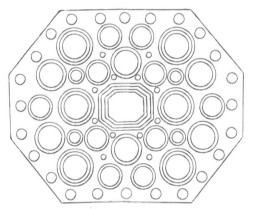

Layout of a table for 20 to 25 guests. The little circles around the outside represent plates for the guests.

Felix Urbain Dubois (1818–1901) was a proponent of the movement to serve food hot and wrote extensively about the use of Russian service, changing the landscape in terms of how Europeans dined. He published the two-volume *La Cuisine Classique* in 1856.

Unlike today's cookbooks where every step of a recipe is explained in great detail, all these books made the assumption that the user was well-versed in techniques that were passed down to them. What Escoffier did changed everything. He extracted the techniques in order to create an *aide memoire*, or quick reference for the young cooks in his kitchens.

The evolution of cooking and changing tastes of consumers can be tracked through cookbooks of the past two centuries. They have gone from books to be shared by cooks, to books for the home cook, to books that appeal to both home cooks and professionals. Topics vary from Country French to different ethnic cuisines to the recipes of celebrity chefs. World events have also had an influence—wars, invasions, travel, and the mixing of cultures have all contributed to the extraordinary development of the celebration of food, cooking, and its chefs.

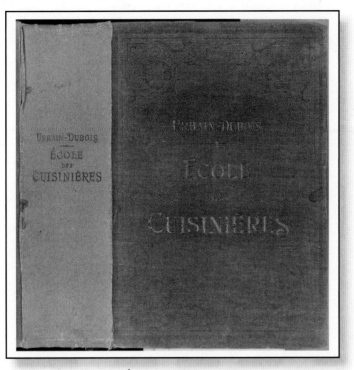

Cover of École des Cuisinières, *Dubois*

The most significant shift was in the 1970s with the *Nouvelle Cuisine* movement, in which two cultures, French and Japanese, discovered a natural affinity between technique and discipline. Nouvelle cuisine chefs strove to create perfection in the minute detail of a plate that pleased the eye as much as the palate. The movement gave way to the excesses of the 1980s and 1990s mixing cooking with media and entrepreneurship giving the world the celebrity chef. During this time, we were probably the furthest away from technique, the focus being on sound bites, photogenics, and public relations—not on the skill of the chef. In the 21st century, the popularity of molecular cuisine through the collaboration of Hervé This and Pierre Gagnaire has brought another element into the kitchen: science. No matter the newness or uniqueness of a technique or type of cooking, it will eventually come out in a book.

Cuisine as we know it today has come a long way. The advances in technology have changed the way we prepare food, from wood burning stoves to convection ovens to refrigeration. Preparation and cooking times have been substantially reduced. Time in many ways has now become the enemy of the kitchen, where everything must be done quicker and faster.

The purpose of this book is to expose the reader to the classic techniques using the traditional recipes that were once common in the restaurants in Europe. Many of the recipes we selected are the same ones that were used by Escoffier and his peers. They, of course, have evolved due to improvements in equipment and changing tastes that have been influenced by contemporary aesthetics, adaptation to new ingredients, and time. However, they are valuable in helping you understand the techniques and provide you with the possibility to create once they are understood. It is then up to you to adapt these techniques to your environment and market without losing the integrity of a well-prepared, flavorful dish.

Chapter 2

parsley

VINAIGRETTE
CRÈME
SAFRAN
CUISSON DES MOULES
HARICOTS BLANCS
GOUSSES D'AIL
VINAIGRE VIN ROUGE
HUILE

COUPER LES ARTICHAUTS EN QUARTIERS
ET ASSAISONNER AVEC LA VINAIGRETTE

BOLS
FOURCHETTE
SPATULE EN BOIS
PASSOIRE

FAIRE TREMPER LES HARICOTS PENDANT
12 HEURES. PASSER ET METTRE DANS UN
MARMITE

À LA MARINIÈRE

Cooking is one of those rare professions that mixes business with pleasure. Make no mistake—life in a kitchen is about hard work and long hours. But what defines this career path compared to others with the same physical demands, is that today most people who choose culinary careers, do so out of their passion for food and cooking. It is true that working in a kitchen is difficult, but the profession, like other professions, evolved as society moved from the Industrial Revolution into the 20th century. For kitchens in particular, the number of work hours have been halved since Auguste Escoffier's time, and technological advances ranging from air conditioning to lightweight clothing have made for a less onerous work atmosphere. Heavy copper cookware has been replaced by lighter, more durable stainless steel and aluminum versions, convection ovens and induction plates reduce the temperature in the kitchen, and steam kettles allow for the preparation of large amounts of stock. As a result, today's chefs and cooks no longer labor under the same physical demands as in the past. In the 1960s with the appearance of *nouvelle cuisine*, cooking took on the faces and personalities of the chefs and chef restaurateurs, changing not only the direction of cooking, but that of the profession of chef.

What is it about cooking that generates a passion for learning and doing? An essential element to human survival, cooking is no longer about just eating but about the appreciation of food. This appreciation can be enjoyed at all levels, ranging from simple home cooking to a gastronomic experience. Nothing compares to the pleasure derived from seeing a smile of satisfaction on the face of the receiver.

In the 1980s, after the novelty as well as the excesses of nouvelle cuisine, a new generation of chef entrepreneurs arrived on the scene. By this time, eating at restaurants had become part of the social scene and these chefs took advantage of the media to promote their restaurants through television and popular restaurant guides. There was a nostalgic return to a more simple style of cooking in the form of bistros, brasseries, and home-style cooking. Later, these same chef entrepreneurs were able to expand their business empires by opening chains of restaurants with different concepts and styles. Once almost exclusively reliant on outside financing, today chefs are able to finance themselves, but are still dependent on investors if they want to pursue even greater ventures with the promise of a good return.

Traditional wood burning stove used in commercial and home kitchens.

To become a chef recognized and respected by your peers, the public, your employees, and managers, knowing how to cook is expected, but your success also depends on having other skills that are shared with professionals in other businesses.

A chef must be versatile and capable of balancing his professional knowledge with his temperament in order to lead, motivate, and manage his employees. He must also have the social skills to go into the dining room and converse intelligently with his clients, in a cultured way and with a sense of humor while always communicating his passion for the art he practices. A chef must be able to work with management and owners in order to fulfill his financial obligations to the business while staying creative and fresh. Furthermore, a chef must maintain his standing and position within the industry by always exhibiting a positive image of not just his profession, but of the establishment he works for—and to do so with pride.

Despite the advances in technology that have taken cooking to new levels, the system of learning essentially remains the same. Like any art, it takes experience to refine and perfect one's skills and, in a kitchen, one's speed. The most successful chefs are those who have invested time in listening to and learning from those who are more experienced, whether on the job or through formal training. Cooking shares a long tradition of the passing on of skills and knowledge from one generation to the next, making for a better rounded chef and one who is prepared to be a future teacher and mentor.

Chefs, based on their experience and age, will naturally become teachers, passing on their knowledge and the heritage of their art. Generation after generation, chefs have shared their tricks—their own techniques that they have cultivated during years of work. They share their personal experiences of working in different kitchens and their travels. The richness of teaching, the passing on of a legacy, and the sharing of their experiences cannot be bought. These values are unique to that individual, collected over many years. These

Chef Patrick Martin teaching the next generation of Le Cordon Bleu Chefs.

Les Compagnons du Tour de France or du Devoir

The *Compagnons du Tour de France ou du Devoir* is the name used to represent several traditional trades dating back to medieval times during the construction of the great cathedrals and châteaux of France. An integral part of a *compagnon's* apprenticeship is the fulfillment of a tour of France of a minimum of 3 years but can last up to 10 years. During his tour, the *compagnon* works with master craftsmen who continue the tradition of passing on their skills to the next generation through mentorship, community, and travel.

Les Compagnons du Tour de France, founded in 1347, representing two trade societies in France, has expanded throughout Europe over the centuries. Though they are different in their organization, the trades practice the same concept and the same values, morals, and professionalism. The *compagnonnage* is a school of life that includes general education in culture and philosophy and *l'art du trait*, which describes a code of honor both in work and the compagnon's personal life that promotes honesty and discipline within each trade including cooking.

The modern family is now made up of two parents who work full-time, and life is about scheduling work, meals, recreation and rest! However, the compagnons live together in a home where traditional family values and customs are encouraged. This practice provides both professional and personal life experiences for each of the young apprentices who devote themselves to becoming part of this brotherhood. Their house is called "La Cayenne" and the person in charge of this "nest" is called the "Mother" (*la mère*). She is the only woman authorized to live among the men who represent the various trades. The Mother represents the family unit in terms of the moral values of each *compagnon* and future *compagnons*, and the image of this woman and what she represents must always be respected even after they leave the house. Like any mother, she also provides a shoulder on which they can lean when they have problems or are feeling low. Overall, she is the heart that provides her charges with reassurance and wise counsel.

After fulfilling the tour, the apprentice must create a masterpiece to demonstrate the skills that he has learned from his masters. If his masterpiece is accepted, he then is admitted as a *compagnon* and given a name that reflects the region from which he hails. The *compagnon* then enters the industry, but continues the teaching tradition by becoming a mentor and future master to following generations of apprentices. More recently, young women have been admitted into the *compagnonnage*.

technical, professional, and moral values are priceless and are not taught in kitchens where the teachers have had limited experience. It is important to inspire creativity by opening a window onto different cultures, different ways of living, and different ways of thinking than what we were raised with. With this perspective on work and life, we can continue to grow and evolve.

Cooking is about discipline, organization, creativity, motivation, passion, a love of sharing, and common sense.

DISCIPLINE AND THE KITCHEN BRIGADE

Auguste Escoffier brought his wartime experience to the kitchen through the formalization of the various roles performed therein. Using the army as his inspiration, he implemented a hierarchical system that continues to exist today in kitchens large and small, all over the world. Most of these titles are recognizable even by the patrons of restaurants, thanks to the popularity of cooking shows and celebrity chefs.

Escoffier was the author and codifier of modern French cuisine through his book, *Le Guide Culinaire*, which was based on the experiences of and knowledge passed on by generations of chefs. Escoffier's hierarchical system, called a "brigade," represented every member of the kitchen, from the chef (the *gros bonnet*, referring to the height of the chef hat compared to others) to the dishwasher. He also applied his system to the dining room, defining the different roles, titles, and functions based on age and experience, from the dining room manager to the busboy.

The original brigade was organized in the manner described below. Today, due to technology, and the salaries and taxes paid to employees, the brigade is not as extensive as it was during the time of Escoffier. One can still find a traditional brigade in France, most often in the large kitchens of five-star hotels and high-end catering firms such as Lenotre, Dalloyau, and Fauchon.

At the end of the 19th century into the beginning of the 20th century, the height of the chef hat (toque) indicated the title and role of each member of the brigade, the tallest hat being worn by the head chef *(gros bonnet)*. Despite one's age, it was the technical abilities, knowledge of the craft, and ability to lead and manage that helped one move up through the ranks. Thus it was often the case that a chef with character (not to be confused with temperament) had a much better chance of obtaining the post of chef. Certain of his peers who might have been his technical equal or even better, might have lacked the respect of their clients and managers because of their attitude and actions (impatience, physical punishment, etc.).

Today the apprentices and young cooks are no longer subject to the same treatment thanks to a society or mentality more attuned to mutual respect. For example, young cooks now receive a formal education where they are taught moral values and principles thanks to an apprenticeship that starts later than it did before. During and even before the time of Escoffier, the *marmitons* (young apprentices) were apprenticed to kitchens after they finished primary school, around the age of 12 or 13. As of the 1970s, by French law, young apprentices begin their apprenticeships at the age of 16, or if they finish their secondary studies early, may receive dispensation to begin at age 15. This additional time spent in school allows the young person to mature intellectually and culturally, resulting in future chefs who are able to express themselves, not just through their art, but with their words as well.

During Escoffier's time and before the popularity of cooking schools, teaching chefs were not highly respected by working chefs. If you compare the chefs Escoffier and Pellaprat, both of them are known for the codification of French cuisine during the same time period and, in fact despite their differences, they often collaborated together. Both were prolific writers, and both received similar training and obtained the same skills. However, Escoffier was better recognized by his peers and the media due to his experience in the kitchens of the Savoy in London and the Ritz in Paris. Pellaprat, on the other hand, devoted 26 years of his life teaching (at Le Cordon Bleu in Paris).

Today's chef instructors are highly respected because in addition to offering theory in their culinary programs, they also offer students practice, which was once only available by apprenticing into a hotel or restaurant kitchen. As a result, a young cook today can explain the process that a product will go through when cooked or treated, compared to the 1900s, when a young cook would never dare to ask a chef or his seniors to explain such details. To ask for a detailed explanation of a technique would have been considered an impertinence, questioning the authority of the chef. At the turn of the 20th century, the art of cooking was still passed down orally without explanation, which allowed the succeeding generations to reproduce recipes automatically without question. This was *gastronomie* with its defined rules and standardized names that were used consistently in all restaurants, and also where specialties changed based on the season and the regions of France.

Another indication of the evolution of the kitchen mind-set was the acceptance of women or young girls in the kitchen. Until recently, the kitchen was considered the exclusive domain of men. Ironically, the roots of French cooking, apart from invasions and wars, came from the mothers of France, who played an important role in the establishment of dishes and the culinary culture of the different regions of France. The rare female French chefs such as La Mère Brasier, La Mère Blanc, and others were known during their generation and earned the respect of their male counterparts. They in turn helped train chefs such as Paul Bocuse, Michel Guerard, and Georges Blanc. These female chefs played an important role by cooking at the same level as men. Their creativity, presentation, and fine touch complemented those of their male peers.

To go further, one must acknowledge the presence of chefs of any and all nationalities in kitchens around the world including France. These diverse chefs bring with them their own culture and experiences and introduce traditional chefs to new products and ingredients, providing another vision of the culinary world. Today, cuisine at the international level is constantly evolving. This new era permits professionals around the world to express themselves not only technically and culinarily, but also as ambassadors of their regions and countries in the same spirit as athletes, musicians, performers, and artists.

Of note is that after the Second World War, children who were not interested in school were directed by educational authorities to enter the restaurant business. Parents readily agreed, ensuring that they and their families would never go hungry. This was a classic reaction resulting from the lack of food after the war.

Chef Pellaprat demonstrating classic French culinary techniques to a class in 1907.

The best example of a mixing pot of international chefs can be found on board luxury cruise lines, which, due to volume, maintain a classic brigade. Managing a galley is difficult because of its space limitations and the amount of food that must be generated within this space. The chefs working on board these vessels are of different nationalities so they must learn to work and cook together in harmony. The experience of working on board a ship is interesting for the following reasons:

- Exposure to different cultures and ethnicities

- Menus that change daily for multiple outlets on board and encompass breakfast, lunch, tea, dinner, and a night buffet, requiring 24-hour-per-day service, not including room service

- The ability to debark and visit different ports and discover different cultures

- The ability to ensure the highest quality by sharing the workload and helping one another for each type of food service

- Sharing community life in a limited space, be it the galley or living quarters for the duration of a contract (three to six months depending on the cruise line)

- After fulfilling several contracts for the same cruise line, the possibility of being offered a permanent position with the responsibility and salary to match.

Previously, being given the title of chef and the accompanying responsibilities wasn't possible before the age of 45 or 50. Becoming a chef was considered a good end to a career depending on the person's professional accomplishments. Many professionals before the 1970s and 1980s never even had the possibility of becoming chefs. The highest post they could hope to achieve was the post of sous chef and, for many others, they would proudly end their careers as a chef de partie. A lack of education and their way of living did not always allow them to evolve differently within the brigade. Some would leave a top kitchen to open a neighborhood bistro or small restaurant and build a reputation among the locals, which would allow them a comfortable life.

Today, with public education systems, as well as the presence of cooking schools (although some young cooks will choose to follow an apprenticeship in a school rather than that of a restaurant or hotel kitchen), aspiring cooks are in school longer than previous generations and they may learn another language, learn to use a computer and other technology, and receive more theory, including hygiene and sanitation theory.

The downside of this educational experience is the lack of practice of the techniques (speed, muscle memory) and doing less cooking, compared to previous generations. Young cooks are becoming chefs at a younger age than ever before, when previous generations only obtained this title toward the end of their careers. As a result, a majority of today's young chefs can only replicate recipes from well-known restaurants or copy celebrated chefs as inspiration that has little to do with the gastronomy of their forebears. Without the foundation, fundamentals, and understanding of the origins of culinary art, a young chef is limited in his ability to create and grow.

We conclude the subject of general training with a discussion of continuing education in the form of competitions. A culinary competition is a challenge given to young professionals or young cooks by industry associations to improve their knowledge, technique, and performance but also to motivate them to win.

The importance of the different competitions more or less depends on the value of the prize. In France, the Meilleur Ouvrier de France as well as the Bocuse d'Or are the best known internationally. A chef who earns one of these titles and the prize—or even both—would be considered not only a very talented chef, but also a highly respected professional who would be recognized in the kitchens of the different countries they might visit. The media would celebrate this individual as a chef above his peers, much like that of world sports.

Culinary competitions vary from country to country. The organization and themes differ depending on whether it is a team or individual competition. In any case, participating individuals must not only be motivated and have good technique and habits, they must also be able to perform under the pressure of competition. The competitor must know how to work within a strict time limit, be quick but precise in the execution of recipes (treatment of ingredients, cooking at exactly the right moment, etc.), and have an artful eye for presentation. Only those competitors who have trained properly and who present their dishes at the precise time they are called for will be crowned for the rest of their career. These chefs will also be trainers of future competitors and will thus pass on their knowledge and experience from generation to generation.

To compete, you have to have daring and be very much aware of what it will take to succeed, but also be prepared to learn from the experience, win or lose. Competing allows one the opportunity to use techniques and products that may be unfamiliar or even unknown. It is a kind of sport that allows a chef to situate himself among the hierarchy of chefs and other restaurant professionals.

THE KITCHEN BRIGADE

We return to our discussion of the organization of the kitchen that began with Escoffier's brigade by taking a look at each position in the modern kitchen. Titles with an asterisk represent new functions and responsibilities (in comparison to before and during the time of Escoffier) given to professionals within today's brigades.

Corporate Executive Chef*

With the development and growth of international tourism, conglomerates of hotel chains, resorts, and restaurants are multiplying at a rapid rate. The corporate chef plays a role as an adviser but most importantly supervises the various establishments in order to maintain quality control. The corporate chef evaluates the staff and the technical results by observing the mise en place and encouraging continuing education for the chefs in each kitchen.

Continuing education today is an important aspect businesses should take into consideration for the long-term success of their enterprise. Establishment of a continuing education program recognizes motivated and loyal employees by sending them to do a "stage" in a top kitchen or attend a short specialization course, which allows the employees to help their own kitchens evolve.

The corporate chef tests chefs' technical abilities and attitudes in order to determine whether their profile corresponds to the needs of the operation. He is also responsible for the creation of the menus that will be used in the various outlets for which he is responsible.

This position requires a professional with considerable experience (technical and personnel management) who is willing to travel extensively and who is responsible for the financial and culinary direction of the operations. He reports to the director of the company.

Executive Chef – *Directeur de Cuisine*

The title of executive chef is fairly new and did not exist during the time of Escoffier. You'll find this title used more often in North America than in Europe. Restaurants have become big business and as a result chefs for larger kitchens require substantially more in terms of business and management skills. An executive chef in a large hotel kitchen, for instance, often attends meetings, deals with the Human Resources department, and crunches numbers on the computer.

Today, the executive chef of a large operation, is rarely found in the kitchen cooking, with the exception of special events, the creation of new menus, training for competitions, or preparing for promotions. The executive chef has become a manager and organizer who is financially accountable to the owner(s) or manager(s). The executive chef is also asked for his counsel and has an understanding of marketing and public relations so that he can maximize sales. Ducasse, Bocuse, and even Escoffier were natural marketers.

A person can take an exam to obtain the title of executive chef. The exam tests for the additional facets of this position that didn't exist during Escoffier's time, when a chef was judged solely on his ability to cook, prepare recipes, and lead his brigade. In Escoffier's time, cooks and chefs of different levels and specialties were able to move from kitchen to kitchen through word of mouth either through clients, chefs, or colleagues. The reputation of a kitchen could be built or broken by the value or character of its brigade.

Note that the executive chef manages all staff connected to the kitchen including pastry, chocolate, candy, and ice cream staff, bakers, butchers, and maintenance and cleaning staff.

Kitchen Chef or Kitchen Manager* – *Chef de Cuisine* or *Gros Bonnet*

Responsible for the overall management of the kitchen, the chef de cuisine supervises staff, creates menus and new recipes, works with the restaurant manager, purchases raw food items, sets menus and controls costs, trains staff, and maintains a sanitary and hygienic environment for the preparation of food. Depending on the size of the kitchen, chefs de cuisine hire employees, oversee scheduling, and establish a system of communication. The chef serves to inspire his or her employees and also participates in marketing and public relations.

A chef de cuisine was the top chef during the time of Escoffier and the title is still used today in Europe. In North America the titles of executive chef, chef, chef de cuisine, and head chef are used interchangeably. Traditionally, the chef de cuisine led the brigade and concentrated on the kitchen of the restaurant whether it was part of a hotel or a stand-alone operation. In a hotel, the chef de cuisine was also the manager of one of any of the specialized restaurants (French, Italian, Spanish, fusion, etc.) on the property.

An average-sized restaurant in Europe is counted by seats and is between 80 and 100 covers, which is greater than that in English-speaking countries. In such a restaurant, the executive chef manages his establishment including banquets, off-site catering, or a smaller outlet in a hotel.

In the traditional brigade, the chef de cuisine or gros bonnet was the contact point between the dining room staff and the cooks as well as between the client and his brigade. He took care of the purchasing and negotiated the salaries of his employees. He had the power to make management decisions on any aspect that related to the running of the kitchen. The chef served many roles that have been separated in today's kitchen's such as human resources, having direct contact with his team in order to lead them and provide them with the necessary motivation to maintain the reputation of the kitchen.

For the past few years, the reputation of a restaurant, whether or not it has been reviewed or recommended by a guide, has relied in great part on the know-how of the chef. As a result the chef serves as the face of the kitchen with the media and journalists and can make or break the publicity given to the restaurant in magazines and newspapers and on television.

Some chefs will also train their dining staff, be it the hostess or dining room director, with respect to the menu because the success of a restaurant depends on the collaboration between the kitchen and the front of the house. It is in this spirit and with respect for the chef and his brigade that the maître d'hôtel proudly presents the finished dishes to clients. Behind each server, from the maître d'hôtel to the busser, there must exist total confidence in the work of the kitchen and its chef. The sincerity of this admiration ensures strong sales, but also brings pleasure to clients, who benefit from a positive environment in which to enjoy their meal.

Deputy Kitchen Chef – *Sous Chef de Cuisine*

The sous chef de cuisine receives orders directly from the chef de cuisine for the management of the kitchen and replaces the chef de cuisine when he or she is not present. In smaller kitchens, the sous chef is often the most senior or experienced chef de partie.

A large brigade may have several grades of sous chef, normally ranging from one to three. This type of organization is often found in large hotels that have several restaurants or do a lot of banquets or catering. The first sous chef is usually in direct contact with the executive chef. The second and third sous chefs will replace the first sous chef and sometimes even the chef when they are absent due to vacation or off-site promotions.

In principle, the role of sous chef in a brigade is considered "ingrat" in the sense that he serves as the intermediary between the workers in the kitchen and the chef, and in the chef's absence, between the workers and management. Sous chefs often receive training in personnel management, which will serve them well later once they become chefs.

In summary, the role of the sous chef is to ensure that the kitchen runs correctly. In a majority of large brigades, the sous chef is not fixed to a particular section; however, in a smaller brigade, the sous chef is often the *chef saucier*.

Announcer/Expediter – *Aboyeur*

The role of aboyeur once was to serve as the bridge between the front of the house and the kitchen. The aboyeur was present during the service, transferred orders to the kitchen, directed the service of dishes as they were ready, and ensured they were correct before being covered with a cloche and served in the dining room. In the modern kitchen, the tasks once performed by the aboyeur are often realized by the chef or sous chef in the kitchen, and from the dining room side by the maître d'hôtel.

In certain brigades the aboyeur is a cook without any specific grade, but an individual who knows how to remain composed during a service and is precise enough to send out the correct orders while at the same time ensuring that the presentation of the plates meets the chef's standards before being served.

Station Chef – *Chef de Partie*

The chef de partie is responsible for the management of a given station in the kitchen, where they specialize in preparing particular dishes, and recipes, sometimes practicing certain techniques with expertise. A chef who works in a lesser station is commonly referred to as a *demi-chef de partie*. Depending on the size of the brigade, there may also be commis and apprentices, not to mention stagiaires.

Note that in earlier times, the chef de partie could establish a reputation within the brigade such that when a more interesting position became available in another restaurant, the chef de partie might be recommended by his chef to the new employer, where he could continue to advance his skills. The professional kitchen could be compared to medicine: After training as a generalist, learning the basics and fundamentals, the professional may, according to his tastes and passion, specialize in a particular area of his choice.

Specific stations that continue to be used today include saucier, garde manger, entremetier, poissonier, rôtisseur, each with specific tasks and skills. These and other positions are discussed next.

Sauce Maker or Sauté Cook – *Saucier*

The saucier prepares stocks and sauces, completes meat dishes, and in smaller restaurants may work on fish dishes and prepare sautéed items. This is one of the most respected positions in the kitchen brigade.

The saucier is also often the chef rôtisseur of the brigade (see later section). In the traditional brigade, the role of saucier was important because it was the saucier who fabricated all of the mother sauces and reductions and finished all sauces before placing them in the bain marie to keep warm prior to service. Normally before each service, the chef or sous chef will visit the sauce station to taste all of the sauces to ensure they have the correct flavor and seasonings. By the way, if the chef or sous chef was in a bad mood, he would often be displeased by the sauces and the chef saucier would have to redo every one!

Today, the saucier must have all of the stocks available (mother sauces are rarely used in modern kitchens) because sauces are often made by deglazing or by reduction "à la minute." Reduction sauces are made at the last minute due to the fact they are often finished with cream or mounted with butter.

Spare Hand or Roundsman – *Tournant*

Larger kitchens have a team of tournants who work all stations in a kitchen, replacing the chefs de partie on their days off or during holidays. The position of chef tournant is often the function of a very experienced chef because he must be able to replace any chef at any station at a moment's notice. In a brigade, this chef is well respected for his knowledge and culinary culture, even by the gros bonnet who needs him—because not all chefs have mastered all stations of the kitchen like that of a chef tournant.

For young chefs who wish to improve their skills and speed, this is a desirable position—albeit one that is hard to obtain—because of the opportunity it offers to work all stations in a kitchen.

Pantry Supervisor – *Garde Manger*

Traditionally the garde manger was responsible for maintaining the stock and preparing ingredients for cooking such as cleaning and filleting fish, butchering meat, and distributing them accordingly to other stations. The garde manger was also responsible for maintaining the cold storage and all cold preparations such as cold hors d'oeuvres, salads, cold sauces, aspics, and other items needed for large buffet displays.

The garde manger has one of the most important positions within a brigade, be it small or large. He doesn't perform any of the cooking, but must provide all sections with the elements they need to complete a client's meal, such as meat, poultry, and in certain brigades, fish.

In some traditional restaurants, the role of garde manger also includes both hot and cold pâtisseries. In smaller establishments, the chef garde manger is also responsible for ordering ingredients, fresh, frozen, and dry.

Butcher – *Boucher*

The butcher treats and prepares meats, poultry, and sometimes fish. This chef may also be in charge of breading meat and fish items and can also fulfill the role of charcutier (see next section).

The butcher's role is to prepare all of the proteins and give them to the garde manger who will then distribute them based on the orders placed by the clients. In general, the butcher prepares all meats such as veal, lamb, beef, poultry, and game during hunting season. If there is a chef charcutier, the butcher will not prepare any pork.

Charcutier

The charcutier in a brigade prepares any and all pork products exclusively. This includes pâtés, pâtés en croûte, rillettes, hams, and sausages. The chef charcutier is responsible for lengthy preparations for which he or she prepares different brines and marinades. The charcutier provides the garde manger with cured meats for clients and buffets.

Roast Cook – *Rôtisseur*

The rôtisseur manages a team of cooks that roasts, broils, and deep-fries dishes. In larger kitchens, the grillardin and friturier would be under his or her supervision. In a smaller kitchen, the rôtisseur would perform all three functions. The chef rôtisseur performs a very specific function in the kitchen and it is considered a position of prestige. The French epicure Jean Brillat-Savarin once said, "One is born a rôtisseur, one becomes a cook."

Before modern kitchens with their ovens that use wood, charcoal, electricity, or gas, there was the rôtisserie, which was placed in an enormous hearth. During this time, the rôtisseurs were the masters of the kitchen because they directed and mastered all of the cooking. The role had them not only cooking meat and poultry, but also producing jus, stocks, and sauces.

Today the rôtisseur still holds a respected position within a brigade due to the precision and exactness that is required when cooking roasts. It is important for the rôtisseur to not only master the cooking of roasts, but also deglazing (in order to finish the jus that will be served with the meats and poultry) and the correct process for allowing meat and poultry to rest before serving.

Grill Cook – *Grillardin*

The grillardin prepares grilled foods. In larger kitchens, this person reports to the rôtisseur. The grillardin also prepares all of the hot emulsion sauces such as hollandaise and béarnaise, as well as the composed butters that accompany grilled meats.

In certain restaurants that specialize in fish, or within a large brigade, the grillardin can play a very important role in the sense that he or she must master the ability to cook on powerful grills, using wood, charcoal, gas, or electricity.

Many people think that grilling is a simple method of cooking. This couldn't be farther from the truth. The grillardin practices very precise techniques that are applied based on the food that is being cooked. The preparation and treatment of an ingredient or protein starts with a marinade, which must be adapted to whatever type of fish, poultry, or meat is being grilled.

Based on the thickness and size of the protein to be cooked, it is necessary to quadriller the element and baste it regularly with an oil-based marinade to prevent it from drying out or burning, then finish cooking it in the oven.

Fry Cook – *Friturier*

The friturier prepares fried foods. In larger kitchens, this person reports to the rôtisseur. Apart from restaurants that feature predominantly fried foods, the role of friturier is performed by the grillardin.

Deep-frying can include vegetables, fish, poultry, and composed recipes such as meat croquettes or pommes dauphine, but this role is not fixed in a brigade.

Fish Cook – *Poissonier*

The role of poissonier is very complex. The chef poissonier is responsible for cooking all fish, shellfish, and other seafood, including fish that is served hot during the service and fish that is cooked for the garde manger.

The poissonier also prepares the fonds, jus, and hot and composed butters that are served with the fish. He must also, depending on the menu of the restaurant, prepare all soups (potages, crèmes, veloutés, etc.) that might normally be prepared by the entremetier (see next section). The poissonier also prepares fish fumet, garnishes, and hollandaise sauce. In a smaller kitchen, these tasks would be performed by the saucier.

Entrée and Hot Appetizer Cook – *Entremétier*

The entremétier prepares soups, vegetable and egg dishes, and other dishes not involving meat or fish. In larger kitchens, the potager and légumier (see following sections) would be under his or her supervision. In smaller kitchens, the entremétier would perform all three functions.

The role of entremétier, like that of the poissonier, is extremely challenging to manage. In this section, cooking is often done to order, for instance, for vegetables, and always done to order for eggs. The entremétier is also responsible for fabricating the consommés, aspics, creams, and veloutés and anything that would be served as a garniture by the rôtisseur or saucier (turned vegetables, artichoke bottoms, etc.) Only the poissonier prepares his own garnishes for his dishes. The entremétier is often assisted by the chefs of other sections once they have completed their mise en place before the service.

Soup Cook – *Potager*

A potager prepares the soups and, in larger kitchens, reports to the entremétier. This role is very rare in today's kitchens, although it might be found within large royal households.

Vegetable Cook – *Légumier*

The légumier prepares the vegetable dishes and, in larger kitchens, reports to the entremétier. Like the role of potager, it is rarely found in today's kitchens.

Junior Cook – *Commis*

A commis works in a specific station, reports directly to the chef de partie, and takes care of the tools for the station.

A second commis is normally an apprentice who has just completed his studies, either at a school or an apprenticeship of two to three years in a restaurant. A second commis can be promoted to first commis based on his experience within the station where he has worked. Such a promotion might be accompanied by a slight raise in pay.

The commis is responsible for all of the tasks assigned by the chef de partie. The tasks are often the tasks that the demi-chef de partie or the chef de partie doesn't want to do himself—but that is part of the apprenticeship!

Apprentice – *Apprenti(e)*

Until the late 20th century, a long tradition of apprenticeship had been practiced in many trades including cooking. Young people, usually in their early teens, would apprentice in a kitchen, working their way through the various stations under the guidance of the chef de cuisine and other experienced members of the kitchen. Today, the apprentices (*apprentis*) are students gaining theoretical and practical training in school and work experience in a professional kitchen. They perform preparatory work and/or cleaning work.

An apprentice who comes out of a serious kitchen or school will be able to enter the industry with the tools and fundamentals to work in any part of a hotel or restaurant kitchen. These apprentices gain experience by working on their feet without regard for time or the hour. In France, the Meilleur Apprenti de France competition motivates young cooks to compete among themselves.

The real challenge for an apprentice is to learn and practice all of the basics and fundamentals of classic cuisine. In many restaurants today, apprentices learn to prepare, cook, and present according to the direction of the chef. In other words, during this time the apprentice is learning to prepare the recipes on a menu created by the chef without really knowing for certain what techniques are being used. If this aspect of his training is missing this will make it difficult for him to recognize, master, and apply the correct techniques, should he move on to another kitchen. This is the fallout of "cuisine l'auteur."

In a large brigade the apprentice spends three years working through all of the different stations acquiring the techniques that will allow him to then be promoted to commis.

Dishwasher – *Plongeur*

The plongeur cleans dishes and utensils and may be entrusted with basic preparatory jobs.

Pot and Pan Washer – *Marmiton*

In larger restaurants, the marmiton takes care of all the pots and pans instead of the plongeur. This title is no longer used.

Communard

The communard prepares the meal served to the restaurant staff. This role is often given to an experienced commis or a newly appointed chef de partie.

Intern – *Stagiaire*

A stagiaire is often a recently graduated student who wishes to obtain exposure to a professional kitchen. Depending on the chef, stagiaires may perform various preparatory tasks (mise en place). The duration and content of a stagiaire's training are not as formalized as those for an apprentice.

Garçon de Cuisine

The garçon de cuisine performs preparatory and auxiliary work to support other kitchen personnel in larger restaurants. This title is no longer in use.

Pastry Cook – *Pâtissier*

The pâtissier prepares desserts and other meal-end sweets for smaller kitchens and also prepares breads and other baked items. The pâtissier may also prepare pasta and savory doughs for the restaurant. The following people report to the Chef pâtissier:

Candy-maker – *Confiseur*

Reports to the pâtissier and prepares candies and petit fours in larger restaurants.

Ice-cream Maker – *Glacier*

Reports to the pâtissier and prepares frozen and cold desserts in larger restaurants. The glacier will also make ice-carvings.

Decorator – *Décorateur*

Reports to the pâtissier and prepares showpieces and specialty cakes in larger restaurants.

Baker – *Boulanger*

Prepares bread, cakes, and breakfast pastries in larger restaurants.

HYGIENE AND SANITATION

The quality of a dish is determined by a combination of presentation, smell, and taste. But there is more to an enticing dish that should always be taken into consideration as well, such as its nutritive qualities and the care taken in its preparation in terms of hygiene and sanitation. A chef has a moral obligation to observe the latter without exception. Having a work ethic that includes paying detailed attention to hygiene and sanitation considerations will ultimately benefit a chef with the assurance that his or her kitchen is a reliable and safe establishment.

A chef in a kitchen must not only maintain the quality of his or her menu but must also ensure that all those who prepare and cook for the restaurant's clients respect and demonstrate a highly professional approach not only in the cleanliness of the kitchen but in their personal habits as well. Such regimentation will result in work habits that are automatic.

The chef's uniform, attributed to French chef Antonin Carême, serves several purposes:

- The white jacket was an assurance to the client that the kitchen was clean.

- The double-breasted design allows the chef to present a clean appearance by switching sides, and the double layer provides protection from hot elements and spills.

- The checkered pants hide stains. Although the "baggy" style is very popular in North America, it presents a safety risk because the loose fabric can get caught or catch on fire.

- The apron should be long enough to cover the knees and be tied in the front with the top folded over. The length protects the legs from hot spills, and the tie in front allows for the quick removal of the apron should it catch fire.

- The toque serves to keep hair from falling into food, and it is said that during the time of Carême, the height of the toque indicated your rank in the kitchen. He is said to have worn an 18-inch-high toque. Also the pleats in a traditional chef's toque are said to represent the number of ways a chef can prepare an egg. Today the toques are made from a disposable cloth-like material and should be absorbent. The open top allows heat to escape, thus preventing cooks from overheating.

- The *tour de cou*, or neckerchief, absorbs sweat and wicks the heat away from the neck of the cook, helping them keep cool in a hot kitchen.

Chef's knife
(couteau chef)

Slicing knife
(couteau émincer)

Paring knife
(couteau d'office)

Serrated knife
(couteau à scie)

Boning knife
(couteau désosseur)

Butcher knife
(couteau à batte)

- Shoes should completely cover the feet, protecting them from hot spills as well as the occasional falling knife. The soles should also be slip resistant. Today, some cooks wear steel-toed shoes for further protection.

- The *torchon*, or side towel, is pulled through the ties of the apron and should be used for handling hot pots and pans. It should not be used for drying your hands because a wet towel increases the risk of burning yourself when handling hot items.

TOOLS OF THE TRADE

The knives and tools of a chef are like the instruments of a musician. Although the tendency of new culinary students is to buy every new knife or gadget they see, you will find that a good basic knife kit will provide you with all of the tools you will need to perform just about any task in the kitchen:

- **Chef's knife** – *couteau chef:* An indispensable tool, the chef's knife comes in various lengths, from 6 to 12 inches. A standard size is 10 inches, which provides the weight and length to cut large pieces and chop.

- **Slicing knife** – *couteau émincer:* With a long thin blade, this knife can be used for cutting thin slices and for carving large roasts.

- **Paring knife** – *couteau d'office:* It never hurts to have more than one of these small knives, which come in different shapes and lengths. They can be used to peel, trim, and carve. The small blade can also be used for deboning small poultry and pieces of meat or fish.

- **Serrated knife** – *couteau à scie:* The "teeth" on this knife can cut delicate items such as bread or sponge cakes that require a sawing action over pressure.

- **Sole filet knife** – *couteau filet de sole:* This knife is useful for filleting round and flat fish. It has a long, thin, flexible blade.

- **Deboning knife** – *couteau désosseur:* A knife with a short to medium blade, it has a small tip that is used to get in between the joints of meats and poultry. They come in various sizes, some specifically for meat or poultry.

- **Butcher knife or cleaver** – *couteau à batte:* This heavy bladed knife uses its weight and thickness in order to cut through bones, and the back or flat side can be used to flatten escalopes.

- **Steel** – *fusil:* Often incorrectly referred to as a "sharpening" steel, this tool maintains the cutting edge on your knife. Like dental floss, it should be used before and after use, or used periodically during the preparation of meals.

- **Roasting fork** – *fourchette:* The fourchette is used to manipulate hot or delicate items. The tines are longer to provide distance from the heat.

- **Trussing needle** – *aiguille à brider:* Like a giant sewing needle, this is used for trussing.

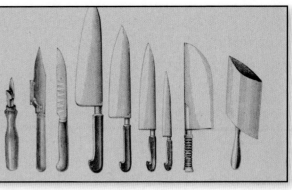

- **Vegetable peeler** – *econome:* This is used for peeling vegetables and fruit. Select one that has a pointed and curved tip that can be used to remove spots and stems.

- **Scissors** – *ciseaux:* Heavy-duty scissors can be used for trimming fish and cutting herbs. Select a pair that comes apart for easy cleaning and sharpening.

- **Channeler** – *canneleur:* This tool is used to create decorative furrows in fruits and vegetables, such as lemons and cucumbers.

- **Dough scraper** – *corne:* Originally made from horn, this tool can be used for scraping particles from the work surface, cutting or portioning dough, or scraping out bowls or pans.

- **Pastry brush** – *pinceau:* This brush is used for coating the interior of recipients with fat, brushing away excess flour, or brushing clarified butter on a finished roast.

- **Rubber spatula** – *maryse:* The rubber spatula has in many ways replaced the dough scraper (corne) and is used to scrape bowls and pans clean. Today, they are made from silicone and are heat resistant so they can be used for cooking.

- **Wooden spatula** – *spatule en bois:* This type of spatula is ideal for stirring hot foods without itself getting hot.

- **Knife kit** – *trousse de couteaux:* A soft knife roll or a hard case allows you to easily transport your knives and tools. A knife roll is light and portable as well as easy to store; however, you must ensure that the knives are secured and fully enclosed. Make sure that the straps and clips are tight enough to prevent the knives and tools from moving. A hard case can carry much more and different types of tools; however, you must ensure that it closes securely and that the cutting edges of your knives are protected. Also observe caution when searching about in the case for something!

Steel (fusil)

Roasting fork (fourchette)

PERSONAL HYGIENE AND APPEARANCE

In a commercial kitchen, these hygiene practices should be followed:

- Be dressed in a complete and clean uniform for each shift.

- Remove all jewelry or secure it underneath your uniform. Dangling earrings, chains, watches, and rings can pose a safety risk by getting caught in machinery.

- Change your jacket, apron, and side towel as often as needed.

- Use the side towel exclusively for handling hot pots and pans.

- Ensure that your hair is enclosed sufficiently, with most of it tucked under a toque, cap, or hairnet. Beards should be enclosed as well.

Scissors (ciseaux)

Channeler (canneleur)

- Wash your hands before and after each task, using designated sinks to do so. Do not use your side towel for drying your hands; instead use paper towels to avoid cross-contamination.

- Keep your nails short and clean.

- Wear safety shoes. Tennis or running shoes are a safety risk as they do not prevent slipping nor sufficiently protect your feet from spilled hot liquids or falling knives.

- Do not wear your uniform outside of the workplace because airborne bacteria can be brought into a kitchen this way.

SAFE AND HYGIENIC WORK HABITS

To keep your place of work safe and clean, you should practice the following work habits:

- Keep your workspace perfectly clean and do not leave tools around when not in use.

- Keep perishables refrigerated.

- Keep your trimmings separate.

- Carefully clean or wash fruits and vegetables before using.

- Never peel vegetables onto your cutting board.

- Carefully wash your cutting board after each use or change your cutting board, especially after working with poultry or fish.

- Immediately discard trimmings, peelings, and trash into a designated recipient with a cover.

- Ensure that products are fresh by consulting expiration and packaging dates.

- Discard or refuse any item that appears questionable such as dented cans or defrosted foods.

- Wash and dry your knives after each use.

- Check each day that the refrigerators and freezers are working properly.

- Do not store goods on the floor; instead transfer them to proper storage containers.

- Systematically remove wrappings and discard or replace.

- Store prepared items in proper containers, never in cooking vessels or service platters.

- Do not store sandy vegetables on the upper shelves.

- Try to minimize the number of days items are stored in the refrigerator.

- Respect the rule of stocking: first in, first out.

- Ensure that the air can circulate properly in the refrigerators.

- Do not store foods in their cooking liquid or sauce.

- Ensure that foods are properly and securely covered before stacking.

- Discard any foods after 24 hours if they have not been cooled rapidly.

- Organize the walk-in by storing similar items together (e.g., dairy, meat, vegetables) and ensure that the temperatures are correct.

- Prepare hot emulsion sauces (hollandaise, béarnaise) as close as possible to service.

- Keep perishables refrigerated until needed for the service.

- Respect all safety rules for grinding meat.

- Never defrost frozen items at room temperature.

- Verify that the thermostat of the fryer is working properly and change the oil regularly.

ADVICE ON EQUIPMENT

The following tips will help you keep the equipment in your kitchen in good working order:

- Regularly check that the lining of copper pans is intact.

- Regularly wash and disinfect the filters on the ventilation hoods.

- Regularly wash, disinfect, and rinse all sponges, washcloths, and mops.

- Carefully wash, disinfect, and rinse all pieces of mechanical equipment (meat grinder, food processor, mixer, slicer, etc.) after use.

- Sterilize pastry bags, piping tips, and strainers by boiling them for 10 minutes.

- Wash, scrub, disinfect, and rinse daily the cutting boards. Do not allow them to dry flat. They should be arranged vertically so that air can circulate around them.

GENERAL SAFETY PRECAUTIONS

These safety precautions should be followed in all kitchens:

- Ensure ovens are empty before heating.

- After a spill on the stove top ensure that pilot lights have not been put out.

- Make sure pan handles are not extending over the front of the burners nor turned so they sit over a heat source.

- After removing a pan from the oven, dust the cover and handles with flour. This lets others know that they are hot.

- Do not place hot utensils in sinks.

- Do not fill recipients to the rim.

- Never run in a kitchen.

- Point the tip of your knives toward the floor when moving about.

- Arrange your knives pointing in the same direction.

- Do not allow foods to cool in copper pots or pans.

- Cover spills with an absorbent cloth immediately, then clean as soon as possible.

- Before leaving the kitchen, ensure that the stoves and ovens are off and the gas has been shut off.

PREPARING YOUR WORK AREA

A work area can be fixed or mobile, depending on the task at hand. An example of a fixed work area would be what is commonly referred to as a station. It is a designated area that is equipped for a specific service. For example, hot entrées would be prepared in a work area that is equipped with burners and an oven, a work table, and cold storage for their mise en place. In this designated area of the kitchen, the chef de partie performs specific tasks related to his specialty.

A mobile work area is a temporary work area based on the task to be realized. It can be in an area that is specific to the preparation of the task (butchery), or in another area of the kitchen that provides some isolation if preventing potential cross-contamination is important. The temperature can also be a factor in determining the placement of a temporary work area.

Because the use of temporary work areas must prevent cross-contamination, these guidelines should be followed when choosing their location:

- Identify the appropriate area or isolated space that is conducive to the accomplishment of the task.

- Identify the different steps required to realize the task.

- Establish a logical order in which to realize the task, taking into account the preparation needed, movement from one part of the kitchen to another, and the different products to be prepared. This allows for each task to be completed rapidly and comfortably, with few errors, thus providing the best results.

- Equip the work area with all of the tools and products that will be needed for each step.

- Return equipment and ingredients to their proper place and then clean, disinfect, and rinse the work area and tools.

To maximize the use of temporary work areas, you must use logic and common sense and select the site accordingly. A well-placed and well-organized work area minimizes unnecessary movement, fatigue, loss of time, and accidents, resulting in work that is completed rapidly and efficiently.

MENU

The act of feeding people is accomplished in all types of flexible business models, from a small 25-seat restaurant to a giant catering establishment serving banquets for 3,000-plus guests. As a private chef, you can prepare food in the client's kitchen or prepare it for pickup or delivery. The food service industry adapts to markets large and small, feeding four mouths or four thousand—you choose the venue based on your aspirations and your determination to get there. Whichever type of food service you choose, being able to establish and manage a menu will be important.

Food Costing

When creating a menu, you must consider not only the cost of the food and the variety, but also the time required to prepare and present it. The menu should reflect the season: stews and game during the fall and winter months, fish and salads in the spring and summer months. The menu should be well balanced between red and white meats, fish and seafood, and offer sufficient variety based on the size of the restaurant and the number of employees in the kitchen. Thought should also be given to the garnishes that will accompany a protein, avoiding too much repetition. A well-planned menu minimizes waste and controls costs both in terms of the ingredients and labor.

It is important to maintain and respect a proper inventory of both fresh and dry stores. A French kitchen makes use of a *bon d'économat*, a type of ingredient list that allows for easy and clear ordering of the ingredients needed for each dish. The list of ingredients is sorted by category:

- Meats (including cured meats and venison)

- Poultry (including rabbit and small game)

- Fish (including shellfish, crustaceans, and mollusks)

- Dairy products

- Vegetables and fruits

- Frozen products

- Dry goods (such as spices, flour, pasta, rice)

- Bread

- Wine

A *bon d'économat* should be prepared for each dish on the menu. This is done to avoid any mistakes in ordering, especially with common ingredients, such as butter. Once the *bon d'économat* has been created for each dish, the information can be combined to create a *bon récapitulatif* in a spreadsheet. The rows list the ingredients, grouped by category, and the columns list the recipes in which the ingredients are used. Another column lists the total amount required for each ingredient.

The completed spreadsheet also serves to help calculate the cost of ingredients for each recipe. To do this, one can add two additional columns, one with the price by weight, volume, or piece, followed by the total price.

In addition to the *bon d'économat*, a *fiche technique de fabrication* is used for each individual dish. This document contains the following information:

Ingredient	Asperges hollandaise	Steak frites	Crème caramel	Recapitulatif	Unit price	Cost
Meats						
Vegetables						
Dairy						
Dry goods						
Total Cost						

- The *bon d'économat*

- Unit price

- Total cost

- Total cost per serving

- Method of preparation

- Description of presentation

- Comments and recommendations.

It can also contain the following additional information:

- Staff required for the preparation

- Total preparation and cooking time

- Required time for cooling and reheating

- Nutritional values.

All of this information is indispensable when calculating the cost of preparing the dish or ordering ingredients and ensures consistency in the realization of each recipe with an established method and presentation.

Note that the prices for fresh items fluctuate, so prices must be updated on a daily basis. This task has been simplified by computerized systems that allow kitchens to link directly with vendors.

The completed fiche de technique is then posted or kept in an accessible area so that the staff can refer to it as required. Different ways are used to prepare a fiche de technique, but each one should contain the information listed above. A sample fiche de technique is shown here in the following table.

Table 2–1 Sample Fiche de Technique

Principal nutritional values		Base of calculation	Number of servings
Glucides	Protides	100	200

RECIPE TITLE	Classification
	Cold first course
	Principal techniques
	Cooking à l'anglaise, cold emulsion sauce

Ingredients	Unit	Basic quantity	Quantity needed for the number of servings	Product category	Price per unit	Total cost
Main ingredients						
Barley	kg	3.8	7.6	Dry goods		- €
Lentils	kg	0.7	1.4	Dry goods		- €
Cooked pork shoulder	kg	1.8	3.6	Meat		- €
Spanish onions, medium	kg	0.7	1.4	Fresh produce		- €
Swiss cheese	kg	0.8	1.6	Dairy		
Seasoning						
Sunflower oil	l	0.9	1.8	Dry goods		
Mustard	kg	0.18	0.36	Dry goods		- €
Wine vinegar	l	0.28	0.56	Dry goods		- €
Parsley	kg	0.07	0.14	Fresh produce		- €
Salt	kg	0.035	0.07	Dry goods		- €
Garnish						
Red leaf lettuce	u	4	8	Fresh produce		- €
			Total	200 servings		- €

Progression

Cook the barley at a low simmer in salted water.

Strain without rinsing and set aside.

Make a classic vinaigrette.

Rinse and drain well the lentils. Dice the pork, tomatoes, and cheese.

Slice the onions. Carefully mix the barley, lentils, pork, tomatoes, cheese, and onions. Stir in the vinaigrette and season to taste.

Store in the refrigerator (0°/+3°) until ready to serve.

Dress on a bed of red leaf lettuce sprinkled with parsley.

Techniques and Basic Preparations

Chapter 3

CLASSIC VEGETABLE CUTS – *COUPE DE LÉGUME CLASSIQUE*

Classic French cooking uses specific vegetable cuts depending on the type or preparation of the dish or the recipe. The size of the cut depends on the amount of cooking time required and the cooking process used. The form depends on whether it will be served as a garnish with the dish or not. In French cooking, two types of garnish are used: *la garniture de cuisson*, often referred to as the aromatic garnish, which is used during the cooking process, and *la garniture de caisson*, which is served with the cooked food. An example would be braised lettuce. Other international cuisines share the same rules, but do not have clear designations for each cut.

Cutting a Block
Hard Vegetable: Carrot

1. After peeling, cut the carrots into even sized pieces.

2. Trim one side.

3. Turn onto the cut side and repeat the same cut.

4. The carrot is now ready for cutting into a julienne or brunoise.

Cutting a Block
Hard Vegetable: Potato

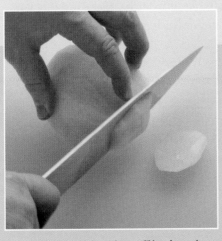

1   Start by trimming off both ends.

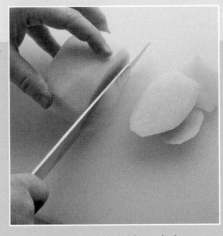

2   Then, slice one side and place the cut side flat onto the cutting board. Cut the two sides straight down.

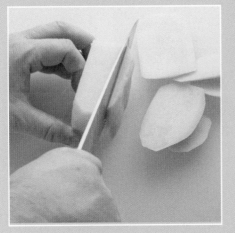

3   Turn the piece and continue cutting straight.

4   Trim as needed until a perfect block has been cut.

Preparing vegetables with attention paid to their size and form ensures that they will cook evenly. When used as an aromatic garnish, proper preparation ensures that the maximum flavor is released before the vegetables begin to break down. When used as an accompanying garnish, the same careful attention to preparation ensures that each piece is cooked to the same degree of doneness and that the vegetables will look attractive when served.

Bâtonnet

Bâtonnet refers to cutting vegetables into sticks. *Bâton* in French means "stick," the *et* indicates a diminutive, and thus bâtonnet means "little stick." Vegetables are cut into bâtonnets when they are to be served as a garnish on the plate or platter as well as the first steps towards cutting a dice (dés) or brunoise. The size of the bâtonnet, therefore, varies according to the size of the main ingredient it will be accompanying, such as poultry, meat, or fish.

Variations of the bâtonnet cut would be *cheveux, paille, allumette, mignonette,* and *pont neuf,* but these cuts are used exclusively with potatoes. Accompanying garnishes such as *jardinière* and *porte-maillot* call for the vegetables to be cut in a bâtonnet.

Bâtonnet
Hard Vegetable: Carrot

1 Cut the carrot block into 1 cm thick slices. Trim off any rounded edges.

2 Stack the slices and then cut into 1 cm slices.

3 Continue cutting.

4 Carrot Bâtonnet

Bâtonnet
Soft Vegetable: Zucchini

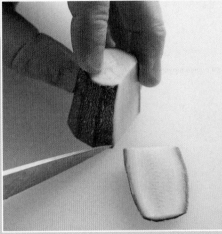

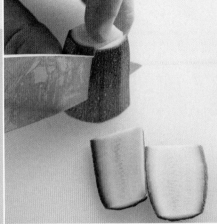

1 Once whole zucchini is cut, place vertically on the cutting board.

2 Cut slices to desired thickness.

3 Square off the edges.

4 Stack the trimmed pieces and cut lengthwise approximately 5 mm.

5 Zucchini Bâtonnet

Bâtonnet
Soft Vegetable: Celery

1 Slice peeled celery into 4 cm long pieces.

2 Cut each piece into even sized bâtonnet, approximately 1 cm wide.

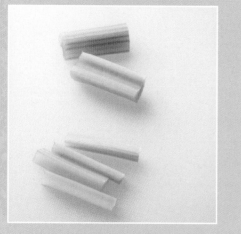

3 Celery Bâtonnet

Bâtonnet
Miscellaneous: Pepper

Pepper Bâtonnet

Brunoise

To describe *brunoise* as a fine dice does not do it justice. Brunoise describes the cutting of a vegetable first into bâtonnet or large julienne (depending on the size of the brunoise) and then into small, precise cubes no larger than 3 mm square. It is often used as an aromatic garnish and can be served with the principal element in the sauce, *jus*, or *fonds de braisage*. It can also be used in stuffings or forcemeat fillings and it is one of the classic garnishes in the soup family. When the brunoise is served with the main ingredient, it is presented on the platter.

Brunoise
Soft Vegetable: Celery

Celery Brunoise

Brunoise
Soft Vegetable: Tomato

1 Following the shape of the tomato, cut thin slices.

2 Lay each slice on a cutting board and cut into thin strips.

3 Pile the strips and cut crosswise into small cubes.

4 Tomato Brunoise

Brunoise
Miscellaneous: Peppers

1 Once the pepper has been trimmed and cut. Cut into thin strips, 3 mm thick.

2 Lay the strips together and cut across, 3 mm.

3 Continue cutting as evenly as possible.

4 Pepper Brunoise

5 Pepper Brunoise (top) and Pepper Brunoisette (bottom)

Brunoisette

Brunoisette describes a very small brunoise, around 1 mm square. This designation is relatively recent and came out of the *Nouvelle Cuisine* movement of the 1970s. French chefs who had traveled to Japan discovered new styles of presentation and cooking and brought these ideas back to Europe where they became incorporated into the cooking style at the time.

The brunoisette is specifically used as a garnish for soups and fillings and as a decoration. The brunoisette is prepared to be presented on a plate due to its smaller size. (The brunoise, on the other hand, is often made to be presented on a platter.)

Chiffonade

The term *chiffonade* has replaced ciseler in referring to the shredding of leafy vegetables and herbs.

Ciseler

The closest translation of the term *ciseler* in English would be "to finely mince." Used in particular with bulbs, such as onions and shallots, it is a methodical way of cutting them very finely. The term originally was used to describe the method of finely slicing leafy vegetables such as sorrel, spinach, or lettuce and also fresh herbs.

Ciseler
Soft Vegetable: Shallot

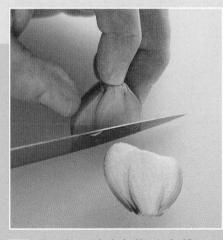

1   Cut the peeled shallot in half.

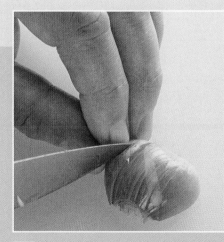

2   Lay one half cut-side down and make thin vertical cuts, cutting as close to the root end as possible.

(continues on next page)

Ciseler
Soft Vegetable: Shallot

(continued from previous page)

3 Make a horizontal cut.

4 If the shallot is large, make a second horizontal cut.

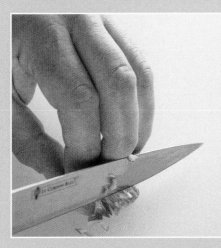

5 Thinly slice crosswise.

6 Continue to the root.

7 Shallot Ciseler

Ciseler

Ciseler
Soft Vegetable: Onion

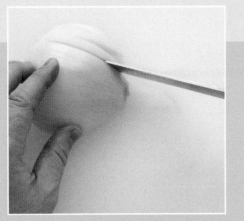

1   Cut the peeled onion in half and lay it cut-side down on the cutting board, root end away from you.

2   Cut vertically across almost to the root end at even intervals, 3–5 mm.

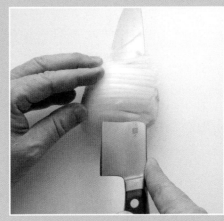

3   Cut horizontally, approximately the same thickness as the vertical cuts.

4   Cut almost to the root end, keeping the onion intact.

5   Holding the onion together, cut crosswise, at the same interval.

6   Continue cutting to the end for a fine dice.

Ciseler
Miscellaneous: Garlic

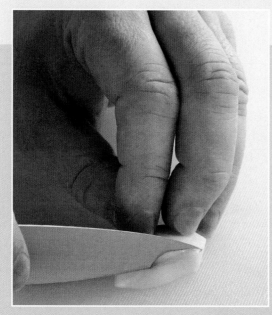

1   Begin by laying the split clove cut-side down and making thin vertical cuts.

2   Depending on the size of the clove, then make one or two horizontal cuts.

3   Begin slicing thinly.

4   Garlic Ciseler

Ciseler

Concasser

Concasser is a coarse chop that can be used for any vegetable. Vegetables cut this way can be served as a garnish for country-style recipes or as a garnish for various cooking processes.

Tomates concassé is a preparation where the tomatoes are chopped before cooking.

Concasser
Soft Vegetable: Tomato

1 Peel and seed tomatoes.

2 Cut into strips.

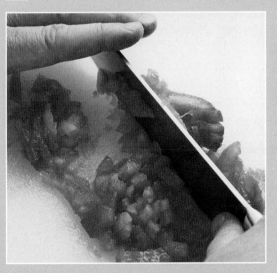

3 Begin chopping by rocking the knife back and forth over the tomatoes.

4 Tomato Concassé

Dés

Dés literally translated means "dice" and this term is applied mainly to the preparation of fresh tomatoes to be used to garnish soups or salads or as a garnish for fish and poultry.

Dés
Soft Vegetable: Tomato

1 Following the curve of the tomato, cut away the outer flesh to desired thickness.

2 Square off the slice.

3 Cut into even strips.

4 Turn and cut crosswise.

5 Tomato Dés

Émincer

Émincer refers to thinly slicing a vegetable or fruit. It is not cut to any specific shape, but the slices should be of the same thinness.

Émincer
Soft Vegetable: Onion

Onion Émincer

Émincer

Soft Vegetable: Shallot

1   Split the shallot in half.

2   If needed remove the center if it has started to become yellow or green.

3   Place the shallot, cut-side down and begin slicing lengthwise, as thinly as possible.

4   Break up the slices.

Hacher

Hacher literally translates to "chop." This term would apply to fresh herbs and other irregularly shaped ingredients that do not need to be prepared to an exact size or dimension, but must be fine and still fairly regular in size.

Hacher
Miscellaneous: Parsley

1 Rinse the parsley well in several changes of cold water. Then separate the leaves from the stems.

2 Hold the leaves in a pile.

3 Then begin slicing using a rocking motion with the knife.

4 Continue slicing.

(continues on next page)

(continued from previous page)

5　Then change the direction of the knife and cut at the horizontal.

6　Using a rocking motion, cut evenly over the parsley, changing angles as you go.

7　Continue rocking back and forth and changing direction to the desired fineness.

Hacher
Miscellaneous: Garlic

1 After removing the germ, begin by crushing the cloves.

2 Once crushed, begin chopping by rocking the knife back and forth.

3 Continue rocking the knife back and forth while moving the knife over the garlic.

4 Continue until the garlic is chopped to the desired fineness.

Julienne

This designation describes cutting vegetables into very thin strips, usually 3 to 5 cm in length and 1 to 2 mm thick. It can be used as an aromatic garnish to be served with the principal element it is cooked with or as a garnish in soups. The julienne is also the cut that is the first step towards cutting a brunoise and brunoisette. Because it is a very fine cut, *julienne* would not be used for braising, roasting, or any extended cooking processes. When used as an aromatic garnish, it is most often used with fish and small pieces of poultry. Vegetables cut julienne style can also be used as a filling or added to forcemeat. The length of the julienne cut can be shorter than 3 to 5 cm if the vegetables are being used in soups to make the pieces easier to consume with a spoon.

Julienne
Hard Vegetable: Carrot

1 Starting with a squared off carrot, cut very thin slices.

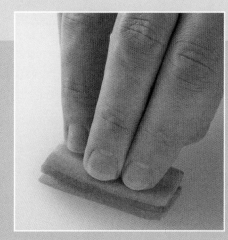

2 Stack the slices.

3 Slice lengthwise the same thickness as the slices.

4 Carrot Julienne

Julienne
Soft Vegetable: Celery

1   Thinly slice the celery at a shallow angle.

2   Cutting at a shallow angle gives longer slices.

3   Stack the slices and slice lengthwise.

4   Celery Julienne

Julienne
Soft Vegetable: Zucchini

1 A julienne is cut only from the exterior of the zucchini.

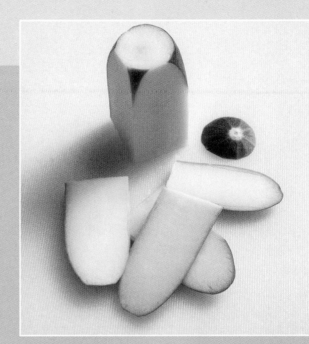

2 Cut the skin in even slices. Discard the spongy center.

3 For a fine julienne, remove a layer of the white flesh.

4 Trim the ends to square off.

(continues on next page)

Julienne
Soft Vegetable: Zucchini

(continued from previous page)

5 Cut thinly lengthwise.

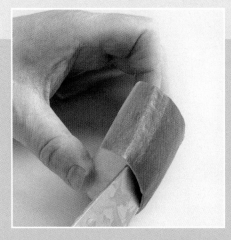

6 An alternate method, cut the skin of the zucchini away in one piece.

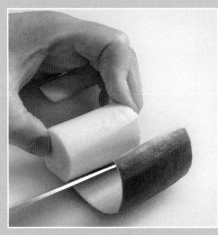

7 Continue all the way around. Square off and cut into same size pieces.

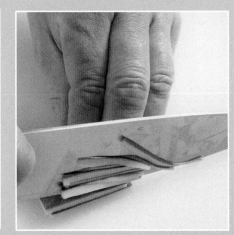

8 Stack and thinly slice lengthwise.

9 Zucchini Julienne

Julienne
Miscellaneous: Leek

1 Cut the leek into 4 cm pieces.

2 Cut each piece in half.

3 Split leek piece.

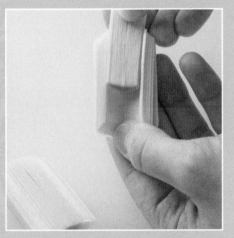

4 Separate each half by removing the center.

5 Flatten the leaves onto the cutting board.

6 Cut lengthwise.

7 Leek Julienne

Dés/Macédoine

Dés describes cutting vegetables (traditionally carrots, turnips, and green beans) and, more recently, fruit into cubes 4 to 5 mm square.

The term macédoine refers to a specific preparation using carrots, turnips, green beans, and peas. The carrots, turnips, and green beans are cut into cubes that correspond to the size of the green peas. A macédoine is served as a cold salad dressed with mayonnaise.

Dés/Macédoine

Hard Vegetable: Carrot

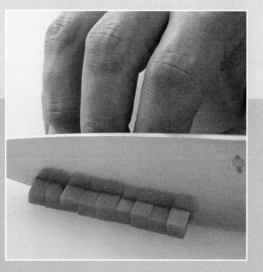

1   Line up a bâtonnet and cut crosswise.

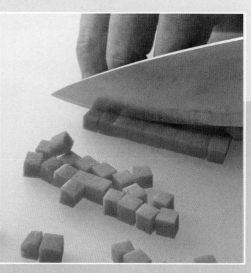

2   Cut the same thickness as the bâtonnet.

3   Carrot en dés/macédoine

Mirepoix

The *mirepoix* cut is one of the most important in classic French cuisine and is used as an aromatic garnish for any cooking process applied to fish, seafood, crustaceans, meat, poultry, marinade, etc. It is cut according to the length of cooking time. The mirepoix is always strained from the cooking liquid and is never served with the main dish.

Mirepoix also refers to a blend of aromates made up of carrots, onions, and/or leeks and celery that are also always cut in a mirepoix.

Basic Vegetable Mirepoix

Mirepoix
Hard Vegetable: Carrot

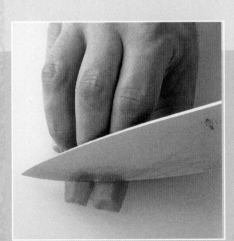

1 Split the carrot in half or quarters depending on the size required.

2 Cut crosswise evenly.

3 The size of the mirepoix would be adjusted according to the cooking time.

Mirepoix
Soft Vegetable: Onion

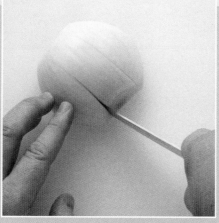

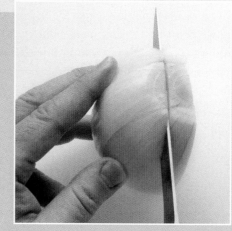

1   Cut the peeled onion in half and lay it cut-side down on the cutting board, root end away from you. Cut vertically across almost to the root end at even intervals.

2   Cut horizontally, approximately the same thickness as the vertical cuts.

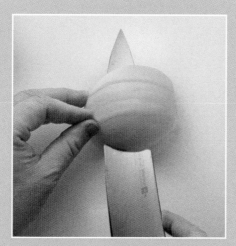

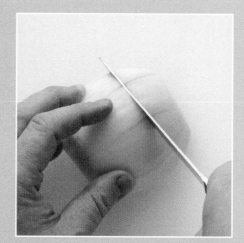

3   Cut almost to the root end, keeping the onion intact.

4   Holding the onion together, cut crosswise, at the same interval.

5   The size of the dice can be adjusted by cutting smaller or larger intervals.

Mirepoix
Soft Vegetable: Celery

1 For a small mirepoix, cut a peeled stalk lengthwise.

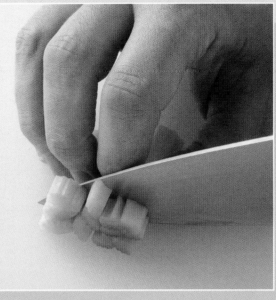

2 Then cut crosswise.

3 The size of the mirepoix would be adjusted according to what it will be used for.

Parisienne

Parisienne refers to forming vegetables into balls of various sizes using a melon baller, called a cuillère parisienne. They come in different sizes from 1/4 to 1 inch (6 to 25 mm) in diameter, and can be round, oval, or fluted. The parisienne cut can be applied to any root or solid vegetable such as potatoes, celery root, zucchini, or cucumbers. It can also be used with fruit such as apples, pears, and melons.

Parisienne
Hard Vegetable: Potato

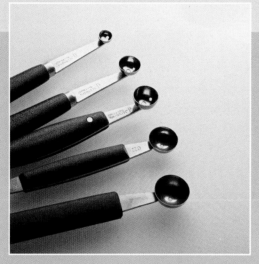

1 Select the appropriate size melon baller for what the potatoes will be accompanying.

2 Press the spoon of the melon baller firmly into the flesh of the potato using your thumb to keep it secure.

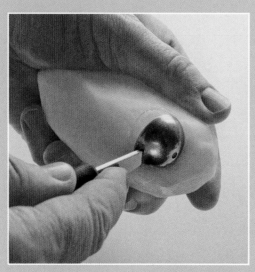

3 Turn the spoon in a circular motion.

4 Keep turning until the potato ball is completely free.

(continues on next page)

Parisienne
Hard Vegetable: Potato

(continued from previous page)

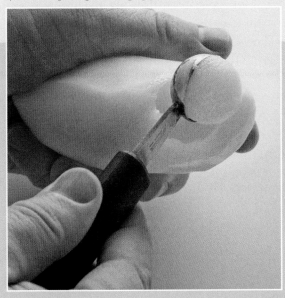

5 Lift out and place in cold water.

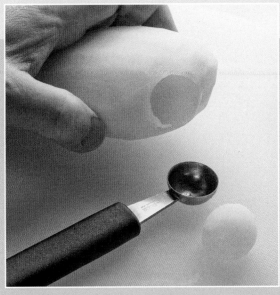

6 Rinse the melon baller in between.

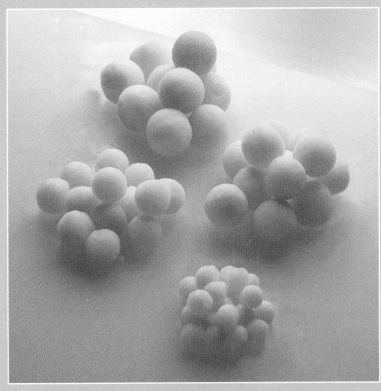

7 Potato Parisienne in various sizes.

Paysanne

Paysanne is a cut used as an aromatic garnish that, like the brunoise, can be served with the dish, or in soups after cooking. It calls for cutting the aromatic vegetables into thin triangular or square shapes and is mostly applied to aromatic vegetables such as carrots, celery, onions, turnips, and leeks.

Paysanne
Hard Vegetable: Carrots

1 Cut the carrot lengthwise into quarters, depending on the size of the carrot.

2 Round off the tip which also removes part of the woody heart which can be bitter.

3 Round off the other edges.

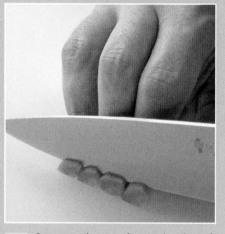

4 Lay together on the cutting board and cut crosswise.

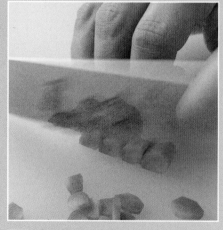

5 Cut approximately 1–3 mm thick, depending on what it is being used for.

6 Carrot Paysanne

Paysanne
Soft Vegetable: Celery

1 Split the peeled stalk lengthwise into four.

2 Thinly slice the cut celery, approximately 1–3 mm thick, depending on what it is being used for.

3 The result should be triangular shaped pieces of equal thickness.

Paysanne

Paysanne
Miscellaneous: Leek

1 Press flat a layer of leek on the cutting board.

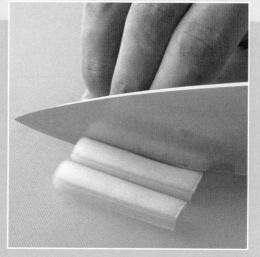

2 Cut into strips 1 cm wide.

3 Take each strip and begin cutting at an angle.

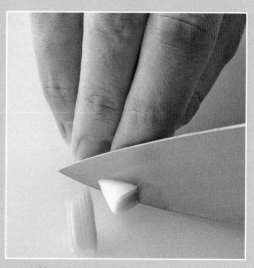

4 Change the angle and cut again, creating triangles.

5 Leek Paysanne

Rouelle

Rouelle describes the method of cutting layered or hollow vegetables, such as onions or peppers, into rings. Onions are thinly sliced, then each slice is carefully separated into rings.

Rouelle

Soft Vegetable: Onion

1 After trimming and peeling place the onion on its side and hold securely. Cut a slice at the desired thickness.

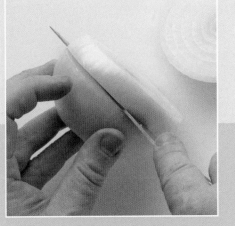

2 Cut parallel to the first cut, cutting as straight as possible.

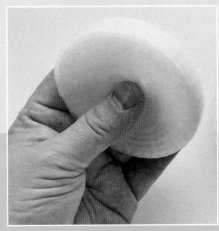

3 The slice should be regular.

4 Slices can be kept whole or separated into rings.

5 For rings, carefully separate the layers.

6 Onion Rouelle

Sifflet

Sifflet literally translated means "whistle." Long, narrow vegetables such as carrots, celery, or leeks are cut at an angle. They are prepared in this way to be served as a garnish. It is also used to cut long breads such as baguettes.

Sifflet
Soft Vegetable: Celery

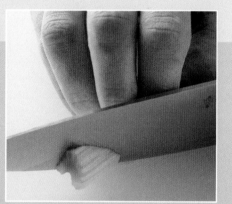

1 After peeling, cut the top at an angle.

2 Continue cutting slices at the same angle about 1 cm thick.

3 Celery Sifflet

Sifflet
Miscellaneous: Leek

1 Once the leek has been cleaned and trimmed, cut at an angle.

2 Continue cutting evenly.

3 Leek Sifflet

Tournés

Based on the verb *tourner,* meaning "to turn," *tournés* describes the method of trimming vegetables and some fruits into an oval shape in various sizes. This method is applied to any hard vegetables or fruits such as potatoes, carrots,

Tournés
Hard Vegetable: Potato

1 Holding a small knife securely in your hand, place the blade at the top of the potato, with your thumb at the bottom.

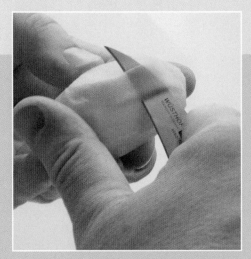

2 Cut down toward your thumb creating a slight curve. Try to cut in one smooth motion.

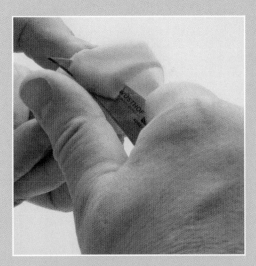

3 Cut through the other end of the potato.

4 Turn the potato slightly and repeat.

(continues on next page)

Tournés
Hard Vegetable: Potato

(continued from previous page)

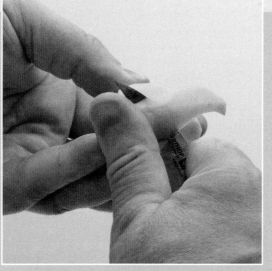

5 Continue cutting around until seven facets have been cut.

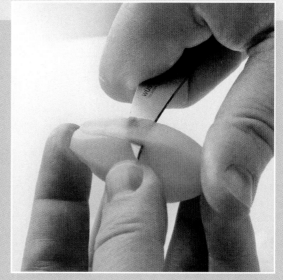

6 Trim to smooth each facet and even out the shape.

7 Store in cold water until needed.

Tournés
Soft Vegetable: Celery

1 Cut the peeled celery into even sized pieces.

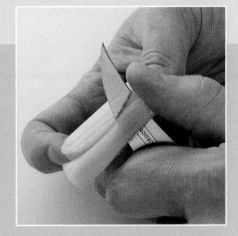

2 Round each side.

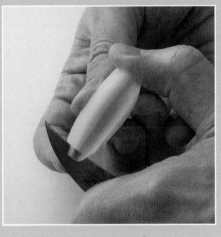

3 Trim the bottom to flatten slightly.

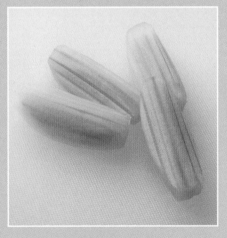

4 Celery Tournés

turnips, zucchini, cucumber, and apples. A classic "turned" vegetable is barrel shaped with seven sides and evenly pointed at both ends. Turned vegetables are served as an accompanying garnish and can be boiled, steamed, fried, glazed, or *cuit à l'étuvée*. They are turned in order to shape the vegetables to exactly the same size to ensure even cooking while being aesthetically pleasing to the eye.

The term "turning" often is inaccurately applied to mushrooms when the caps are lightly fluted in an attractive spiral, which is a classic decorative garnish for fish. The more correct term is *champignon cannelé* (channeled mushroom). A *champignon tourné* describes a mushroom that has been peeled using a paring knife and where the skin has been removed by turning the head and peeling in a spiral.

Tournés
Soft Vegetable: Zucchini

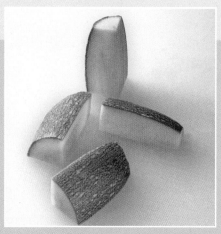

1   Cut the zucchini to desired length then cut into quarters.

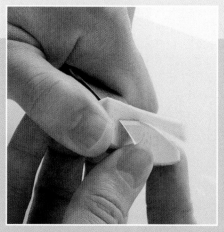

2   Round off and remove the spongy middle.

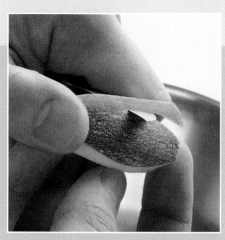

3   Curve each side forming a long oval.

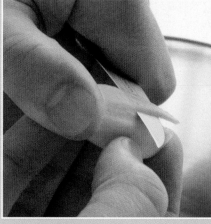

4   Trim off the white flesh on the sides.

5   The finished product should have three to five facets.

6   Make sure that they are of the same size and shape.

Triangle

Triangles are similar in shape to the paysanne but larger. This cut is used to make garnishes out of nonaromatic vegetables, such as zucchini.

Triangle
Soft Vegetable: Zucchini

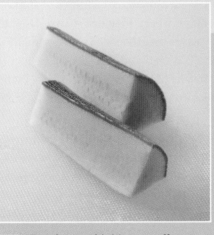

1 Cut the zucchini into small wedges.

2 Using a vegetable peeler, remove the point which is the spongy center of the zucchini and will most likely disintegrate during cooking.

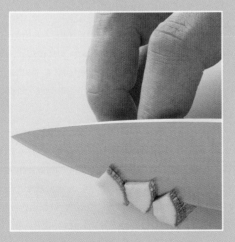

3 Line up the zucchini and thinly slice, around 2 mm thick.

4 Zucchini Triangle

VEGETABLES AND FRUITS

The term *vegetable* is neither botanical nor scientific, but a culinary term that refers to parts of plants that are consumed, sometimes raw, and, when cooked, prepared as a savory dish or accompaniment. The plants themselves belong to different families and species, and different parts are consumed, ranging from the roots to the stalk to the seeds. For instance, mushrooms, which we usually think of as a vegetable, are actually fungi in that they grow as a result of a symbiotic relationship with a plant.

Many of the vegetables we eat today once grew in the wild and were cultivated by different cultures. Some are hybrids, which are the offspring that result when crossing different plants. With our current abilities to ship vegetables efficiently, we often don't even know where they originated. How many people remember from their history classes that the potato was virtually unknown in Europe until the discovery of the New World? And that corn, a staple of the North American diet, is still considered animal feed elsewhere in the world, but is consumed globally in its derivative forms? What might be shunned in one culture is prized in another.

With modern science and technology, anything can be grown just about anywhere, but despite such progress, the quality and flavor of a garden tomato grown in the summer sun cannot be replicated. Appreciation of the changing of the seasons and the bounty each season brings is being lost—but not completely. A new breed of chefs is bringing food from the farm to the table and reintroducing a new generation to the changing seasons and changing variety of available ingredients and their inherent flavors that have been enhanced by the climate and soil. In some parts of the world, people's eating habits are still tied to the seasons, and they wait with anticipation for the first melons of the season or accept and enjoy fresh cepe mushrooms for just a few weeks a year.

In this chapter we have provided the botanical names or families of the various vegetables to give you an idea of how they are related, but we have presented them by separating them into different categories: bulbs, root vegetables, shoot vegetables, leafy greens, mushrooms, brassicas, potatoes, fruit vegetables, and pods and seeds.

Unlike the term *vegetable*, the term *fruit* is a botanical designation that refers to the reproductive part of the plant, the ovary. An easy rule of thumb is to remember that fruits usually contain seeds, although there are exceptions. Vegetable fruits include tomatoes, cucumbers, squash, eggplant, peppers, and chilies. Botanically speaking, the presence of seeds defines them as fruits, but culinarily speaking, they are prepared as a vegetable; that is, they are traditionally used in savory preparations.

We have also provided the botanical names and families for fruits as well, but have organized them into the following categories: citrus fruits, stone fruits, grapes and berries, and exotic fruits.

In 1893, in the case of *Nix v. Hedden,* the U.S. Supreme Court formally recognized the tomato as a vegetable, thus taxing it according to the 1883 Tariff Act, which placed a duty on imported vegetables. Although the court acknowledged that, botanically speaking, the tomato was a fruit, it stated that in commerce and the common language of the people, the tomato was considered a vegetable and that it was "usually served at dinner in, with, or after the soup, fish, or meats which constitute the principal part of the repast, and not, like fruits generally, as dessert."

In this chapter, the terms *fruit* and *vegetable* do not designate the actual botanical designation of these plants, but how they are used in the kitchen. There are many gray areas, where a fruit is referred to as a vegetable (tomato) and a vegetable as a fruit (rhubarb). In the culinary sense, vegetables are used for savory preparations; fruit for sweet.

VEGETABLES

Brassicas

Brassicaceae is a family of plants belonging to the mustard family. Plants belonging to this plant genus are often referred to as mustards or cabbages. Brassicas are native to the temperate regions of Asia, Western Europe, and the Mediterranean. The resulting crops are often referred to as *cole crops* and contain more agricultural and horticultural plants than any other genus. The word *cole* is from the Middle English word *col* meaning the "stem" or "stalk" of the plant.

A cole crop refers specifically to the species *Brassica oleracea*, cool-weather vegetables that are easily hybridized. They are also self-incompatible, which means that flowers of the same plant cannot pollinate among themselves. Hybrids are generally hardier and grow more rapidly, are more uniform in their maturity, and are more disease resistant than open-pollinated varieties. That is why they are often preferred by growers. Brassicas grow best between 15° and 20°C (59° and 68°F). Most will stop growing at 0°C; however some plants of this variety are able to withstand cooler temperatures as low as −10°C (14°F). Brassicas require soil that provides a continuous supply of water during the growing season or they will not develop or flower properly. Crops do not require much manual labor, because they can be easily harvested by machine, making them more profitable than crops that have to be harvested by hand.

Broccoli

Species name: *Brassica oleracea italica*

The cultivation of **broccoli** dates back to ancient Rome and it takes its name from the Latin word *brachium*, which means "branch" or "arm." Broccoli has dark or bright green florets with a compact head; the stem should be cleanly cut. Broccoli contains substances called *indoles*, which are attributed to have some cancer-fighting properties. Both the head and stalk of this plant may be eaten. The most commonly known and consumed broccoli is green, and is known in the United Kingdom as *Calabrese broccoli*.

Did you know?

Broccoli is a very good source of vitamins A and C; is rich in potassium, calcium, phosphorus, and folate; and contains some iron. A 1-cup (250-mL) serving of cooked broccoli contains about 45 kilocalories.

Broccoli Preparation

1 Remove the leaves from the stem.

2 Using a paring knife, cut at the base of each cluster.

3 Remove the smaller head.

4 Continue working your way around.

5 Broccoli Florets

Brussels Sprouts – Choux de Bruxelles

Species name: *Brassica oleracea gemmifera*

Brussels sprouts possibly get their name from the fact that they were first grown as early as 1200 in Belgium. Leafy green buds that resemble small cabbages, Brussels sprouts have a bad reputation, mainly due to improper cooking. Overcooking Brussels sprouts releases sulfur compounds in the vegetable that give it a distinctly off-putting odor. They possess a delicious nutty flavor when cooked properly.

Did you know?

Brussels sprouts are an excellent source of vitamins A and C and are rich in potassium and folate. They also possess other nutrients in small quantities. A 1-cup (250-mL) serving contains 58 kilocalories.

Brussels Sprouts

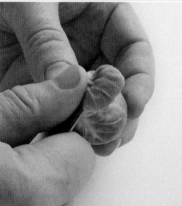

1   Remove any leaves that are damaged or wilted.

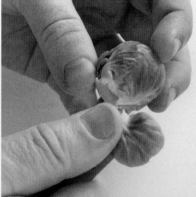

2   Remove any loose leaves.

3   Trim the bottom, by cutting the stem with a small knife.

4   Score the bottom with a cross.

5   Trimmed Brussels Sprouts

Cabbage – Choux

Species name: *Brassica oleracea* var. *capitata*

The term **cabbage** is thought to be taken from the Normandy-Picardy word *caboche*, meaning "head." Cabbage is a leafy mustard plant with each variety differing slightly. Cabbage color will vary depending on the region and the pH level of the soil. Cabbage contains a pigment called anthocyanin. If grown in acidic soil, the cabbage will develop deep red leaves; however, if grown in alkaline soil, the leaves will be yellowish green.

Once growing in the wild, cabbage was cultivated early in the history of human civilization and is considered to be one of the most ancient of cultivated vegetables. Historical evidence suggests that cabbage farming began in the Near East more than four millennia ago. In its earliest known form, the cabbage was regarded as an herb. Centuries of careful cultivation has led to an expanded family that includes broccoli, kale, and Brussels sprouts.

Trimming White Cabbage

1 Remove the outer leaves.

2 Cut off the stem.

3 Split in half.

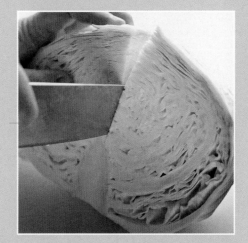

4 Then cut each half in quarters.

(continues on next page)

Trimming White Cabbage

(continued from previous page)

5 Cut away the hard core.

6 Separate the leaves.

7 White and red cabbage leaves have a thick central vein.

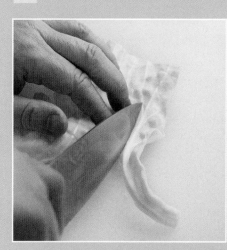

8 Lay the leaf on the cutting board and cut away the hard center vein.

Head cabbage is the most important variety economically and what most people visualize when they think of cabbage. Head cabbage originates from a wild variety that grew on the Mediterranean and the Atlantic coasts. Developed around 1200, white and red head cabbages possess a firm, tightly closed round head with thick, silky smooth leaves. White and green cabbages are the same vegetable, with a subtle difference in how they are harvested.

Did you know?

Cabbage is an excellent provider of vitamins B and C, potassium, and calcium. A 1-cup (250-mL) serving of raw cabbage contains 21 kilocalories; cooked, 58 kilocalories.

Cooking Cabbage

1 Cut the head of cabbage in half.

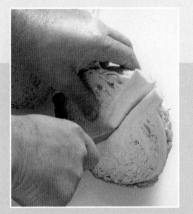

2 Cut each half into quarters.

3 Immerse the cabbage quarters into boiling salted water.

4 Cook until tender, then remove and place in an ice bath to stop the cooking.

5 Once cabbage is cooled, squeeze out excess water.

6 Trim off the core.

7 Lay the cooked cabbage on a paper-lined tray to drain.

Blanching Cabbage Leaves

1 Preparing cabbage leaves: Cut around the stem of the cabbage with the point of the knife angled toward the center.

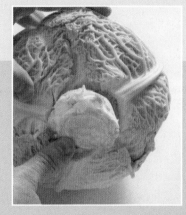

2 Continue all the way around until the core detaches itself.

3 Begin removing the outer leaves.

4 Place the leaves in a bowl of cold water with vinegar.

5 Immerse in the vinegared water.

6 Rinse well under cold running water.

7 Immerse the leaves in boiling salted water.

8 Use a wire skimmer to keep the cabbage submerged.

(continues on next page)

Cooking Cabbage Leaves

(continued from previous page)

9 Once tender, remove from the boiling water and transfer to an ice bath.

10 Immerse completely to cool.

11 Remove one leaf at a time and shake off excess water.

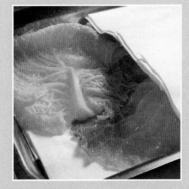

12 Lay on a paper-lined tray.

13 Arrange additional leaves in a single layer then cover with more paper towel.

14 Continue layering cabbage leaves and paper towel.

15 Once all the cabbage leaves are arranged, place a final layer of paper towel and press firmly and evenly over the tray.

16 Excess water is absorbed by the paper without crushing the leaves.

Red Cabbage – *Choux Rouge*

Species name: *Brassica oleracea* var. *capitata*

Although similar to the white variety, **red cabbage** possesses a more potent flavor. The leaves of the red cabbage are tinted brownish red. Similar to all red, blue, and purple vegetable plants, the red cabbage contains a pigment called anthocyanin. Botanists from the Middle Ages were aware of this characteristic and learned to encourage the growth of this feature by monitoring the level of anthocyanin in the soil, thus influencing the color of the cabbage. The color may be preserved during the cooking process by adding an acid, such as lemon or vinegar. Red cabbage may be eaten raw or cooked, and may be prepared similar to white cabbage.

Savoy Cabbage – *Choux de Savoie*

Species name: *Brassica oleracea*

Tender and sweet with a round head and loose, crispy crinkled leaves, **savoy cabbage** possesses a mild flavor compared to white and red cabbage. Versatile, savoy cabbage is used in soups, stews, salads, and the leaves can also be stuffed and baked.

White Cabbage – *Choux Blanc*

Species name: *Brassica oleracea* var. *capitata*

Actually creamy yellow to light green in color, **white cabbage** may be eaten both raw and cooked. There are more than 100 different varieties of head cabbage. Growers remove the heads from the plant base and bury them in small field trenches. This serves two purposes. The first is to *blanch* the cabbage; by burying the cabbage, it is no longer exposed to sunlight, thus limiting the development of chlorophyll. The second is to insulate the cabbage from freezing so that cabbages may be harvested year-round. White cabbage is buried in the fall when it is fully grown, and is then preserved for the entire winter. To cultivate a green cabbage, the heads are simply removed from the field and sent to suppliers.

Cauliflower – *Choux Fleur*

Species name: *Brassica oleracea*

Unlike other members of the Brassicaceae family, which produce leafy greens, **cauliflower** possesses a white flowered head with surrounding leaves and a large stalk. In French, *choux fleur* literally translates as "cabbage flower" and the origin of the name is attributed to 13th-century monks in southern France. In English, "cauli" is taken from *cole* plus "flower" due to the appearance of its head.

Did you know?

Cauliflower contains vitamin C, folate, and potassium, and it yields diminutive measures of various minerals and other nutrients to the diet. A 1-cup (250-mL) serving of cauliflower supplies 26 kilocalories.

The head of the cauliflower is eaten and the leaves and stalk are discarded. This vegetable is crunchy, possesses a nutty flavor, and can be consumed both raw and cooked. In the late 1980s, the first purple cauliflower was grown from a mutated plant in a cauliflower field in Denmark. After its first spontaneous growth, the plant was perfected, tested, and proven to be adaptable and productive in many temperate and subtropical areas. Purple cauliflower is produced mainly in southern Italy, Spain, and the United Kingdom.

Cauliflower Preparation

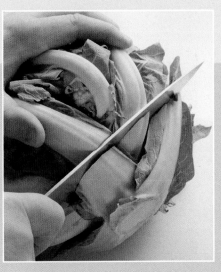

1 Cut off the stem end of the cauliflower.

2 Remove the inner leaves remaining.

3 Cut around the hard core to remove.

4 Cauliflower with core removed.

5 Using the tip of the knife, cut at the base of a floret.

6 Like with the broccoli, continue cutting small flowerets from the outer stalks.

(continues on next page)

Cauliflower Preparation

(continued from previous page)

7   Once the bottom section has been cut, trim away the heart.

8   After the stem is trimmed, you can continue to cut florets.

9   Trim the stems of the florets.

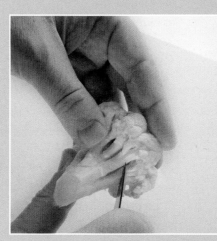

10   Keep in acidulated water until ready to use to maintain the whiteness.

11   To make *inflorescences* or small buds, take each floret and cut into smaller bouquets.

12   Continue working around each floret.

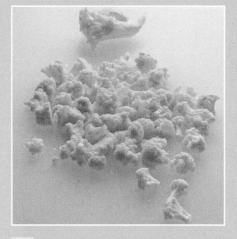

13   Cauliflower *inflorescences* or buds.

14   Depending on what it will be used for, whether for a gratin or a garnish for a soup, the cauliflower can be cut into different sizes.

Peeling Garlic

1 Cut the base of the clove which was attached to the bulb.

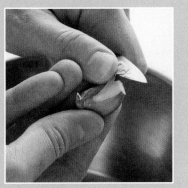

2 Do not cut all the way through and pull the skin.

3 From the cut end, continue to pull the skin away.

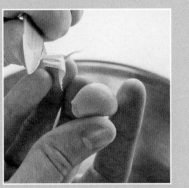

4 Peeled garlic.

Bulbs

The edible portion and the most nutrient-rich part of some vegetables grows underground in a bulbous shape. This shape is comprised of many fleshy layers that overlap and act as a sponge to bring nutrients into the plant. Onions, which are bulbs, have excellent keeping abilities and will not deteriorate—even lasting throughout the winter months.

The bulb is a flavorful and versatile vegetable that is an important aromatic element in the culinary world. An excellent addition to most preparations because of their perfume and texture, they enhance any dish in which they are used. Because there are so many varieties of bulbs to choose from, the flavor combinations are endless. Onions, leeks, garlic, and shallots all belong to the bulb family and are thought to have originated from Central Asia. We discuss each of these types of bulbs next.

Garlic – Ail

Species name: *Allium sativum*

Garlic is the most pungent and spicy member of the bulb family. When cooked, however, its flavor sweetens and mellows. The bulb of the garlic is comprised of numerous fleshy sections called cloves. The individual cloves are covered with a thin papery membrane, or skin. The leaves, stems, flowers, and cloves of this plant are edible, and they are usually eaten before they have matured. The only portion that is not palatable is the papery membrane that covers certain parts of the plant, and the roots of the bulb. The germ is removed because it is difficult to digest.

De-germing Garlic

1   After peeling the garlic, split in half.

2   The sprout will be like a comma.

3   Gently insert the tip of the knife at the tip of the sprout and lift.

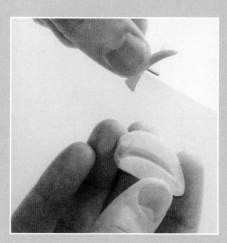

4   Remove and discard.

5   De-germed garlic.

Leek – Poireau

Species name: *Allium porrum*

Despite its shape, the **leek** is also a member of the bulb family. Instead of developing a round bulb like the onion, the leek produces a long cylinder of bundled leaves, which are paled by the soil pushing around them. The edible portion of the leek is the white onion-like base and the light green middle stalk. The dark green leaves are too tough for consumption but are used for adding flavor, such as in a *bouquet garni*. Leeks possess a more delicate flavor than that of onions.

Bouquet Garni

1   A classic bouquet garni is made up of parsley stems, celery, thyme and bay leaf, wrapped in the green part of the leek and tied securely with string.

2   Gather the parsley stems and place the celery in the center.

3   Add the thyme and bay leaf on top of the celery and parsley stems.

4   Carefully wrap the green part of the leek around the stems, making sure to enclose them completely and tightly.

(continues on next page)

Bouquet Garni

(continued from previous page)

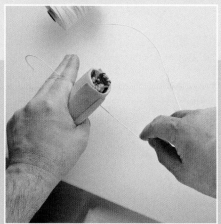

5 Using butchers' string, secure the cut end of the string and start wrapping around one end of the bouquet garni.

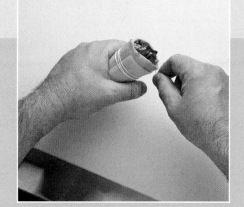

6 Wrap several times.

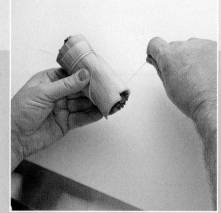

7 Then turn the bouquet garni and begin wrapping string around the other end.

8 Once the other end has been tied, cross the string over to tie with the loose end.

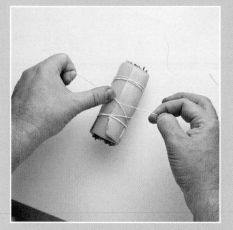

9 Loop twice in order for the knot to hold well.

10 The size of the bouquet garni can be adjusted according to its use. Large bouquet garni may need two pieces of green leek to completely wrap around the other elements.

Classic knife cuts for leeks.

Onions – Oignons

Species name: *Allium*

There are nearly 1,250 species of onion in the bulb family. The three varieties of onion that are familiar to most people are the spring onion, the common onion (yellow and white), and the pearl onion.

The **spring onion** (*Allium fistulosum*) is also referred to as a green onion or scallion. It possesses an undeveloped slender white bulb from which long, tender green leaves extend. Onions are believed to be indigenous to Asia; however, it is entirely possible that they have grown wild on every continent.

The **common onion** (*Allium cepa*) is a more complex onion due to its higher sulfur content. The sulfur in an onion is what makes your eyes water and there are several suggested remedies to avoid this, although none work especially well. This onion has a fully developed bulb that has yellow-white flesh, and the outer layers are covered in white to yellowish brown papery skin.

The **pearl onion** (*Allium proliferum*) is one of the sweetest varieties of onion. The pearl onion is a type of tree onion that is available in red, yellow, and white varieties. Tree onions produce bulblets, whereas a regular onion produces flowers. A pearl onion tree will take approximately two years to produce onions sweet enough for sale. Pearl onions are used in cocktails, salads, and stews.

Peeling an Onion

1 Onion should be dry and firm.

2 Start by cutting the top of the onion. To limit irritation to your eyes, use a very sharp knife that will cut rather than crush the onion.

3 Remove the root end by inserting the point of a small knife at an angle pointed toward the center of the onion.

(continues on next page)

Peeling an Onion

(continued from previous page)

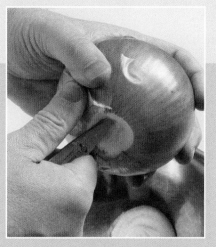

4   Cut in a circular motion cutting a cone-shape at the root end.

5   Lightly score along the latitude of the onion.

6   Loosen a corner of the skin with the point of the knife and pull the skin away.

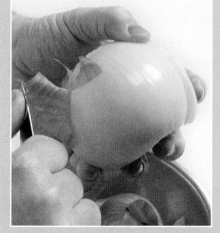

7   Continue, removing a second layer if needed.

8   A peeled onion should not have any of the brown skin remaining.

Onion Concasser

1. Cut the peeled onion in half and lay it cut-side down on the cutting board, root end away from you.

2. Cut vertically across almost to the root end at even intervals.

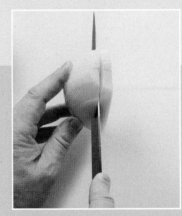

3. Cut horizontally, approximately the same thickness as the vertical cuts.

4. Cut almost to the root end, keeping the onion intact.

5. Cut parallel to the first horizontal cut.

6. Holding the onion together, cut crosswise, at the same interval.

7. Move your hand holding the onion, down as you cut.

8. The size of the dice can be adjusted by cutting smaller or larger intervals.

Mirepoix

Rouelle

Concasser

Rouelle

Ciseler

Émincer

Classic knife cuts for onions.

Shallots – Echalote

Species name: *Allium oschaninii*

Shallots look like a cross between garlic and an onion. A shallot has a coppery, reddish, or gray skin and when the outer skin is removed, the shallot will separate into large cloves like garlic. There are two shallot types: "True" or French gray or griselle shallots (*gris* means "gray" in French) are considered to have a more subtle flavor than the "false" or Jersey shallots, which are larger. They are called Jersey shallots because they were first cultivated on the Isle of Jersey. The name is derived from the ancient city of Ascalon in Canaan. Shallots possess a sweeter, milder taste than onions.

Did you know?

In keeping with an old English rhyme, the thickness of an onion skin is said to predict the severity of the winter. A thin skin is indicative of a moderate winter, whereas a thick skin is said to indicate a difficult winter ahead.

Peeling a Shallot

1 The recommended tool is the paring knife.

2 Start by cutting off the root end.

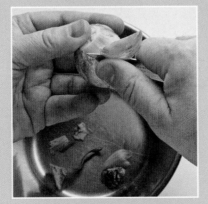

3 Remove the outer layer. It may be necessary to remove more than one layer.

4 The peeled shallot will be violet in color and it should be smooth with no dry or papery layers remaining.

Ciseler

Whole, *en chemise*

Concasser

Émincer

Classic knife cuts for shallots.

Fruit Vegetables

The main component of a flower's reproductive structure is the ovary. When fertilization occurs, the flower opens, exposing a ripened and matured ovary. A fruit is a ripened ovary that contains seeds, unless it has been cultivated specifically without them.

Some fruits have become widely known as vegetables. This is mainly due to the assumption that vegetables are used for savory preparations, while fruits are used for sweet preparations. This was officially acknowledged in 1893 by the U.S. Supreme Court, which officially identified the tomato as a vegetable based on its use (see the sidebar on page 78).

Since then, certain fruits have been considered vegetables based on their culinary use. For instance, the tomato, eggplant, and bell peppers are all actually fruits and not vegetables! And rhubarb, used almost exclusively in sweet preparations, is actually a vegetable.

Avocado

Avocado – Avocat

Species name: *Persea americana*

The **avocado** is a fruit vegetable belonging to the Lauraceae family. Native to Meso-America, the avocado has celebrated ties to the Incans. Commercially available in most parts of the world, this fruit grows in tropical and subtropical climates only.

The etymology of the word *avocado* stems from the Nahuatl (Aztec) word (from the Nahua people in Central Mexico) *ahuacatl*, meaning testicle, due to its shape and because the avocado grows in pairs. The Incans believed that the avocado would increase fertility in anyone who consumed it. The word *guacamole* is derived from the Nahuatl word *ahuacamolli*.

An avocado is a medium-green, pear-shaped fruit. The fruit ripens off the vine and contains a large pit at its center. As the avocado ripens, its alligator-like skin darkens and the fruit softens. The flesh will be medium chartreuse to golden when ripe. The flesh possesses a rich buttery texture that is both nutty and mild tasting. Like apples, avocado flesh oxidizes rapidly and will begin to brown once in contact with air. Rubbing lemon or lime juice on the flesh will immediately slow down the oxidation process.

The avocado that we know today stems from three varieties; Mexican, Guatemalan, and West Indian. The Mexican variety is the size of a plum and possesses smooth skin. The skin is purple to black in color with yellow-green–colored flesh. The leaves possess an anise-like perfume; they can be dried and used to season black bean dishes.

The Guatemalan variety is slightly larger than the Mexican variety. The skin may range in color from green to purple, and sometimes black. The leaves

Assorted Bell Peppers

of the Guatemalan variety are used in folk medicine to treat respiratory ailments, as a stomach tonic, and to regulate and induce menstruation. The natural oils produced from the leaves are very similar to anise, and are used for both medicinal and culinary purposes.

The West Indian variety is the largest, and can weigh up to 2 pounds each. They possess smooth skin, are usually light green, and possess unscented leaves. Hass and Fuerte avocados are hybrids of the Guatemalan and Mexican varieties and are most readily available in North America.

As most fruits ripen, their sugar content rises. This is not true with the avocado. The avocado will decrease in sugar content as the fruit matures, but will continue to yield more potassium, beta-carotene, magnesium, thiamin, riboflavin, folic acid, and vitamins E and K than most other fruit. The avocado is also high in protein, natural oils, and vitamins A and C. The vitamins contained in this fruit belong to the antioxidant group that protects and builds cells in human tissue. An avocado-rich diet is also said to lower bad cholesterol and increase good cholesterol. Avocado oil is richly flavored with hints of fruit and pleasing nutty undertones.

Bell Peppers – Poivrons

Species name: *Capsicum annuum*

Although cultivars of capsicum are commonly referred to as peppers, they are in no way related to pepper of the *Piper* genus. **Bell peppers** belong to the capsicum family. In fact in countries such as the UK and Australia, bell peppers are called capsicums. They are indigenous to Central America, South America, and Mexico. Pepper seeds collected by Spanish explorers were taken back to Spain in 1493, and from there the popularity of the bell pepper spread through Europe and reached as far as Asia. The pepper was found to adapt to a vast array of climates, further promoting its popularity wherever it would grow. The bell pepper is easily grown in temperate regions, either in green rooms or under glass. The bell pepper is now used internationally, and is a staple in many cultural dishes.

The pepper is said to have been named for its resemblance to a bell. Bell peppers are as recognized for their shape as they are for their flavor. The longer the pepper is permitted to ripen, the sweeter it will become. The bell pepper is one variety of capsicum that possesses a recessive gene that cancels out the effects of capsaicin. Capsaicin is the component that gives peppers heat, and without its activation, the resulting flavor is greatly tempered. As a pepper ripens, it will go through a series of color changes as well, beginning first as green, then yellow, and eventually red. Bell peppers are available in a spectrum of colors—even purple.

Bell peppers can be prepared in many different ways. They can be used in salads, puréed for use in vinaigrettes, grilled, stuffed, or baked. The bell pepper lends itself especially well to dry heat methods. Due to the versatility of this fruit, its culinary options are endless.

Evolutionary Advantages

The avian nervous system functions differently than that of a mammal; one difference is that birds have immunity to capsaicin. In their natural environment, chili peppers are among the favored forms of sustenance for birds, providing a healthy dose of vitamin C. It is thought that the chili pepper has been widely distributed throughout its native territory by birds, either as the seeds travel through the bird's digestive system or as the bird eats the seed pod in flight. If placed in bird feeders, capsaicin is known to deter squirrels and other mammals.

Classic knife cuts for bell peppers.

Cucumber – Concombre

Species name: *Cucumis sativus*

Native to India, the **cucumber** has been propagated for more than 3,000 years. A member of the gourd family, of which squash is also a member, the cucumber belongs to the same genus as muskmelon. The cucumber plant is a creeping vine and grows on trellises or supporting frames. It has large foliage that shades the growing fruit. The fruit is oblong with tapered ends and can grow up to 24 inches (60 cm) long.

Because it develops from a flower and has an enclosed seed, cucumbers are categorized as fruits, though like tomatoes and squash, cucumbers are prepared and consumed as vegetables. Cucumbers that are grown in a greenhouse are almost always seedless. If the grower would like the fruit to contain seeds, they will either pollinate each flower by hand, or allow bees into the greenhouse to do the work for them. Cucumbers are vitamin and nutrient rich, containing folic acid, vitamins A and C, magnesium, and phosphorus. The edible portion of the cucumber is the fruit itself, skin, flesh, and seeds, but not the plant.

In 1494 Christopher Columbus imported cucumbers to Haiti, and in 1535, Jacques Cartier discovered "very great cucumbers" grown in and around what is now Montreal. Toward the end of the 1600s, an aversion to uncooked vegetables and fruits began to develop among consumers. In a number of health publications it was stated that ingesting uncooked plants would cause any number of summer diseases and should not be consumed by children. Originally called the *cowcumber*, it is believed that the cucumber was at one time thought to be suitable only as cow feed.

Cucumbers can be pickled, which produces a very different flavor from their natural flavor. Pickling cucumbers are usually shorter and thicker than regular cucumbers and have bumpy skin. During the pickling process, much of the nutrient content is removed or degraded. The cucumbers are soaked in a solution that is a combination of brine, vinegar, and spices. In North America, pickled cucumbers are simply known as pickles; in the United Kingdom they are known as gherkins or "wallies." Cucumbers can be added to salads or sandwiches and are often cut and used in crudités with dips.

Cucumber–Dépépiner

1 After peeling, cut the cucumber in half lengthwise.

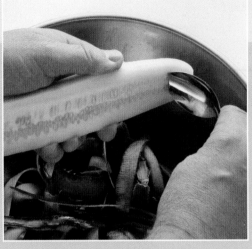

2 Using a teaspoon, begin to loosen the seeds from one end.

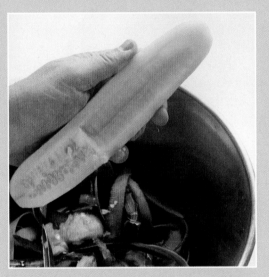

3 Work your way down the length of the cucumber.

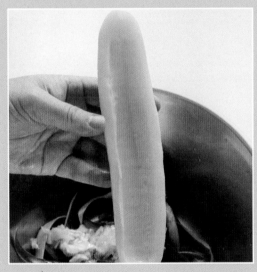

4 The cucumber is now ready to be cut for other uses.

Cucumber Dégorger

1 Place sliced cucumber into a large colander and season well with coarse sea salt.

2 Toss well to ensure the salt is distributed evenly.

3 Place the colander on a shallow plate and cover the cucumber with a small plate.

4 Place a weight on top of the plate, such as a small bowl of water, and leave to degorge. The water will collect on the bottom of the larger plate.

Eggplant – *Aubergine*

Species name: *Solanum melongena*

The **eggplant**, or aubergine, belongs to the Solanaceae family, also known as nightshade and is closely related to the tomato and potato. Native to India, the plant grows 16 to 57 inches (40 to 145 cm) tall with white to purple flowers and yellow stamens. Botanically classified as a berry, the eggplant contains numerous small, soft seeds. These seeds are edible but can be quite bitter because they contain small amounts of nicotinoid alkaloids, which isn't surprising since the eggplant is a close relative of tobacco.

The name *eggplant* was first used in North America, Australia, and New Zealand because the fruits of 18th-century cultivars were yellow or white and looked like goose or hen's eggs. In Britain, the word *aubergine* comes from the

French word of the same name. Aubergine is derived from the Catalan word *alberginia*, which comes from the Arabic word *albadinjan*. In India and South Africa, the plant is known as *brinjal*.

Though eggplant becomes tender when cooked, the raw fruit has a bitter taste. After it is cooked, eggplant develops a rich, complex flavor. Degorging (salting and rinsing) the eggplant can soften and reduce this bitterness. Because it can absorb large amounts of sauces and cooking fats, the eggplant can produce very rich dishes. The skin of the fruit is also edible so it does not need to be peeled before cooking. Because it is native to India, eggplant is widely used in Indian cuisine. Used in chutneys, curries, and achaar (a pickling method in India), it is often described as the "King of the Vegetables" and is used in everyday and festive Indian food. Eggplant can be stewed, as in *ratatouille*, the Italian dish *melanzane alla parmigiana*, or the Greek dish *moussaka*. In the Middle East, eggplant is used in *baba ghanoush*, where it is blended with other ingredients such as lemon, garlic, and tahini.

Because the eggplant belongs to the nightshade family, it was at one time believed to be dangerous for human consumption. Because some eggplants are bitter, they can irritate the stomach lining, causing gastritis. Eggplant makes an excellent meat substitute for vegetarian cooking.

Eggplant Dégorger

1. After cutting the ends, split the eggplant lengthwise.

2. Score down the length of each half.

3. Score horizontally at a slight angle.

4. Sprinkle the surface with coarse salt.

5. Sprinkle the bottom of a paper-lined pan with rock salt and place the eggplant cut-side down.

6. Leave the eggplant to degorge.

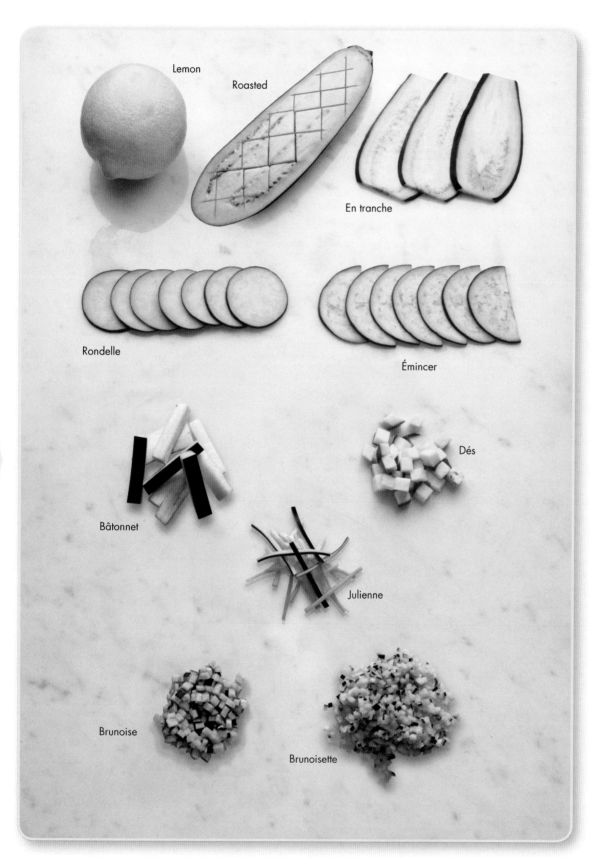

Classic knife cuts for eggplant.

Squash

Species name: *Cucurbita pepo*

All squash are indigenous to the Americas and have been cultivated for more than 10,000 years. Squash crops were cultivated by the Incas, Aztecs, and Mayans in Latin America usually alongside corn and bean crops. This type of planting is called *companion planting*, because these three crops benefit from growing together. The corn provides a tower for the climbing beans, eliminating a need for poles. The beans enrich the soil with nitrogen (see page 134 under Pods and Seeds) and the low-growing squash plants cover the soil bed, blocking the sunlight and preventing the growth of unwanted weeds. The broad leaves of the squash plant also provide shade, keeping the topsoil cool and moist, and the spiny hairs of the squash vine help keep pests away.

Most varieties of squash are classified as either summer squash or winter squash, as determined by the storage life of the squash. The summer varieties are picked from the vine when they are very young, whereas the winter varieties are picked only when they are fully ripe. Squash varieties include pattypan squash, spaghetti squash, acorn squash, butternut squash, pumpkin, and zucchini.

Pattypan Squash

Pattypan Squash – Pâtisson

The **pattypan squash** is a summer squash that is best when small, smooth, firm, and with good coloring. They measure between 3 to 4 inches (7 to 10 cm) in diameter and are distinctively shaped. This particular type of squash has a soft, sweet flavor similar to that of an artichoke. Pattypans cannot be kept for a long period of time because as they age, the flesh lightens and toughens considerably.

Spaghetti Squash – Courge spaghetti

Spaghetti squash is an elliptical-shaped winter squash that has large seeds at its center. The skin can be orange, green, ivory, yellow, or orange with white streaks. When uncooked, the flesh will look like any other squash. When cooked, the flesh is transformed, falling away from the skin in ribbons, much like spaghetti.

Acorn Squash – Courge

The **acorn squash** is commonly classified as a winter squash; however, it is in fact a summer squash like zucchini. The acorn squash is ridged from top to bottom and is shaped like an acorn. The flesh of this squash is sweet and yellow to orange in color. The skin is usually dark green, but with new varieties on the market, you may find some that are white or golden yellow.

Butternut Squash – Courge Musquée

The **butternut squash** is considered a winter squash and can be stored from 30 to 180 days. They are ripe enough to enjoy when they are approximately 8 to 12 inches (20 to 30 cm) long, and 4 to 5 inches (10 to 13 cm) in diameter, and have a lovely orange color. A slightly green skin is an indicator that the squash has not yet fully ripened.

Pumpkin – Citrouille

The **pumpkin** is pulpy, possessing a very thick skin, and is considered to be a winter squash. The flesh has a softened sweetness and its seeds are exquisitely nutty in flavor.

Zucchini – Courgette

The **zucchini** fruit is mild, sweet, and takes on the flavors of whatever it is cooked with. The flavor and quality of zucchini will decline as the fruit matures. Zucchini has a thin, smooth skin with cream-colored flesh and a varying amount of seeds. The skin can be either yellow or green and will sometimes have grayish-green or yellow-green striations. Zucchini can be eaten raw, baked, grilled, or sautéed. The zucchini flower is even more flavorful than the fruit itself, possessing a rich and savory taste. Zucchini flowers are used in salads, deep-fried, or used as a garnish for cooked zucchini.

Zucchini Canneler Émincer

1 Rinse the zucchini to remove any dirt.

2 Trim off the ends of the zucchini.

3 Holding it firmly, place the tooth of the channeling knife at the cut end.

4 Firmly pull toward you.

5 Continue to the other end, cutting as straight as possible.

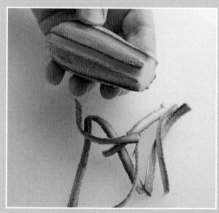

6 Continue around the zucchini.

(continues on next page)

Zucchini Canneler Émincer

(continued from previous page)

7 Place on the cutting board and cut into thin slices.

8 Zucchini Canneler Émincer

Zucchini Tonnelet

1 Cut whole zucchini to desired length.

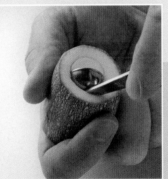

2 Using a melon baller, carefully scoop out the flesh leaving a 3-4 mm border.

3 Continue scooping, keeping the walls even.

4 Do not scoop too far, there should be at least 1 cm of flesh at the bottom.

5 Zucchini are now ready for filling.

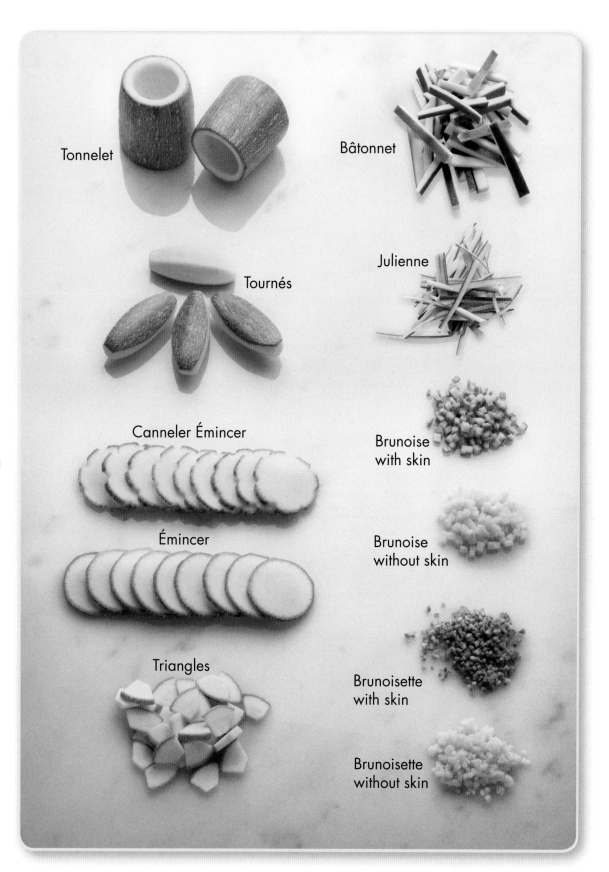

Tonnelet

Bâtonnet

Tournés

Julienne

Canneler Émincer

Brunoise
with skin

Émincer

Brunoise
without skin

Triangles

Brunoisette
with skin

Brunoisette
without skin

Classic knife cuts for zucchini.

Tomato – Tomate

Species name: *Solanum lycopersicum*

The **tomato** belongs to the Solanaceae or nightshade family. The tomato's close relatives include tobacco, potatoes, eggplants, and chili peppers. A vine plant that has countless variations in shape, color, and taste, this plant generally grows to heights reaching 3 to 10 feet (1 to 3 meters) with 4- to 10-inch (10- to 25-cm) leaves and yellow, 0.4- to 0.8-inch (10- to 20-mm) flowers. Native to South America, the species we know today, *Solanum lycopersicum*, was brought to Mexico and eaten by prehistoric humans. Evidence suggests that the first deliberately farmed tomato was a small yellow fruit, likely an ancestor of the cherry tomato. The exact date of this cultivation remains a mystery. It was grown by the Aztecs of Central Mexico who called it *xitomatl* (zee-toe-má-tel), which means "plump thing with a navel." The word *tomato* comes from the Nahuatl word *tomatl*. The species name, *lycopersicum*, means "wolf-peach," because in South America the tomato is the main food source for wild dogs.

Some schools of thought suggest that the Spanish explorer Hernán Cortés (1485–1547) was the first to bring the small yellow tomato to Europe, while others believe that Christopher Columbus discovered it in 1493. However, the earliest written mention of the tomato in Europe was in 1544 by Pietro Andrea Mattioli (1501–1577), an Italian physicist and botanist. He called the tomato *pomo d'oro*, which literally translates to mean "golden apple."

Tomatoes were not grown in Europe until the middle of the 16th century, and in places like Florence, tomatoes were used as a tabletop decoration rather than a foodstuff until the late 17th century. John Gerard was one of the earliest cultivators, and he believed that the tomato was poisonous, even though it was common for them to be grown in English gardens in the late 1500s. Gerard's views were largely influential and so for many years in places like Great Britain (and her North American colonies), the tomato was considered unsafe for consumption. By the early 1700s, tomatoes were being grown in British North America. By the mid-18th century tomatoes were being cultivated as ornamental plants more often than as a food item. Thomas Jefferson is said to have eaten a tomato in Paris and after sending some seeds back to America, the full potential of this fruit was realized, and they were finally planted as a food crop.

Tomatoes range in size from cherry tomatoes, which are about 1/2 to 1 inch (1 to 2 cm), to beefsteak tomatoes, which can exceed 4 inches (10 cm) in diameter. The most popular commercial tomatoes are about 2 to 2.5 inches (5 to 6 cm) in diameter. While most cultivars produce red fruit, there are a number—especially heirloom plants—that produce yellow, orange, pink, purple, green, black, and white fruit. An heirloom plant is a cultivar that was grown during early periods of human history, but is not widely used in modern times. They are grown through open pollination and not by hybridization.

Tomatoes are now consumed worldwide and are used extensively in Italian, Middle Eastern, and South American cuisines. Though botanically a berry and therefore a fruit, the tomato is commonly classified as a vegetable. Because *vegetable* is not a botanical term, there is no discrepancy in the plant botanically being a fruit while at the same time treated as a vegetable. (See the sidebar on page 78 about the *Nix vs. Hedden* court case for more on the vegetable vs. fruit debate.)

More than 7,500 varieties of tomatoes are grown for a number of purposes. The more popular varieties are discussed next.

Although tomatoes come in an almost infinite amount of varieties in all shapes, colors, and sizes, there are two main types that one is likely to come across. These are the classic red, round tomato and the plum tomato.

Round tomatoes contain many seeds in a large number of juicy compartments, known as locular cavities. They are best used in cold preparations and salads. The most popular tomato of this type in North America is the beefsteak tomato. The plum tomato, also known as the Roma and Italian tomato, is a small, red, oblong tomato. It was developed specifically for use in canning and sauce making. It is ideal for cooking because it only has 1–2 locular cavities and is much fleshier than other varieties of tomato.

Tomato Emondée

1 Remove the stem of the tomato.

2 Place in boiling water.

3 Leave in the water until the skin begins to blister.

4 Immediately remove.

5 Place in an ice water.

6 Once cooled, peel away the loosened skin.

(continues on next page)

Tomato Emondée

(continued from previous page)

7 Peeled tomatoes should be completely smooth with no skin remaining.

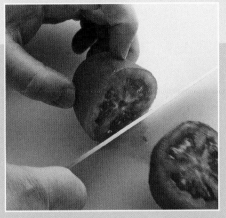

8 Cut the tomato in half.

9 Gently squeeze.

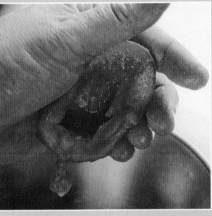

10 Loosen the seeds and excess liquid.

11 Tomato Emondée.

Tomato Vidées

1 After removing the stem, cut the tomato in half.

2 If needed, trim the bottom and top of the tomato to keep it from rolling.

3 Using a melon baller, trim the interior ribs and seeds.

(continues on next page)

Tomato Vidées

(continued from previous page)

4 Tomatoes should be completely cleaned with no holes or punctures to the bottom.

5 Sprinkle the interior with salt to degorge.

6 Place upside down onto paper toweling to drain.

Tomato Julienne

1 Place the whole peeled tomato on the cutting board. Following the natural curve of the tomato, cut thin, even slices.

2 Continue around the tomato until only the core and seeds remain.

3 Trim the rounded ends of the slices.

4 Lay each slice flat on the cutting board and cut lengthwise.

5 Tomato Julienne

Leafy Greens

Leafy vegetables include Swiss chard, spinach, sorrel, watercress, bok choy, curly endive, radicchio, and various types of lettuce. They are delicious and can be eaten raw, pickled, cooked, or marinated. With a myriad of flavors, there is a leafy green to complement every palette.

The leaves and stems of a leafy vegetable plant are used for food and seasoning, and are often referred to as pot herbs. Pot herbs were commonly used in recipes dating from the 16th to the 19th century. This term was used to describe any plant with edible leaves and stalks that could be boiled as greens, used in soups, or used as cooking herbs.

Curly Endive or Frisée

Butterhead — *Laitue pommée, Laitue beurre*

Species name: *Lactuca sativa* var. *capitata*

Butterhead is a small-headed lettuce with soft leaves. Butterhead is one of two main varieties of lettuce, the second being crisphead. There are several varieties of butterhead, two of which are bibb and Boston lettuce. All lettuce varieties contain trace amounts of lactucarium, a known sedative, which has similar side effects to opium in higher amounts. Butterhead lettuce is known for its buttery texture and sweet flavor.

Curly Endive – Frisée

Species name: *Cichorium endiva*

Curly endive is native to Europe. Sometimes called chicory in North America, or *chicorée frisée* in France, it is not to be confused with the common chicory plant or its roots. Curly endive and chicory are two different species of the same genus. It is easy to get confused because the terms *chicory* and *endive* are often used interchangeably.

Curly endive, as its name suggests, has curly, bitter-tasting leaves. The outer leaves are dark green and more bitter than the creamy yellow inner leaves. One variation of curly endive is escarole.

Iceberg Lettuce – Laitue Iceberg

Species name: *Lactuca sativa* var. *capitata*

Iceberg, or crisphead, lettuce has a large round, tightly packed head of pale green leaves. **Iceberg lettuce** is crisp, juicy, and hardy with a neutral taste. Iceberg is commonly used for salads and to garnish foods. Iceberg lettuce was referred to as crisphead lettuce until the early 1900s—it became known as iceberg lettuce when California began shipping large quantities of the lettuce to other parts of the United States under piled ice.

Lettuce has been growing in China since the 5th century, and is considered by the superstitious to bring good luck. In fact, it is customary to serve lettuce on special occasions, such as birthdays and the Chinese New Year. During his second voyage to the New World, Christopher Columbus was said to have brought with him several varieties of lettuce. In the 17th century, Spanish missionaries planted lettuce in what is now known as the "Lettuce Capital of the United States"—California. Centuries later, with the development of new transportation technologies, lettuce is readily available year-round and has been popularized throughout North America.

Radicchio

Leaf Lettuce – Laitue, Laitue Frisée

Species name: *Lactuca sativa var. crispa*

Red and green **leaf lettuce** feature wide, curly leaves. These varieties are delicate tasting and possess a mildly crisp texture with firm leaves. Both red and green leaf lettuce contains small amounts of antioxidants such as beta-carotene and lutein, as well as vitamins A and K.

Lamb's Lettuce – Mâche

Species name: *Valerianella locusta*

Corn salad, **mâche** or lamb's lettuce grows wild in Europe, northern Africa, and western Asia. A common cultivar in France and Germany, it is a low-growing plant with wide, rounded leaves that are tender and succulent. It is considered a winter salad because it grows well in colder temperatures. It grows easily and can often be found growing like a weed in cultivated fields (in particular corn fields) and open spaces.

Mesclun Greens – Mesclun

Species name: Mixed varieties

Mesclun greens are a bitter-tasting mix that varies depending on the area where it is purchased. Traditionalists in Provence, France, use a mix of chervil, endive, arugula, and lettuce in equal proportions. The North American mixes include arugula, endives, mustards, lettuces, purslane, chicory, parsleys, fennels, escarole, and tender greens such as bibb or Boston lettuce.

Oakleaf – Feuille de Chêne

Species name: *Lactuca sativa*

Oakleaf lettuce should have crisp, firm leaves that are deeply colored and oak shaped. Oakleaf lettuce is delicate tasting and pairs well with other delicate flavors without overwhelming the palette.

Radicchio – Trévise

Species name: *Cichorium intybus*

Known for its small head and violet-colored leaves, **radicchio** is part of the common chicory family. Common chicory is cultivated in two forms—for its leaves or for its roots. Radicchio belongs to the former category, as does Belgian endive. The roots of common chicory are often dried, roasted, and ground to be used to replace coffee or mixed with coffee.

Did you know?

In ancient times, the populace of the Mediterranean considered lettuce to be little more than a noxious weed. However, by 55 BC the nutritional values of lettuce had begun to be recognized, and it began to be found on the dinner plates of Persian royalty. The name *lettuce* is said to come from the Latin words describing its "milky juices."

Romaine Lettuce – Romaine

Species name: *Lactuca sativa var. longifolia*

Romaine lettuce was one of the first varieties to be used in salads during Roman times. The leaves can grow to 9 inches in length. The leaves are medium green and tightly folded, and have a sweeter flavor compared to other lettuce varieties. It is the lettuce used to prepare a traditional Caesar salad.

Sorrel – Oseille

Species name: *Rumex acetosa Linn*

Sorrel is native to Europe. Sometimes referred to as spinach dock, sorrel contains varying levels of acidity and sourness due to the presence of oxalic acid. Sorrel is cultivated as either an herb or leafy vegetable.

Spinach – Epinard

Species name: *Spinacia oleracea*

Spinach is native to southwestern Asia. It possesses a similar taste profile as beets. Spinach that is fresh and uncooked will have a sweet taste, whereas cooked spinach will have a decidedly more astringent and full-bodied flavor.

Watercress – Cresson

Species name: *Nasturtium officinale*

Watercress is native to Europe and western Asia. The watercress plant is cultivated for its smooth, thick, dark green leaves. The leaves are pungent, bitter, and peppery. Watercress encourages digestion and is a known diuretic. It also contains more vitamin C than an orange, more folate than bananas, more iron than spinach, and more calcium than milk.

> Lettuce is indigenous to the Eastern Mediterranean region and parts of Western Asia. Conveyed through paintings in Egyptian tombs, lettuce has been a recorded part of history since at least 4500 BC. The ancient Greeks and Romans believed lettuce to be an important food source and medicinal ingredient.

Blanching Lettuce

1 Add vinegar to the cold water and wash the lettuce well.

2 Generously salt boiling water with coarse salt.

3 Holding by the stem, immerse the lettuce into the boiling water.

(continues on next page)

Blanching Lettuce

(continued from previous page)

4 Push under using a wire skimmer.

5 Once wilted, immediately transfer to ice water.

6 Cool completely, then squeeze out excess water.

7 Squeeze from the root end to the tip.

8 Lay them out on a work surface.

Mushrooms – Champignons

Mushrooms belong to the Fungi family. The word *mushroom* comes from the old French word *moisseron*, which comes from mousse, or "moss." This word also existed in old English as *mos*, meaning a swamp or bog. Although there are many mushroom varieties, many are toxic, which limits our consumption to those wild types that are trusted or to commercially grown mushrooms.

Although for purposes of cooking, we consider mushrooms to be vegetables, they are not plants. Unlike plants, mushrooms do not contain seeds, leaves, roots, or chlorophyll. Fungi draw their nutrients from other living things, living off the material of plants and plant remains. Mushrooms reproduce by releasing spores into the air. After being carried by the wind, new mushrooms grow where the spores have landed. They grow, reproduce, and thrive in dark, moist spaces.

Mushrooms are cultivated worldwide, and although most growing regions are located in the Northern Hemisphere, there are a few in the Southern Hemisphere.

It is not possible to commercially grow all mushrooms. Some varieties, such as the truffle, survive by forming a symbiotic relationship with living plants or trees. The fungi will collect needed nutrients from the soil and share it with the plant or tree roots, which in turn will share their sugars with the mushroom.

Many delicious mushrooms are available for culinary use. The white button or *champignon de Paris* is a common, widely used member of the fungi family. There are also wilder varieties; the oyster, crimini, chanterelle, shitake, porcini, and morel are among the most prized. Always remember the old mushroom adage when purchasing or selecting your mushrooms: "If you cannot smell the mushroom, you will not be able to taste the mushroom."

Chanterelle Mushroom – Girolles

Species name: *Cantharellus cibarius*

The **chanterelle mushroom** grows wild in thick forests and develops a symbiosis with the pine and deciduous trees in these areas. Chanterelles are not commercially cultivated and can only be found in the wild. When eaten out of hand, chanterelles possess a peppery flavor, but this flavor will dissipate with cooking. A cooked chanterelle has a more delicate taste. Chanterelles that are translucent are poisonous and should not be eaten.

Morel Mushroom – Morilles

Species name: *Morchella esculenta, Morchella conica*

Morels are among the most difficult mushrooms to find, making them quite expensive. They are most commonly found in moist areas, in proximity with dying and decaying trees. Their nutty flavor and meaty texture make the effort to find them well worth the trouble. If you are lucky enough, morels can be found in some specialty stores from April through June and are sometimes available dried throughout the year. Some mushroom growers have succeeded in cultivating the morel, but they are still one of the most difficult mushrooms to grow.

Oyster Mushroom – Pleurotte

Species name: *Pleurotus ostreatus*

The **oyster mushroom** is characterized by its appearance, scent, and oyster-like flavor. This variety possesses a very small stalk and grows sideways in clusters. Oyster mushrooms are moist, hairless, and are light to dark gray in color. The color of the oyster mushroom will darken as it ages. The fan-shaped cap can be 2 to 8 inches (5 to 20 cm) in width. Oyster mushrooms have long been cultivated in Asia.

Porcini Mushroom – Cèpe

Species name: *Boletus edulis*

The **porcini mushroom** is characterized by a firm white stalk, and a wide, dark brown cap that can grow up to 30 centimeters in diameter. Porcini mushrooms possess a nutty flavor and are one of the most prized by mushroom gatherers the world over. This variety is best used while very fresh because they deteriorate quickly after being picked. Purchasing dried porcini is very common. When using the dried variety, ensure that they remain fragrant. If the dried variety is dry and crumbly, they will most likely be old and flavorless. Porcini are prized for their versatility in cuisine.

Shitake Mushroom

Species name: *Lentinus edodes*

The **shitake mushroom** is also known as the Japanese black forest mushroom and is medium brown in color with a flat cap. They are cultivated commercially and can also be found in the wild. The first shitake mushrooms were found growing on hardwood trees more than 2,000 years ago in Japan, and are now commercially grown on artificial logs. The shitake mushroom has a distinctively thick umbrella-shaped cap, chewy texture, and earthy flavor when fresh. Dried shitake mushrooms that have been rehydrated are used regularly in Asian cuisine and possess a smoky, meaty flavor.

White Button Mushroom – Champignon de Paris

Species name: *Agaricus bisporus*

The **white button mushroom** is a cultivated field variety and the most cultivated worldwide. White button mushrooms are grown commercially in mushroom houses where both temperature and humidity are carefully monitored and controlled. The rich compost they are grown in is a combination of cottonseed, gypsum, straw, corncobs, cocoa seed hulls, and nitrogen supplements. Within the first few weeks of the growing process, peat moss is applied to the compost. Mature mushrooms are ready for harvesting approximately three weeks after the peat moss is applied.

Peeling Mushrooms

1 Hold the mushroom by the head.

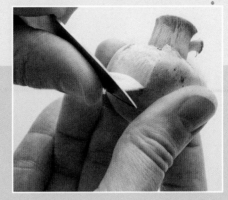

2 Using a paring knife, begin pulling the loose skin from the bottom of the cap.

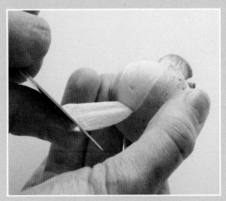

3 Pull gently, and pulling off as much as possible.

4 The cap should be firm and white.

Mushroom Émincer

1 Once the stem has been removed, place the cap on the cutting board and hold securely.

2 Begin cutting thin, even slices.

3 Mushroom Émincer

Mushroom Julienne

1   Thinly slice the peeled mushrooms at a slight downward angle.

2   Continue cutting the peeled mushroom in slices of even thickness.

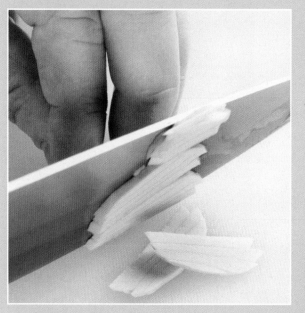

3   To cut a julienne, stack the slices and cut into strips.

4   Sprinkle with lemon juice to prevent oxidization.

Mushroom Brunoise

1 To make a brunoise, stack the julienne.

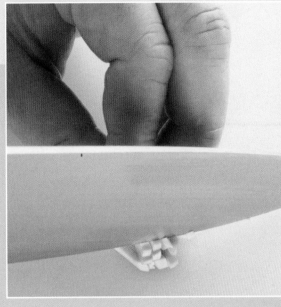

2 Cut crosswise.

3 Continue to cut the mushroom brunoise quickly and carefully.

4 Clockwise from top center: step 1 peeled mushrooms, step 2 sliced mushrooms, step 3 mushroom julienne, and step 4 mushroom brunoise.

Destemming Mushrooms

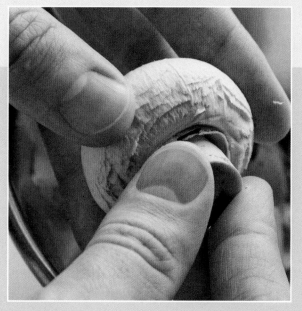

1 Method One: Holding the cap, gently pull the stem.

2 Break off at the base.

3 Method Two: Cut the stem straight across at the base of the mushroom.

4 Cut stem is flush with the cap.

Mushroom Évider

1 Once peeled, rub the mushroom with lemon juice to prevent it from oxidizing.

2 Break off the stem.

3 Using a melon baller, scoop out the gills (the brown part) of the mushroom cap.

4 Remove as much of the gills of the mushroom as possible.

5 Rub with lemon juice during the process.

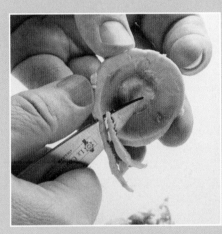

6 Once finished, trim the ends.

7 Save the trimmings for stock and sauce making.

8 Mushroom Évider

Turning Mushrooms

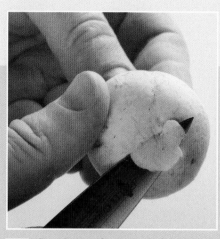

1 Starting at the center of the mushroom cap, begin peeling, cutting in a circular pattern.

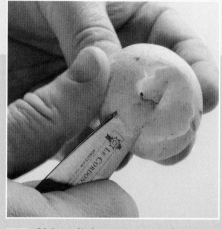

2 Using slight pressure with your thumb, turn the mushroom as the knife slices through.

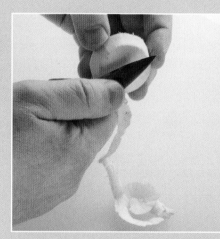

3 Continue turning, as the knife moves outward.

4 Finish by trimming the bottom of the cap.

5 Once finished, rub the cap with lemon to keep it from discoloring.

Quartering a Mushroom

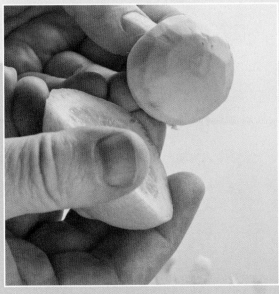

1 After peeling, rub the cap with lemon juice.

2 Cut in half through the stem.

3 Cut each half into quarters.

4 Quartered Mushrooms

Mushroom Canneler—Right Handed

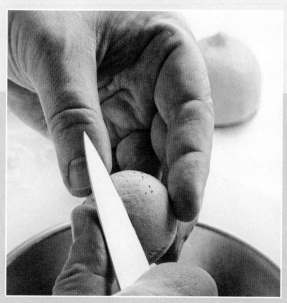

1 Hold the mushroom with your left hand and place the cutting edge of the knife on top facing away from your body. The blade should be approximately at a 45 degree angle and touching the center of the head of the mushroom

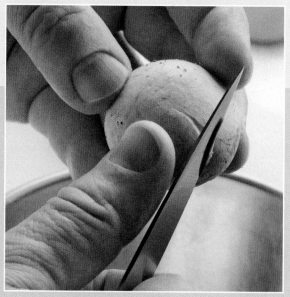

2 As you turn the mushroom toward you, turn your right hand with the knife away from you, keeping the blade against the mushroom.

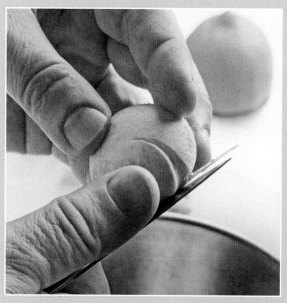

3 The blade should follow the curve of the mushroom head, and the action of "turning" your hands will result in a small groove being made in the mushroom head.

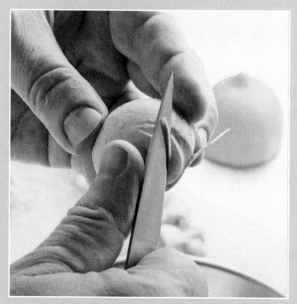

4 Place the knife below the first cut and repeat the movement.

(continues on next page)

Mushroom Canneler—Right Handed

(continued from previous page)

5   Each cut should be close enough to the next to ensure that the skin is completely removed.

6   The cut should be made in one movement, so do not worry about cutting off the strips of mushroom.

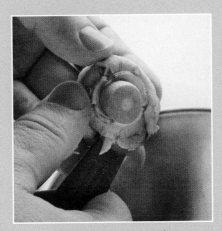

7   Continue all the way around the mushroom.

8   Once completed, turn the mushroom over and cut straight across the bottom to remove the stem and any remaining strips.

9   Rub with lemon juice to keep the mushroom from discoloring.

Mushroom Canneler—Left Handed

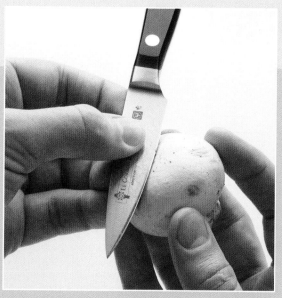

1. Holding the blade with your left hand, place it at a shallow angle so that it is touching the middle of the top of the mushroom.

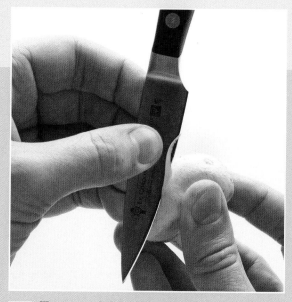

2. Turn your left hand toward you, while turning your right hand away from you, making sure that the blade is always in contact with the mushroom. It will automatically dig into the mushroom.

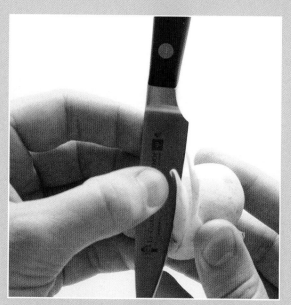

3. Place the blade back on the top of the mushroom, next to the first groove, and repeat the same movement.

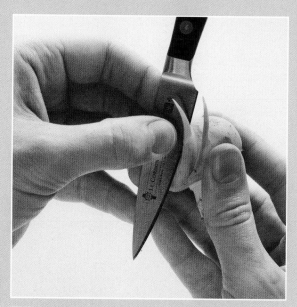

4. You may need to adjust the angle of the knife in order to remove the skin, but not cut too deeply where the mushroom might break off.

(continues on next page)

Mushroom Canneler—Left Handed

(continued from previous page)

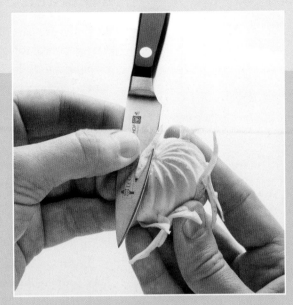

5 After a cut, always lift the knife and replace it back at the top.

6 Continue around the mushroom. Don't worry about the peelings that remain attached. They can be removed at the end.

7 If done correctly, all the skin should be gone leaving a white, fluted cap.

Choosing Dried Mushrooms

Mushrooms are one of the few ingredients that can be used equally fresh or dried. In fact, dried mushrooms often possess more intense flavors. Moisture evaporates during the drying process, and because mushrooms are comprised of mostly water, the end result is a concentration of flavor.

Prior to purchasing dried mushrooms, smell them if you can—they should possess a rich aroma. You should also choose darker colored varieties, because they possess more flavor. Select mushrooms without tiny pinholes, because that usually means that insects have been living there.

Pods and Seeds

Legumes are part of an economically significant plant family that falls into the vast botanical category of *Eudecots*. Known also as the pea family, bean family, or pulse family, legumes are cultivated as a food source but are equally important to farmers as they are used to improve the nitrogen content of the soil.

A **legume** is a simple dried fruit that is contained in a long pod that opens along a seam on two sides. Legumes live in a symbiotic relationship with bacteria that live in nodules on their roots. These bacteria help feed the plant by processing nitrogen from the air into compounds that the plants can use, enriching the soil in which they grow. This is why farmers alternate their crops in the fields. A legume crop is used to enrich the soil with nitrates, and the following year the same crop bed will be used for a different crop that will benefit from being planted in the nitrate-enriched soil.

Legumes are celebrated for their nutritional properties. Most are rich in fiber, protein, B vitamins, iron, and vitamin C. Some examples of legume plants are string beans, shelling beans, sweet green peas, snow peas, and corn.

The green bean variety of the bean plant was named so because the pods are harvested prior to reaching full maturity. Most green beans are not actually green; some varieties are yellow.

Corn – Maïs

Species name: *Zea mays*

Unlike beans and peas, which are considered part of the Fabaceae family, **corn** is a member of the Poaceae family. Corn is also not technically a legume but due to its pod shape and cooking methods it tends to be categorized as such by food distributors. Corn is grown on every continent in the world with the exception of Antarctica. The two most popular varieties are white and yellow. As soon as corn is harvested, the sugars begin to turn to starch. Corn is not only a popular food item, but also the foundation of many common by-products, including bourbon, corn flour, corn meal, corn oil, cornstarch, corn syrup, corn whiskey, and laundry starch.

Peas – Pois

Species name: *Pisum sativum*

Peas are native to Asia and central Europe. They are considered a super food because they are rich in protein, fiber, folic acid, vitamins, and minerals. A pea will begin to convert its natural sugars into starch the moment that it is picked. It is for this reason that it is best to eat peas soon after they are removed from the plant.

There are many varieties of pea, including the sweet green pea and the mange tout or snow pea. The **sweet green** variety is also known as the English pea, the garden pea, or petits pois. The pod is plump and bright green in color. When immature, the sweet green pea seed is delicious. The seeds are crunchy and sweet. As the pea pod matures, it will lose its sweetness and will not be as desirable.

Gregor Mendel (1822–1884), an Austrian monk known as the "father of genetics," propagated and analyzed 28,000 pea plants for the sole purpose of studying plant variations. Through a series of simple tests and experiments, he conceptualized the idea of heredity. This later became known as Mendel's laws of heredity or **Mendelian inheritance.**

The **mange tout** or **snow pea** is consumed whole. The pods are harvested prior to reaching full maturity while the pod is still flat and undeveloped. This variety of pea is very sweet.

Shelling Beans

Species names: *Phaseolus lunatus* (lima); *Glycine max* (soy); *Pisum sativum* (pea)

Shelling beans are indigenous to Japan, India, Central America, and the Mediterranean. Shelling beans are beans that have reached full maturity and are then removed from the pod before they have dried. The pod is not consumed. When the bean is grown for the seed only, it may be considered a shelling bean. Some shelling beans include Lima, soy, peas, and fava or broad beans.

Root Vegetables

Sometimes the part of the plant that grows underground is the most delicious and desirable culinary treasure. Roots, tuberous roots, and taproot vegetables are all used for their nutritional properties and myriad of flavors.

To understand the difference between root and bulb vegetables, consider the bulb vegetable to be a storage unit, similar to an underground parking lot. The nutrients are taken in by the roots at the base of the bulb and are absorbed into a concentrated mass, comprised of many fleshy layers. They remain in this storage area until dispersed at a slow rate, allowing for some greenery to grow above the soil. However, the bulk of the nutrients lie just beneath the soil, in the edible bulb that grows much larger than the roots. The greens that grow above the soil, closest to the bulb, contain the most nutrients. The greens that grow the farthest away from the fleshy layered bulb will be too tough for consumption. They may, however, be used as a flavor enhancer. In fact, the darker greens of the leek are used in bouquet garni. Bulb vegetables are known for their strong perfume and pungent taste, in varying degrees. This is due to the presence of sulfur compounds, and some are so potent they will make the eye tear, as with onions. This is characteristic of the *Allium* genus, the plant family to which bulbs belong.

If the bulb vegetable is thought of as a parking lot for nutrients then the root vegetable could be compared to a road. It is the part of the plant that is eaten, and sometimes the greens that grow above the soil are eaten too. The nutrients are absorbed by the roots and transferred throughout the entire plant, traveling at an even rate. As a result, both the root and the greens are nutrient rich, and although not every root vegetable is utilized for its greens and root, the nutrients are dispersed evenly. Root vegetables contain a complex mix of carbohydrates that results in varying levels of sugars and starches. When the plant begins to grow, the leafy tops seemingly steal the road. However, as the root develops beneath the soil, it also enlarges, developing both sugar and starch.

Did you know?

It is a surprising fact that the enzyme for digesting the broad bean is lacking in some 100 million people worldwide. This condition, known as favism, is a form of hemolytic anemia and affects mainly people of Mediterranean and Middle Eastern descent.

Root vegetables have become an important staple in lieu of cereals. West Africa, Central Africa, and Oceania use root vegetables as a staple in their diets. They are either used whole or mashed to make foufou or poi.

This type of vegetable will house the nutrients in the root of the plant, where they are transformed into carbohydrates. Each root vegetable contains a mixture of starches and sugars. Next, we discuss the following root vegetables: beets, carrots, celery root, potatoes, radish, and turnips. Horseradish, crosnes, Jerusalem artichokes, manioc, parsnips, and salsify are examples of other root vegetables.

Beets — Betteraves

Species name: *Beta vulgaris*

Beets are native to the Mediterranean, the Atlantic coast of Europe, the Near East, and India. Firm and round with green leafy tops, beets range in color from red to white, with the most common and widely known being garnet red. Beets are high in sucrose and have been used to manufacture sugar. The beet top can also be eaten. The leafy top of a beet contains three times more iron than the root of the plant.

Carrots — Carottes

Species name: *Daucus carota L.*

Carrots are native to Europe and southwestern Asia. Most often orange, the carrot has a crisp texture when fresh. The carrot plant grows a rosette of leaves in spring and summer, while building roots which store large amounts of sugars that allow the plant to flower in the second year. The stem will produce a cluster of white flowers. Carrots are now selectively bred to produce different colors.

Demilune

Mirepoix

Bâtonnet

Sifflet

Émincer

Dés (Macédoine)

Paysanne

Brunoise

Julienne

Brunoisette

Julienne for Soup

Classic knife cuts for carrots.

Celery Root – *Céleri rave*

Species name: *Apium graveolens*

Celery root, also known as celeriac and celery rave, is indigenous to Europe. It is an edible root vegetable that belongs to the celery family and is grown specifically for its fleshy white and spherical root. In general, the roots are large and attached to a turnip-like bulb. Smaller roots have better flavor, while larger roots are more fibrous and better suited to longer cooking.

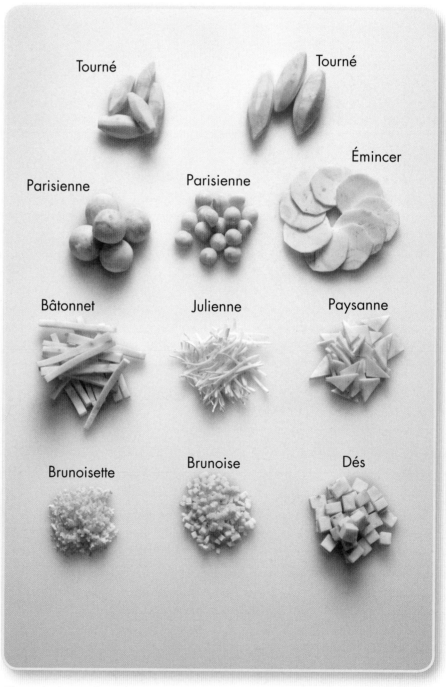

Classic knife cuts for celery root.

Potatoes – *Pommes de Terre*

Species name: *Solanum tuberosum*

The potato is a tuber from the perennial *Solanum tuberosum* of the Solanaceae family. The Solanaceae family includes tobacco, nightshade, nettles, tomato, eggplant, and pepper plants. A tuber is an engorged, nutrient-storing stolon or bud, located just below the soil surface and the stem of the plant. As a tuber, the potato is not technically a root but falls into the root-vegetable category in terms of its appearances, the fact that it is grown underground, as well as its culinary use. The external parts of the potato plant are toxic and should not be eaten. The sprouts that develop on the tuber during germination should also be avoided.

The potato plant is a perennial that grows approximately 60 centimeters high. The flowers, which range from white, pink, and red to blue and purple, resemble those of other plants in the Solanaceae family, a distinctive five-pointed star. After flowering, some varieties will produce small green fruits resembling cherry tomatoes. Each of these fruits contains 300 true seeds and high amounts of toxins. Therefore, they are not suitable for consumption. However, the potatoes that are produced from this plant are extremely safe and nutrient rich.

Although the origin of the potato has been traced to Southern Peru, today's cultivars are from a subspecies native to Chile that was cultivated 10,000 years ago. There are approximately 5,000 potato varieties worldwide; 3,000 are found in the Andes alone, mainly in Peru, Chile, Bolivia, Ecuador, and Colombia. Brought to Europe in 1536, by the Spanish, the potato was initially thought to be poisonous, and it took some time before it was universally accepted in Europe as an important food source. Famines and climate change during this time helped accelerate the potato's acceptance into the European diet. When most other crops were failing, potatoes could still be relied upon to grow. France was one of the last countries to accept the potato, and it is believed that some of the infamous famines during the 1600s could have been avoided if the potato had been accepted as a food source earlier. (See inset Parmentier page 24 *Classic Recipes.*) The potato has been celebrated by many cultures over the centuries, and has provided sustenance to generations of families worldwide.

Potato blight struck Irish potato crops in 1845. Potato blight is caused by the fungus *Phytophthora infestans*. The fungus infests the leaves, stems, and tubers, making them inedible. Blight is spread through wind and rain; wind spreads the disease for miles and the rain helps it seep into the soil. The Irish potato blight, from 1845 to 1852, reduced the entire population of Ireland by an estimated 20 to 25 percent through starvation, starvation-related diseases resulting in death, and emigration.

At the time of the famine, the Irish relied heavily on potato crops for food—a working man could consume up to 14 pounds of potatoes a day!

Most, if not all, farming land was British owned and rented out to Irish farmers. The British-owned farms would be divided into smaller plots of land and then leased to several farmers to either grow crops or raise sheep and cattle. The size of the rented farming land was so small that only potato crops could provide enough food to feed a family. This provided very little security for the Irish tenants, and the rents were very high. The tenant could be evicted if the land owner decided to raise animals on his land, in lieu of crop growing, or vice versa, or if the tenant was unable to pay his rent. Most paid their rent by cultivating and harvesting the land owner's crops.

Potatoes can be prepared any number of ways: skin on or peeled, whole, sliced, or diced, seasoned or unseasoned. Some potato dishes are served hot, some cooked and then served cold. Very common preparations include mashed, baked, boiled, sautéed, deep-fried, and roasted.

Potato Categories

A majority of the dry matter contained in a potato is made up of starch and the starch content will vary among the different varieties, thus giving potatoes different properties when cooked. Some potatoes are better for boiling or baking, but they can be used for both. Potatoes can be categorized by their usage such as baking, boiling, or all-purpose, or their physical properties, such as firm, fairly firm, and mealy (starchy).

Potato Preparation
Peeling a Potato

1   Rinse the potato under cold water to remove any remaining soil.

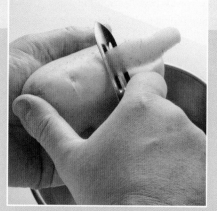

2   Peel the potato first lengthwise.

3   Finish by peeling the ends and removing any blemishes with the tip of the peeler.

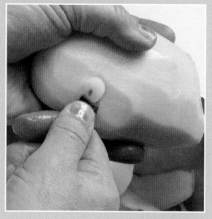

4   To remove eyes, use the tip of the peeler. Insert at a shallow angle.

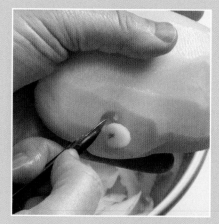

5   Turn to remove.

6   Peeled potatoes should be stored submerged in cold water until ready to use.

Cutting a Block

1 Start by trimming off both ends.

2 Then, slice one side and place the cut side flat onto the cutting board. Cut the two sides straight down.

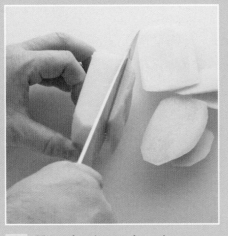

3 Turn the piece and continue cutting straight.

4 Trim as needed until a perfect block has been cut.

Firm

According to the European system, a firm potato (firm-fleshed ware variety) is best for use in salads, a fairly firm potato (ware variety) has a multipurpose use, and a mealy (starch variety) type will produce a floury textured product, usually desired in a baked or deep-fried potato. The latter is also used for making starch. Depending on what the potato is being used for, the variety of potato should be taken into consideration for a better end result.

The firm-fleshed ware variety, also referred to as the boiling potato, is of medium size with good flavor and fine-textured flesh. They are best for salads, but also in stews and ragouts because they do not break down during cooking. Varieties include the fingerling (North America), the Ratte (Europe), the BF 15 (Europe), the Belle de Fontenay (Europe), and the round white, yellow, and red (North America).

The United Nations declared 2008 the "International Year of the Potato." In a worldwide strategy to address hunger for the poor, the cultivation of the potato is ideal in developing countries, where there is an abundance of labor, but limited available land for farming. Potato crops provide a nutritious food source quickly and can be grown in a wide range of climates. Eighty-five percent of the plant provides edible food, compared to the 50 percent provided by cereal crops.

Potato Frying Cuts
Potato Cheveux

1 Thinly cut potato into 1 mm slices.

2 Slices should be as regular as possible.

3 Stack the slices and slice into 1 mm lengths.

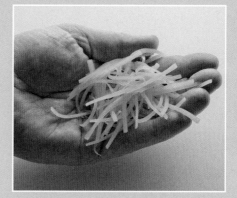

4 Potato Cheveux

Fairly Firm

The ware variety, also known as the all-purpose and baking potato, is medium to large in size and has a good to bland flavor and coarse-textured flesh. It is suited for a broader range of uses, such as baking, mashing, and deep-frying, than the firm potato. It has a tendency to break down during cooking. Varieties include the Bintje (Europe), the russet, the Yukon Gold (North America), and the Kennebec (Europe and North America).

Mealy (Starchy)

The mealy or starch variety are larger in size than the other two types, bland in flavor, and used for making starch.

Potato Frying Cuts
Potato Paille

1 Thinly cut the potato into 2 mm slices.

2 Slices should be as regular as possible.

3 Stack the slices and slice into 2 mm lengths.

4 Potato Paille

Sweet Potato

Although called a potato, the sweet potato (*Ipomoea batatas*) is in fact a very distant relative of the potato. Both belong to the same botanical order of Solanales, but each belong to different plant families. Sweet potatoes are usually long and tapered and covered by a smooth skin that ranges in color from brown to red and purple. The flesh of a sweet potato can range from yellow to purple.

Unlike potatoes, the sweet potato has edible shoots and leaves that are best eaten while immature. Sweet potatoes are never eaten raw, and are best prepared baked because most of the nutrients lie just beneath the skin. The sweet potato is often confused with the yam, but they are not even distantly related to one another. The yam (*Dioscorea*) comes from the Dioscoreaceae family. The yam contains more moisture and possesses more natural sugars than a sweet potato.

Potato Allumettes

1 Cut the potato into 3 mm thick slices.

2 Stack the slices and slice into 3 mm lengths.

3 Potato Allumettes

Potato Mignonettes

1 Cut the potato into thick slices 1/2 cm thick.

2 Stack the slices and cut 1/2 cm lengths.

3 Potato Mignonettes

Potato Pont Neuf

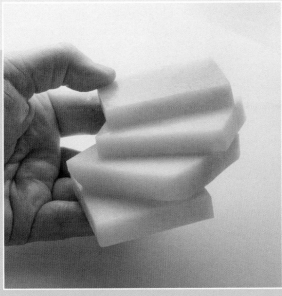

1 Cut the potato into thick slices 1 cm thick.

2 Stack the slices and cut 1 cm lengths.

3 Potato Pont Neuf

Pont neuf

Pont neuf

Migonette

Allumette

Paille

Cheveux

Potato frying cuts.

Potato Savonettes

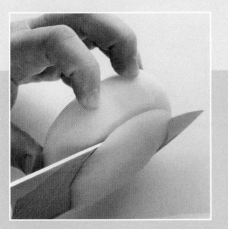  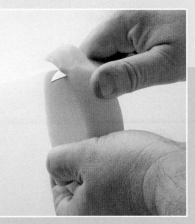

1   Cut about 1/4 of the peeled potato lengthwise.

2   Cut the other side parallel to the first cut.

3   Hold the potato and cut around the edge.

4   Continue all around until the sides are smooth.

5   The result is a perfect oval.

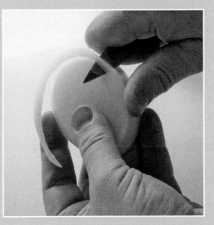 

6   Bevel the cut corners on both sides.

7   Potato savonettes can be cut in different sizes.

Potato Bouchon Émincer

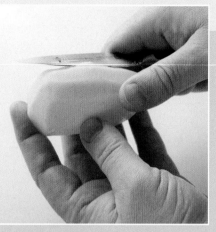

1 Select long shaped potatoes. After peeling, hold the potato firmly, holding your knife horizontal to the potato.

2 Continue around the potato until the potato takes on the shape of a cylinder.

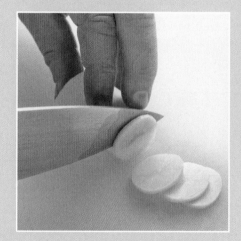

3 Cut off both ends.

4 To cut rounds, slice at desired thickness.

5 Potato Bouchon Émincer

Potato Fondante

1 | Cut approximately 1/3 of the potato lengthwise.

2 | Trim both ends.

3 | Starting at one of the trimmed ends, begin shaping the potato.

4 | Cut in an even curve.

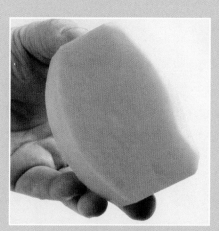

5 | The curve should be even and smooth.

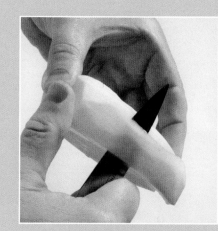

6 | Turn and cut the other side the same way.

7 | The curve should be the same as the first side.

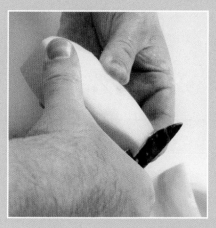

8 | There are five facets, starting from one side, cut a second facet in order to give a dome shape.

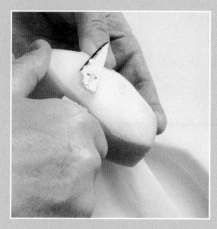

9 | Take off only the minimum.

(continues on next page)

Potato Fondante

(continued from previous page)

10 Now cut the center facet.

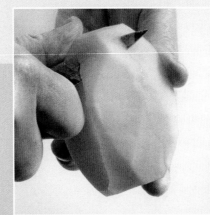

11 Cut with one even stroke.

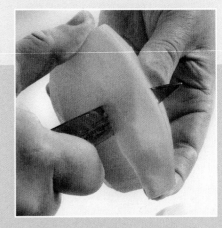

12 Continue to the last facet.

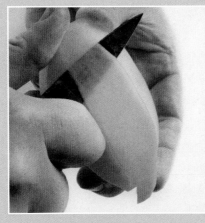

13 If necessary, trim the potato to even out the facets.

14 The potato should be an elliptical curve from the side.

15 The bottom is flat.

16 The top clearly has five facets.

Potato Soufflée

1 Cut the potato in a square or rectangular block.

2 Trim off the corners.

3 Finish by peeling the ends and removing any blemishes with the tip of the peeler.

4 Cut 3 mm slices.

5 Cut evenly.

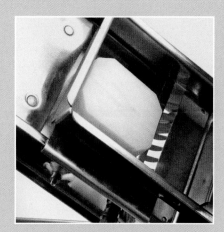

6 To use a mandoline, after trimming the corners, place in the guard.

(continues on next page)

Potato Soufflée

(continued from previous page)

7 Place the cover of the guard over the potato.

8 Holding firmly and applying even pressure, move the guard down against the blade in one motion.

9 Slices should be 3–4 mm thick.

Potato Champignon

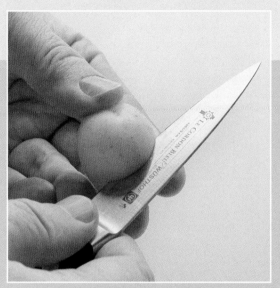

1 | Make an incision around the middle of the potato.

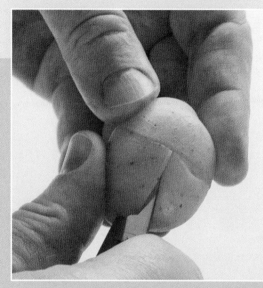

2 | With the point of the knife, cut around below the incision.

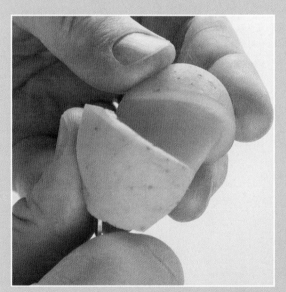

3 | This will form the stem of the mushroom.

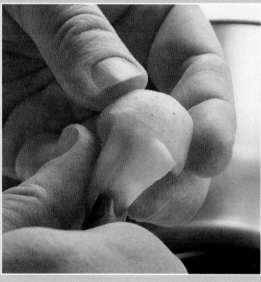

4 | Continue trimming down to the desired size.

(continues on next page)

Potato Champignon

(continued from previous page)

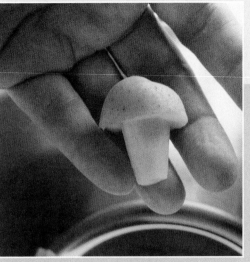

5   You now have the stem of the mushroom.

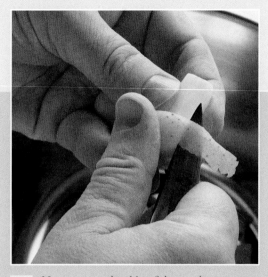

6   Now remove the skin of the mushroom cap.

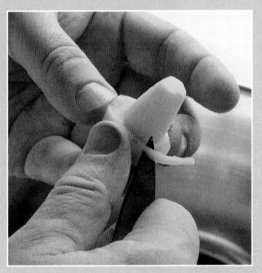

7   Continue in a circular motion until all the skin is removed.

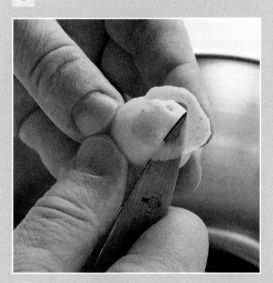

8   Round the edges.

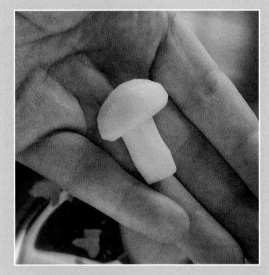

9   Potato Champignon

Classic knife cuts for potatoes.

It is ironic that Peru, the birthplace of the potato has one of the highest poverty rates in the world. The T'ikapapa initiative is a social grassroots project that provides access by poor farmers in the Andes to sell their crops in the big city markets. Since 2004, T'ikapapa has improved the income and quality of life for 500 farming families in the high Andes of Peru. Not only are their potatoes available in urban markets, but they are also sold for commercial purposes such as the manufacture of potato chips. The T'ikapapa initiative was the winner of the 2007 BBC World Challenge, which seeks to recognize development projects that are not only financially successful but also support a community in need.

Classic knife cuts for potatoes.

Radish – *Radis*

Species name: *Raphanus sativus*

The **radish** is native to Europe. The radish family boasts several varieties that vary in size, color, and duration of time required to cultivate. A radish possesses a firm, compact texture, and short, bright green leaves. It has a spicy, earthy flavor. The greens of the radish root are also nutritious to eat. Radishes, despite their peppery flavor, contain three times as much natural sugar as corn, tomato, and carrots.

Radish

Some anthropologists theorize that roots and tubers may have helped fuel human evolution, when the climate of the African savanna cooled about two million years ago and fruits became scarce. Raw starch granules resist our digestive enzymes, while the gelated starch that results from the cooking process does not. Because tubers were plentiful and far more nutritious when cooked, they may have offered a significant advantage to early humans who learned to dig for them and roast them in the embers of the fire.

Turnips – *Navets*

Species name: *Brassica rapa*

Turnips are native to West Asia and Europe. The turnip most commonly used is the white-skinned variety. The top of the turnip that is exposed to sunlight can be green, red, or purple tinged. The main edible portion of this cone-shaped vegetable is underground and will remain white skinned. Turnip leaves, however, are also edible; in the United Kingdom they are referred to as turnip tops and are eaten as a side dish. In fact, some turnip varieties are grown only for their tops, such as the Chinese cabbage. The Chinese cabbage and the turnip are both from the Brassicaceae and are also related to the common cabbage. Both the leaves and root of this variety of Brassicaceae possess a pungent flavor, but become milder tasting after cooking.

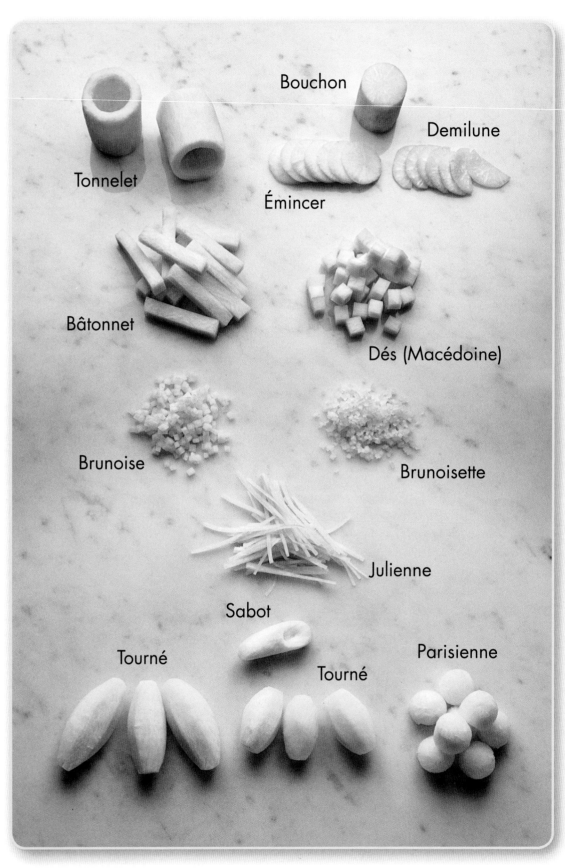

Classic knife cuts for turnips.

Shoot Vegetables

Shoot vegetables more often than not contain a large amount of fibrous vascular tissue. Imagine the stalk as a highway taking nutrients that are essential to a plant's growth to and from each end of the plant. This constant traveling causes a fibrous buildup, which creates a pulpy stalk. The fibrous tissue continues to build as the plant matures. Selecting a less fibrous variety of the plant you wish to use will assist you in creating a successful dish. Artichokes, asparagus, Belgian endive, Celery, and fennel root, discussed next, are all classified as shoot vegetables.

Artichoke – Artichaut

Species name: *Cynara scolymus*

The **artichoke** is native to Southern Europe. Artichokes have long spiked leaves beginning at the base of the plant. The edible parts of the artichoke are the heart and the leafy bottoms of the bud of the plant. There are several varieties of artichoke, some of which are available year-round. Although harvesting the artichoke before the winter months will prevent frost damage to the exterior leaves of the plant, making them more pleasing aesthetically, frost damage will actually enhance its characteristic nutty flavor. Varieties of artichokes include the green globe, the desert globe, the big heart, and the imperial star.

The green globe artichoke is available year-round and possesses a compact appearance. This artichoke, as its name suggests, is globe shaped. In summer and fall, the artichoke is cone shaped with pronounced thorns, and in winter and spring the thorns are less developed, thus giving it a more rounded shape.

The desert globe artichoke is available in the beginning of winter until early spring. Like the green globe, its shape varies from conical to round throughout the growing season. The desert globe has thorns, but they are not very pronounced.

The big heart artichoke is a thornless variety that possesses a large heart. It is cone shaped and possesses an enhanced nutty flavor.

The imperial star artichoke is a thornless variety available year-round. Developed in the 1990s it can be grown in colder climates. It is cone shaped, compact, and possesses an edible stem.

Turning an Artichoke—Variation 1

1 You will need a very sharp knife and fresh lemon.

2 Break off the stem. If the artichoke is fresh, it should snap off cleanly.

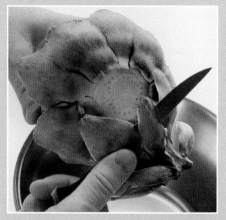

3 Using a very sharp knife, trim the bottom and rub with lemon.

4 Cut around the side of the artichoke in order to remove the outer leaves.

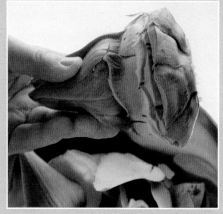

5 The artichoke should look like this once the outer leaves have been cut.

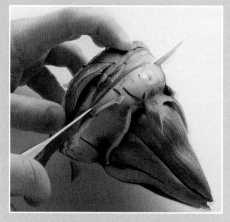

6 Cut the exposed top of the artichoke.

(continues on next page)

Turning an Artichoke—Variation 1

(continued from previous page)

7 Be careful not to cut too much from the top. It should be level with where the choke begins.

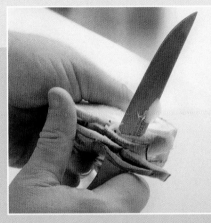

8 Cut again around the outside of the artichoke in order to remove any traces of green.

9 The artichoke bottom should resemble a disc, perfectly round and flat on the top.

10 Turn the artichoke over and repeat the process on the bottom.

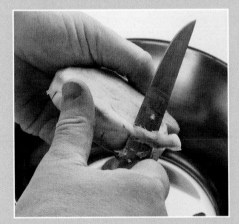

11 Continue trimming as needed, rounding off the cut corners.

12 Very little of the green should remain.

(continues on next page)

Turning an Artichoke—Variation 1

(continued from previous page)

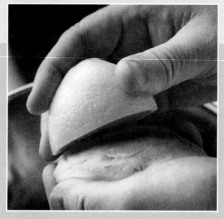

13 The artichoke should be generously rubbed with lemon juice throughout the entire process to prevent discoloring.

14 Trimmed artichokes should be kept in acidulated water to maintain their color.

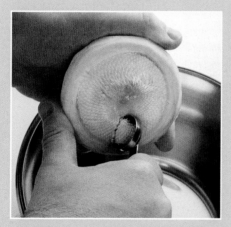

15 Use a melon baller to remove the choke.

16 Scrape around, keeping an even edge.

17 Generously apply lemon juice during and after the process to prevent discoloration.

18 Finished bottoms should be kept in acidulated water until ready to cook.

Turning an Artichoke—Variation 2

1 Using a serrated knife, cut off the bottom.

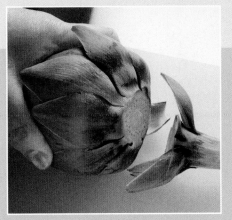

2 Do not cut off too much from the bottom of the artichoke.

3 Cut off the top portion.

4 The cut should be at about where the choke begins.

5 Place the artichoke on its side, and using a sawing motion slice away the outer leaves while turning the bottom.

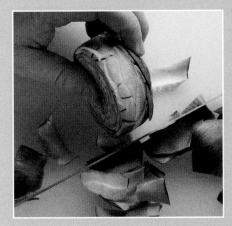

6 Continue cutting around, being sure to cut away the tough outer leaves.

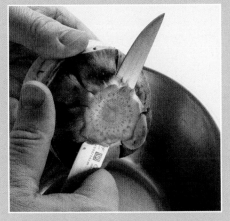

7 Using a smaller knife, trim the bottom.

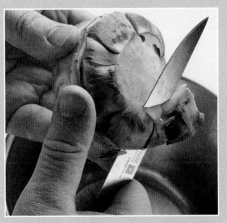

8 Cut away the remaining green following the natural curve of the bottom.

9 Continue turning the bottom until all the green has been removed.

(continues on next page)

Turning an Artichoke—Variation 2

(continued from previous page)

10 Trim the top again.

11 Cut into the choke.

12 Rub with lemon to prevent discoloration.

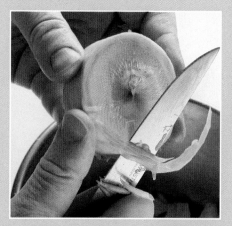

13 Bevel the edges.

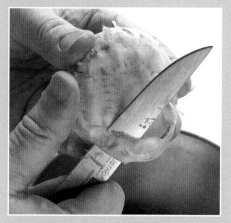

14 Shave off any remaining green areas.

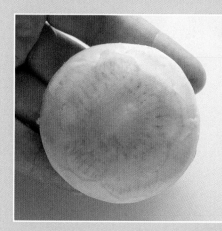

15 The finished bottom should be round and even with no green remaining.

16 The bottom with the choke is now ready for cooking.

Blanc de Cuisson

1   Gather equipment and ingredients.

2   Sift flour into cold salted water.

3   Whisk to ensure that there are no lumps.

4   Squeeze the juice of cut lemon and leave the empty lemon in the water.

5   Add the artichoke bottoms.

Cartouche

1   Fold the parchment in half.

2   Then fold it in half again.

3   Hold the folded corner down with a finger and fold one in toward the center. Repeat on the other side, then fold in half to form a narrow triangle.

4   Measure the circumference by placing the point of the triangle in the middle of the pan. Pinch the triangle where it touches the outer edge.

5   Trim off the excess with a pair of scissors.

Asparagus – Asperges

Species name: *Asparagus officinalis*

Asparagus has been around since the beginning of civilization and is native to parts of Russia, the Mediterranean, and the British Isles. It was written about in the first known recipe book, *De Re Coquinaria, Book III*, by Apicius in the third century. Asparagus is the immature, green sprout of the asparagus plant. There is more than one variety of asparagus, with white and green being the most common. The green variety has a stronger grass-like flavor.

White asparagus is both succulent and delicious and its discovery may be more legend than fact. It is said to have been discovered in Bassano del Grappa near Venice during the 16th century. A large crop of green asparagus was destroyed after a hailstorm, and the people were compelled to find sustenance beneath the soil, salvaging whatever they could find. It was then that they found white asparagus. White asparagus is grown beneath the soil, so it is not exposed to the sun, which prevents the development of chlorophyll, thus giving them a creamy white appearance. White asparagus is more tender than the green variety and possesses a sweeter, nutty flavor. It is sometimes referred to as *spargel*, which is German for asparagus because most asparagus in Germany is white.

Asparagus en Botte

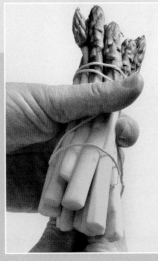

1 Starting at the top of the bunch hold the end of the string and wind it around 2 or 3 times. Leave enough on the end for tying.

2 Cross over to the bottom of the bunch.

3 Wind the string around the bottom 2 or 3 times.

(continues on next page)

Asparagus en Botte

(continued from previous page)

4 Cut the string and bring the two ends together.

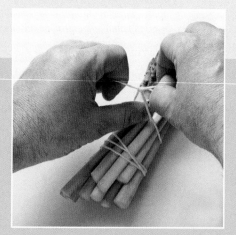

5 Make a butcher's knot by looping the string around the other two times, and pull.

6 Secure with your thumb, then make a second loop.

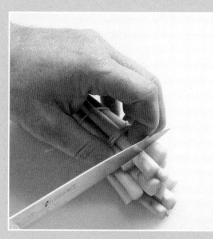

7 Trim the bottom to even out the ends.

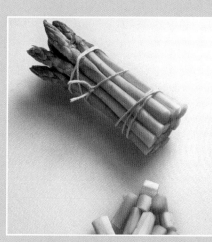

8 Asparagus with ends trimmed evenly.

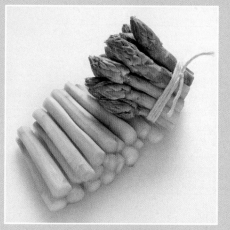

9 To prepare asparagus tips, tie the bunch at the top.

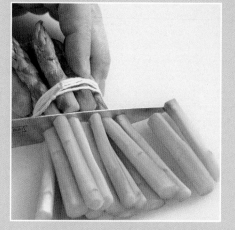

10 Cut just below the string.

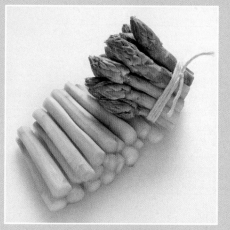

11 Prepared asparagus tips.

Belgian endive – Endive

Species name: *Cichorium intybus*

As the name indicates, **Belgian endive** is native to Belgium and is also known as French endive or witloof. The plants are roughly 6 inches (15 cm) in length and possess a lightly colored, tubular-shaped head with many tightly bunched leaves. The leaves are slightly bitter in taste. Commercially grown endives are started in a field and harvested by machine before they are fully grown. The endives are then placed in sterile soil in stacked pallet boxes. Some growers prefer to use artificial soil because it allows for better drainage, with less chance of root rot or fungal diseases. The space and temperature within each box are carefully controlled and utilized. Once the shoots begin to grow, the roots are replanted into a second growing media for harvesting. Belgian endive is cultivated in this way so that when the shoot is finally cut from the root it will be clean and require no washing, saving time and labor. To maintain its creamy white coloring, the Belgian endive is grown in complete darkness. Belgian endives are used for salads and braising.

Endive Preparation

1. Leaves should be a creamy yellow with a hint of green.

2. Trim off the bottom.

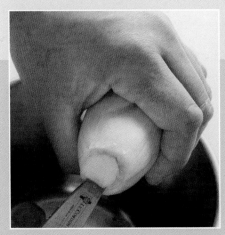

3. Using the tip of a paring knife, remove the bottom of the core.

(continues on next page)

Endive Preparation

(continued from previous page)

4   Remove any loose or wilted outer leaves.

5   Split the endive in half lengthwise.

6   Cut away the bitter core.

7   Cored endive.

8   Turn and begin slicing thinly.

9   Prepared Endive

Celery – Céleri Branche

Species name: *Apium graveolens dulce*

Celery, which is indigenous to the Mediterranean, is one of the most popular vegetables eaten in the Western world. Two varieties are used: Pascal and golden celery. Pascal celery is bright green and the most widely cultivated. Golden celery has delicate whitish-yellow stalks and leaves and is used less and is, therefore, less common than Pascal celery.

Celery grows in bunches of large, leafed ribs that encompass the tender heart. Golden celery is grown under the soil to avoid the sun and chlorophyll production, resulting in celery that is light in color and more tender.

Celery Preparation

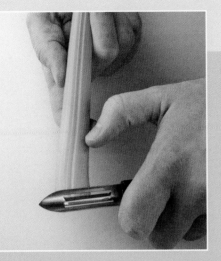

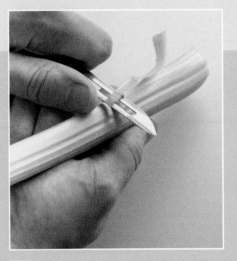

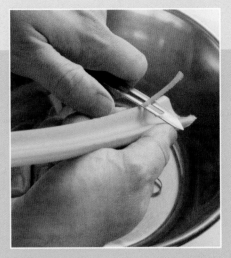

1. Trim the stalk of its leafy top and wide bottom. Using a vegetable peeler, starting at one end, thinly peel off the stringy outer layer.

2. The purpose is to remove the outer fibers which are tougher. Be careful not to remove too much.

3. Finish by the outer corners of the celery stalk.

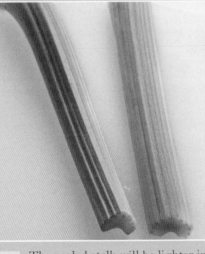

4. The peeled stalk will be lighter in color with a smoother surface.

5. Keep the peeled celery immersed in ice water until needed.

Fennel Root – Fenouil

Species name: *Foeniculum vulgare azoricum*

Fennel root is native to the coast of the Mediterranean. The name is derived from the Latin *foeniculum*, meaning "little hay," most likely referring to its fine, feathery strands. It was spread throughout Europe by Imperial Rome. It is now grown in India, Australia, and South America and is naturalized in the United States. It has a bulb-shaped white base that is slightly divided. Each side of the bulb has two to three thick, flat layers. Fennel tastes like anise and is used often in Italian and French cuisine, in particular with fish. It is also used in distilling absinthe, aquavit, and gin.

Classic knife cuts for celery.

PEARS AND APPLES

Pears and apples belong to the botanical family Rosaceae, or the rose family. The bark, foliage, and the form of the flower cluster in both types of trees are quite similar; however, the fruit produced by each is, of course, very different.

Apart from color, shape, texture, and taste, apples and pears differ quite dramatically in terms of their shelf life as well. Through tomographic imaging, plant biologists have found that breathing pathways in fruit affect the rate of decomposition and that, specifically, apples and the pears retain oxygen at different rates. Apples, for example, have cavities between their cells, whereas pears have tiny interwoven channels. With the availability of this knowledge, growers and suppliers can estimate ideal storage temperatures and extend the shelf life of each fruit.

Anjou Pear

Pears – *Poire*

Under the skin surface of a pear are minute cell clusters. These specific cell structures are known by the wood-like taste that a pear possesses before it has had a chance to soften off of the vine. A pear will continue to ripen and soften after it has been harvested, and should be harvested prior to reaching full maturity. If harvested too late in the season, the pear will be brown at the core and will possess an unpleasant taste. The many pear varieties on the market include Anjou, Bartlett, and Bosc.

Anjou

The Anjou pear is thought to have first been produced in the Anjou region of France, sometime during the 19th century. The two main varieties are red and green. The red variety develops a characteristic red skin that darkens as the pear matures. The green variety retains its green coloring even after it has reached full maturity. They are both tangy and sweet and possess a fragrant, white flesh. Reaching what can be considered a medium to large size, Anjou pears possess a wide base and short stem.

The Bartlett or Williams' Bon Chrétien

The Bartlett pear is known by several names: the Williams' pear, the Williams' Bon Chrétien pear, and the Williams' Good Christian, among others. The first of this cultivar was found growing in the yard of an English schoolteacher in the mid to late 1700s. The variety is large and possesses a smooth skin. It is supple and luscious and lends itself well to dessert making. The Bartlett is green while immature, but upon reaching maturity, the fruit ripens into a golden yellow color or, in some instances, develops into a deep red color.

Bosc or Beurré Bosc

The Bosc pear is also known as the Beurré Bosc or the Kaiser pear. It is known for its wide base, elongated neck, and crisp, smooth skin. This fruit is grown on the west coast of Canada, in northwestern parts of the United States, in Australia, and in parts of Europe. The Bosc usually has a darkish yellow color with a russet blush. The Bosc does not change color as it ripens. Bosc pears are fragrant and sweet and are sometimes described as being slightly spicy. This pear is an excellent fruit to use in baking, grilling, poaching, and eating out of hand.

Apple – *Pomme*

As mentioned earlier, beneath the skin of an apple are irregular cavities between each cell of the fruit. The spaces between the cell structures allow for gas exchange and for oxygen to flow, increasing an apple's life span.

The apple is harvested when it has reached full maturity. A mature apple will be crisp, lush, and very juicy. The taste, texture, and look of the apple will vary depending on the variety. Some apple varieties include the Red Delicious, Golden Delicious, Granny Smith, Royal Gala, and Macintosh.

Red Delicious

The Red Delicious apple possesses a rich red skin with some light yellow streaking and a creamy pale flesh. This apple should be firm with taut, smooth skin and is best eaten fresh or in salads.

Golden Delicious

The Golden Delicious is a large apple with delicate yellow skin that bruises easily. This fragrant apple is mildly sweet and pleasant tasting. The Golden Delicious is excellent when eaten fresh, in salads, and when used in baking. This cultivar is slow to brown and presents well.

Granny Smith

The Granny Smith is lime-green with sporadic rose-colored blushing. It possesses firm, smooth skin with sweet and tart flesh that does not brown quickly like most apples. This cultivar is delicious eaten fresh, in salads, or when used in cooking or baking.

Royal Gala

The Royal Gala is pinkish red with some green or yellow-green vertical striping and is considered a dessert apple. The Royal Gala is a small variety that is very hardy and is fairly resistant to bruising. It is a thin-skinned cultivar with soft flesh, making it very easy to bite into. It possesses a grainy textured flesh, a mildly sweet flavor, and a delicate perfume. The Royal Gala was developed in 1920 by hybridizing a Golden Delicious and a Kidd's Orange Red cultivar.

Macintosh

The Macintosh apple is predominantly red in color with traces of green. The flesh is white and possesses a tart flavor. The Macintosh apple is considered to be a superior eating apple by apple enthusiasts and is one of the most widely available.

Granny Smith Apple

CITRUS FRUITS

Genealogically a wild and unruly family, all citrus fruits are believed to be descendants of the mandarin, the pomelo, and the citron. All citrus fruits share the same genus, *Citrus* and belong to the Rutaceae family. They prefer to grow in temperate to tropical regions. Citrus fruits are native to Asia and to tropical and subtropical regions. These fruit types are high in vitamin C, flavonoids, and water-soluble fibers and have varying degrees of acidity.

Many of the fruits as we know them today are hybrids, or crosses between the sweet orange, pomelo, and mandarin, or mutations arising from interbreeding or cross-cuttings. Oranges are used to make everything from juices to honey and marmalade. The rind can be grated to produce orange zest, which is popular in cooking. In Spain, fallen orange blossoms are collected and made into tea, and orange flower water is used as an ingredient in bakery and pastry making. Orange blossom honey is made by placing beehives in orange groves, and orange peel is used by gardeners to keep slugs away.

Citron – *Cédrat*

Citrus medica

The citron, not to be confused with the lemon (which also bears the name "citron" in French), is native to the Himalayan foothills and has the honor of being the first of the citrus fruit to make its way out of Asia in approximately 700 BC. A long and lumpy fruit that is pale-green in color, the citron has pulp that is both bitter and dry. It is not eaten raw and has few culinary applications aside from being candied and used in marmalades. The aromatic rind, however, is used in making perfume for both cosmetics and religious ceremonies.

Grapefruit – *Pamplemousse*

Citrus paradisi

As one of the larger citrus species, the name *grapefruit* seems odd at first—that is until it is seen hanging in grape-like clusters from its tree branches. This hybrid was created by crossing a pomelo with a sweet orange, though by its color and size, it is evident that the pomelo is genetically dominant.

Although several varieties exist, the white-fleshed and seedless Marsh and the red-fleshed and seedless Redblush are two of the more popular North American sellers. Popular enough to warrant its own specialized knife (curved to follow the contour of the skin when carving out the flesh), the grapefruit is often enjoyed for breakfast but can also be sliced, broiled, and served as an amuse-bouche.

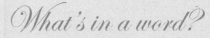

What's in a word?

Flavonoids are plant-based pigments that are gaining acceptance by the medical establishment as having antioxidant properties. There is mounting evidence to suggest that antioxidants protect cells from cancer-causing molecules. The citrus flavonoid "tangeretin" has caught the attention of researchers as being particularly effective in this domain.

Ruby Red Grapefruit

Lemon – *Citron*

Citrus limon

Although the exact origin of the lemon is unknown, it is believed that it was first grown in India, northern Burma, and China. In approximately 700 AD the lemon was introduced to Persia, Iraq, and Egypt, and was first recorded in literature in the 10th century. In the first century AD, the lemon was introduced to Europeans through southern Italy, but was not widely cultivated until the middle of the 15th century in Genoa. Christopher Columbus brought lemon seeds to the Americas in 1493; however, lemons were only used for ornamental and medicinal purposes until the 1700s. The name *lemon* comes from the Arabic *limun*, and the Old Italian and Old French *limone*.

The lemon is green until it fully ripens into a beautiful yellow color. Lemons vary in size but generally remain around the size of a tennis ball. Possessing a tart taste, the lemon contains 5 percent citric acid.

The lemon has both sweet and savory uses. Pickled lemons are a delicacy in Morocco and lemon marmalade is popular in England. Many drinks, such as soft drinks, iced tea, mixed drinks, and water, are often served with a slice of lemon on the rim of the glass. Marinating fish in lemon juice will neutralize the odor of the fish and "cook" the flesh. Squeeze some lemon juice on cut fruits that easily oxidize—apple, bananas, and avocados for example—and the acid in the juice will act as a short-term preservative, allowing the fruits to keep their natural color for a longer time.

Lemons also have non-culinary uses. Dip a lemon half in coarse salt or baking powder and use it to scrub copper cookware. Use lemons to deodorize your kitchen—a halved lemon will remove grease stains and act as a bleach and disinfectant. Add some baking soda and rub on plastic food containers to remove food stains.

Dent de Loup (Wolves Teeth)

1 Trim both ends of the lemon.

2 Start by making an angled cut along the equator of the lemon. Cut deep enough to the center of the fruit.

3 Changing the angle of the knife, make the next cut to form a "V."

(continues on next page)

Dent de Loup (Wolves Teeth)

(continued from previous page)

4 Continue around the lemon, then gently pull the two halves apart.

5 Remove any seeds with the tip of the knife.

6 A sprig of parsley can be placed in the center for some color.

Panier (Basket)

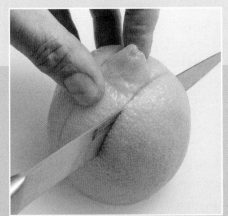

1 Cut the stem end of the lemon so it stands straight up. Cut two parallel lines to the equator of the lemon. This will form the handle.

2 Make the angled cuts between the ends of the handle.

3 Gently remove the two pieces.

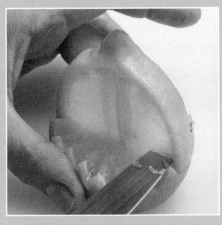

4 Cut straight across the middle to separate the flesh.

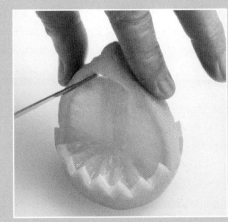

5 Carefully cut between the flesh and the zest to remove the center.

6 Remove any seeds with the tip of the knife. Fresh herbs can be used to "fill" the basket.

Lime

Lime – *Citron vert*

Citrus latifolia, Citrus aurantifolia

The lime is the smallest fruit of the citrus family. Limes are picked while still green, but if limes are left on the tree, they will ripen to an orange color. Some limes will exhibit a degree of yellow when left to mature. The lime is extremely tart, containing one to one and a half times the amount of acid of a lemon by weight.

The three most common types of lime are the Tahitian (*Citrus latifolia*), the Mexican (*Citrus aurantifolia*), and the Key lime (*Citrus aurantifolia*). The Mexican and Key limes are referred to as "true limes, whereas the Tahitian is considered to be a hybrid." The Key lime is native to Southeast Asia and found its way through the Middle East to North Africa and then to Sicily and Andalusia. Spanish explorers brought the lime over to the West Indies and the Florida Keys in the 1500s where cultivation spread, hence the name *Key lime*. Key limes are smaller than the Tahitian variety, and the Key lime in particular is known for its distinctive flavor and juiciness. It was the primary lime crop in Florida until the 1920s when it was destroyed by a hurricane and replaced by the Tahitian lime.

The Tahitian is also known as the Persian and Bearss lime. It is larger than a Key lime—roughly the size of a hen's egg—and is seedless with light green pulp. Although not as fragrant as Key limes, Tahitians are the most commonly found commercial variety.

Orange – *Orange*

Thought to originate in the Malay Archipelago (between Australia and Southeast Asia), the orange proliferated in the Mediterranean as a result of the Roman conquests. Attesting to its universal appeal, shortly after Christopher Columbus introduced the orange to the New World, the succulent fruit was already being packed on hunting trips by Native Americans in the Florida region.

Although common enough today in contemporary North American and European households, the sweet orange and its varieties were once considered a great luxury. The orange graced the tables at Roman feasts, it was a delicacy and a symbol of wealth on the aristocratic tables of the Renaissance, and even into the early 20th century, oranges were cherished more than candy by children at Christmas time.

The United States is the world's largest producer of oranges (closely followed by Brazil) with more than 40 percent of its crop being dedicated to the domestic consumption of frozen concentrated orange juice, although freshly squeezed is preferable to frozen. To name but a few of its nutritional properties, the orange is a significant source of vitamin C, calcium, and iron with fructose making up nearly half of the fruit's chemical components.

In terms of its culinary uses, the orange's versatility is referenced in the following words of 18th-century British poet Jonathan Swift:

"Come buy my fine oranges, sauce for your veal,

And charming, when squeezed in a pot of brown ale;"

Of course, sauces and beer only scratch the surface of the orange's many uses, both savory and sweet. The flavor of an orange can range from sweet to tart and may be categorized into two groups: sweet oranges (*citrus × sinensis*) and bitter or sour oranges (*Citrus aurantium*).

Bitter or Sour Orange Varieties

Bigarade Orange – *Bigarade*

alternate name: Seville Orange – *Séville*

Citrus aurantium

The bigarade or Seville orange is native to South Vietnam and is valued for its essential oils, which are used for perfumes and as flavorings. In particular, it is used in the production of orange liqueurs. The Seville orange is also preferred in the making of marmalade because it contains more natural pectin than the sweet orange. Orange flower water is also derived from its blossoms. The bitter orange is also used in herbal medicine.

Bergamot Orange – *Bergamote*

Bergamia risso

The bergamot orange is primarily cultivated in Italy for its oil which is used in perfume, confectionaries, and tobaccos. It is also the flavoring used in Earl Gray tea.

Mandarin Group of Sweet Oranges

Mandarin – *Mandarine*

Citrus reticulata

The mandarin first made its way from India to China and was likely introduced to Europe by early Spanish or Portuguese explorers. The cultivation of the mandarin in southern Europe was several centuries later, in the 1850s, and it was not until the 1900s that the mandarin was firmly rooted in Californian and Floridian soil. The Chinese language known as *Mandarin* lends its name to this delightfully flavored fruit. Esteemed for its sweet and juicy flesh, as well as for its loose-fitting peel, mandarins are sometimes referred to as "kid-glove" oranges.

The majority of mandarin crops today are grown in China, Japan, India, and in the East Indies; however, certain varieties have also been grown commercially in the United States and Mexico. While generally measuring slightly smaller than a tennis ball, the mandarin's shape tends to be more of a flattened sphere. A great number of cultivars and hybrids fall under the mandarin classification. For example, the tangerine, the Clementine (itself a tangerine variety), the Robinson,

Blood Orange

and the Satsuma all claim the mandarin as their parent. A gathering of all the cousins and distant relatives of the mandarin would make a family reunion of this fruit group a confusing and possibly scandalous affair! But not to denigrate *Citrus reticulata*, we should mention that the mandarin is considered one of only three "parent species" in the entire citrus family.

Satsuma – *Satsuma*

Citrus unshiu

A Japanese hybrid of the mandarin, the Satsuma is remarkable for its ability to survive colder weather. Known to withstand temperatures as low as 12°F (–11°C), it also outperforms other sweet oranges in fending off crop-destroying diseases. This natural resistance of the Satsuma may account for its prevalence as an "organic" crop. The one downfall of this sweet and seedless fruit is that its thin skin makes it a little more fragile and susceptible to damage. Although a little more care is advisable when choosing satsumas, shipping practices have improved in terms of the use of small boxes and the individual wrapping of fruit.

Tangelo – *Tangelo*

Citrus tangelo

The tangelo is a cross between a grapefruit and a tangerine and is mildly sweet and low in acidity. It is easily identified by the bump at the stem end of the fruit. Two common varieties are the Minneola and the Orlando, and both offer the flavor of a tangerine, profuse juiciness, and a generous size.

Tangerine – *Tangerine*

Citrus tangerina

After more than two thousand years of cultivation in China, the tangerine made its way to Morocco and finally set sail for Europe in the mid-1800s. The name of the Moroccan port city was Tangier and, predictably enough, this is where the tangerine got its name. The most commercially successful variety of Tangerine is the *Clementine*. Unlike the mandarin, the skin of the Clementine is tighter fitting, but the flavor and juiciness are no less enticing. Named in the early 20th century after its inventor, Father Clement Rowdier, the Clementine was mainly consumed in France, but is now commonly available throughout Europe and North America.

Sweet Orange Varieties (Citrus sinensis)

Blood Orange – *Orange Sanguine*

The mutation of the sweet orange into the blood orange appears to have occurred in Sicily between the 7th and 10th century AD. The variety was developed in Sicily under the cultivation expertise of the Moors, who were Muslims that once ruled throughout North Africa and parts of the Mediterranean.

Less successful in the United States (due mainly to unfavorable growing conditions), this variety is mostly grown in the Mediterranean, with a concentration of crops in southern Italy. To achieve its distinctive coloring, the blood orange needs the cooler temperatures and specific soil conditions that can be found in the Mount Etna growing region of Sicily. Pakistan, on a smaller scale, also has suitable conditions for producing the blood orange.

The Tarocco, Moro, and Sanguinello are sweet varieties of blood orange that can be enjoyed freshly peeled and in desserts, whereas the Maltese blood orange has higher acidity and is therefore more suitable for savory applications such as sauces. The terms *full-blood* and *half-blood* refer to how deep red the flesh of the blood orange is, Tarocco being an example of the lighter and Moro the darker. The evocative name and the striking color of this variety certainly make it stand out against other sweet orange varieties.

Navel Orange – *Navel*

Some sources claim that the navel orange made its way to the United States via Brazil from China; others claim that a single mutation of the sweet orange occurred in Brazil alone. What is clear, however, is that the fruit was introduced to Florida in 1835 and that its popularity subsequently exploded. The original Californian tree, planted in 1870, was still bearing fruit in Riverside, California, in 1911.

The naval orange is both seedless and easily peeled, making it a well-loved fruit to be eaten out of hand. Due to a chemical reaction that occurs when its cells are ruptured, the navel orange is not particularly suited for juicing. Not surprisingly, the navel orange takes its name from the navel-like depression where an underdeveloped second orange will be found. As a sterile cultivar, the navel is a tricky crop to grow, requiring grafting (the process of fusing one cultivar to another) for its propagation.

Persian Orange – *Orange Douce*

Once a bitter variety that originated in northern India, the Persian orange has gradually become sweet through centuries of propagation. Sometimes this variety is referred to simply as the sweet orange.

Valencia Orange – *Valence*

In late April in Orange County, California, a sweet, almost overwhelming odor permeates the air. This is the odor of Valencia orange blossoms and the promise of a good crop. As a juice orange, the Valencia is ideal because it has few seeds and, under the proper conditions, holds its color and flavor. No less enjoyable when eaten out of hand, it does, however, take some perseverance to peel. One little note of interest: finding a green tinge on the skin of the Valencia has no bearing on the quality or ripeness of the fruit, but is instead part of a natural process called *regreening*. Although named after the Spanish port city of Valencia, this member of the citrus family hails originally from China.

Valencia Orange

Pomelo

Pomelo – *Pomélo*

Citrus maxima

As one of the three parent species and by far the largest citrus fruit (growing anywhere from the size of a softball to that of a basketball), the pomelo gives the impression of being the matriarch of its unruly family. In addition to its range of sizes, the specifications for this fruit are incredibly variable: from round to pear shaped; with skin ranging from green to yellow hues; and translucent pulp, colored anywhere from yellow to red. Accounting for this diversity are the 25 known varieties, none of which have had much growing or commercial success in North America. That being said, the pomelo can be found in local Asian markets and is finding its way into a broader spectrum of culinary traditions.

BERRIES

There isn't a stringent set of botanical rules for classifying berries and fruits. Similar to the way that vegetables are sometimes classified as fruit for their intended culinary use, berries are classified for their appearance. Terms like simple fruit (true berry), aggregate and multiple (false berries) describe the way that the ovary will grow into a fruit. The term "accessory" is applied to fruit like the strawberry and the blackberry for the way they hang on the bush. In other words, the term accessory is a nod to the way that the fruit presents itself; much like an earring would accessorize an ear. Truth be told, the strawberry and blackberry are at once aggregate, accessory, and false berries but for the sake of simplicity, they are most likely to be referred to as an accessory (See chart below).

Berries are small, round or oval shaped, usually brilliantly hued, and can be either sweet or sour. Examples of berries include the strawberry, raspberry, blackberry, blueberry, loganberry, boysenberry, cranberry, huckleberry, red currants, and black currants.

Table 3–1 Berry Classification Chart

Common Parlance	Botanical classifications:			
	True Berry (Single fruit produced from a single ovary)	False Berry (Flower parts remain attached close to the top of the ovary)	Aggregate Fruit (Several fruit produced from one ovary)	Other Accessory Fruit (Fruit produced from ovary and other parts of the plant)
Berry	Black currant Red currant	Cranberry Blueberry	Blackberry Raspberry Boysenberry	Strawberry
Not a Berry	Grape			Apple Peach Cherry

Bilberry – *Myrtille*

Vaccinium myrtillus

The bilberry or whortleberry is indigenous to Europe. Bilberries resemble the North American blueberry and in fact are closely related, although the bilberry grows on a much larger bush that can reach 15 feet (4.5 meters) in height. The bilberry bush produces either single or paired berries but never clusters like the North American blueberry bush. The berries are black-blue in color with a deep reddish purple pulp. They are smaller than a blueberry and said to be more flavorful. Bilberries are eaten fresh; made into jams, juice, and pies; and used as a base for liqueurs and to flavor sorbets. Called *myrtille* in France, *bleuet* refers to the North American variety.

Blackberry – *Mûre*

Rubus fruticosus

The blackberry is native to North and South America, Asia, and Europe. Dark purple in color with sleek, delicate skin, this particular fruit possesses a light green core that extends throughout the berry and remains intact when picked. Blackberries have been used in Europe for more than two thousand years for medicinal purposes and for food. They were also used as prickly hedges to keep out intruders. In the United States, meats are labeled with a harmless purple-hued dye that is made from the juice of North American blackberries.

Black Currant – *Cassis*

Ribes nigrum

Black currants are indigenous to northern Asia and central and northern Europe. They are also known as the cassis berry. Black currants grow on small fragrant shrubs that are 3 to 6 feet (1 to 2 meters) tall. The berries, which are a glossy purple-black color, grow in clusters similar to those of the grape. The black currant is used predominantly to make liquor, wine, and soft drinks and in meat dishes, sauces, and baked goods.

Black Raspberry – *Framboise Noire*

Rubus occidentalis (eastern North American variety), *Rubus leucodermis* (western North American variety)

Black raspberries are native to the wilds of North America. They are most prevalent in the east and the Gulf States, but can also be found in the west. Due to the popularity of the red raspberry and the abundance of other fruit available, the black raspberry was not domesticated until the 1850s. The black raspberry has never gained the same popularity of the red raspberry, so its commercial production is minor compared to the production of red raspberries

Blackberries

During World War II fruits that were high in vitamin C were very difficult to come by. Because black currants contain high amounts of vitamin C and could be grown in the climate in the United Kingdom, the British government encouraged the cultivation of this fruit. Beginning in 1942, a large amount of the British black currant crop was made into black currant cordial. The cordial was provided to the children of Britain for free.

and blackberries. They are sometimes crossed with the red raspberry to make the purple raspberry.

Oftentimes mistakenly called a blackberry, it tastes like neither a red raspberry nor a blackberry. Oddly, a mutation of the black raspberry is a yellow berry, with its own distinct flavor.

Chambord liqueur is made from black raspberries.

Blueberry – *Bleuet*

Vaccinium section *Cyanococcus*

The blueberry is indigenous to eastern North America and is of the low-bush type, reaching 12 inches (30.5 cm) in height. The blueberry is small and round with smooth, gray-blue skin. The blueberry is a sweet and juicy fruit that contains many soft, tiny seeds that are virtually unnoticeable.

Blueberries are considered to be rich in antioxidants due to the presence of high levels of anthocyanins and polyphenol antioxidants. This is also true of other berries, such as red grapes, cranberries, and raspberries, which get their color from the presence of anthocyanins.

Did you know?

Native Americans call the blueberry the starberry and believe that this delectable fruit was sent from the Great Spirit. They believe that starberry was sent from the stars to feed the people and to keep them healthy. The bottom of each small fruit was marked with a star so that they would never forget where this fruit came from. Native Americans used the blueberry for food preparation as well as medicine. Blueberries were probably used in one form or another during the first Thanksgiving meal.

Boysenberry – *Mûre de Boysen*

Rubus ursinus × *idaeus*

The boysenberry is a hybrid that was developed in California by Rudolph Boysen. The boysenberry is a large glossy berry, reddish-purple in color, with a tart taste.

Rudolph Boysen was a berry farmer who believed in experimenting with different berry crosses in the 1920s. In 1923, he crossed a blackberry, loganberry, and raspberry with amazing results. The hybrid plant that was produced flowered and bore fruit. It was named the boysenberry after its inventor. By 1935 the rights to the plant were secured by Walter Knott, a Southern California berry farmer, and he began to sell the fruit commercially.

Cranberry – *Canneberge, airelle*

Oxycoccus palustris

The cranberry is indigenous to the Northern Hemisphere. It is a wetland fruit that grows in bogs. Cranberries grow on low, creeping vines with wiry stems and evergreen-like leaves. The vines grow and thrive in a special combination of soils and nutrients that is specific to wetlands. The wetlands act like a sponge, storing and purifying water, making them nutrient rich.

Cranberries are white until fully matured, when they develop their characteristic color. Depending on the variety, the cranberry can be a light pink or a bright red hue. The cranberry possesses a tart taste that overpowers its delicate sweetness.

There are four varieties of cranberry worldwide: the common cranberry, small cranberry, large cranberry, and southern mountain cranberry. The most commonly used are the common cranberry and the large cranberry.

The common cranberry is also known as the northern cranberry. This variety is indigenous to the Northern Hemisphere: northern Europe, northern parts of North America, and northern Asia. They possess a strong acidic flavor. The fruit produced is relatively small, with a light pink hue. The plant has small 5- to 10-mm leaves, and develops dark pink blooms.

The large cranberry is also known as the bearberry and the American cranberry, and is indigenous to eastern Canada, the eastern United States, and North Carolina (in high altitudes only). The leaves of the large cranberry are larger than those of the common cranberry, and are between 10 and 20 mm long. The large cranberry has a sweet-tart flavor that is reminiscent of apples.

The name *cranberry* comes from German and Dutch settlers, who called the fruit the "crane berry." In late spring when cranberries begin to bloom, the light pink petals twist and resemble the head and bill of the sandhill crane. Over time the name was abbreviated to cranberry.

The cranberry is now grown commercially in the northern areas of the United States and the bordering areas of Canada. They are available dried, fresh, and in processed forms. Cranberries are used in cereals, soft drinks, yogurt, salsa, sauces, muffins, and energy bars. The Native Americans ate fresh cranberries in a sweetened sauce with maple sugar and used them to add additional flavor to existing dishes. Cranberries were also used for medicinal purposes as poultices for wounds and as medicine for various ailments. The juice was also used as a natural dye to color rugs, clothing, and blankets.

Grape – *Raisin*

Vitis vinifera

The grape is a true berry belonging to the *Vitaceae* family. Grapes are often classified according to how they will be used: as a table fruit, as a baking or cooking fruit, for the purpose of winemaking, or for the manufacture of raisins. The grape is a fruit that grows in clusters of 6 to 300 fruits on deciduous woody vines. Grapes are generally smooth skinned and juicy, and have been cultivated with or without seeds.

The varieties of grapes number in the thousands, some having been modified to suit the needs of consumers by taste and color. The seedless and the slip-skin varieties provide examples of these modifications. Of all fruits, the grape has been one of the most often mentioned fruit in historical records and one of the most widely shared. It is not certain where grapes originated, but it

Champagne Grapes

is believed that grape vines were grown as early as 2375 BC by the Egyptians, or even earlier by the Chinese.

Loganberry – *Mûroise*

Rubus × loganobaccus

The exact origin of the loganberry is undetermined. Some botanists believe that the loganberry is a distinct species of fruit, whereas others believe it to be a hybrid of the raspberry and the blackberry. The loganberry is shaped like a blackberry, red in color, juicy, and sweetly tart.

In the case of the accidental hybrid, the loganberry has an interesting story. Some believe that the loganberry was created in the early 1880s by James Harvey Logan in Santa Cruz, California. During this time, berry growers had begun to cross different varieties of raspberries and blackberries to produce better commercial varieties. Logan accidentally planted a cross between two blackberry varieties next to an older variety of red raspberry. All of the plants fruited and flowered together producing a rather interesting hybrid.

Raspberry – *Framboise*

Rubus idaeus (European variety), *Rubus strigosus* (American variety)

Raspberries are grown on bush-like plants with woody, thorny stems. The raspberry is comprised of many connecting bead-like fruits, surrounding a central core. When the berry is plucked, the core remains on the plant, and will leave a hole at the top of the raspberry. Raspberries are very fragile and are considered to be the most potently flavored berry. The fruit can be yellow, red, purple, or black.

The raspberry is indigenous to the Caucasus Mountains of Asia Minor and to Europe and North America. Red and black varieties of the raspberry are thought to be the first to grow wild. The red variety was prevalent in Asia Minor and Europe, whereas the black variety grew wild only in North America.

Red raspberries were found in the wild and collected by the people inhabiting Troy and Mt. Ida, Crete during the first century. Roman agriculturist Palladius wrote in the fourth century of the domestication of red raspberry. Seeds have been unearthed in Roman forts in Britain, leading experts to believe that the Romans were most likely responsible for spreading its cultivation throughout Europe. The British improved and popularized this delicate berry throughout the Middle Ages and eventually sent red raspberry plants to New York in 1771.

Red Currant – *Groseilles*

Ribes rubrum

Red currants are native to Western Europe, but can be found growing throughout the Northern Hemisphere. The red currant grows on small shrubs that

Raspberries

closely resembles that of the black currant. Red currants are palatable, even if tart; they can be eaten fresh without the addition of sugar. Red currants are a hardy shrub. They are able to take root and grow when other plants are unable to do so.

Red currants are available fresh only for a short time in the summer, but can be purchased frozen. Red currants are used to make jams, tart fillings, fruit soups, and summer puddings.

Strawberry – *Fraise*

Fragaria ananassa

The strawberry is indigenous to the Pacific Coast of the Americas. The strawberry grows on the stem of the plant very close to the ground in groups of three. Not every flower produces a berry. The fruit is light green at first and then develops into a lush, red color as it matures. As the strawberry develops the petals of the flower fall and all that remains is the calyx, or the leafy star-shaped top of the berry. The strawberry is unique because the seeds of the fruit develop on the outside. The strawberry is known as an accessory fruit. (See Berry Classification Chart – Pg. 182).

MELON

Melons belong to the Cucurbitaceae family and grow on vines. Ranging in shape from round to oblong, melon varieties are classified as either summer or winter melons. Summer melons have skin with tiny craters whereas winter melons have smooth skin and will keep longer after they have been harvested. Melons are high in vitamins A and C and calcium. The cantaloupe, honeydew, watermelon, and Crenshaw are all examples of melon.

Melons are believed to be indigenous to either Africa or Asia Minor, but no one knows for sure. Archaeological digs have proven to be of little help because melon seeds closely resemble cucumber seeds. To the best of their knowledge, archaeologists have been able to identify melon seeds found in India dating back to 2000 BC and in Egypt around 2400 BC.

It would be safe to assume that melons grown in 2000 BC were very different from the melons of today. At that point in history, our ancestors classified the melon alongside cucumbers because of their similar appearance and flavor. The melons of yesterday were not the flavorful, sweet, aromatic melons that we have come to love and depend on today. Through innovation, civilizations have changed the course of the melon through cultivation and cross-breeding. It wasn't until the sixth and seventh centuries that melons were generally agreed to be different from the cucumber. Through careful hybridization, the melon evolved into a sweeter and more aromatic variety.

The melon was introduced to England during the 16th century. Initially considered rare and, hence, only found in the gardens of the privileged classes,

It would be natural to assume that dried currants are made from fresh currants, but they are in fact made from sweet Black Corinth grapes. In their fresh form, they are known as champagne grapes and are often found decorating buffets and fancy cheese platters. The reference to "currants" thus comes from the word *Corinth*. In French, dried currants are called *raisins de Corinthe*.

Cantaloupe

the fruit increased in popularity when it eventually became more available to commoners. Spanish explorers in the 1400s were responsible for the distribution of the melon in the West Indies and the Americas. The melon became very important to the first settlers in America. By the 18th century the melon was common in many parts of the world.

Cantaloupe – *Melon*

The cantaloupe is one of two muskmelon varieties: the European cantaloupe and the North American cantaloupe. The cantaloupe is an aromatic, rough-skinned fruit. The flesh of a cantaloupe can be both soft and firm to the touch and is pale orange in color. When fresh and ripe, the cantaloupe possesses a sweet smell that will be most noticeable at the severed stem. The cantaloupe is considered a summer melon and will continue to ripen when left at room temperature.

Honeydew – *Miellée*

Honeydew melons have a round to oblong shape and weigh 4 to 5 pounds (1.8 to 2.3 kg). When the melon has reached full maturity, it has a smooth, creamy yellow exterior and light green-colored flesh. The honeydew melon has been grown in France for many years, but is known there as the "White Antibes." The honeydew is considered to be a winter melon.

Watermelon – *Pastèque, melon d'eau*

The watermelon is firm and evenly shaped. The exterior of a watermelon should be firm and have a hollow sound when hit lightly with an open hand. This is indicative of a perfectly ripe watermelon. The part of the watermelon that rests on the ground should have a yellow spot where it sat and matured. The edible rind may be used safely as a vegetable. In China, after the rinds have been deskinned and defruited, they are cooked with oil, garlic, chilli peppers, scallions and sugar. Pickled watermelon is common in the southern United States, Russia, the Ukraine, and Romania.

Watermelons are thought to be indigenous to the Kalahari Desert of Africa, and are thought to have been first discovered some 5,000 years ago. The first reference made to a watermelon-like fruit was in the ancient buildings of the Egyptians, in hieroglyphic form. Watermelons were often placed in the burial chambers of Egyptian kings. Merchant ships would also carry the melons by way of the Mediterranean, diffusing the succulent treasures to communities along the coastal areas. By the 10th century the watermelon had arrived in China. The watermelon had spread throughout Europe by the 13th century, and eventually to the United States on slave ships sailing from Africa.

Yellow Watermelon

Crenshaw – *Crenshaw*

The Crenshaw is a sweet and spicy tasting melon with a yellowish rind and salmon-colored flesh. A hybrid of the casaba melon and the Persian melon, the Crenshaw is an excellent source of vitamin C.

STONE FRUITS

All stone fruits belong to the Rosaceae family and are called such due to the presence of a single hard pit or stone at the center. The apricot, cherry, nectarine, peach, and plum are all included in this particular genus of *Prunus*. Stone fruits are produced in the summer and are also referred to as drupes. A drupe is a botanical designation for stone fruits. Drupes develop from a single pistil of the flower. As the fruit develops, it forms thick flesh around a hard shell (the pit), which is the hardened wall of the ovary surrounding the seed.

Apricots

Apricot – *Abricot*

Prunus armeniaca

The apricot is thought to be indigenous to northern and western China, as well as parts of Central Asia. The fruit was cultivated extensively in prehistoric times, making it difficult to track its exact origin.

The apricot is graced with many names: apricot, abricot, and apricock. The exact etymology is unknown. One suggestion is that the origin stems from the writings of Pliny the Elder (AD 23–AD 79). Pliny wrote: "The Asiatic peach ripens at the end of autumn, though an early variety (*praecocia*) ripens in summer—these were discovered within the last thirty years…." A second suggestion is that it is derived from the Catalan *abercoc*, which was an adaptation of the Arabic *al-birquq*, itself a derivative of the Byzantine Greek *berikokkia*. Finally, to complete the long journey of this word back to its roots, *berikokkia* came from the Latin *(malum) proecoguum*, meaning "early ripening fruit." *Prunum* or *Malum armeniacum* are the older Latin names that are meant to reference the apricot's origin, Armenia. It has not been proven that the apricot is indigenous to Armenia, but the apricot is still known in many parts of the world as the *Armenian apple*.

The apricot is a plump fruit with a golden orange color when ripe. The apricot's delicate flavor is sweet and the fruit, when fresh, should be very juicy. The apricot is a delicate fruit that unfortunately is very difficult to transport. For this reason the fruit that you purchase out of season is harvested before it has reached perfection (with the thought being that it will "ripen" on the way to its final destination). Unfortunately, as with other stone fruits, once plucked from the tree, the fruit no longer increases in sugar content. Whenever possible, you should purchase local produce while it is in season.

Cherries

Cherry – *Cerise*

Prunus avium, Prunus cerasus

The cherry is indigenous to Eurasia and has been cultivated since antiquity. The cherry is a fleshy drupe that possesses a single stone at its center. This stone fruit boasts hundreds of varieties, all of which belong to two edible and noticeably different species: sweet and sour. Some cherry varieties are grown exclusively for ornamental purposes, such as the Japanese flowering cherry (*Prunus serrulata*).

Sweet cherries (*Prunus avium*) belong to two different groupings: Bigarreus and Geans/Guines. Sweet cherries are generally larger, firm fleshed, and heart shaped compared to sour cherries. Those that belong to the Biggareus variety, like the Napoleon, have firm, crisp flesh. They are generally large and are pale with a light blush, possessing a slightly tart flesh. Other varieties include Bing, Royal Anne (also known as White Napoleon), and Black Schmidt. They are best eaten out of hand, in pastries, and in preserves. The Geans or Guines varieties are softer, have fragrant and juicy flesh, and come in a variety of colors. Popular Geans varieties include Black Tartarian, Rainier, and Swiss Black.

The Royal Anne, Rainier, and Gold cherries are currently used to make a sweetened, preserved cherry that is known to dessert lovers as the maraschino cherry. The cherries are bleached and then bottled in artificially flavored and colored liquid. Traditionally, the maraschino dessert cherry was made from one of two sour varieties grown in Croatia, called *wild damasca* and *wild amaresca*. In the original recipe, the cherries are infused in a sweet colorless Italian liqueur that is aptly called *maraschino*.

Sour cherries (*Prunus cerasus*) are smaller, softer, and more rounded than the sweet varieties, and should be medium firm to the touch. The two main varieties of sour cherry are light and dark. The lighter colored cherry is known as the *amarelle*, and the darker is the *morello*.

The *morello* cherry tree is much larger than the *amarelle* tree and is not suited for small gardens. The *morello* cherry tree fruits earlier than its counterpart, the *amarelle* tree. *Morello* cherries remain popular in France. They have a dark-colored juice and are used in confectionary items such as *griottes*, a specialty food of the Franche-Comté. They are utilized exclusively to make black cherry jam and are used in many popular dessert dishes.

The smaller *amarelle* tree produces cherries that have a light juice that is almost devoid of color. Much like the tree on which they grow, *amarelle* cherries are smaller than *morello* cherries. They possess a sweet-sour combination and are very popular in Canada. One of the most prevalent varieties is the Montmorency, which is used in both savory cuisine and dessert items.

The sour varieties are too tart tasting for most people. However, in the Middle East, they are eaten fresh, out of hand. Sour varieties are better suited for pastries and preserves. Sour varieties include the Evans cherry, and the Nanking cherry. Sour cherries are also referred to as "tart" cherries.

Cherries were popularized by King Henri VIII during the 16th century. Due to increased demand, Kentish farmers had developed many new cultivars by 1640. When the colonists arrived in Massachusetts, they brought with them and planted the sour cherry seed, aptly named the *Kentish Red*.

Common uses for the sour cherry include cooking them in soups and pork dishes and combining them with sugar to make syrup that is used in liqueurs, preserves, desserts, and beverages.

Nectarine

Nectarine – *Brugnon*

Prunus persica

The nectarine is indigenous to China and was first cultivated in ancient Persia, Rome, and Greece. Historians believe that the nectarine arrived in Great Britain in the late 16th or early 17th century. It was later introduced to North America by the Spanish. The name *nectarine* is thought to be inspired by the German word *nektarpfirsich*, meaning "nectar peach."

The nectarine is genetically similar to the peach; a recessive gene in the nectarine is what gives its skin a smooth composition. Like the peach, the nectarine has a hard seed at the center. It has a fragrant smooth skin and flesh that deepens into a rich red at the center. The flesh color of the nectarine will not reflect the taste of the fruit in any way. When perfectly ripe, nectarines should be as sweet as nectar.

The ripening process for a nectarine includes softening and the development of juices and flavor. Once a nectarine has been harvested from the tree, however, its sugar content will not increase. So the fruit must be at its ripest at the time of harvest to ensure a high sugar content. Green nectarines should be avoided because they have been harvested prior to reaching full maturity and will not ripen or taste particularly palatable.

Some of the fruit that is produced from the seeds of peach trees, either by means of cross-pollination or self-pollination, will produce both nectarine trees and peach trees. In fact, nectarines will grow on peach trees, and peaches will also grow on nectarine trees. It is almost impossible to predict what will grow from which seed. Commercial growers often graft the branches of nectarine trees onto peach trees, and the peach trees will continue to produce nectarines from those branches.

The nectarine is delicious when paired with pork, poultry, and seafood. They can be used in salads, eaten fresh, or oven baked.

"Talking of *Pleasure*, this moment I was writing with one hand, and with the other holding to my Mouth a Nectarine—how good how fine. It went down all pulpy, slushy, oozy, all its delicious embonpoint melted down my throat like a large, beatified Strawberry."

John Keats (1795–1821)

Peaches

Peach – *Pêche*

Prunus persica

Peaches are a species of *Prunus* and are indigenous to China. Prior to the Common Era, peaches were imported to Persia and the Mediterranean area by travelers using the Silk Road.

White-fleshed peaches (actually a very pale yellow) are the sweetest and contain less acidity. This variety is most popular in Asia. The yellow-fleshed variety is sweet, but with varying levels of tangy acidity. Yellow-fleshed peaches are most popular with European and North American consumers. The skin is velvety and delicate, and susceptible to bruising. The seed, or stone, is a reddish brown color and oval shaped. Peaches may be eaten fresh, but also have many culinary uses in pastries, jam, chutney, salad, and wine.

Peaches that are cultivated can be separated into three separate groups: clingstone, freestone, and semi-freestone. Each variety has red markings to varying degrees on their skin and have either white or yellow flesh. When ripe, the flesh should be fragrant, sweet, and juicy. A peach is categorized by how the flesh "clings" to the stone or pit of the peach.

Clingstone peaches ripen May through August and are the first to be brought to harvest. Peaches in this category are the "clingiest" of the bunch in that the flesh literally clings to the stone at its center. Clingstones typically possess a yellowish flesh that turns slightly crimson in color right around the pit. They are sweet and juicy and perfect for desserts, but average consumers will have a very difficult time trying to find them. They are removed from the fields when ripe, delivered to companies within the canning industry, and processed within 24 hours. This peach variety is perfect for jams, jellies, and canning.

Freestone peaches are the easiest to eat, because the flesh is easily removed from the hard pit at the fruit's center. Freestones are harvested May through October and are consistently larger than the clingstone variety. They possess a firm composition, are not as juicy as the clingstone, and are sweet tasting. Freestone peaches are perfect for baking and canning.

The semi-freestone variety of peach is relatively new. A hybrid of the clingstone and the freestone, it is a culmination of the positive attributes that both fruits possess. It is known as a general-purpose fruit; great for canning and baking.

Industry improvements have led to the introduction of refrigerated transport in the form of tractor trailers, boxcars, and air freight. New peach varieties have also been developed since the 1900s, a welcome innovation that has created produce that is hardier and more disease resistant. These transportation options and modifications have assisted and heightened the marketing potential for many commercial crops.

Plum – *Prune*

Prunus domestica, Prunus salicina

More than 2,000 years ago, the Assyrians were the first to cultivate the wild plum, and a short time later the Romans hybridized them. Plums were brought to the west coast of the North American continent by Spanish missionaries and to the eastern coastline by English Colonists.

The plum is a soft round fruit, with sweet flesh and smooth skin. There are many varieties of plum, developing from separate species, each indigenous to different parts of the world. Because of the many varieties, plums vary in size and color. For instance, the flesh of plums can be white, yellow, green, or red, with variations in skin color. At the center of the plum, as in all stone fruits, there is a stone or pit. This stone is somewhat flat and pointed. At present, all plums fall under one of two groupings: European or Japanese.

The European plum (*Prunus domestica*) is often referred to as a prune because it can be dried without the removal of its pit. European plums are also known for their sweetness. When dried, they retain much of their original flavor and sugars. The European plum grows on large trees that can reach 40 feet in height, of which there are approximately 950 different varieties. Varieties of European plum include Victory, Vision, and Valour.

The Japanese plum (*Prunus salicina*) can be eaten fresh, canned, and in jams or jellies. Varieties of Japanese plums include Red Beauty, Black Beauty, Black Amber, and Simka. The Japanese plum variety is indigenous to China, where it has been cultivated for thousands of years. The fruit was introduced to Japan only 200 to 400 years ago. This cultivar was introduced to America in the late 19th century and has now been hybridized to produce more than 100 specialized varieties. This plum is now available worldwide, and is deceivably known as the *Japanese plum*, even though it was first grown in China.

The Plumcot is a hybridized plum, a cross between a plum and an apricot. Plumcots are burgundy colored and possess red flesh. This hybridized fruit has the perfect ratio of sweetness to acidity, and is recognized as being sweeter than both the plum and the apricot.

Prior to today's technological advances, prunes were made by drying the plums while they were still hanging from the tree. Now they are dried by gas heat in air tunnels, resulting in a more uniform appearance. Plums that are picked to be dried are collected at a much later date than plums that are destined for canning, or that are meant to be eaten fresh. This ensures commercial fruit growers fruit with a higher sugar content, yielding a more profitable product. Prunes have been popularized for their fiber content. The European plum or *Prunus domestica*, is the variety that is used to produce the prune.

Plums are used to make wine, jam, and plum brandy.

Black and Red Plums

Plant Type Definitions

Annual: a plant that lives for only one year and regenerates from seed.

Biennial: a flowering plant that takes two years to complete its life cycle.

Perennial: a plant that dies back in the winter and grows from its root stalk in the spring.

HERBS AND SPICES

"A dash of this and a sprig of that." Cooks the world over have come to favor certain herbs—bay leaf, thyme, dill, marjoram, oregano, basil, coriander, mint, rosemary, sage, and savory. As long as humans have been gathering plants for their meals, herbs have been helping us develop our palettes as well as the refinement of flavor in our cuisine.

Spices are made from the bark, seeds, stems, roots, buds, fruits, or flowers of a multitude of distinctively scented trees and plants. Spices have played an important part in history through their use in medicine and cosmetics, as preservatives, and for culinary purposes.

A certain mystique surrounds the use of herbs and spices mainly because of their uses for healing and their role in superstition. Most herbs and spices were first used for their medicinal and mystical powers before they were used in the kitchen. They played a major role in forming political alliances, as well as opening the door to exploration and travel. From Marco Polo to Lewis and Clark, countries sought to gain power and wealth through the spice trade.

Let's take a look at some of the more common herbs and spices used in the kitchen.

Allspice – *Piment de la Jamaïque*

Scientific name: *Pimenta dioica*

Available forms: Whole and ground

Allspice is the dried berry of the *Pimenta dioica* tree (from the myrtle family), which is native to the West Indies and parts of Central and South America. The berries are harvested just before reaching full maturity and are left to dry in the sun. Allspice is available whole or ground. Whole allspice can be preserved for a very long time in airtight jars, but once it is ground it will lose its flavor quickly.

Allspice is pungent and aromatic with a bouquet that is comparable to a combination of clove, nutmeg, cinnamon, and ginger. The flavor of allspice is like that of its bouquet, only with peppery overtones. Allspice is used to flavor pâtés, terrines, smoked and canned meats, cakes, fruit pies, and even ice cream.

Anise – *Anis*

Alternate name: Aniseed

Scientific name: *Pimpinella anisum*

Available forms: Whole and ground

Anise is native to the Mediterranean and is one of the oldest known spices, having been used since ancient times. Anise seeds can range in color from grayish green to brown, and the seeds are ribbed and oval shaped. The seeds lose their flavor quickly, so storing them in airtight containers will help retain their flavor. It is best to purchase the seeds whole and then grind them as needed. The bouquet is fragrant and sweet and possesses a mild licorice taste—that should come as no surprise considering that licorice is flavored with anise. Anise is used to flavor poultry, fish, root vegetable dishes, soups, and alcoholic drinks and cordials.

Basil – *Basilic*

Scientific name: *Ocimum basilicum*

Available forms: Fresh and dried

Basil

Growing wild in prehistoric Africa, cultivated for more than 5,000 years in Asia, and used in ancient Greece, basil has only been readily available in North America since the 1970s. Even then, popular North American recipes often called simply for "basil" assuming that what was at hand was dried. Now there is almost universal agreement that to attain the full breadth of basil's flavor, it should be used fresh. Note, however, that when cooking with fresh basil it is generally best to add it toward the end of the cooking process because of the fragile nature of the glands that contains the herb's aromatic and flavorful essential oils.

Basil is a perennial in warmer climates, but is considered an annual where frost occurs. It grows anywhere from 8 inches (20 cm) to 24 inches (61 cm) high. Basil can be identified by its square stem and its leaves, which are wrinkled and oval. Its color ranges from deep-green to purple.

The flavor of basil varies depending on the cultivar. "Sweet basil," used mainly in European-influenced cuisine (for example, in Italian pesto or the French soup called *pistou*), tastes of mild licorice and cloves. Thai basil and Indian "holy" basil are similar but with more pronounced hints of tarragon. Another factor influencing the flavor of basil is the age of the plant; because the oils become muted over time, the newer leaves are more flavorful than the old.

Reflected in the history of its name (a derivative of *basileus*, which is the Greek word for "king"), basil is known as the king of herbs. Greek legend decreed that basil must be harvested with a golden scythe in the hands of the king. The French call basil *l'herb royale*.

Bay Leaf – *Feuille de Laurier*

Scientific name: *Lauraceae, Laurus nobilis*

Available forms: Fresh leaf, dried leaf, and ground

Laurus nobilis, or true laurel, is a family of trees and shrubs found mainly in Southeast Asia, but native to the Mediterranean. Many plants have been given the laurel name because of their dark, glossy leaves, but these generally come from the unrelated heath family. Though similar in appearance, their leaves are not edible; examples include cherry laurel, which is from the rose family, and California laurel (*Umbellularia californica*), also known as pepperwood, bay tree, and Oregon myrtle. A native of California and Oregon, these laurels provide wood and are used ornamentally; their leaves and fruit are used for medicinal purposes by Native Americans and should not be used as a substitute for true laurel.

Bay Leaves

True laurel is sold commercially as bay leaf and is used in cuisine as a seasoning. Mediterranean bay leaf is a staple in European and North American cuisine. An integral flavor in French preparations such as bouillabaisse and bouillon, bay leaf is also used in stews, meat, seafood, and vegetable dishes. When dried, the leaves have a slightly floral scent similar to that of oregano and thyme. When used in a dish, usually whole and removed before serving (as in a *bouquet garni*), it will add a fragrance and flavor that may be described as woody and floral.

In ancient Greece a garland made of bay laurel leaves was bestowed on scholars and poets; this is where we get the modern academic term *baccalaureate*. In England and Italy, it was believed that bay leaves warded off evil and brought good luck.

Caraway – *Carvi*

Scientific name: *Carum carvi*

Available form: Whole

Native to Europe, North Africa, and western Asia, caraway is a biennial plant that grows from about 15 to 23 inches (40 to 60 cm) tall and has feathery, finely divided leaves. Caraway seeds (which are actually the fruit) are 2 mm long and crescent shaped. Having been found in foods dating back to 3000 BC, caraway is one of the oldest known cultivated spices. Ancient Egyptians buried their dead with the seed to ward off evil spirits.

Caraway may turn bitter when cooked for too long and for this reason it is often added after a dish is cooked. Its warm, sweet aroma is reminiscent of fennel and aniseed, making it a popular spice in German, Austrian, Scandinavian, and Eastern European cuisines. It is essential in sauerkraut and rye bread, and its flavor accents smoked and skimmed milk cheese, such as Havarti. Havarti cheeses from Austria, Germany, Hungary, Holland, and Scandinavia contain whole seeds.

The essential oils in caraway are often used to flavor mouthwashes, toothpastes, and chewing gums, as well as some liqueurs, including aquavit, gin, and schnapps. Used as a digestive, caraway can be chewed after a heavy meal, or used to settle an upset stomach. Roots may be cooked as you would a root vegetable such as carrots or parsnips.

Cardamom – *Cardamome*

Alternate name: Cardamon

Scientific name: *Elettaria* and *Amomum* cardamoms

Available forms: Whole and ground

What do Scandinavian pickled herring and a good Indian curry have in common? Cardamom of course! Although the similarities of these two culinary traditions end here, it is nonetheless fascinating to imagine Vikings (circa 800 AD) sailing back from their exploration of the Middle East with a supply of cardamom pods—altering the course of Nordic culinary history in the process.

Indigenous to the Malabar region on the southwest coast of India, cardamom is part of the ginger (*Zingiberaceae*) family and is sold in two varieties, black (*Amomum*) and green (*Ellateria*). In both cases it is the dried seed pod from the cardamom plant that has the aromatic and flavoring properties. Brown pods have a shriveled husk and are approximately half an inch long, whereas green pods (the variety more commonly found outside of India and the Middle East) are slightly smaller. Both are pungent and fruity and if used too liberally can be overpowering. This spice is most often found as whole pods because this form holds its flavor best; however, inside the pods are a number of tiny black seeds that can be ground with a mortar and pestle. This process is time consuming and the resulting ground spice should be used immediately.

Used sparingly to intensify the flavor of basmati rice and added as a flavor component in some curries, a couple of cardamom pods may also be used in the preparation of Indian chai (tea with scalded milk and spices). In Middle Eastern traditions, cardamom is ground with coffee adding a mild eucalyptus flavor to the hot drink. Getting back to our Vikings and their ancestors, in Scandinavia cardamom is used in baking and savory dishes alike, and is even infused in the alcoholic beverage called aquavit.

Celery Seed – *Graines de Céleri*

Scientific name: *Apium graveolens*

Available forms: Whole and ground

Not only are the stalks as well as the taproot of celery used in cooking, but celery is also grown for its seeds. The seeds are actually very small, round fruit, and the volatile oils contained within them are used in both the cosmetics and pharmaceuticals industry. Celery seeds are used whole or ground, and often mixed with salt to make "celery salt," which is used as a seasoning on its own.

Celery seed is an important ingredient in Indian cuisine, though it did not start appearing in European recipes until the 19th century. Before that it was commonly used in Eastern herbal remedies to treat colds, flu, water retention, digestion, and some diseases of the liver and spleen. It was prescribed as a pain reliever as early as 30 AD in Rome.

Chervil – *Cerfeuil*

Scientific name: *Anthriscus cerefolium*

Available forms: Fresh and dried

Chervil is indigenous to Russia and is often referred to as "rich man's parsley." This comparison is made because it is similar to parsley in appearance but more fragile and therefore more expensive. Chervil belongs to the Apiaceae family and possesses bright green leaves and a fresh, subtle flavor that is similar to tarragon. Some varieties have edible roots that taste like small turnips. It is best to use this herb fresh, because chervil loses most of its flavor when it is dried.

Chives – *Ciboulette*

Scientific name: *Allium schoenoprasum*

Available forms: Fresh and dried

Chives

Chives are native to Europe, Asia, and North America; in fact, the species *Allium schoenoprasum* is the only species of *Allium* native to the New World and the Old World. Chives are a perennial plant with edible tubular leaves that grow 12 to 20 inches (30 to 50 cm) tall. The flowers are purple and grow on stems that rise up through the leaves.

Chives do best in well-drained soil, rich with organic matter, and in full sun. In colder regions, they will die back in winter to their underground bulbs and in early spring will produce new leaves. Because they grow in clumps and not as individual plants, chives are always referred to in the plural. Chives are the smallest species in the onion family. The name of the species comes from the Greek *skhoinos* ("sedge," a plant resembling grass) and *prason* ("onion"). The English name comes from the French *cive*, which was derived from the Latin word for "onion," *cepa*.

In cuisine, chives provide a milder flavor than that of any of their *Allium* cousins. They are one of the four ingredients in *fines herbes* (along with tarragon, chervil, and parsley). Signs of its use can be traced back 5,000 years, and chives have been cultivated in Europe since the Middle Ages. Also used medicinally throughout history, chives were thought by ancient Romans to be a balm for sunburn, and Romanian gypsies believed the herb could ward off evil.

Cinnamon – *Cannelle*

Scientific name: *Cinnamomum zeylanicum, Cinnamomum cassia*

Available forms: Stick and ground

Cinnamon

Cinnamon is the dried inner bark of trees sharing the genus *Cinnamomum*. Native to the Asian tropics, the cultivation of cinnamon is to this day a predominantly East Asian enterprise. Although *Cinnamomum* has numerous varieties, two types are generally available in spice form: Sri Lanka cinnamon and Chinese cinnamon. Note that Chinese cinnamon is also known as cassia and, although the two varieties exhibit subtle differences, they are both suitable for most culinary applications.

The cultivation of cinnamon is said to have been kept a secret for hundreds of years. The bark of the tree is thin, smooth, and possesses a light brown color. Cinnamon is harvested from two-year-old trees that are cut and pruned to encourage new growth; the following year, shoots will grow from the roots. The young shoots will then be stripped and the bark left to dry. Once dry, the inner bark will curl into rolls, or quills, and that is how cinnamon sticks are produced for sale. Cinnamon is also ground to a fine powder for use in baking and cooking and in beverages, stews, and sauces. One stick of cinnamon is equivalent to ½ teaspoon of cinnamon in powdered form. Cinnamon possesses a warm, sweet flavor.

Cloves – *Clou de Girofle*

Scientific name: *Syzygium aromaticum, Eugenia aromaticum,* or *Eugenia caryophyllata*

Available forms: Whole and ground

An evergreen, the clove tree ranges in height from 33 to 66 feet (10 to 20 meters) and it is from this tree that the unopened flower buds are harvested, dried, and sold as a spice. Until the last couple of hundred years, cloves grew mainly in the Molucca Islands, historically known as the Spice Islands (see sidebar). Now the cultivation of cloves has expanded into parts of South America the West Indies, East Africa, and India. Indonesia, however, remains the single largest producer of cloves in the world.

Whether used whole or ground, clove is a spice that can easily dominate other flavors, but when used in moderation adds a delightful sweet cinnamon-like flavor. Cloves are used in Indian and Mexican cuisines, where they are often combined with cumin and cinnamon. In Northern India, ground cloves are used in almost every sauce or side dish and are usually mixed with other spices. In Southern India, whole cloves are used to enhance the flavor of rice in biryani, a dish similar to pilaf. Cloves and green cardamom are also key ingredients in chai tea. In Western cuisine the clove is mainly used in sweet preparations.

Coriander – *Coriandre*

Alternate name: Cilantro, Chinese parsley

Scientific name: *Coriandrum sativum*

Available forms: Fresh, dried, whole seed, and ground

When talking about fresh coriander leaf, there are two types of people: people who love it and people who hate it. Considering it is one of the most consumed fresh herbs in the world, the people who dislike it appear to be in the minority! Native to the Middle East, this annual herb has been cultivated for centuries in Southeast Asia and Latin America, and is well represented in these regions' cuisines. Coriander has had less success being adopted into the European or North American culinary traditions—references to fresh coriander as having a "soapy" taste come mainly from this camp. Still, many Westerners enjoy the fresh aroma and characteristic flavor that coriander brings to food.

Since 300 BC, the Spice Islands had long been the epicenter of competition for traders vying for cloves and nutmeg. Chinese, Indian, and Arab traders sought out the spices of the Spice Islands long before the Europeans. By the early 1500s, the Spice Islands were known as *Jazirat-al-Muluk* meaning "Land of Many Kings." The fight over control of the Spice Islands finally ended in the early 1800s when the French and British managed to smuggle plants to their equatorial colonies. The Arab connection is still evident, however, because a very large population of Muslims lives in the Moluccas.

Much like basil and parsley, fresh coriander leaves do not cook well and are either mixed into curries and chilies in the final stages of cooking or are sprinkled on top once the dish has been finished.

Dried coriander seeds are quite different in flavor to the fresh leaf but are no less distinctive. Coriander seeds are often ground and mixed with cumin, cinnamon, clove, and other tropical spices to form a paste to thicken and flavor curries. In other applications the whole seed is left to simmer in dishes. Unlike coriander leaf, the seed has found a number of applications in European cuisine; for example, in charcuterie and pickling and infused in liquors such as the French Chartreuse.

Cumin – *Cumin*

Scientific name: *Cuminum cyminum*

Available forms: Seeds and ground

Cumin is an herbaceous annual, growing about 11 to 19 inches (30 to 50 cm) tall. The plant has thread-like leaves 2 to 4 inches (5 to 10 cm) long with small, white or pink flowers. Cumin is native to Eastern India and the Mediterranean. The cultivation of cumin requires three to four months of summer heat with daytime temperatures reaching at least 86°F (30°C). The main international cumin exporters for cumin are India and Iran.

Because cumin draws out the natural sweetness of many dishes, it is traditionally used in Tex-Mex, Cuban, and northern Mexican cuisines. It is also a main ingredient in curry and can be found in the Dutch cheese Leyden, as well as some traditional French breads. Not only does cumin play a large role in Latin American cuisines, it's an important flavoring in Thai, Vietnamese, Afghan, Moroccan, and Indian cuisines. An important ingredient in chili powder, it is also found in garam masala, curry powder, adobos, and Bahārāt, a Middle Eastern spice mixture. The ancient Greeks kept cumin on the dining table—much like we do pepper—and this continues today in Morocco.

Cumin is sometimes confused with caraway and, indeed, many languages do not distinguish clearly between the two. This confusion arises because cumin and caraway (not to mention anise and fennel) are visually quite similar to one another—which is not surprising considering they all belong to the same botanical family, Apiaceae. Despite the similarities, the flavoring outcomes can be radically different.

Dill – *Aneth*

Scientific name: *Anethum graveolens*

Available forms: Fresh and dried

From the Norse *dilla* meaning "to lull," dill grows to about the height of 16 to 24 inches (40 to 60 cm) with slender stems and delicate leaves between 4 and 8 inches (10 and 20 cm) long. Dill is native to Eastern Europe, but is cultivated in northern and southern climates alike.

Dill seed is harvested by removing the flower tops from the stem of the plant. The flower tops are then placed in humidity- and temperature-controlled sheds where they will be dried until the seeds detach from the stalks.

Both fresh and dried dill leaves are available, but because dried loses its flavor quickly it is best used fresh. Dill flavors many foods including cured salmon (gravlax), borscht, and pickles.

Dill

Fennel – *Fenouil*

Scientific name: *Foeniculum vulgare*

Available forms: Fresh leaf and whole seed

Native to India and Egypt, the fennel plant grows up from an edible bulb. (For the culinary importance of the bulb, see the Vegetables section, page 171.) It has feather-like leaves and hollow stems that are topped by clusters of small yellow flowers.

From these flowers tear-dropped shaped seeds are produced. Ranging from green to brown, the seeds have an anise-like flavor that can be found, for example, in curry and Northern European rye breads.

The bulb and the fern-like leaves of fennel are used (often in Italian cuisine) to flavor both hot and cold preparations such as soups, salads, pastas, and risottos.

Ginger – *Gingembre*

Scientific name: *Zingiber officinale*

Available forms: Whole, crystallized, and ground (dried)

Ginger is native to Asia and is available fresh or ground for culinary purposes. Ginger is a root with thin brown skin and pale yellow flesh; in botanical terms this chunky root is referred to as a rhizome. While ginger is mild tasting when young, its pungency increases as it matures. Fresh ginger and ground ginger also have different potencies and are not interchangeable; use 6 parts fresh ginger for 1 part ground ginger.

Ginger is commonly used in Chinese cuisine, in Western baking, and in the creation of some Western sweets. Ginger can be pickled, boiled for tea, used in carbonated beverages, and paired with garlic for stir-frys and curries. Oils that occur naturally in ginger aid in the digestive process to help eliminate flatulence, nausea, and cramping.

Juniper Berry – *Baie de Genièvre*

Scientific name: *Juniperus communis*

Available form: Whole berries (dried or fresh)

Junipers are from the genus *Juniperus* from the *Cypress* family, Cupressaceae. Between 50 and 70 species of juniper can be found growing from the Arctic to the mountains of Central America. Junipers can vary in size and shape, from 66- to 131-foot (20- to 40-meter)-tall trees to low-spreading shrubs. Considered an evergreen, they have needle or scale-like leaves.

The juniper berry is actually a female seed cone and is only called a berry because it is unusually fleshy and berry-like. Juniper berries are green when immature and usually turn purple-black over a period of 18 months. Gin is flavored with the immature green berries, whereas the dark, mature berries are commonly used in food and cooking. The younger berries have a piney taste that is accompanied by notes of citrus as the berries mature.

Common in Scandinavian cuisine, juniper berries are used to flavor meat dishes, particularly wild bird and game meats—blackbird, woodcock, boar, and venison, for example. The berries are also used to flavor pork, cabbage, and sauerkraut dishes. The traditional recipe for the Alsatian dish *choucroute garnie* (made of sauerkraut and cured meats) includes juniper berries. Juniper berries are sometimes used in German, Austrian, and Hungarian cuisines, usually with roasted meat.

First intended as a medication, gin was developed in the Netherlands in the 17th century. In fact, the name *gin* comes from either the French *genièvre* or the Dutch *jenever*, which both mean "juniper." There is also a Finnish drink called *sahti*, which is a rye- and juniper-flavored beer.

Juniper berries have been found in ancient Egyptian tombs, including that of King Tutankhamun. Though they are not known to grow in Egypt, the berries may have been imported from Greece, because the Greeks were using juniper berries as a medicine long before they were used in cooking. Because juniper was thought to increase stamina, the ancient Greeks used it in many of their Olympic events.

Mace – *Macis*

Scientific name: *Myristica fragrans*

Available forms: Whole and ground

Mace is made from the waxy red covering of the nutmeg seed (see Nutmeg, page 204). When dried whole, mace is known as a blade. Both the blade and the ground spice should be stored away from moisture. To ensure they are cooking with the freshest possible spice, chefs prefer to grind mace as needed.

While the flavor of mace is both milder and more complex than that of nutmeg, it can be used in a similar fashion—in baked goods such as pies, cookies, and scones. It is also commonly used in curries, soups, roasts, and sauces.

Marjoram – *Marjolaine*

Scientific name: *Origanum majorana*

Available forms: Fresh and dried

Marjoram, also referred to as sweet marjoram, comes from the same family as oregano (*Origanum vulgare*). Similar in appearance and flavor, marjoram is sweeter and milder than oregano. Considered a perennial, it can be grown outdoors, but most species are considered to be cold sensitive and will wither away from exposure to frost.

Marjoram is used with a variety of foods including lamb, beef, pork, chicken, fish, stuffing, bread, and tomato dishes. It is also prevalent in spice blends such

Marjoram

as *fines herbes* and in sausage and pickling mixes. Because its oils are destroyed by heat, marjoram should be added to a dish just before serving.

Mint — *Menthe*

Scientific name: *Mentha spitica* (spearmint), (peppermint)

Available forms: Fresh and dried

Mint

The mint family, Lamiaceae, comprises more than 180 herb varieties (including the familiar basil, oregano, marjoram, rosemary, sage, savory, and thyme), and it is at best confusing to try and discuss Lamiaceae's family politics! Suffice it to say, members of the mint family, native to both Europe and Asia, have a reputation for vigorous hybridizing and indiscriminant reproduction—earning the botanical category of perennial "invasive species."

To simplify things, however, when mint is mentioned in a recipe it will generally refer to one of two varieties: peppermint and spearmint. In terms of its flavor, peppermint is more intense than spearmint and comes with a particular "cooling" sensation when eaten fresh. This sensation is caused by the chemical menthol that is concentrated in the plant's essential oil. Menthol, it may be noted, is used medicinally to ease respiratory and other ailments. From a culinary point of view, peppermint tends to be the preferred mint as an accompaniment for fish and meat dishes. It is most commonly (particularly in the United Kingdom) associated with lamb in the form of mint sauce or jelly. Peppermint is also an ingredient in candies—the festive candy cane, for example, or the chalky bon-bon that may be found in the bottom of grandma's purse, known simply as "the peppermint."

Spearmint does not come with the same hot-and-cold complexity of peppermint but offers a more distinctive, if somewhat milder, flavor. Spearmint tends to be the preferred mint in Southeast Asian, Indian, and Middle Eastern cooking. Spearmint leaves may be found in a tall glass of hot sweet tea, or torn and sprinkled in a yogurt marinade for goat or lamb.

A number of other varieties of mint are enjoyed and grown in backyard gardens. Apple mint, blue balsam, and water mint are notable but the list goes on and on.

Mustard Seed — *Graine de Moutarde*

Scientific name: *Sinapis hirta* (white mustard), *Brassica juncea* (brown mustard), *Brassica nigra* (black mustard)

Available forms: Whole and ground

Mustard means different things to different people. To the boy in Paris spreading mustard on his baguette as he prepares his ham and cheese sandwich, mustard is a sharp-tasting condiment. To the girl in Calcutta, mustard seeds are those little black grains popping in the pan, telling her it's curry night. As different as these two experiences are, the plant source (Brassicaceae) for these two products is the same.

Because mustard seeds have been found in archaeological digs throughout Europe and Asia, the origin of this plant is hard to pinpoint. It is generally accepted to be native to both continents. The three commonly used varieties of mustard seed are black mustard, brown mustard, and white mustard.

Black mustard produces a small black seed that has the highest pungency of the three. The intensity of its volatile oils and the fact that it is prone to crop failure does not make it ideal for prepared mustard production. It is primarily sold in whole-seed form and is the preferred seed for curries and other Indian dishes. **Brown mustard** is a more reliable crop whose plants produce a larger brown seed that is a little less pungent. This is the seed favored by European mustard producers. In some coarsely ground preparations, the brown husks may be evident. **White mustard** is the mildest of the three and is used in American-style mustard. This variety is also used as a pickling spice.

In European-based cuisine, mustard is generally understood to be a yellow to pale-yellow condiment with varying degrees of acidity and pungency. Dijon and Meaux are two well-known French mustards, and Tewkesbury is a favorite in the United Kingdom. Prepared mustard is generally made by grinding water-soaked mustard seeds and adding an acidic liquid such as wine or vinegar. Powdered mustard seeds can also be purchased; this form is prepared by adding water to form a paste that is served immediately. In both cases the pungency in mustard seed is only released when water is added.

The word *pungency* in relation to mustard, horseradish, and wasabi refers to the powerful sensation that occurs when the volatile oils of these plants reach the nasal passage. It is also used to describe the spicy heat in peppers though the sensation in this case is more focused on the tongue.

Nutmeg

Nutmeg – *Noix de Muscade*

Scientific name: *Myristica fragrans*

Available forms: Whole and ground

Native to the Molucca Islands, or Spice Islands, of Southeast Asia, nutmeg is a large, tropical evergreen tree that grows an average of 40 feet (12 meters) high. The tree only comes to fruit-bearing age after 15 years, at which point it may produce as many as 2,000 fruits a year. The part of the nutmeg fruit that is used as a spice is the dark brown nut-like seed and its thin reddish membrane. This membrane is removed and processed into mace (see Mace, page 202). Whole nutmeg can be identified by its hard and wrinkled ovate exterior, its brown color, and its size, which is usually no larger than a grape.

Before Vasco da Gama claimed the Moluccas for Portugal in 1512, the Arabs were the only ones importing nutmeg. Even though the Portuguese and later the Dutch had a stronghold on the importation of nutmeg, Pierre Poivre, the French botanist also known as Peter Piper, smuggled nutmeg seedlings onto the island of Mauritius where he established a healthy crop. When the British took over in 1796, they successfully spread the cultivation of nutmeg to the East Indies and the Caribbean. In Grenada, nutmeg found ideal growing conditions and to this day Grenada calls itself "Nutmeg Island" and proudly displays an image of a nutmeg seed on its flag.

With its sweet peppery flavor, nutmeg (whether ground or freshly grated) is used in desserts containing milk, cream, and eggs. In terms of savory dishes, nutmeg can be found to accompany meat (most notably lamb) in Middle Eastern cuisine and is found in concert with coriander and black pepper in mortadella sausage from Italy. It can also be found in the Moroccan spice blend *ras el hanout*. And finally, what are cider, mulled wine, and eggnog without a little nutmeg?

Did you know? In the Middle Ages, people carried nutmeg everywhere—some even carried mini graters made of silver or ivory, with a compartment for the nuts. Nutmeg was also worn as an amulet to protect against evil as well as ailments ranging from boils and rheumatism to broken bones.

Oregano – *Origan*

Scientific name: *Origanum vulgare*

Available forms: Fresh and dried

"To ornament the mountain" is roughly how the word *oregano* translates from the Greek. True to its name, oregano grows wild in the Mediterranean highlands. In terms of commercial cultivation, however, its range has jumped continents and expanded into Mexico—although Turkey remains the world's largest producer. Also, finding oregano in kitchen herb gardens has become common in North America and Europe alike.

For its popularity as the "pizza herb," North Americans can thank returning World War II soldiers. Having grown to love the flavor of oregano on pizza while stationed in Italy, these soldiers brought the herb home for domestic use. Subsequent waves of Italian immigration can take credit for its popularity as well.

Although pizza was the vehicle by which oregano traveled to the shores of North America, the herb also brings to life many dishes from a variety of culinary traditions. Greek salad, lamb, different kinds of tomato sauces, grilled fish, and ratatouille all benefit from its flavor. Possessing mildly bitter qualities, oregano is similar to, though generally more potent than, its cousin marjoram. Oregano is available ground, crumbled, or fresh. As is usual with other mint family herbs, for uncooked applications fresh oregano is preferable. Dry leaf oregano, however, is good in sauces because it releases its flavor over time; this process can be sped up by rubbing or "bruising" the herb between the thumb and index finger.

Oregano

Paprika – *Paprika*

Scientific name: *Capsicum annuum*

Available forms: Ground

Paprika is made by drying and grinding any one of the milder peppers of the species *Capsicum annuum*. While peppers in this botanical class are native to the New World, the processed powder we call paprika is an invention of the Turks that was adopted by the Hungarians in the early 1600s. Although it is the national spice of Hungary, the bright red or orange powder is not exclusive to that country. In addition to the Hungarians, the Spanish also produce a version of paprika that tends to be less pungent than the Hungarian version.

The variability in paprika intensity is determined by two main factors: (1) As in all pungent spices, the volatile oils in paprika evaporate, so pungency is affected by storage procedures and age. For this reason, the spice should be stored in airtight containers and should be used within six months of grinding. (2) The pungency level of paprika is also determined by which variety of *Capsicum* pepper is being used. The peppers chosen range from mild to pungent but never as pungent as, for instance, cayenne pepper. As a spice, paprika not only adds color and flavor but it also serves to thicken Hungarian sauces as well.

While paprika is a standard in the arsenal of spices at a cook's disposal, it is often used as a garnish because of its vibrant color and for a hint of flavor. In contrast, and earning its place as Hungary's national spice, paprika is a principal flavor in goulashes, sausages, and paprikash.

Parsley – *Persil*

Scientific name: *Petroselinum crispum* (curly leaf), *Petroselinum neapolitanum* (Italian or flat-leaf)

Available forms: Fresh and dried

This biennial herb is native to southeast Europe and western Asia and its culinary uses are as vast as its natural habitat. The herb was readily used in ancient Roman cuisine and has been appreciated through the ages both in food and medicine. The botanical name for parsley, *Petroselinum*, comes from the Greek word for "stone," *petro*, because it was found growing near rocky hillsides in ancient Greece.

Because its fresh taste is both distinctive and subtle, parsley finds its way into numerous preparations. It can be used in omelets, soups, and sauces, as well as in a multitude of vegetable dishes. Attesting to its cultural flexibility, parsley features in Lebanese *tabbouleh* as well as in the classic French *bouquet garni* and *fines herbes*.

Fresh parsley should be bought in bunches that have springy, erect leaves and should be stored in the refrigerator stem down in a glass of water to maintain crispness. If it is absolutely necessary to use dried parsley (it is inferior to fresh in both taste and texture), make sure the flakes are dark green and free of stalks. Dried parsley should be stored away from direct light.

The two common varieties of parsley are *curly leaf* and *Italian*. Named for its tightly bunched leaves, curly parsley has a fresh, almost fruity taste, is crispy, and has bright green leaves. Italian or flat-leaf parsley has a more delicate leaf pattern and does not hold up well as a garnish; however, its taste is almost interchangeable with curly parsley.

Curly and flat-leaf parsley

Pepper – *Poivre*

Scientific name: *Piper nigrum*

Available forms: Whole, crushed, and ground

Assorted Peppercorns

Native to the Indian coastal region of Malabar, black pepper is the fruit (bcrry) of the climbing vine *Piper nigrum.* Climbing up neighboring trees to a height of 13 feet (4 meters), this vine produces tiny flowers that issue into peppercorns.

Although pepper is a common feature on our tables today, in its early trade history it was literally worth its weight in gold. For example, after the sack of Rome in 410 AD, the invading Visigoths demanded more than 3,000 pounds (1,400 kg) of black pepper (along with other riches) as their spoils of war. Considering that at this time the berry was still being hand picked from wild vines and transported mostly by land from India, 3,000 pounds was a colossal amount. By the late 1400s the spice had been integrated into aristocratic European cuisine to the extent that a more efficient trade route was needed to keep up with demand. This demand for pepper was largely responsible for motivating explorations in search of sea routes from Europe to southwest India where the crop was, by this time, being cultivated. With the sea route as his objective, Christopher Columbus famously set sail in the wrong direction and found America instead, leaving Vasco da Gama to chart the route in the name of Portugal. Since then, the demand for pepper has only increased and the transportation and cultivation of the spice have become more and more streamlined. The world's major producers of pepper today are India, Indonesia, and Brazil.

The processing of pepper berries (peppercorns), from a tiny grape-like cluster into individual whole-spice form, depends on what color of berry is desired. **Black pepper** is from a semi-ripe berry that has been blanched and then dried until the outer skin turns black and wrinkled. The peppercorn reaches its aromatic peak just before ripeness, which explains why the berry is picked when it is. Black pepper is ground into sauces and onto red meat (such as in the recipe for pepper steak); however, it is most effective when ground directly onto food that has been plated. **White pepper** is made from a ripe berry that is soaked in water to facilitate the removal of its dark skin before drying. White pepper is used on white meat, in white sauces, as well as in clear soups. Its color allows it to blend visually with these lighter colored foods. Also, as a result of chemical changes that occur as the berry ripens, white pepper is less aromatic but slightly more pungent than black pepper. **Green pepper** is made when pepper berries are picked before they have begun to ripen. This process does not involve drying but rather preservation in brine. **Rose-colored pepper** is similar to green pepper except that it is made to ripen until the skin turns red, at which point it is also preserved in brine.

Rosemary

Rosemary – *Romarin*

Scientific name: *Rosmarinus officinalis*

Available forms: Fresh and dried

Native to the Mediterranean, rosemary is a perennial herb with small blade-like leaves and a woody stem. This aromatic herb has had a presence in lore, in medicine, and in the kitchen since at least 500 BC. When Shakespeare wrote the line from Hamlet in 1602 "There's rosemary, that's for remembrance," he was drawing on the herb's potency as both a symbol of love but also as an agent for improving memory. Proving that the health benefits of rosemary have survived into the present, in Provence rosemary tisane is still taken as a digestive after a heavy meal.

The culinary uses of rosemary have not changed too dramatically over the years either. Soups, vegetable dishes, meat (lamb in particular), and stuffings all benefit from seasoning with rosemary. Mainly an herb for savory dishes, rosemary has some limited applications in sweets. Lemon-rosemary sorbet may sound odd to some but is in fact quite refreshing. Another sweet place that a hint of rosemary can be found is in the renowned "honey of Narbonne" produced in southern France. This honey is made by bees that collect nectar from rosemary's purple flowers.

Saffron – *Safran*

Scientific name: *Crocus sativus*

Available forms: Whole threads and ground

Resembling the flower of the common garden crocus, the saffron flower distinguishes itself by the three red threads that droop down over the purple petals. The spice we know as saffron is made from these precious filaments (stigmas) that are in fact the female part of the flower's reproductive system.

Native to Asia Minor, saffron spread naturally from Palestine all the way to Kashmir. It continued its journey into Europe with the help of Arab traders in medieval times. Enthralled by its magical color and unique flavor, Spain and France quickly became prime saffron producers. Spain is famous to this day for its high-quality saffron.

Saffron is the most expensive spice in the world. The cultivation of saffron is a labor-intensive process, involving the hand planting of bulbs, the hand pollination of flowers, and the hand picking of threads. Also, it takes 70,000 flowers to produce just 5 pounds (2.25 kg) of stigmas, which dry to only 1 pound (450 g) of saffron—all of which more than justifies the high cost of the spice.

The main flavor component in saffron is *safranal*, which gives the spice its elusive aroma and flavor. It has been lovingly described as possessing "earthy," "mildly bitter," and "hay-like" qualities. Although the uncooked spice is red, saffron gives a yellow hue to soups like bouillabaisse and adds an even more vibrant gold to rice dishes such as pilaf. Only a scant amount is necessary in these preparations because the pigment in saffron is so strong that even at 1 part per million, it will still color water.

Saffron can vary greatly in quality and it is important to stay vigilant when purchasing this spice. The highest quality saffron is deep red and contains only stigmas. Lower grade saffron can be made from the tasteless orange/yellow saffron "styles" (saffron's male reproductive organ) or other substitutes that are ineffective and sometimes, as is the case with "meadow saffron," even poisonous. Finally, ground saffron is not recommended because it has probably been mixed with lesser spices such as turmeric or safflower.

Sage – *Sauge*

Scientific name: *Salvia officinalis*

Available forms: Fresh leaf, dried whole leaf, and ground

A small perennial shrub with dusty-green leaves and purple flowers, sage is native to Turkey and parts of southern Europe. Due to its hardiness it can be cultivated in cooler climates as well. Its slight peppery flavor makes it ideal for many culinary uses, including flavoring fatty meats, poultry, pork, and sauces. In French cuisine, sage tends to be used for cooking white meat, and it is often added to vegetable soups. In England sage is the main flavoring in English Lincolnshire sausage. It is also frequently used in Italian cuisine, where it is added to pasta filling, and in Middle Eastern cuisine, where it is used in lamb and mutton dishes.

Sage

The word *sage* derives from the Latin *salvia*, which means, literally, "to heal." Sage has been used as an antiseptic, an antibiotic, and an antifungal for hundreds of years, although it can be toxic when used to excess.

Salt – *Sel*

Scientific name: *Sodium chloride* (NaCl)

Available forms: Granulated, iodized, flake, kosher, unrefined, *fleur de sel*, flavored, and colored

One of the five fundamental flavors of the human palate, salt is a chemical compound that is essential to the proper functioning of the human body. The balance between salt and water determines the way our body metabolizes proteins and carbohydrates and it is essential to the functioning of our central nervous system. The connection, however, between salt (sodium) and heart disease (as well as hypertension) seems at times to contradict our physiological need for salt. While it is true that the fast-food and pre-prepared food industries hide excessive amounts of sodium in everything from hamburger buns to ice cream, the salt used for seasoning in most "from scratch" cuisine is acceptable—not to mention crucial in terms of flavor!

Kosher Salt

Sea Salt

Fleur de Sel

Sea salt is much richer in minerals than rock salt, containing potassium, magnesium chloride, calcium, and other minerals. The differences in composition of the water in different parts of the world is the main reason why we have such a variety of gourmet salts at our disposal. Depending on the different organisms and minerals in the water, we obtain salt colors that vary from white to green to gray.

The history of salt is too vast and complex to be detailed in this short space, so what follows are just some highlights to show the mineral's cultural and economic importance through the ages. Approximately 800 years ago, the Chinese were already mining salt by pumping water into underground salt deposits. Once the salt crystals in the mine were dissolved, the salt-saturated water was pumped back up and transferred into shallow pans where the solution evaporated in the sun. The residue in the pan was a solid block of salt. These blocks of salt were stamped with the insignia of the Chinese emperor and were used as a currency. Similarly, Roman soldiers were given daily salt rations that they exchanged for money. They called these rations *salarium*, which evolved into the modern word *salary*. Likewise, medieval French soldiers were paid with salt coins called *sol*, which is where we get the word *soldier*.

Today, the three main sources for natural salts are seawater, mines, and natural salt springs. Most of the table salt that we consume today is mined, iodized, and coated with anticaking agents. Iodization of salt has gone a long way toward eradicating goiter (a disfiguring thyroid disorder); however, cooks prefer kosher salt, which is not iodized and tends not to discolor clear broths. Also, because kosher salt comes in larger crystals it dissolves more slowly and permeates ingredients evenly. Other salt formats also have their place in cuisine: salt flakes sprinkled on food at the last minute give food a crunchy texture, and *fleur de sel* is the most delicately flavored of the salts that are harvested from the sea.

Savory – *Sariette*

Alternate name: Savoury

Scientific name: *Satureja hortensis*

Available forms: Fresh and dried

Closely related to rosemary and thyme, savory is native to temperate climates. This herb can grow from 6 to 20 inches (15 to 50 cm) in height, with leaves from 0.4 to 1.2 inches (1 to 3 cm) in length, and has white to pale pink flowers that form on the stem. Savory is often a prominent flavoring for stuffing, stews, and meat pies.

Star Anise – *Badianne*

Scientific name: *Illicium verum*

Available forms: Whole and ground

Native to China and Vietnam, star anise is a small to medium evergreen in the magnolia family. Reaching up to 26 feet (8 meters) in height with yellow flowers, the fruits are harvested just before they ripen and are then dried in the sun until they reach a rust color. As the name would suggest, star anise are star shaped and have 5 to 10 boat-shaped sections that measure up to 1.2 inches

(3 cm) long. Star anise is available whole or ground. Today, star anise is grown almost solely in southern China, Indo-China, and Japan.

First introduced to Europe in the 17th century, star anise oil was substituted for aniseed in commercial drinks. With its licorice-like flavor, star anise is reminiscent of aniseed, though its flavor is stronger and more pungent. In Asia, star anise is used in everything from confections to meat and poultry. It is used in Chinese red cooking (where the ingredients are simmered for a lengthy period of time in a dark soy sauce), it is almost always added to beef and chicken dishes, and it pairs nicely with pork and duck. In the West, star anise is sometimes added to jams and is a common flavoring for medicinal teas and cough drops. Star anise is one of the ingredients of Chinese five-spice powder.

Star Anise

Tarragon – *Estragon*

Scientific name: *Artemisia dracunculus*

Available forms: Fresh and dried

Tarragon, also called dragon's wort, is native to western and northern Asia. Growing from 47 to 59 inches (1.2 to 1.5 meters) tall, the tarragon plant has slender, branched stems with broad glossy leaves measuring from 0.7 to 3 inches (1.8 to 7.6 mm) in length. Tarragon flowers grow in clusters of up to 40 yellow or yellow-green florets.

In the Middle Ages, tarragon was called *tragonia* or *tarchon*. These words are believed to be on loan from Arabic. Today, the Arabic word for tarragon is *at-tarkhun*. This origin is not clear, but may have come from the Old Greek *drakon*, which means "dragon" or "snake." This may have come from the belief that tarragon could not only ward off dragons and serpents, but that it could actually heal snake bites.

Alongside parsley, chives, and chervil, tarragon is one of the four *fines herbes* in French cooking. It pairs well with chicken, fish, and egg dishes and is the defining flavor in béarnaise sauce. French tarragon is sweet with notes of fennel, anise, and licorice. In contrast, Russian tarragon has a bitter taste and is not at all fragrant. Mexican tarragon is used as a substitute for French tarragon and has many of the same flavor properties.

Tarragon

"I believe that if ever I had to practice cannibalism, I might manage if there were enough tarragon around."
~James Beard

Thyme – Thym

Scientific name: *Thymus vulgaris*

Available forms: Fresh and dried

Native to the Mediterranean, the name derives from the Greek *thumos*, meaning "odor." Best cultivated in a hot, sunny location, thyme is usually planted in the spring and grows between about 4 and 12 inches (10 and 30 cm). Because thyme is able to tolerate drought very well, it retains its flavor when dried better than most herbs.

Thyme

With its delicate taste and slight clove aftertaste, thyme is one of the elements in a *bouquet garni* and in its dried form helps make up *herbes de provence* (see page 214). Used in European as well as in Creole and Cajun cuisine, thyme works well with lamb, veal, poultry stuffing, pâtés, sausages, stews, soups, and breads to name only a few of the possibilities.

When ancient Greeks used the phrase "to smell of thyme," they meant it as a compliment inferring gracefulness. The Egyptians and ancient Greeks both appreciated thyme's antiseptic properties. The Egyptians used it in the embalming process, and the ancient Greeks used it as a fumigant. The botanical suffix for wild thyme, *serpyllum*, is from the Greek "to creep," referring to its entwining, low-growing habit.

Turmeric – *Curcuma*

Scientific name: *Curcuma domestica*

Available forms: Whole and ground

The spice called turmeric is made from the root of the turmeric plant, which is a tropical perennial native to Southeast Asia. Growing from 24 to 39 inches (60 to 100 cm) tall with bright green, lily-like leaves that surround conical clusters of yellow flowers, turmeric thrives in its hot, moist climate. The root is yellowish-brown with a dull orange interior that becomes bright yellow when powdered.

Turmeric has an earthy taste to it, with a bitter undertone, and is only used in its ground form. The powder will maintain its color indefinitely; however, the flavor will diminish over time. It should be stored in an airtight container away from sunlight. Turmeric is mainly cultivated in Bengal, China, Taiwan, Sri Lanka, Peru, Australia, and the West Indies.

Turmeric is an ancient spice with its use dating back 4,000 years to the Vedic culture in India. It was used as a culinary spice, as well as having some religious significance. In fact, it is still used today in Hindu rituals and as a dye for holy robes. Though it is similar to saffron as a coloring agent, the culinary uses of the two spices should never be confused. In other words, turmeric should never replace saffron in a preparation. Turmeric gets its name from the Latin *terra merita*, which means "meritorious earth," referring to the color of ground turmeric.

Turmeric is best known in Eastern and Middle Eastern cuisines as a spice and culinary dye. It is widely used in Moroccan cuisine to spice meat, especially lamb and vegetable dishes. In India it is used as a tint for many sweet dishes. However, its principal place is in curries and curry powder. Because it successfully masks the strong odor of fish, it is commonly used in fish curries. It is generally one of the main ingredients in curry powder, providing the yellow color associated with this spice blend.

Vanilla – *Vanille*

Scientific name: *Vanilla planifolia*

Available forms: Whole bean, ground, and liquid extract

Vanilla Beans

Vanilla is a highly aromatic flavoring derived from the vanilla orchid, referred to as the *tlilxochitl* vine that is native to the Veracruz region in Mexico. It is a climbing vine that grows on trees or poles and will climb as high as the tree or pole that is supporting them. In cultivation, the height of the plant is limited in order to facilitate harvesting. Vanilla was originally found only in Mexico and Central America until it was successfully cultivated outside of these regions through hand pollination.

Highly prized for its flavor, vanilla is the second most expensive spice or flavoring in the world. Vanilla cultivation is a labor-intensive process and it is often grown in areas that are subject to tropical storms and political instability. Furthermore, until the late 1970s, a cartel of vanilla growers controlled the price and distribution, thus limiting the availability of vanilla on the market. The breakup of the cartel allowed other areas such as Madagascar, French Polynesia, and the Caribbean to enter the once exclusive market.

There are three cultivars of vanilla today that all derive from the original *tlilxochitl* vine: *Vanilla planifolia*, *Vanilla tahitensis*, and *Vanilla pompona*. The most commonly available is *V. planifolia*, better known as Madagascar Bourbon vanilla.

Vanilla is used in commercial and domestic baking, candies, and perfumes. It comes in many forms: whole bean, liquid, and ground whole dried beans. Due to its high cost, most commercial vanilla-flavored products are flavored with synthetic vanillin made from lignin, a chemical compound derived from wood.

EXOTIC SPICES AND SPICE BLENDS

Fines Herbes

Fines herbes are the pillar of French cuisine. Parsley, chives, chervil, and tarragon make up the spice composition known as *fines herbes*. They release a subtle flavor over a short period of time.

Five-Spice Powder – *Cinq Épices*

One of the strengths of five-spice powder—in its many variations—is that it takes into account the five basic flavors of Asian as well as European cuisine: sweet, sour, bitter, savory, and salty. Recipes for this spice blend vary depending on the tastes and regional background of the person blending it. One recipe includes a mixture of ground Chinese cinnamon (cassia), star anise, anise, ginger root, and cloves, while another recipe consists of ground Sichuan pepper, star anise, cassia, cloves, and fennel seeds.

Five-spice powder is most commonly used for Cantonese roasted duck and beef stew. This spice is used on a regular basis in commercial kitchens and, in some restaurants in Hawaii, five-spice powder in a shaker is a regular part of the table setting.

It is worth noting that different cultures have different versions of a five-spice blend. The French have one called *quatre-épices*, made with black peppercorns, whole cloves, nutmeg, and ground ginger. Alternatively, the peppercorns can be replaced with allspice and the ginger may be replaced with cinnamon. There is also a Jamaican jerk seasoning that consists of chilies, thyme, cinnamon, ginger, allspice, cloves, garlic, and onions. Curry powder is also a popular spice blend with many variations because up to 20 different spices can be used in a curry blend.

Garam Masala – *Garam Masala*

The literal translation for garam masala is "warm spice," referring to the warmth it brings to food as opposed to a "piquant" pungency. It is a blend of spices that is usually added to food just prior to being served and its purpose is to complement existing spices and flavors.

Common in Indian, Pakistani, and Bangladeshi cuisines, garam masala is prepared in many different ways and there is no particular authentic or standard recipe. In Northwest India, for example, it is usually prepared with cloves, green or brown cardamom, cinnamon (or cassia), and mace or nutmeg. In other regions, similar spices will be used with variations in terms of the quantity of one spice or another. Commercial mixes may include less expensive spices like red chili peppers, dried garlic, ginger powder, mustard seeds, turmeric, coriander, star anise, and fennel. Although these mixes can be bought already ground, they do not keep well and will eventually lose their aroma. For this reason many Indian chefs will not use commercial garam masala but instead will grind small batches of the blend to be used over a short period of time.

Herbes de Provence

Herbes de Provence is a combination of herbs that is said to reflect the flavors of southern France. The mixture was developed in the 1970s by spice wholesalers, and consists of savory, fennel, basil, thyme, and lavender. Prior to prepackaged herb combinations, chefs would collect herbs growing in the countryside for their herbes de Provence.

"Sweet, sour, bitter, pungent— all must be tasted."
~Chinese proverb

LES FONDS – BASIC STOCKS

Les fonds, or the basic stocks, in French cuisine fall under five main categories: fonds, fumets, essences, glaces, and jus. The different types of stock are then classified by color—typically brown and white—which is determined by the ingredients, cooking time, texture, and consistency. Les fonds serve as a canvas for sauces and families of soups (crèmes, veloutés, etc.), and are also used as the liquid when braising or poaching. Les fonds are primarily used as a background, thus their flavoring should be rather generic so as to not overpower the final preparation.

Fonds

Until well into the beginning of the 20th century, fonds were usually made by boiling different meats and fowl together. But today, the flavor of a fonds generally corresponds to the ingredient it is accompanying. For example, veal fonds would be used for veal and beef preparations. (Note that mature beef is not used for beef preparations because as an adult animal, its flavor is considered too strong for use in fonds. This is true of the mature pig also.)

The color of the fonds should also correspond with certain preparations, so if desired a fish fumet could be used with chicken, such as for a poulet marengo, and fond d'agneau is sometimes used with similar meat types in order to highlight the flavor of certain recipes.

All chefs, from Carême to Gouffé to Escoffier to today, agree that nothing exceptional can be accomplished without fonds that have been prepared with attention and care!

Fonds Brun or Estouffades – Brown Stocks

Fonds brun are used with meat, game, and certain fowl such as duck. There are three types of fonds brun:

Fonds brun de veau–brown veal stocks

Fonds brun de volaille–brown poultry (duck, quails, squabs, etc.) stocks

Fonds brun de gibier–brown game stocks.

Fonds Brun de Veau – Brown Veal Stocks

Fonds bruns de veau and, in some countries where veal is expensive and difficult to obtain, fonds de boeuf (beef), are made by coloring the trimmings (nerves, some fat) and bones in a very hot oven (*pincer les os*) until well roasted and the bones are nicely browned, being careful not to overcolor.

An aromatic garnish can be used and would include a mirepoix of leek, carrot, onion, and celery, along with a whole head of garlic, tomato paste, cut fresh tomatoes, thyme, bay leaf, and whole peppercorns. These would be added three-quarters through the roasting time of the bones and allowed to brown as well. This process adds additional color as well as flavor to the stock.

Making a Brown Stock Browner

For additional color, many chefs will add browned onion slices to their stock. Cut whole onions in thick slices and place on a flat burner until dark brown. The browned onions are added after the water has been added to the roasted bones and aromates.

The bones and vegetables are then transferred to a large stock pot and cold water is added until the mixture is completely covered. The stock is then simmered, degreased, and skimmed of impurities, fat, and any surface skin that might form while it cooks for several hours—at least 8 hours for maximum flavor, depending on the volume being prepared. The stock is then strained—a well-made stock should not require any additional skimming after it is strained. However, if residual fat does remain, it should be skimmed off.

Fond Brun de Volaille or *Fonds Bruns de Gibier* – *Brown Poultry or Game Stocks*

To make a brown chicken or game stock, the same process of roasting and the same aromatic garnish just described for a veal stock would be used to provide color and flavor. The cooking time, however, is much shorter because poultry bones are much smaller than veal and beef bones. Take care when browning the bones, because overcoloring can produce a bitter overtone to the final stock.

Fonds Brun

1 Roast the bones in a hot oven until well-colored.

2 Add the aromates and place back in the oven.

3 Continue roasting until the aromates begin to color.

4 Spread the tomato paste over the bones and place back in the oven.

5 Roast for at least 5–10 minutes in order to cook the acidity out of the tomato paste.

6 Transfer to a large stock pot.

(continues on next page)

Fonds Brun

(continued from previous page)

7   Add the fresh tomatoes, bouquet garni, and peppercorns.

8   Place the roasting pan on the heat and add water. Stir well to dissolve the cooking juices. Then pour into the stock pot.

9   Add enough cold water to cover.

10   Place on medium heat and prepare a container of water with a ladle and skimmer. When a foam forms on the surface begin skimming it off into the water.

11   Skim off any fat that rises to the surface.

12   Allow to gently simmer, 4–6 hours over low heat, skimming regularly.

Fonds Blanc – White Stock

White fonds are used with white meats such as fish, chicken, and sometimes veal and pork. There are three types of fonds blanc:

Fonds blanc de veau–white veal stock

Fonds blanc de volaille–white poultry stock

Fonds de légumes–vegetable stock.

Fonds Blanc de Veau or *Fonds Blanc de Volaille* —
White Veal or Poultry Stocks

Instead of browning the bones or trimmings as with the brown stocks, they are first blanched and simmered for 5 to 10 minutes depending on the size of the bones and the quantity of stock to be prepared. This removes the impurities that rise to the surface, which should be skimmed off. An aromatic garnish of carrot, leek, onion, celery, thyme, and bay leaf is then added and the stock is finished by gently simmering it to minimize any cloudiness. The stock should be skimmed regularly while it simmers. You can also add mushroom peelings if desired.

The cooking time depends on the quantity being prepared, but a white poultry stock should cook for at least two hours, but not more than four. Special care is taken to ensure that the flavor elements of the fonds do not take on any color during the cooking process, resulting in a more subtle, neutral flavor. The stock is then strained through a fine sieve and skimmed of any excess fat.

Fonds Blanc

1 First blanch the bones by placing them in a large stock pot.

2 Add enough water to cover.

3 Place over the heat and bring to a low boil. Prepare a container with water and a ladle and skimmer.

4 When the impurities rise to the surface, skim them off as well as any fat.

5 After skimming, refresh with cold running water.

6 Continue until the water runs clear. Drain.

(continues on next page)

Fonds Blanc

(continued from previous page)

7 Place the blanched carcasses back into the cleaned stock pot.

8 Add the aromates.

9 Add enough cold water to cover.

10 Place over medium low heat to simmer, skimming off any remaining impurities and fat.

Fonds de Légumes – Vegetable Stock

The latter half of the 20th century saw the use of vegetable stock become more common in professional kitchens. Vegetable stocks are used to prepare dishes for vegetarians, the health conscious, and for certain categories of soups. Apart from first sweating the vegetables in oil or butter before adding the liquid, the preparation of a vegetable stock follows the main principles of other white stocks. Sometimes, the pure juice of the vegetables is added to enhance or concentrate the stock's flavor depending on its final use.

Fumets

A fumet is a much lighter preparation than a fonds in which the flavor elements and liquid are cooked for a limited amount of time, generally 20 minutes. A fumet is often prepared using fish and shellfish because a longer cooking time would result in overpowering flavors and bitterness. It can also be used for small-boned game. The two basic types of fumet are:

Fumet de poisson–fish fumet

Fumet de crustacés–shellfish fumet.

Fumet de Poisson – Fish Fumet

To make a fish fumet, it is preferable to use bones from white fish such as whiting, sole, or turbot, because of their natural gelatin. Using an oily fish such as salmon will result in a fumet with a distinct flavor of salmon, which is okay if you are preparing a salmon dish, but not okay for more delicate fish such as turbot.

The fish bones are first soaked in ice water (*dégorger*), changing the water several times during the soaking period in order to remove any blood from the bones and trimmings that might give the final product a bitter taste and cloudy appearance. After degorging, the bones are strained. An aromatic garnish of onion, celery, mushroom peelings, thyme, and bay leaf is gently cooked in butter to which the bones are added. White wine is added and reduced by half. Enough cold water is added to cover the bones and the fumet is then allowed to cook at a low simmer for 20 minutes; then it is strained through a fine sieve. When straining, the bones should never be pressed because this will give the fumet a cloudy result.

Fumet de Poisson

1 Prepare ingredients.

2 Sweat the onions and shallots, once they begin to soften, add the celery and leek. Add the bouquet garni and stir well.

3 Add the drained fish.

(continues on next page)

Fumet de Poisson

(continued from previous page)

4 Stir well and cook the fish until it begins to firm up.

5 Add the white wine.

6 Bring to a boil and skim.

7 Add cold water and stir well.

8 Strain, tapping well to recuperate the maximum amount of liquid without pressing.

9 Reserve fumet de poisson for later use.

Variation: A fish fumet, called *fumet de poisson au vin rouge*, can also be made using red wine. The same process as above would be followed, replacing the white wine with red wine.

Fumet de Crustacés – Shellfish Fumet

The same process described above can be applied to the shells of crabes, écrevisses, homards, crevettes (crab, crawfish, lobster, shrimp) and other crustaceans. The shells are crushed, then roasted in the oven or gently cooked on the stove with the same aromates as a brown stock, and then flambéed with

Cognac. Tomato paste is a key ingredient because it provides a desirable red color and, depending on the quality of the tomatoes, adds additional flavor and taste to the shellfish stock.

Essences

Essences, as the name implies, are more pronounced than fonds or fumets, having a more concentrated flavor. This is achieved by reducing the ratio of liquid to the flavor elements. In some cases, an essence is prepared based on a single flavor such as mushroom or celery.

Glaces – Glazes

There are as many different types of glaces, or glazes, as there are stocks. Glaces are essentially fonds that have been reduced down to a syrupy consistency. As a result, they have several different uses compared to an ordinary stock. The reduction results in a concentrated flavor and color so they can be used to add flavor or color to a sauce or stock. They can also be brushed onto a finished piece in order to give it a lustrous appearance, or they can be made directly into a sauce through the addition of butter or cream (see the Reduction entry in the *Les Sauces* section).

Jus

A jus is traditionally served with a roast. It is included here because it is made by adding water to the aromatic elements after roasting. The water dissolves the browned juices (sucs) that form during roasting. After the roast is finished cooking, it is removed from the roasting pan and the juices and accompanying aromates are further colored before water is added. Traditionally a jus was made by repeating the process several times, allowing the water to reduce 3–4 times, resulting in a flavorful jus, then finished with browned butter. The pan is scraped and then the jus is strained through a fine sieve and seasoned. It can be considered a sauce, *jus lié*, through the addition of a thickening agent (traditionally arrowroot).

LES SAUCES – BASIC SAUCES

In general, a sauce is defined by its flavor, the basic stock used to prepare it, its cooking process, cooking time, and its final texture and consistency.

Les Liaisons – Thickening Agents

In modern cuisine, reduction (see later entry) is used to get the right consistency for a sauce, but historically and more traditionally the right consistency is reached by adding a thickening agent. Several types of thickening agents are used that specifically correspond to the preparation and the cooking of the sauce.

Roux

A roux blanc, blond, or brun (white, blond, or brown) is a cooked mixture of equal parts by weight of flour and butter, oil, or any other type of fat. It is considered one of the primary liaisons in making sauces that require medium to long cooking times. A longer cooking time is required for a sauce using a roux to remove the taste of the raw flavor of flour. The different roux are cooked slowly to obtain different degrees of color that will correspond to the final color of the sauce.

Roux can be used hot or cold. The general rule of thumb is that a cold roux is used with a hot liquid, and a hot roux is used with a cold liquid. It is whisked into the liquid, and the more roux that is added, the thicker the sauce will be. When adding the roux to the liquid, it is very important for the liquid to be brought to a boil so that you can verify the proper thickness of the sauce. The quality and gluten content of flour vary from country to country, so the quantity of roux needs to be adjusted to accommodate these differences (120 g of roux will normally thicken 1 liter of liquid).

Roux

1   Prepare your ingredients and equipment.

2   Melt the butter over medium heat.

3   Once melted and foamy, add the flour all at once.

4   Stir well and allow to cook at least 1 minute.

5   For roux blond, continue cooking until it begins to color.

6   For roux brun, continue cooking until a darker color is achieved.

(continues on next page)

Roux

(continued from previous page)

7 From top to bottom, roux blanc, roux blond, and roux brun

Beurre Manié

Beurre manié is an uncooked mixture of equal parts by weight of flour and butter. It is used for sauces with shorter cooking times and in particular in fish and seafood sauces.

Beurre manié is whisked into hot liquids, and the more that is added, the thicker the sauce. Because the flour is uncooked in a beurre manié, it is important to allow the sauce to boil or simmer for a few minutes after it has been incorporated. It should be tasted to ensure that the taste of the flour has been cooked out (120 g of beurre manié should thicken 1 liter of liquid).

Beurre Manié

1   Gather ingredients and equipment.

2   Beat the butter in a large bowl.

3   Beat until smooth and homogenous.

4   Stir in the flour.

5   Continue stirring until all the flour has been incorporated.

6   Beurre Manié

Egg Yolk

Egg yolk adds a silky finish to a sauce and is used in white and blond sauces. The egg yolks are usually mixed with cream, and then tempered by adding some of the hot liquid (stock) before being incorporated into the sauce to be thickened. Because egg yolks will begin to coagulate over 85°C (185°F), they are incorporated off the heat and never put back on the heat. Sauces thickened with egg yolk need to be served immediately and are difficult to reheat for later use. However, they can be prudently heated in a hot, but not boiling, bain marie.

Cream

Cream is added to sauces to provide extra richness and color. It will give a sauce an opaque appearance. For further consistency and a richer taste, the cream can be reduced before being incorporated into the liquid.

Starch

The term *starch* refers to arrowroot, corn, potato, and rice flours that are first mixed with cold water, called a slurry. Once cooked, they provide the sauce with a certain translucence.

Cornstarch, which has become more common due to its low cost, is less stable than the other starches, and can lose its thickening abilities if added to an acidic sauce or cooked too long.

Blood

Blood is used in traditional dishes such as a civet (game stew), where the blood of the game is used to thicken the sauce. To prevent the blood from coagulating, it is usually mixed with some vinegar, lemon juice, or alcohol such as Cognac before being introduced to the hot liquid. As with egg yolks, the blood needs to be tempered first by mixing it with a small quantity of the hot stock before being added to the remaining quantity to be thickened.

Reduction

Reduction is a late 20th-century technique used to thicken a sauce through evaporation, but also to concentrate the sauce's flavor. A result from the *Nouvelle Cuisine* movement, its consideration as a sauce does not fit the traditional definition. The use of reductions in modern kitchens has even changed the way stocks are prepared. The reduction is made from a "court" or short stock. The stock is prepared with less liquid (water, stock, or wine) than a traditional stock, and once strained is reduced to a glaze consistency. Often cream is added until the desired consistency is obtained (ranging from thick to light based on the recipe and chef's preference). The sauce is then mounted with butter (*monter au beurre*) right before serving. Once prepared the sauce should be used immediately; if that is not possible, it can be kept heated in a bain marie.

Les Sauces Mères – Mother Sauces

The term *mother sauces* was first used by Antonin Carême. Mother sauces are the primary sauces that are used as a base for a myriad of other sauces called derivatives that have spanned the evolution of French cuisine.

Sauce Espagnole Grasse

Elements

Stock: Fonds brun

Liaison: Roux brun

Ingredients: Bacon, carrot, onion, thyme, bay leaf (bouquet garni), tomato paste

Derivatives: Sauce demi-glace with the addition of tomato paste and a longer cooking process

The sauce demi-glace is considered a mother sauce by Escoffier, however, if one applies the system of categorization, it is in fact a derivative of the sauce espagnole grasse.

Escoffier might have decided to consider a demi-glace a sauce based on the fact that it also serves as an intermediary sauce for many other sauces (bordelaise, Madère, périgourdine, poivrade), however, if you go back to the origins of the demi-glace, all sauces made from it make them derivatives of the sauce espagnole. This may explain why, up until Escoffier, sauce espagnole was sometimes referred to as *la grande espagnole*. Its role in sauce making was such that Jules Gouffé suggested that it was more appropriate to call it sauce Française.

Sauce Espagnole Maigre

Elements

Stock: Fumet de poisson

Liaison: Roux blanc or blond

Ingredients: Butter, onion, mushroom peelings, thyme, bay leaf (bouquet garni), white wine

Jus de Veau Lié

Elements

Stock: Fonds brun de veau reduced by three-quarters

Liaison: Arrowroot

Velouté – Sauce Blanche Grasse (de Volaille, de Poisson, de Veau)

Stock: Fond de veau blanc, fonds de volaille, or fumet de poisson

Liaison: Roux blanc or blond

Derivatives: Allemande or Parisienne, suprême

Sauce allemande or parisienne and sauce suprême, though considered by Escoffier to be mother sauces, are basically derivatives of the sauce velouté to which egg yolks or cream have been added, respectively.

Sauce Espagnole

We have included information on sauce espagnole as it is one of Carême's original mother sauces, however, they are no longer used regularly in a majority of modern kitchens. The cost of ingredients, the length of preparation and the higher cost of human resources have made some of these sauces too expensive for the average restaurant. With the popularity and ease of reduction sauces, jus de veau lié is rarely found in today's kitchens as well.

Sauce Velouté

1 Make a roux blanc and allow it to cool. Heat the chicken stock.

2 Pour the hot stock into the cold roux.

3 Whisk until the roux has dissolved and the mixture begins to thicken.

4 Add the mushroom peelings and bouquet garni. Allow the velouté to come to a low boil.

5 Carefully skim the foam from the surface.

(continues on next page)

Sauce Velouté

(continued from previous page)

6   Leave to simmer until thick.

7   Remove the bouquet garni.

8   Strain through a fine chinois.

9   The velouté should be thick enough to coat the back of a spoon.

10   Sauce Velouté

Sauce Béchamel

Elements

Liquid: Milk

Liaison: Roux blanc

Ingredients: Lean veal, onion (thyme), crushed peppercorn, nutmeg, salt, bouquet garni

Derivatives: Mornay, soubise, crème, etc.

Today's béchamel is an abridged version of the original béchamel, which was a much richer, more flavorful sauce than the ubiquitous bland version used today. Originally, once the milk was added to the roux, the béchamel was finished slowly in the oven with the addition of veal, aromates, and seasonings. The present-day sauce béchamel might be a simplified version created for the home cook (cuisine bourgeoise) around the end of the 19th century.

Sauce Béchamel

1. Line an oven proof pan with barding fat and add an onion stuck with a clove, bay leaf, white peppercorns, and a bouqet garni.

2. Heat the milk with an onion stuck with a clove and a bay leaf.

3. Strain half of the hot milk over cold roux blanc.

4. Whisk well over medium heat until smooth.

5. Add the remaining milk and whisk well.

6. Season with grated nutmeg.

(continues on next page)

Sauce Béchamel

(continued from previous page)

7 Bring to a low boil, and cook, stirring constantly, until it thickly coats the back of a spoon.

8 Strain through a fine sieve into a clean pan.

9 The béchamel moderne is ready for use.

10 For the béchamel à l'ancienne, pour the strained béchamel into the prepared pan. Add the mushroom trimmings, cover and place in a hot oven for 90 minutes.

Sauce Tomate

Elements

Liquid: Fond blanc

Liaison: Flour (singer)

Ingredients: Tomatoes, bacon, carrot, onion (thyme, bay leaf), bouquet garni, butter, white stock, garlic, salt, sugar, pepper

Unless you grow them in your own garden, tomatoes can vary enormously in terms of flavor, color, and quality, so today's tomato sauce may require the addition of tomato purée or tomato paste. Sugar is used to offset the acidity of some tomatoes.

Sauce Tomate

1. Sear the bacon in some oil, then add the onions and carrots and stir until well-coated. Once they begin to soften, add the celery.

2. After stirring in the celery, add the leeks and mix well.

3. Add the tomato paste.

4. Stir until well mixed and allow to cook 1–2 minutes to remove the acidity.

5. Add the fresh tomatoes.

6. Season with salt, pepper, and sugar, and stir.

7. Sprinkle with the flour, then stir over the heat 1–2 minutes.

8. Add the bouquet garni and the bacon rind.

9. Cover and place in the oven.

(continues on next page)

Sauce Tomate

(continued from previous page)

10 After 25-30 minutes, remove from the oven.

11 Add chicken stock, cover and place back in the oven for 1 1/2 to 2 hours.

12 Once cooked, remove the bouquet garni.

13 Place a food mill into a large pan, and ladle the sauce in.

14 Turn the food mill, until the mixture has been pressed through. Work in small increments.

15 Continue until only the solids are left in the food mill, scraping down the sides as necessary.

16 Scrape down the sides of the pan.

17 Transfer the sauce to a fine chinois and work the ladle in an up-and-down motion to force the mixture through.

18 The remaining pulp from the tomatoes will remain in the chinois.

(continues on next page)

Sauce Tomate

(continued from previous page)

19 Whisk in the butter and season to taste.

20 The finished sauce will be a rich amber, and should be completely smooth.

Fondue Tomate

1 Melt the butter and add the tomato paste.

2 Cook the tomato paste 2–3 minutes to cook off the acidity.

3 Add the fresh diced tomatoes.

4 Add the bouquet garni and season with salt and pepper. *(continues on next page)*

Fondue Tomate

(continued from previous page)

5   Cover with a paper cartouche and place in the oven.

6   Once thick, remove the cover and bouquet garni.

7   The fondue tomate can now be used for different applications.

Sauces Emulsifiée (Froide et Chaude)— Emulsified Sauces (Cold and Hot)

Emulsified sauces are sauces in which an amount of fat, in the form of oil or butter, is introduced into a water-based liquid. Emulsified sauces can be both hot and cold. In this category of sauces the fat is always incorporated off the heat; this step insures that the fat emulsifies rather than just melts. In order to make the fat molecules small enough to mix with the water, the sauce needs to be whisked with a wire whisk when it is being incorporated.

A third important ingredient in emulsified sauces is the presence of a protein that will stabilize the emulsion and keep it from separating, or breaking. The protein in most hot and cold emulsified sauces is egg yolk. Egg yolks contain lecithin, which acts as a stabilizer.

Mayonnaise

Mayonnaise can be referred to as the mother of the cold emulsified sauce. It is made with egg yolks that have been seasoned with salt, mustard, and some lemon juice or vinegar. While whisking, oil is gradually incorporated until the mixture is thick and unctuous. Variations on mayonnaise are aïoli, tartar sauce, rémoulade, and gribiche.

Mustard was not an original ingredient of mayonnaise, but is more of a modern addition due to the difference between the quality of commercial eggs and farm eggs. It also acts as a stabilizer with the egg yolks.

Mayonnaise

1 Prepare equipment and ingredients.

2 Put the mustard into a deep bowl and add the vinegar.

3 Whisk together.

4 Season with salt and pepper.

5 Whisk in the egg yolks.

6 Gradually whisk in the oil.

7 The mayonnaise will begin to thicken.

8 Once the oil is incorporated, the mayonnaise will be thick and light yellow in color.

9 Mayonnaise

Vinaigrette

Vinaigrettes are classified as stable and unstable, the latter not being a classic emulsion. Stable vinaigrette contains mustard, which acts as the stabilizer. An unstable vinaigrette of just oil and vinegar does not maintain its emulsified state for very long before separating.

Vinaigrettes can also be made using reductions of jus or fonds of meat, poultry, fish, or shellfish.

Sauce Hollandaise

Hollandaise sauce is a hot emulsified sauce. Egg yolks are diluted with an infusion of water and black ground pepper, and then gently heated while being whisked and once they begin to thicken, clarified butter or cubes of cold butter are gradually incorporated. Béarnaise is a derivative of hollandaise to which a reduction of shallots, tarragon, and vinegar with a bouquet garni is added.

Hollandaise

1 Bring the water and crushed peppercorn to a boil and allow to reduce by one-quarter.

2 Strain into a clean pan.

3 Whisk in the egg yolks.

4 Place the pan into a bain marie and continue whisking. The yolks will become foamy.

5 Continue whisking until the mixture thickens and traces of the whisk are left when lifted.

(continues on next page)

Hollandaise

(continued from previous page)

6   Gradually whisk in the clarified butter.

7   Once all the clarified butter has been incorporated, season with salt, cayenne pepper, and lemon juice to taste.

8   The Hollandaise sauce should be thick like a mayonnaise.

Sauce Béarnaise

1   Place the shallots, peppercorns, and first quantity of herbs in a pan.

2   Add the white wine vinegar.

3   Season lightly with salt.

4   Place on the heat and bring to a boil.

5   Allow to reduce by two-thirds.

6   Off the heat, add the egg yolks.

(continues on next page)

Sauce Béarnaise

(continued from previous page)

7 Whisk well, then add about one-third of the butter.

8 Whisk until the butter has been incorporated and the sauce becomes thick and light in color.

9 The texture of the sauce will be thick and hold its shape in a spoon.

10 Add the second portion of chopped herbs.

11 Strain through a fine sieve.

12 Finish with finely chopped tarragon.

13 The sauce can be kept warm in a bain marie but should not be reheated.

Sauce au Beurre

A butter sauce is a seasoned butter that is served hot. As in a classic beurre nantais, red wine and shallots are reduced and seasoned with salt and pepper before whisking in cold butter. The liquid can vary but its presence is more as a flavor and a complementary ingredient to the sauce than a primary ingredient of the sauce.

Derivatives of the sauce au beurre are beurre nantais, beurre blanc, and the use of different wines and aromates in the reduction.

Sauce Nantaise

1 Add the red wine vinegar to the shallots.

2 Bring to a boil.

3 Allow to reduce by half.

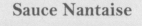

4 Whisk in the butter in two parts.

5 Whisk well after each addition.

6 Continue whisking until all the butter has been incorporated.

(continues on next page)

Sauce Nantaise

(continued from previous page)

7   Season to taste.

8   Sauce nantaise is not as thick as other hot emulsions and should just coat a spoon.

Beurre Composé

Composed butters are cold seasoned butters where the butter is softened to the point where flavors, such as lemon juice or Cognac, and chopped herbs can be incorporated. The butter is then rechilled. It is usually served with grilled meats, poultry, and fish, where a slice is placed on top to soften and melt. Some examples of composed butters are beurre d'escargots (snail butter), beurre maître d'hôtel (lemon juice and parsley), and beurre d'anchois (anchovy butter).

EGGS

When we step out to the grocery store for eggs, it is generally expected that the eggs we bring home will have come from a chicken. In other words, *egg* is the generic term for *chicken egg*. Duck eggs, goose eggs, and eggs from other fowl and poultry all have their own culinary strengths—so why all this chicken-egg favoritism? As much a coup on the part of modern chicken-egg marketers, this preference goes as far back as 6000 BC in Thailand where the chicken was favored for its abundant egg production.

Because they were able to lay eggs continuously, the predominance of the chicken and its egg really took off in the 20th century. A population boom in urban centers and its accompanying increased demand for eggs made vast chicken ranches (containing in excess of 1 million laying hens) economically viable. Although successful in meeting the demand for eggs, the factory-like nature of these ranches has caused a number of people to seek alternative sources. As a result, farms using free-range and free-run chicken coops have jumped in to get a sliver of the egg market.

Despite negative attitudes toward the large commercial chicken ranches, the chicken egg remains a central feature in our diets and, from the point of view of this book, an absolutely vital ingredient in classical French cuisine. From the multitude of preparations where it is front and center to the numerous applications where it is a hidden yet indispensable ingredient, the egg, to answer an ages-old question, absolutely comes before the chicken!

Biological Function

On its most basic biological level, the egg's function is to provide a hospitable environment for the development of a chick. The process of creating a fertilized egg involves two things: (1) The rooster must copulate with the hen in order to deposit sperm inside the reproductive organs of the hen. (2) The hen must then produce an egg. In its early form, an egg has no shell, which allows the sperm to come in contact with the germ cell. Contact between the sperm and the germ cell causes an embryo to be formed.

To develop into a chick, the embryo needs certain nutrients, nutrients that are provided by the white and the yolk of the egg. Another aspect of the egg is the shell. This hard but porous outer layer of mostly calcium both protects the embryo and allows for the transfer of air—this is why eggs can take on the smells inside a refrigerator.

Although it is important to understand the biological purpose of a fertilized egg, we cannot overemphasize that the eggs we use in the kitchen are not fertilized and will never become chicks. A hen lays eggs (approximately one a day) regardless of whether or not there is a rooster lurking about! Therefore, the eggs we consume are from hens that have never come in contact with a rooster and are therefore unfertilized.

Nutrient Value

Considering the fact that an egg contains all of the nutrients needed to transform an embryo into a chick, it should come as no surprise that it is richly endowed with nutrients beneficial to humans as well. A large egg—approximately 2 oz (55 g)—contains approximately 0.2 oz (6.6 g) of protein, 0.1 oz (3 g) of unsaturated fats, nine essential amino acids (essential, that is, for building protein in the human body), and a whole host of vitamins and minerals. In addition, eggs also contain two vegetable-based antioxidants, lutein and zea-xanthin, both of which are considered by some scientists to be effective in cancer prevention.

Egg Sizes

Unless otherwise specified, when a recipe calls for one egg it means one large egg. The average large egg is approximately 2 oz (55 g). This weight varies from egg to egg, which is why eggs are sold by a minimum weight per dozen. For example, a dozen large eggs must have a combined weight of at least 24 oz (680 g), but no more than 27 oz (765 g). Other sizes (also classified by weight per dozen) include jumbo, medium, and small.

Grades/Freshness

When the freshest, highest grade egg (grade AA) is cracked onto a flat surface, its white will hold its shape and will spread very little. Similarly, its yolk will have a strong membrane that will prevent it from breaking easily. When a standard fresh egg found in the grocery store (grade A) is cracked on the same surface, it will be a little less firm and well formed than grade AA but will, nevertheless, be perfectly acceptable for all egg preparations. Grade B eggs are not available at grocery stores. These eggs end up being processed into liquid, frozen, and powdered form.

Liquid, Frozen, and Powdered Eggs

Depending on the preparation, pre-separated whites and yolks can be purchased in containers at grocery stores as liquid eggs. In addition to removing the step of separating eggs for baking and sauces, liquid eggs come with the added advantage of being pasteurized (see the Eggs and Salmonella section). Frozen and powdered eggs can also be purchased in whole or separated form.

Egg Tips

- Break individual eggs into a small container before adding them one at a time to a preparation. This allows for a quick inspection and prevents one bad egg from spoiling the entire preparation. In the 19th century (before "best-before" standards were in effect), this procedure was absolutely necessary; however, the modern cook still benefits from the practice as it provides a chance to remove any bits of shell that may have broken off.

- Very fresh eggs do not peel well when hard cooked.

- Slightly older eggs are better for foaming.

- Other than the obvious signs (such as an off smell), another way to tell that an egg's freshness is questionable is to submerse it in a pot of cold water. If it sinks it is fresh; if it floats it is likely not. As an egg ages, the air pocket inside it expands and causes the egg to become buoyant.

Specialty Eggs

For consumers with ethical and/or dietary concerns with respect to large commercial chicken ranches, smaller egg producers offer the following alternatives:

- *Organic:* eggs produced by hens that are fed certified organic grains only

- *Vegetarian:* eggs produced from hens that are fed a diet consisting exclusively of plant-based ingredients

- *Free run:* eggs produced by hens that are able to walk around the floor of the barn and have access to nesting boxes and perches

- *Free range:* eggs produced by hens who have access to an outdoor run. In Canada and parts of the northern United States, free-range eggs are only seasonally available

- *Omega-3 enhanced:* eggs produced by hens fed a diet containing 10 to 20 percent flaxseeds. Flax contains omega-3 polyunsaturated fatty acids, which have been associated with reducing the risk of heart disease

Eggs from Fowl Other Than Chicken

With different flavor outcomes, duck, goose, and quail eggs can be used in much the same way chicken eggs can. Clearly, due to size differences, adjustments to existing recipes need to be made. A bit of common sense tells you that a soufflé made from tiny quail eggs would be extremely expensive, not to mention laborious. Quail eggs do, however, come pickled to be served as a cocktail snack. Also, there are specific recipes calling for quail eggs which generally involve aspic. Ostrich and emu eggs can be hard cooked or scrambled but remain somewhat of a culinary curiosity. Gull eggs, considered a delicacy in England, are also popular in Scandinavian countries, particularly Norway.

Basic Cooking Techniques

Coagulation

One factor common to all egg cookery is coagulation. Whether it is a yolk binding a Hollandaise sauce or the perfect texture of an expertly scrambled egg, the degree of coagulation defines how well an egg preparation has been executed. On a chemical level, coagulation occurs when the free-flowing proteins in raw eggs link together when subjected to heat. The linking together of proteins results in thickening and setting. Following is a list of approximate egg coagulation temperatures:

Egg white: 140° to 149°F (60° to 65°C)

Egg yolk: 149° to 158°F (65° to 70°C)

Whole egg (beaten): approx. 154°F (68°C)

Eggs mixed with other liquids: 175° to 185°F (79° to 85°C)

Clarification with Egg Whites

Consommé derives its clarity from coagulating egg whites in stock. As the egg-white proteins come together in the stock, they trap other fine particles. The egg whites eventually rise to the surface and are skimmed off taking any cloud-causing particles with them.

Oeufs au Plat

1. Place a heat-proof dish over medium-low heat. Add clarified butter and season with salt and pepper.

2. Break eggs individually into a ramekin.

3. Gently pour the egg into the heated dish.

4. Allow to gently cook, then once the whites begin to set, place in a hot oven.

5. Remove occasionally to baste with the hot butter.

6. The whites should be barely set and the yolks runny.

Egg Yolks as Binding Agent

Egg yolks bind as they coagulate. As the proteins link together, they trap other solids (such as milk solids) and, in so doing, thicken sauces or set custards. Sauces, such as crème Anglaise and Hollandaise sauce, and set custards, such as crème brûlée and crème caramel, all rely on egg yolks to reach their desired consistency. Egg yolks can also thicken velouté sauces such as a bâtarde or allemande sauce. In cooking, a binder is called a *liaison*.

Scrambled Eggs (Oeufs Brouillés)

1 Place some butter in the pan set in hot water.

2 Break the eggs individually and pour into the bowl.

3 Whisk the eggs together with salt and white pepper.

4 Pour the eggs into a pan set in a bain marie while stirring.

5 Continue stirring, as the eggs begin to coagulate.

6 Once the eggs have coagulated, remove the pan from the heat and add the remaining butter.

7 Stir in the cream.

8 Stir in the fresh chopped herbs.

9 Serve immediately, or keep warm in a bain marie.

Deep-Fried Eggs (Oeufs Frits)

1. Heat oil to 160°C. Place two wooden spatulas or spoons in the hot oil.

2. Break the egg into a small container and carefully pour into the hot oil.

3. The hot oil will bubble, and using the wooden spatulas, turn the egg.

4. Continue to turn the egg so that it colors evenly.

5. Once cooked, approximately 3 minutes, place on a napkin or paper to absorb excess oil.

6. Trim the crisp bits of egg white to give the egg an even, rounded appearance.

7. Season with salt and pepper and serve while still hot and crisp on the outside.

Omelettes: Filled, Rolled, Stuffed (Farcie, Roulée, Fourée)

1   Brush a plate with clarified butter and season with salt and pepper. Keep warm.

2   Heat some clarified butter over medium heat. Beat the eggs, season and pour into the preheated pan.

3   Using a fork, gently stir allowing the uncooked eggs to flow to the bottom of the pan.

4   If using a filling (*farcie*), when the eggs are just set, evenly sprinkle with the filling, in this case, ham and cheese.

5   While the eggs are still soft, tilt the pan and with the fork, roll it over onto itself.

6   Keep rolling until the egg is folded in half.

7   Pour some clarified butter along the folded edge of the egg to loosen it from the pan.

8   Lift the pan almost vertically and give it a couple of firm taps. The eggs should move toward the edge of the pan and extend about ¼″ over the edge.

9   Center the egg over the buttered part of the plate.

(continues on next page)

Omelettes: Filled, Rolled, Stuffed (Farcie, Roulée, Fourée)

(continued from previous page)

10 Fold the egg over itself onto the plate.

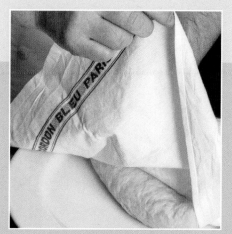

11 Place a towel over the omelette.

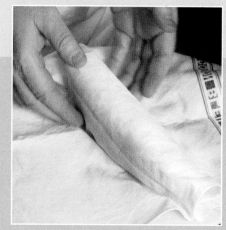

12 Tuck the omelette along the sides in order to give it an even torpedo shape. This also absorbs any excess clarified butter.

13 The omelette can be served plain, or is now ready for filling for an omelette farcie.

14 For an omelette fourrée, cut down the center of the omelette, about halfway down.

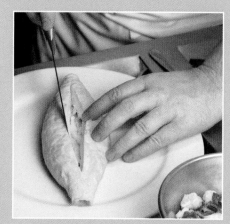

15 Gently pull it open.

16 Spoon a warm filling of your choice into the opening, in this case, shrimp and spinach.

17 Brush with clarified butter and serve.

Omelette Plate

1 Heat clarified butter in a pan over medium high heat. Add the filling, in this case, potatoes and onions.

2 Beat the eggs together and season with salt and pepper. Pour over the garnish.

3 Use a fork to stir the eggs so that they cook evenly and are evenly distributed.

4 Lightly press the sides to make even edges.

5 Once the egg is almost set, cover the pan with a plate and flip the omelette over.

6 Slide the omelette back into the pan.

7 Allow the other side to cook 1-2 minutes.

8 Slide onto a warm serving plate.

Overheating, Curdling, and the Addition of Starch

There is a fine line (or split second) between thickening and curdling in egg-based sauces. Too little heat will result in a thin and unsterilized sauce. Too much heat will curdle it. Curdling occurs when excessive heat causes the egg proteins in a sauce to bond together too quickly. If, however, a sauce needs to be heated beyond 185°F (85°C), adding the right amount of flour or cornstarch will do the trick. Starch not only absorbs heat, it also interferes with the bonding of egg proteins—which is to say that the sauce will withstand higher temperatures (even up to the boiling point) without curdling. One fairly serious drawback to adding starch, however, is that it alters the texture and dilutes the flavor of a sauce.

Foaming

Heat is not the only thing that causes eggs to coagulate; agitation can also bring about coagulation. Whipping not only adds air to an egg white, it also opens the proteins and causes them to link together to form an interconnected web.

The reason foaming is done with egg whites and not with yolks is because yolks have a high concentration of fat and fat inhibits foaming. Foaming is used to make soufflés, meringues, mousses, and sponge cakes such as génoise. The texture of mousseline preparations also benefits from this technique.

Cooking Eggs in Their Shell

In everyday cuisine, most people say that they "boil" eggs. However, a perfectly done egg in the shell is not boiled; it is instead simmered on the very cusp of the boiling point. A rolling boil is to be avoided because the physical action of the water tends to crack the egg, which in turn causes some of the egg white to leak out. Also, using a water temperature above the coagulation point of egg whites leads to rubbery whites.

Hard cooked and *soft cooked* are terms that accurately describe this cooking process. The following is a list of cooking times for eggs cooked in their shell:

Oeuf à la coque: 2 to 3 minutes

Coddled or soft cooked: 3 to 5 minutes

Mollet: 5 to 6 minutes

Hard cooked: 10 to 15 minutes

Cooking Eggs Out of Their Shell

Once out of the shell, eggs are prepared in many different ways:

Au plat: cooked on the stove top in a heat-resistant dish

Scrambled (brouillé): lightly beaten, cooked in a bain marie with constant stirring

Deep fried (frit): submerged and cooked in hot oil

Molded (moulé): oven baked in a mold that is submerged in a water bath

Omelette: Lightly beaten, stirred over heat and generally, but not always, folded (with or without a filling). The four types of omelette are: rolled (*roulée*); filled (*farcie*); stuffed (*fourée*); and flat (*plate*).

Poached (poché): cooked in simmering liquid (generally acidulated water, although milk, wine, and stock are also used)

Cocotte: placed in a ramekin and oven baked

Poached Eggs (Oeufs Pochés)

1 Add vinegar to the water.

2 Season with salt and bring to a boil.

3 Once the water comes to a gentle boil, crack an egg into a small container and slip into the hot water.

4 Check the doneness of the egg by gently pressing with a finger.

5 For oeufs pochés chaud, the cooked eggs are slipped into a bowl of warm water until ready to serve.

6 For oeufs pochés froids, the eggs are slipped into an ice bath.

(continues on next page)

Poached Eggs (Oeufs Pochés)

(continued from previous page)

7   Once the eggs are cooled, trim off the loose whites.

8   Trim off any additional uneven edges if needed.

9   After trimming they should be smooth and nicely egg-shaped.

10   Place on paper toweling or a kitchen towel until ready to use.

Eggs and Salmonella

It is estimated that 1 in 10,000 eggs have *Salmonella* bacteria living on their surface or inside their shell. Not bad odds . . . but why gamble? Speedy refrigeration of eggs is an obvious kitchen precaution, and because salmonella infection is associated with raw eggs, cooking them to a temperature of 140°F (60°C) and higher is another. For raw egg preparations such as mayonnaise, pasteurized eggs can be found in whole-shell, frozen, and liquid form.

Frequently Asked Questions about Eggs

Q. If I find a blood spot on my egg does it mean the egg has been fertilized?

A. Blood spots are simply blood vessels and have nothing to do with fertilization. They can be easily removed and are harmless to eat if left on.

Q. Does the color of the yolk indicate the freshness of an egg?

A. Yolk color is determined by the diet of the hen who laid the egg and not by its freshness.

Q. Can the eggs I buy at the supermarket ever hatch into chicks?

A. Even if properly incubated, supermarket eggs can never hatch. This is because they are unfertilized.

Q. Are brown eggs more nutritional than white eggs?

A. There is no nutritional or flavor difference between brown and white eggs; the difference is simply that brown-feathered hens lay brown eggs and white-feathered hens lay white eggs.

FISH AND SHELLFISH

Seafood can be categorized into two very distinct groups: fish and shellfish. Fish possess a backbone to sense changes in their aquatic environment, gills that enable them to breathe oxygen, and limbs in the form of fins. Shellfish, on the other hand, possess an exoskeleton, or shell. Shellfish include crustaceans, such as shrimp and lobsters, and mollusks, such as clams and oysters. Sea urchins fall under the category of shellfish but are echinoderms and are related to sand dollars, starfish, and sea cucumbers, the latter being the other echinoderm consumed by humans.

Fish

Fish are categorized primarily by their habitat and then by body shape and fat content.

Habitat

Fish can be divided into two primary groups: freshwater and saltwater (or marine) fish. Our oceans hold 48 percent of the world's fish population, whereas 41 percent inhabit lakes, rivers, and streams. One percent of fish inhabit both and are referred to as anadromous fish.

Fish breathe oxygen by pushing water through their gills, by either gulping the water or by moving through the water with their mouths open. The functioning of the gills, kidneys, and air bladder differs between marine fish and freshwater fish based on their response to the amount of salt in their environment. Interestingly enough, both fishes and all vertebrates for that matter have the same salinity content in their bodies. Marine fish are thus in an environment where they are surrounded by more salt than their bodies can support. The process of osmosis, going from low salinity to high salinity, forces the fish to expel the excess salt in their system and, ironically enough, stay hydrated.

Freshwater fish, in contrast, have more salt in their bodies than in the water, so must prevent the water from diluting the salt they need to survive.

Remember that osmosis is low salinity going to high salinity, so the freshwater naturally wants to invade the body of the fish. The scales on a fish act as a barrier that prevents too much water from being absorbed. The scales are arranged like shingles on a house, overlapping each other. Have you ever noticed the sliminess of fresh fish? That slime acts as a sealant to further protect the fish from the water. The sliminess of a fish is a sign of its freshness. A dry fish indicates a fish that has been out of its watery habitat too long.

Body Shape

The shape of a fish's body is influenced by its environment, whether the fish lives at the bottom of the ocean, in open water, or in rivers and lakes. **Round fish** are tubular in shape and the term describes fish that move in open and moving water. Their shape is sometimes further described as torpedo shaped, especially for fish that must be able to move quickly such as tuna. Salmon, trout, whiting, and sardines are other examples of round fish. The body is symmetrical with the eyes located on both sides of the head. Round fish will produce two equal-sized fillets.

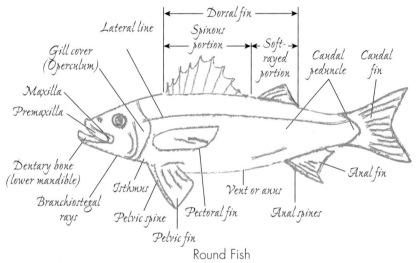

Round Fish

Flatfish on the other hand, tend to be more stationary, lying flat against the bottom of their watery habitat. They are nonsymmetrical in that they produce four fillets of different sizes and both eyes lie on one side of their head. The tops of these types of fish are usually mottled or pigmented so that they blend in with the ocean's bottom, whereas their undersides are white to protect them from predators from below when moving.

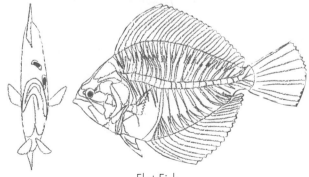

Flat Fish

Forty-one percent of fish are freshwater fish; however, freshwater (containing less than 0.05 percent salt) makes up only 1 percent of the water on the planet.

When flatfish are born, their eyes are placed on either side, but as they mature, one eye will slowly migrate to join the other eye!

Fat Content

Fish with less than 3 percent fat are considered lean and their flesh is almost white in color and mild tasting. Oils are concentrated in the liver of these fish. Cod, sole, and halibut are considered lean fish and their rich livers are considered a delicacy by many. Fatty fish, in contrast, contain 12 to 30 percent fat and distribute their body's oils throughout the flesh. The flesh is therefore darker in color, with a firm texture and stronger flavor. Salmon, mackerel, and eel are considered fatty fish. However, many fish will fall between these two categories, which explains the variety in flavors and textures experienced when preparing and cooking fish.

Cleaning Fish

1. Open the gill cover of the fish to expose the gill. A fresh fish will have bright red gills.

2. Pull the gill cover as wide open as possible.

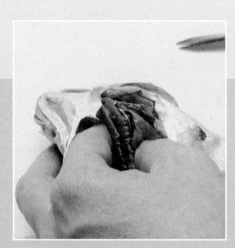

3. The gill is arc shaped, so slip your finger underneath.

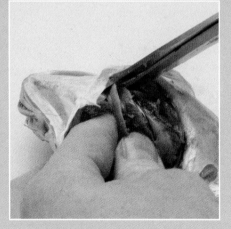

4. With a pair of scissors, snip the gill off at the bottom of the chin of the fish.

5. Carefully pull the gill to remove the guts of the fish. Discard. Remove the gill from the other side.

Round Fish

Anchovy – *Anchois*

Anchovies are part of the Engraulidae family and are closely related to herring. The Atlantic, Pacific, and Indian Oceans are inhabited by 140 species of anchovies. They are considered an oily fish and can range in size from 3/4 inch to 16 inches (2 to 40 cm) in length. They travel in schools and are a significant food source for other fish, as well as for sea mammals and birds. The use of fine-mesh nets has resulted in overfishing.

Anchovies prefer temperate waters and are most abundant in the Mediterranean, where they are prepared fresh and cured. They are most commonly salted and packed in oil or salt. The majority of cured anchovies come from Italy.

The use of anchovies in cooking dates back to Roman times where they were served as a base for *garum* which is a fermented fish sauce. Today, they are consumed fresh, although in many parts of world flesh anchovies can be difficult to find because they are highly perishable. More commonly, they are salted and tend to be used as a garnish or condiment.

Illustration of Round Fish

Illustration of Salt Water

Poisson à l'anglaise

1. Trim off the pectoral fin using a pair of scissors.

2. Snip off the pelvic fins.

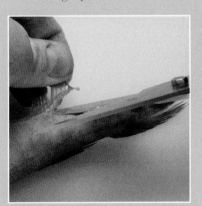

3. Snip off the anal fin.

4. Cut along the top to remove the dorsal spines.

(continues on next page)

Poisson à l'anglaise

(continued from previous page)

5   The fish is now ready to be filleted *à l'anglaise*.

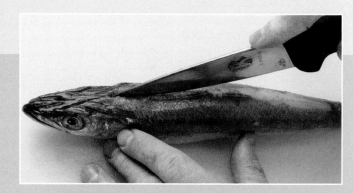

6   Start by making an incision at the base of the head.

7   Cut down the length of the spine.

8   Cut down one side of the spine, following the bones.

9   Continue cutting all the way down, being careful not to puncture the belly.

10   Repeat the same process on the other side of the spine.

(continues on next page)

Poisson à l'anglaise

(continued from previous page)

11 Be sure to disengage the spine completely.

12 Carefully cut the bottom to disengage the spine at the belly, again, being careful not to puncture the skin.

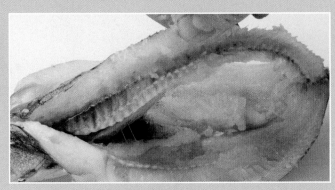

13 The spine should now be connected only to the head and tail.

14 Using the scissors, cut at the tail end.

15 Pull the spine over the head of the fish, and cut as closely as possible.

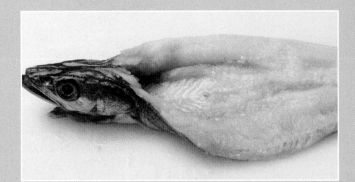

16 The fish is now ready for cooking.

Roundfish

Salt Water

Cod – *Morue*

Fresh Cod – Cabillaud

Scientific name: *Genus gadus*

The Atlantic cod has been a popular food fish ever since its use by the Norse in the first century. In fact, the word *fish* comes from the Norse *fiskr*, which at the time referred to the plentiful cod on which they were dependent. Today, cod is still important in Norway, where the traditional Christmas meal is not a roasted goose or turkey, but boiled cod.

Cod became a commodity when the Basque were the first to expand the cod market by following the cod runs to Georges Bank off the coast of Newfoundland and Labrador. Instead of just drying the fish as the Vikings had done, they salted it so that it would last indefinitely, allowing them to survive long ocean voyages.

Cod weigh 10 to 25 pounds (about 5 to 11 kg) and have a meaty white flesh that flakes nicely when cooked and is low in fat. It can be prepared in several ways: baked, poached, broiled, fried, and braised, as well as dried, smoked, and salted. Cod has traditionally been the fish in fish and chips. Cod liver oil, once a standard in every nursery, is high in vitamins A and D and omega fatty acids.

For the last 500 years, cod has supported European and North American economies and fed millions. The stocks were considered to be so vast that no one imagined that they would one day be depleted. Unfortunately, with the advancement of technology the cod populations have been overfished and are now endangered.

Salt Cod – *Morue*

The economic importance of cod in European history can be attributed to salt cod, which was a storable, nutritious, and inexpensive food. Today, most salt cod is produced in Canada, Norway, and Iceland. Due to its long history, salt cod has become an important ingredient in cuisines on both sides of the Atlantic.

The Vikings dried fish to provide sustenance during long voyages, but the Basques learned that by salting the fish as well, it could be stored for several years. It was traditionally dried by the wind and the sun on wooden racks. Nowadays, however, it is dried indoors using fans and heaters.

Today, due to overfishing, imitation salt cod products are made from other white fish such as pollock, haddock, and blue whiting. It is sold at varying grades depending on the quality, thickness, and size of the pieces. Salt cod is graded by quality, with the highest quality being from cod that are line caught during the spawning season.

To prepare salt cod, it is soaked overnight in several changes of cold water. It is then poached and served as is or mixed with other ingredients. The best known French dish is *brandade de morue*, salt cod mixed with potato purée and olive oil.

Haddock – *Aiglefin*

Scientific name: *Melanogrammus aeglefinus*

Haddock, also referred to as offshore hake, is a member of the cod family and can be found on both sides of the North Atlantic. It is smaller than cod, averaging 1.8 to 4 pounds (0.8 to 1.8 kg) in weight and 43 inches (1.1 meter) in length. The highest concentration of these fish can be found in the same areas as cod, off Georges Bank in the Northern Atlantic. Next to cod, it is one of the most popular fish used in fish and chips. Due to its similarity to cod, haddock has also suffered from overfishing.

Unlike cod, haddock does not take well to salting. It is sold fresh, but also dried and, in particular, smoked. Fresh haddock has white flesh that becomes whiter upon cooking. It has a finer flake than cod with a slightly sweeter taste.

Monkfish – *Lotte*

Scientific name: *Lophius americanus* (North America), *Lophius piscatorius* (northern Europe)

Monkfish, also called goosefish, anglerfish, or allmouth, is a bottom-dwelling fish found in coastal waters of the Atlantic Ocean. *Lophius americanus* dwells mainly in North America, whereas *Lophius piscatorius* can be found in the waters around northern Europe.

The monkfish is a grotesque fish, with a large head and huge, gaping mouth. The rest of its body appears only as an appendage, and it has three filaments coming from the middle of its head. These are actually the detached three first spines on the dorsal fin. With most anglerfish, the central filament is the longest and ends in an irregular growth of flesh, called an esca. The esca is used as a lure to attract and catch other fish, which the monkfish will eat whole. The monkfish grows to a length of 5 feet (1.5 meters), though on average they are caught at 3 feet (0.9 meter).

The texture of the tail meat of a monkfish has been compared to the meat from a lobster tail and is sometimes referred to as the "poor man's lobster."

Mullet – *Rouget*

Scientific name: *Mullus*

The mullet is a bright red fish native to the European and North African coastlines. Mullets are small fish, the largest only reaching 16 inches (40 cm) in length. Both the English term mullet and the French term rouget cover many families of fish in the order perciformes, that includes the family mullus.

The two different species of mullet are fished for consumption. The red mullet (*rouget barbet; Mullus barbatus*) is a mud fish found off the Atlantic shores of France, Spain, and North Africa. It reaches a size of 12 inches (30 cm) and is easily recognizable by its mottled pattern and steeply sloping forehead. The striped mullet (*surmulet; Mullus surmuletus*) is a rock fish found in the coastal regions of the Atlantic Ocean from England down to North Africa as well as in the Mediterranean Sea. It is slightly larger than the red mullet, measuring up to 16 inches (40 cm), and is differentiated from it by its striped flanks and dorsal fin, as well as by the much gentler slope of its forehead.

Mullet has been prized since Roman times for its lean and tender white flesh. Mullet has a pungent fishy flavor and very delicate flesh. It is a scaly fish and care should be taken when scaling since its skin is fragile and easily torn. Mullet spoils quickly so it is best eaten as fresh as possible. The best way to tell the freshness of a mullet is from the color of its skin. A fresh fish will be vividly colored, whereas an older one will have more muted skin tones. Mullet is appropriate for baking, deep frying, sautéing, grilling, and cooking in a papillote, but it should not be poached because this cooking method reduces its flesh to a pulp.

The liver of the mullet is much sought after and, accordingly, in many classical preparations, the fish is not gutted before cooking. This way the diner may appreciate the liver as part of their dish. If the fish is gutted, the liver may be used in preparing the accompanying sauce.

Red Snapper – *Vivaneau (in Quebec) / Rouget (Equivalent in France)*

Scientific name: *Lutjanus campechanus*

The red snapper is a reef fish that is native to the Atlantic and Pacific Coasts of the Americas and the Gulf of Mexico, and is part of the snapper family (mangrove, mutton, and dog).

Snappers have sloping profiles, spiny fins, and sharp teeth. They are considered a rock fish due to their preference to inhabit rocky bottoms, ledges, and reefs.

What's in a word?

Rouget (*Mullus barbatus*) is caught in the Mediterranean and is not available in North America. Red snapper is the closest to rouget in terms of cooking and taste and is available on the North American market. This is why recipes that call for rouget in France are made with red snapper in North America.

Red snappers, as their name indicates, have pink- to red-colored skin, with white, translucent flesh. They get their color from the presence of carotenoids due to the large amount of shrimp that make up their diet.

Salmon – Saumon

Scientific name: *Salmon* is the common name for several species of fish in the Salmonidae family.

Salmon can be found in the Atlantic and Pacific Oceans, as well as lakes, rivers, and streams. Salmon are anadromous, that is, they are born in freshwater, migrate to the ocean, and then return to their birthplace to spawn.

The different species share common traits, although their exterior markings change. They can adjust to their changing environment, providing the needed camouflage to protect them from predators. Although the life spans of the various species differ in length, their life cycles are very similar.

Salmon lay their eggs in the gravel of riverbeds. Once the eggs hatch, thousands of baby salmon, around 2 cm long, are released with their egg sacs still attached. The baby fish remain in the gravel until the egg sac has been completely absorbed. Once they emerge, they may remain in freshwater 1 to 6 years before migrating out to sea. During the migration their internal organs will begin to change in preparation for life in saltwater.

Depending on the species, salmon spend one to four years at sea, during which time a majority of their feeding and growth will take place. They then return to their native waters to spawn, either in the fall or spring. Studies have shown that they return to the exact spot from where they hatched, but have not been able to explain how this happens. Most salmon die after spawning, although some species are iteroparous, meaning that they do not die automatically; they instead return to sea. Steelhead salmon are the only species known to return for multiple spawnings.

Salmon are carnivorous, feeding on small crustaceans and other small fish and species of salmon.

Filleting a Round Fish

1 Cut just below the gills to the bone.

2 Turn the fish and repeat on the other side.

3 Cut along the dorsal line using a thin bladed knife.

4 Follow the bones, cutting as close as possible in order to remove the maximum amount of flesh.

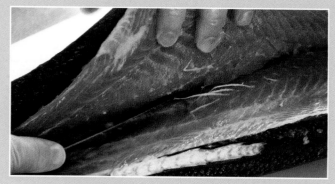

5 Continue following along the bones while gently pulling the fillet back.

6 Continue sliding the knife to the tail, and cut along the stomach.

(continues on next page)

Filleting a Round Fish

(continued from previous page)

7 Flip the fish over and repeat the same process on the other side.

8 Remove the fatty section from the top, following the natural curve of the fillet.

9 Cut away the fatty area from the stomach.

10 Slice off any remaining fat and discard.

11 Use a pair of fish tweezers to remove the pin bones.

(continues on next page)

Filleting a Round Fish

(continued from previous page)

12 Using your fingertip, feel for the pin bones in the fillet.

13 Using the fish tweezers, gently pull the pin bones in the direction that they lay.

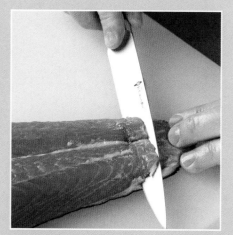

14 Make a small incision at the point of the tail, keeping the knife at a shallow angle.

15 With a gentle sawing motion, move the knife up toward the head of the fillet.

16 Continue to work towards the "head" of the fillet, folding it back as you go if it is a large fillet.

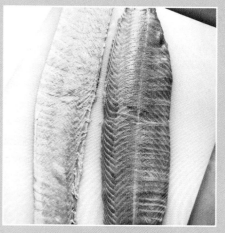

17 If your knife is at the proper angle, very little flesh will remain on the skin.

Atlantic Salmon

Sometimes called the king of fish, the Atlantic salmon is the only species of salmon that lives in the Atlantic. The fish spawn in rivers in Western Europe from Portugal up to Greenland and in North America from Connecticut to Arctic Canada. When migrating to sea, they swim in the waters off of western Greenland.

They will spend 1 to 2 years in the Atlantic before returning to their home rivers, a journey that can cover up to about 2,500 miles (4,000 km) of open water. Between April and November, Atlantic salmon navigate upstream, leaping as high as 10 feet (3 meters) over waterfalls or other barriers so that they can spawn in late fall.

Atlantic salmon are highly aggressive compared to other salmon species, and where they have been introduced to other habitats such as lakes and the Pacific Ocean, they have been known to hunt other species of salmon.

Pacific Salmon

Six species of Pacific salmon are found primarily along the west coast of North America, from California to Alaska. The six species are described below:

Chinook Salmon

Scientific name: *Oncorhynchus tshawytscha*

The Chinook salmon is the largest of the Pacific salmon, weighing on average 30 pounds (13.6 kg). They are also called *spring salmon* because they return to spawn earlier than other species. Due to their size and preference for coastal waters, they are common prey for whales and commercial fishermen.

Their flesh varies from light pink to deep red.

Coho Salmon

Scientific name: *Oncorhynchus kisutch*

The Coho salmon is often found off the northern coast of the Pacific Northwest. Coho salmon spend up to 18 months at sea before returning to freshwater to spawn, but unlike other species, they do not migrate far. They are jumpers and dodgers and, thus, are popular with sport fishermen. During spawning, they develop distinctive hooked jaws.

Salmon is an extremely healthy food source: One 4-oz (113-gram) serving provides a full day's worth of vitamin D, and it contains more than half of the necessary vitamin B_{12}, niacin, and selenium. It is also an excellent source of vitamin B_6 and magnesium. Salmon is also high in omega-3 fatty acids, which are thought to reduce inflammation in the body, which in turn helps prevent heart disease, diabetes, and blood clots that may cause strokes.

Sockeye or Kokanee Salmon

Scientific name: *Oncorhynchus nerka*

The Sockeye salmon is one of the best known salmon of the Pacific Northwest and the first to be commercially harvested. They are a fatty fish with deep-colored flesh and high oil content due to their diet of shrimp and other crustaceans. Sockeye will spend a year or more in freshwater, but once they migrate to the ocean, they can be found over a vast area of the Pacific Ocean.

Pink Salmon

Scientific name: *Oncorhynchus gorbuscha*

The pink salmon is the most abundant species of salmon. They spawn in streams and rivers from Alaska to California. The most significant pink salmon fishery, however, is off the coast of Alaska and Northern British Columbia.

Unlike other salmon species, pinks spawn relatively close to the coast, sometimes even in river estuaries. They are also distinguished by the fact that once they have developed into juvenile fish they swim directly to the ocean from their spawning beds.

Pinks return to spawn between July and October and have a fixed two-year life span. In the ocean, they travel in schools feeding on zooplankton and krill, which gives the flesh its pink tone. Despite their small size and short life span, pink salmon migrate thousands of kilometers before returning to their home streams. Pinks are also called *humpbacks* or *humpies* due to the large hump on their dorsal side.

Chum Salmon

Scientific name: *Oncorhynchus keta*

Also known as *dog salmon* due to its sharply pointed, hooked upper jaw and canine teeth, chum salmon are found not only along the west coast of North America but also as far as Japan and Korea.

Chum salmon are the poorest jumpers of the Pacific salmon species—waterfalls that do not impede other species can often slow or stop their upstream migration.

This salmon is preferred for cold smoking because of the low oil content of its flesh.

Steelhead Salmon

Scientific name: *Oncorhynchus mykiss*

The steelhead salmon is actually an anadromous subspecies of the coastal rainbow trout. They both spawn in the same waters, but the steelhead migrates to the ocean, growing to an average of 20 pounds (9 kg), whereas the coastal rainbow trout remains in its freshwater environs and grows to about 1 lb (453 grams).

Despite its close relation to coastal rainbow trout, the steelhead is always referred to as a salmon. It is the only salmon that does not die after spawning, returning to the ocean after laying and fertilizing its eggs. Approximately 10 to 20 percent return to spawn a second time, with some spawning up to four times during their lifetime.

> The building of dams and increased logging have had a negative impact on the salmon's ecosystems, adversely affecting the streams and rivers and even completely blocking the passage of migrating salmon. Since the 1990s efforts have been made to ensure that these waterways remain clear.

Sea Bass – *Bar, Loup de Mer*

Scientific name: *Dicentrarchus labrax*

Sea bass are part of the Serranidae family, which includes groupers. There are 450 species, all having a "bass-like" appearance: compact, thick bodies with one dorsal fin, large mouths, and a lateral line that extends the entire length of the body to the tail.

They are bottom dwellers, preferring rocks and reefs, and are voracious predators feeding on smaller fish and crustaceans.

Black Sea Bass

Scientific name: *Centropristis striata*

The black sea bass is a type of grouper (Serranidae family) that is found in the Atlantic Ocean, most abundantly off the coast of New York. The black sea bass also inhabits the coasts of Maine to Florida and the eastern Gulf of Mexico. They live in inshore waters such as bays and sounds as well as in offshore waters to a depth of about 430 feet (130 meters). These fish spend most of their time close to the seafloor and congregate close to bottom formations such as rocks, jetties, man-made reefs, piers, and bridge pilings.

As their name would suggest, the black sea bass is black; however, like many other types of fish, they have the ability to change their color to be able to blend in with the bottom of the sea. Their most distinctive feature is their skin, which resembles a fish net. This is due to the lighter color underneath their scales in contrast with the dark color in the margin of their scales. Most sea bass weigh approximately 1.5 pounds (680 grams), though the largest sea bass on record weighed 9 lb 8 oz (4.3 kg). As the sea bass matures, it will experience slight changes in its proportions—smaller sea bass are often nicknamed *pin bass*, whereas the larger ones are nicknamed *humpback bass* because as they grow, they will bulk up just behind the head. The dorsal fin is usually folded close to the body; it can be spread out in an aggressive posture toward other sea bass.

White Weakfish (Sold as White Sea Bass)

Scientific name: *Atractoscion nobilis*

The white weakfish is grouped with a category of fish called *croakers*, which are named because of the repetitive croaking sounds they make. This fish has a habitat that ranges from the coast of California to the coast of Alaska and has an elongated body with a somewhat pointed head and a lower jaw that projects slightly. This fish is the only member of the croaker clan that exceeds 20 pounds (9 kg). The largest weakfish ever recorded was 5 ft long (1.5 meters) and 93.1 pounds (about 42 kg). The maximum legal harvesting size for this fish is 28 inches (71 cm) and 7.5 pounds (3.4 kg). It must also have reached five years of age and have been sexually mature for at least one spawning season.

Patagonian Toothfish (Sold as Chilean Sea Bass)

Scientific name: *Dissostichus eleginoides*

The habitat of the Patagonian toothfish is the waters of the Southern Atlantic, Southern Pacific, Indian, and Southern Oceans between depths of 0.2 mile to 2.2 miles (45 to 3,580 meters). Weighing an average of 20 to 22 pounds (9 to 10 kg), a large adult can exceed 441 pounds (200 kg). They will reach a length of up to 7.5 feet (2.3 meters) and can live up to 50 years. The Patagonian toothfish feeds mostly on squid, fish, and prawns and factors largely in the diets of sperm whales, Southern elephant seals, and colossal squid.

The Chilean sea bass is currently on many consumer watch lists, and the illegal capture and sale of this fish has led to several arrests and fines. Overfishing is threatening the species because it is a slow-growing fish and doesn't reach maturity until it is 10 to 12 years old. Chilean sea bass are caught using longlines, a fishing method that has long been criticized for the drowning of thousands of sea birds such as the Albatross. Although illegal fishing is still a problem in certain areas, the Marine Stewardship Council has certified a fishery in South Georgia for sustainable management.

The total allowable catch for this fishery is 3,307 tons per year by approximately 10 vessels, although illegal catches are estimated to be up to five times

The white weakfish does not share the bass family name of Serranidae but does share the larger order Perciformes. It is not, scientifically speaking, a bass.

The Patagonian toothfish does not share the bass family name Serranidae, but does share the larger order Perciformes. Like the white weakfish, it is not, scientifically speaking, a bass. Marketers created the name *Chilean sea bass* to avoid international criticism and consumer boycotts due to the unsustainabiltiy of the toothfish fishery.

the legal catch limit. Because of this, some researchers predict a total collapse of the fishery in two to five years (from time of publication). Illegal toothfish are called the "white gold of the Southern Ocean"—they are unloaded at pirate ports in countries such as Namibia and Mauritius then sold on the black market. A single sashimi-grade piece can be sold for as much as US$1,000. Although France once sold some fishing rights to Japanese and other foreign fisheries, fishing is now reserved for fisheries from Reunion Island. The French navy patrols this zone and has made arrests and numerous seizures.

Sea Bream – *Dorade*

Sea bream refers to a group of fish species that share a similar body type. Resembling a slightly more rounded red snapper, the external color of this fish varies depending on the variety of fish and temperature and salinity of its waters. Where rivers empty into the ocean, for example, the presence of freshwater darkens the sea bream's skin. Generally, however, the skin is silver with a pink hue and the meat is white and mild flavored. The species that fits this description most accurately is generally known as the European sea bream. This highly marketable species, weighing an average of 1.2 pounds (550 g) is found in waters off the coast of Norway and as far south as the western Mediterranean.

Illustration of Freshwater

Sea Trout – *Truite de Mer*

Scientific name: *Salmo morpha trutta*

Although the sea trout is a species that is distinct from the salmon, its migratory patterns are quite similar. Like the salmon, the sea trout starts its life in freshwater, comes to full maturity in the ocean, and returns to its birthplace to spawn, and often to die.

One fascinating aspect about the sea trout is that it is almost identical to the freshwater "brown" trout. The two fish will commingle in the same river until the sea trout starts to feel the pull of the ocean. The biological difference between the sea trout and the brown trout is not well understood by scientists; they do know, however, that slightly more females than males make the trip to the ocean.

Although there are a number of varieties of sea trout (mainly inhabiting waters of the United Kingdom, United States, and Canada), a general description of the fish is as follows: Similar to the salmon with its long body, the sea trout's skin is silver with tinges of brown or pink and is variably speckled. Reaching lengths of 38 inches (97 cm) and weights up to 19 pounds (9 kg), the sea trout's flesh is lean, tan to pink in color, and mild in flavor.

Trout – *Truite*

Scientific name: *Trout* is the common name of a number of species of freshwater fish in the Salmonidae family.

Trout living in different environments will have dramatically different colorations and patterns. These colors and patterns form a sort of camouflage based on their surroundings and will change if the trout moves to a different habitat. Trout have fins without spines and a fatty fin on their backs, near the tail. Lake trout belong to the char genus and inhabit the larger lakes in North America. Lake trout will live many decades, outliving the rainbow trout, which lives a maximum of seven years.

Found in cool [10° to 15°C (50° to 59°F)], clear streams and lakes, trout are distributed throughout North America, northern Asia, Europe, and England. In the 19th century, several species of trout were introduced to Australia and New Zealand, resulting in the displacement and endangerment of several native fish species.

Trout are members of the Salmonidae family, and is the name commonly given to species in three of the seven genera in the subfamily:

- *Salmo*, the Atlantic species, includes the brown trout, flathead trout, and Adriatic trout.

- *Salvelinus* includes Arctic char, brook trout, bull trout, and lake trout. It also includes the now-extinct silver trout and sometimes includes fish called char or charr.

- *Oncorhynchus*, the Pacific series, includes the rainbow trout, cutthroat trout, and Mexican golden trout.

Because of their popularity and consequent overfishing, trout are now often raised on fish farms in order to stock rivers as well as fish shops and grocery stores. Fly fishing is a distinct method of fishing that was developed primarily for catching trout. While trout tend to be a little bony, their flesh is considered quite appetizing, making them a popular culinary fish. Trout can be poached, fried, baked, steamed, grilled, or boiled. It can also be canned, smoked, and kippered, and is often stuffed prior to cooking.

What's in a word?

A breakfast of kippers is one of those meals that sets the British apart from the rest of the world! There's nothing quite like a plate of smoked, salted, and split (not deboned) fish with a side of fried eggs, fried tomatoes, and fried bread to wake up the old taste buds. We make fun, but in truth the kipper has an enjoyable flavor and is not so very different from other smoked fish. Trout can be kippered but it is herring, with its finer more easily swallowed bones, that is more commonly used for this preparation.

Tuna – *Thon*

Tunas are fast swimmers, having been recorded at speeds of 45 miles (72 km) per hour. Unlike most species of fish, tuna have pink to dark red flesh, which comes from the muscle tissue's higher quantities of myoglobin (an oxygen-binding molecule).

Some species of tuna can even raise their blood temperature above the water's temperature, which helps them live in cooler waters, thereby surviving in a wide range of environments.

The eight species in the *Thunnus* genus are discussed next.

Albacore

Scientific name: *Thunnus alalunga*

The albacore tuna is the only tuna species that can be marketed as "white meat tuna" in the United States. It lives in the open waters of all tropical and temperate oceans, as well as the Mediterranean Sea. The pectoral fin of the albacore is very long, consisting of as much as 30 percent of its total length. The albacore tuna can grow as long as 55 inches (1.4 meters) and weigh as much as 132 pounds (60 kg).

Yellowfin

Scientific name: *Thunnus albacares*

The yellowfin tuna is found in tropical and subtropical waters all over the world. It is an epipelagic fish, meaning it lives in the top 650 feet (198 meters) of the ocean. The yellowfin gets its name because its second dorsal fin and anal fin are both bright yellow. Its body is a dark metallic blue.

The yellowfin doesn't necessarily school with its own fish and has been known to school with other fish of the same size, especially different species of tuna and some larger fish—they are often seen with dolphins, porpoises, whales, and whale sharks. The size and length of the yellowfin can vary, but some have been recorded as being as long as 94 inches (2.4 meters) and 440 pounds (200 kg).

Blackfin

Scientific name: *Thunnus atlanticus*

Found only in the Atlantic, from Cape Cod to Brazil, the blackfin tuna is the smallest in the *Thunnus* genus, weighing a mere 46 pounds (21 kg) and growing to a maximum length of 39 inches (1 meter). Their bodies are football shaped, with black backs and yellow on either side of their body. They do not have a very long life expectancy—a five-year-old fish would be considered "old." The blackfin prefers warmer waters [more than 68°F (20°C)], and will spawn in

Tuna is a popular canning fish due to its mild taste (the reason it is often referred to as "chicken of the sea"), but also because it is easier for canneries to process than other species. Skipjack, yellowfin, and longtail tuna are the species most likely to be canned and distributed to supermarkets. Albacore can also be found canned, but at a considerably higher price.

the open sea during the summers. Though they are small in size, they make up for it in numbers and readiness to bite!

Southern Bluefin

Scientific name: *Thunnus maccoyii*

The Southern bluefin, as its name would suggest, is found in the open waters of the Southern Hemisphere. One of the largest of the bony fishes, the Southern bluefin can reach 8.2 feet (2.5 meters) in length and 882 pounds (400 kg) in weight. They are a large, streamlined fish, and can swim very fast. Their bodies are completely covered in scales. They have blue-black backs and silver-white flanks and bellies. The largest bluefin ever recorded was a little longer than 12 feet (3.7 meters) and weighed more than 2,000 pounds (907 kg).

Northern Bluefin

Scientific name: *Thunnus thynnus*

The Northern bluefin, or giant bluefin, is native to the western and eastern parts of the Atlantic Ocean, as well as the Mediterranean and Black Seas. Although it is not native to the Pacific Ocean, the Northern bluefin is now commercially cultivated off the coast of Japan. The Northern bluefin has a robust body and conical head with a large mouth. They are dark blue on their topside and gray on their underside, and can be easily distinguished from other members of the tuna family by their short pectoral fins.

The Northern bluefin can live for up to 30 years, but because of overfishing there are very few known specimens that grow to a mature age. The typical caught fish weighs an average of 770 pounds (349 kg) and is 6.5 to 7 feet (2 to 2.1 meters) long, although they can reach a length of 14 feet (4.3 meters). The largest Northern bluefin on record weighed 1,496 pounds (680 kg)!

These fish have enormous muscular strength, channeled through two tendons connected to the sickle-shaped tail. As opposed to most other fish, the body of the Northern bluefin will stay rigid while the tail flicks back and forth, thus increasing the efficiency of each stroke.

The Northern bluefin tuna provides most of the meat used in sushi and is an important food source in Japan, where it is considered a delicacy. There, the price of one giant tuna can exceed US$100,000 in the Tsukiji Fish Market in Tokyo. Because of its popularity, most bluefin fisheries are considered overfished. Due to the bluefin's slow growth rate and late maturity, the Atlantic population has decreased almost 90 percent since the 1970s.

Pacific Bluefin

Scientific name: *Thunnus orientalis*

The Pacific bluefin can be grouped with the other bluefin species. They have the same streamlined bodies and mature slowly, not reaching sexual maturity until the age of five. They can reach up to 10 feet (3 meters) in length and weigh up to 1,200 pounds (544 kg). Like most tuna species, they are overfished.

The Pacific bluefin is native to the waters between Okinawa and the Philippines and the Sea of Japan, but migrates more than 6,000 nautical miles (11,000 km) to the eastern Pacific, eventually returning to their birth waters to spawn.

Bigeye

Scientific name: *Thunnus obesus*

The bigeye tuna, so called for its oversized eyes, swims deeper than any other tuna species, frequently visiting deep canyons and peaks, 800 feet (243 meters) or deeper. Satellite imagery has recorded the bigeye spending prolonged periods deep below the surface during the day, making occasional dives as deep as 1,640 feet (500 meters).

They are native to tropical and temperate oceans from Chile, Ecuador, and Peru to the Canary Islands, Hawaii, and New England. The bigeye tuna lives longer than its cousin, the yellowfin, with a life span of 10 to 12 years. They reach sexual maturity at the age of four. They, like most tuna, are overfished and therefore ranked as vulnerable on the conservation status list.

Longtail

Scientific name: *Thunnus tonggol*

The longtail tuna is native to the waters of eastern Australia, from Queensland to the Northern Territories.

Whiting – *Merlan*

Scientific name: *Merlangius merlangus*

This fish is also known as *English whiting* in the United States. Because of the whiteness of their flesh or underparts, several marine food fish have been given the name *whiting*. The common whiting weighs on average 2 pounds (1 kg), reaches up to 12 inches (30 cm) in length, has a long, slender body with two spiny dorsal fins, and is a silver-gray color. The common whiting is found along the Atlantic Coast, from Brazil to the northeastern United States. In early May, the whiting will approach the coast and spawn, returning to deep water and strong currents shortly thereafter. The whiting feeds on crabs, shrimp, and other crustaceans.

Whiting is sold fresh or frozen, whole or in fillets. A versatile fish, whiting can be baked, poached, steamed, broiled, pan-fried, salted, or smoked.

Flatfish

Brill – *Barbue*

Illustration of Flat Fish

Scientific name: *Scophthalmus rhombus*

Brill is a species of flatfish native to the North Atlantic, the Baltic and the Mediterranean Seas. Living mostly in deep, offshore waters, brill has a thin flat body with brown skin. Except for the tail, the skin is covered in light and dark spots and the underside of the fish is a pinkish white or cream color. Like other flatfish, brill is able to change its color depending on its surroundings.

Often confused with turbot (brill and turbot belong to the same family, Scopthalmidae), brill can be distinguished by its smaller size; turbot can reach weights of 33 to 37 pounds (15 to 17 kg), whereas brill is full grown at approximately 7 pounds (3 kg) [measuring between 1.3 and 2.5 feet (40 and 75 cm)].

Halibut – *Flétan*

Scientific name: *Pleuronectidae hippoglossus* (Atlantic), *Pleuronectidae californicus* (Pacific), *Pleuronectidae stenolepis* (Alaska)

There is good reason why the fully mature halibut is referred to by marine biologists as a "whale." With the potential to grow as large as 500 pounds (227 kg), this flatfish is truly the king of its kind. From a commercial point of view, however, halibut are more commonly found anywhere from 5.5 pounds (2.5 kg) to 121 pounds (55 kg).

This large range in size accounts for an equally large range of halibut sub-species. The Atlantic halibut is the largest variety and can be found from the northeastern coast of Canada all the way to Maine in the United States. The Pacific and Alaskan halibut are both a little smaller than the Atlantic, but are more abundant and therefore preferable as a commercial fishery.

Because of its large size, the halibut is a versatile fish to cook with; halibut steaks, roasts, and loins are all commonly available at market. Halibut flesh is sweet and flaky, not to mention it holds together nicely, making it excellent for grilling.

Plaice – *Plie*

Alaska Plaice

Scientific name: *Pleuronectes quadrituberculatus*

Caught in the cool waters off the coast of Alaska and Russia, the Alaska plaice is most often a bycatch, picked up by trawlers gathering other fish. Reaching a maximum length of 24.5 inches (62 cm) and a maximum weight of 7.5 pounds (3.5 kg), Alaska plaice is visually remarkable for its mother-of-pearl skin contrasted by its red rays, the "rays" being the equivalent of fins for flatfish. Due to its overall size, the fillets of this fish are generous and the flesh is enjoyed when smoked, among other preparations.

American Plaice

Scientific name: *Hippoglossoides platessoides*

Although it has a superb camouflage reflex, the American plaice has not evaded overfishing. As a result, a moratorium on American plaice was in effect as of 2009, allowing for only a small bycatch to reach the market. Broadly speaking, its habitat is the northwest Atlantic and its commercial and culinary appeal tends to be North American. The brownish-red exterior, prominent lateral line down the center, and a large mouth are defining features of this species. Although the American plaice can grow larger than the Alaska plaice, due to its scarcity it is marketed at between 2 and 3 pounds (1 and 1.4 kg).

European Plaice

Scientific name: *Pleuronectes platessa*

With its mottled green skin punctuated by red or yellow spots, its red tail fin, and its dorsal rays fanning out, this is an extravagant looking fish! Measuring up to 39 inches (100 cm) and weighing as much as 15.5 pounds (7 kg), the European plaice has long been a favorite for European consumers. In England, for example, it is commonly, though by no means exclusively, battered and used in fish and chips. Although it has been heavily fished in other parts of Europe, plaice stocks are in relatively good shape off the coast of Germany.

Sand Dab

Scientific name: *Citharichthys sordidus* (Pacific), *Limanda limanda* (Atlantic)

Among the smaller varieties of the flatfish [sometimes brought to market at under 10 inches (25 cm)], the sand dab has otherwise typical flatfish characteristics; that is, a flat body with eyes on one side of its head. The Pacific sand dab is grayish brown with sparse black speckles, whereas the Atlantic variety is a deeper brown with slimy skin.

Most sand dabs found on the North American market are caught through bottom trawling along the U.S. and Canadian west coasts. In the United Kingdom the sand dab is also harvested primarily through bottom trawling; however, the habitat-respectful hook-and-line method is gaining in popularity. For culinary purposes the sand dab is too small to fillet, so the common dressing method is simply to scale the fish then cut away the head and internal organs. The flavor of this fish is buttery and sweet.

Sole – *Sole*

Scientific name: *Solea solea*

The sole is a flatfish from the Soleidae family; however, outside of Europe the name *sole* is applied to other similar flatfish and members of the flounder family. The common sole, or *Dover sole*, is born like all other flatfish—with one eye on each side of its body. When the young reach approximately 1 cm long, they metamorphose into a flatfish, with small, close-set eyes on the right side of the body. The Dover sole can reach up to 2.3 feet (70 cm) in length. With its preference for shallow water with a sandy or muddy bottom, sole is found in the eastern Atlantic Ocean, from Norway to Senegal, and practically all areas of the Mediterranean Sea.

The name *Dover* comes from Dover, England, the English fishing port that was the main source of sole in the 19th century. The name *sole* comes from the Latin *solea*, meaning "sandal," probably due to its resemblance to that type of footwear. In German and Spanish, it is named for the tongue (*zunge, lenguado*).

Because of its mild, buttery flavor, chefs use sole for its versatility and ease of filleting, allowing it to go well in a number of recipes. Sole can be poached, steamed, baked, broiled, or sautéed.

Skinning Sole

1 Score where the tail meets the body and scrape away from the tail.

2 Loosen enough skin to make a small flap.

3 Hold the tail securely with the aid of a kitchen towel, and grab the small flap of skin with the other hand.

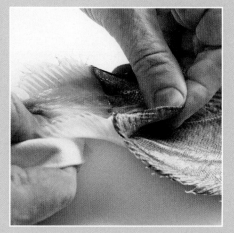

4 Pull the skin away from the tail.

5 As you pull away the skin, hold down the lower half of the body for a better grip.

6 Pull all the way over the head.

7 Turn over and repeat with the white side.

8 Trim off the tail with a pair of scissors.

9 Cut the dorsal fin from the tail to the head.

(continues on next page)

Skinning Sole

(continued from previous page)

10 Repeat with the anal fin.

11 Place trimmings in a bowl to use for fumet.

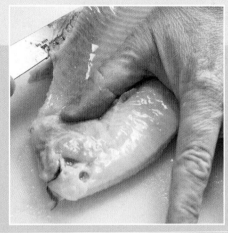

12 Slip the knife through the opening below the head and cut along the belly.

13 Remove the roe sack.

14 Remove the eyes using the tip of a small knife.

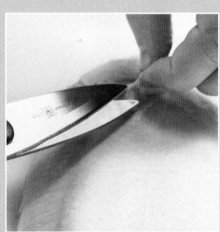

15 Remove the pectoral fin with a pair of scissors.

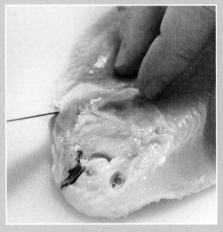

16 Make an incision below the jaw of the sole.

17 Feel around for the gill.

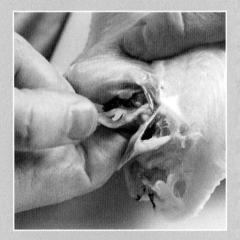

18 Pull the gill out enough to expose it.

(continues on next page)

Skinning Sole

(continued from previous page)

19 Cut both sides with a pair of scissors.

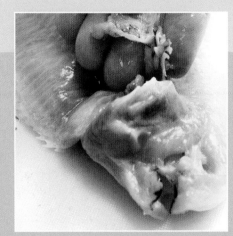

20 Remove and discard.

21 The "top" of the sole, skin removed.

22 The "bottom" of the sole, skin removed.

Lemon Sole – Limande

Scientific name: *Limanda ferruginea* (northwest Atlantic), *Microstomus kitt* (European lemon sole), *Parophrys vetulus* (northwest Pacific)

Lemon sole refers to three fish varieties:

1. *Limanda ferruginea:* Caught along the U.S. and Canadian Atlantic coastal shelf, this fish is also known as a *yellow tail flounder*. It is brown hued with dark brown spots and a tail fin with a yellow tinge.

2. *Microstomus kitt:* This is the variety of lemon sole known by European fish lovers. It is mainly fished off the coast of England and Ireland and its habitat is the rocky sea bottom of the continental shelf.

3. *Parophrys vetulus:* Representing a small northwest Pacific fishery, this variety is sometimes referred to as *California sole* or, confusingly enough, *English sole.* Carrying the distinction of producing a substantial fillet, this lemon sole is unfortunately susceptible to absorbing pollutants and has suffered stock decreases as a result.

As a general note on the three varieties, the name *lemon sole* does not come from the presence of a lemony flavor to the fish, but rather it is an anglicization of the French word *limande,* which translates as "flatfish."

Skinning and Trimming
Filleting Sole Filets

1 A thin bladed knife, usually referred to as a filet de sole knife is the best tool for filleting flat fish.

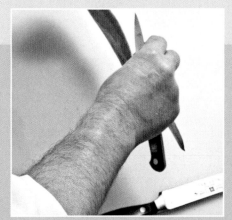

2 Filets will be removed from both sides of the fish. Filets on the white side are considerably smaller than the dark side.

3 With the dark side up, feel for the center bone.

4 Gently run the tip of your knife down the center.

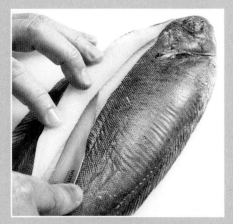

5 Following the side bones, continue cutting with the knife blade at a shallow angle to disengage the fillet.

6 Continue running the knife down until the bones are exposed.

(continues on next page)

Skinning and Trimming
Filleting Sole Filets

(continued from previous page)

7   Find the edge and pierce with the tip of your knife. Repeat moving the knife up the side.

8   Cut at a 45-degree angle at the side of the head to detach the fillet.

9   Make the same angled cut on the other side of the head.

10   Cut well around the head to make sure all of the fillet has been detached.

11   Now, follow down the central bone, using the bones to guide the tip of the knife.

12   Having a flexible knife will give you the ability to cut very closely to the bone.

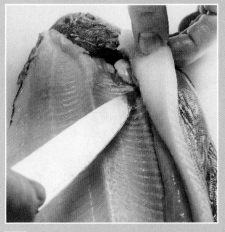

13   Continue slicing while lifting the fillet, until the roe sack is revealed. Be careful not to pierce it.

14   Disengage the roe sack with your fingers and move it away.

15   Pierce the outer edge of the fillet and cut down to disengage.

(continues on next page)

Skinning and Trimming
Filleting Sole Filets

(continued from previous page)

16 Lift the roe sack and carefully remove it.

17 There should be barely any flesh left on the bones.

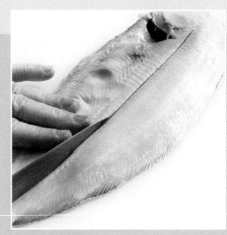

18 Turn the fish over and run the tip of the knife down the center.

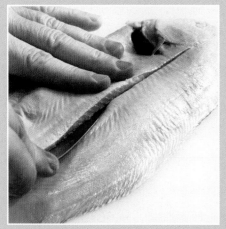

19 Follow the same procedure, using the tip of the knife to loosen the flesh from the bones.

20 The filets are much smaller and less meaty.

21 Follow the bones cutting the skin to disengage the filets.

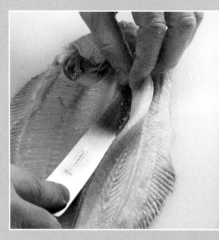

22 Repeat on the other side.

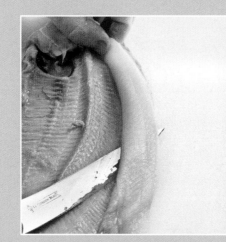

23 Cut through the skin.

24 Four filets of sole, the two roe sacks. The carcass can be used for making fumet after degorging.

(continues on next page)

Skinning and Trimming
Fileting Sole Filets

(continued from previous page)

25   To skin: lay the filet skin-side down on the cutting board. Make a small incision at the small end and slip the blade at a shallow angle between the flesh and the skin.

26   Holding the skin securely with one hand, use a gentle sawing motion while moving the knife down toward the other end.

27   If done properly the skin should be completely clean of any flesh. Discard the skin.

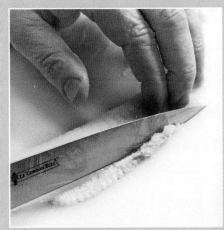

28   Trim the sides.

29   The filet should be trimmed of any dark areas.

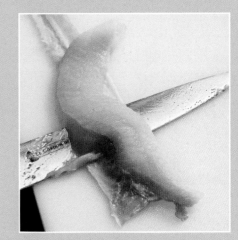

30   Repeat the same procedure with the white side.

31   Trim off the dark portions from the flesh.

32   The filets are ready for cooking. The trimmings can be degorged and used for making fumet.

Sole Meunière

1 Prepare the sole (habiller) and remove the gray skin.

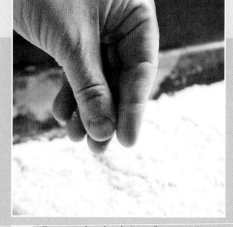

2 Season the dredging flour with salt and pepper.

3 Lightly season the sole.

4 Heat clarified butter in a fish pan or frying pan.

5 Place the fish in the seasoned flour.

6 Turn over.

7 Cover with flour pressing lightly.

8 Lift the fish and tap off any excess flour.

9 Lay the fish, skinned-side down, in the hot clarified butter.

(continues on next page)

Sole Meunière

(continued from previous page)

10 Baste the top with the hot butter.

11 Check to see if the fish is colored a golden brown.

12 Using a wide spatula, carefully turn the sole over.

13 Continue basting while the other side cooks.

14 Check the doneness by inserting a small knife in the middle to loosen the fillet.

15 Once cooked, transfer to a warm serving dish.

16 Discard the butter from cooking the sole. Place the pan back on the heat and add cold butter.

17 Once the butter has melted, add the lemon juice.

18 Allow to foam up.

(continues on next page)

Sole Meunière

(continued from previous page)

19 Immediately pour over the sole and serve.

20 Sole Meunière

Tilapia

Scientific name: *Tilapia* is the *common* name for approximately 100 species of cichlid fish from the tilapiine cichlid tribe.

The name *tilapia* comes from the name of the cichlid genus *Tilapia*, which is a latinization of *thiape*, the Tswana word for "fish." (Tswana is the national language of Botswana, written in the Latin alphabet.) Because tilapia has been introduced all around the world for human consumption, they are often referred to by different names in various languages and dialects. There are also some species of tilapia called *St. Peter's fish*, taken from the passage in the Christian bible about Peter the apostle catching a fish carrying a coin in its mouth. (It is important to mention that, although no species was named in the passage, there is a type of tilapia that can be found in the Sea of Galilee, where the story took place.)

After carp and salmon, tilapia is the most important fish in aquaculture—in 2002, production reached 1,505,804 metric tons! The three species of tilapia—*Oreochromis*, *Sarotherodon*, and *Tilapia*—are known collectively as tilapia. The fish is popular for commercial and artisanal fisheries alike. (An artisanal fishery is a term used to describe small-scale commercial fishing practices, particularly coastal or island ethnic groups using traditional methods such as rod and tackle, arrows, harpoons, and traditional boats.)

The majority of the tilapia fisheries were at one time located in Africa. However, because of introductions of tilapia (accidental and deliberate) into

Due to the abundance and resulting low cost of farmed Asian tilapia, there is an increasing problem with tilapia being sold as red snapper in restaurants. In a recent fraud in Chicago, 14 sushi restaurants had their "snapper" DNA tested. All 14 cases turned out to be tilapia.

The most common food allergy is to shellfish.

freshwater lakes in Asia, outdoor aquaculture in countries with tropical climates such as Papua New Guinea, Indonesia, and the Philippines have increased. In nontropical climates, tilapia farming operations need energy to warm the waters to the tropical temperatures the fish require.

Turbot – *Turbot*

Scientific name: *Psetta maxima*

This flatfish is native to the North Atlantic. The name derives from the Old Swedish word *tōmbut*, meaning thorn, butt, or stump. It was adapted to the English and French in the 13th century. The word is often mispronounced as *tur-bo*, likely due in part to the French pronunciation of words ending in *–ot*. The correct pronunciation is *tur-bit* or *tur-but*.

The European turbot is a large flatfish with close-set eyes on the left side of the body. Turbot are found close to shore in sandy, shallow waters throughout the Mediterranean and the Baltic Sea, the Black Sea, and the North Atlantic. It can reach a weight of 30 to 40 pounds (13.7 to 18 kg). The Greenland turbot, also called the blue halibut, is usually found in the cold waters off Greenland, in waters 3,280 feet (1,000 meters) deep.

The turbot is prized for its delicate flavor and the fact that it retains its bright white flesh when cooked.

Turbot are among a handful of fish species that were experimentally farmed in the early 1970s in France. Hatcheries in Europe now produce 5,000 tons of turbot a year and supply juveniles to the growing Asian turbot farming industry.

Preparing Turbot

1 Using a serrated knife, cut the tail in half.

2 Use a cleaver to split the base of the tail.

3 Have someone hold the two sides of the tail.

(continues on next page)

Preparing Turbot

(continued from previous page)

4 Chop at the opening to split the fish in half.

5 Chop all the way to the head.

6 Chop at the gill to disengage one side.

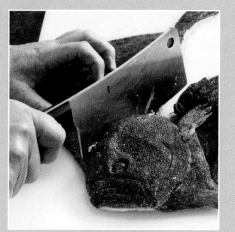

7 Chop the top of the head to separate the other side.

8 With the head removed, the two sides can be cut into thick steaks.

9 Square off the uneven end where it had been cut from the head for an even-shaped piece.

10 Cut away the outer fin using a serrated knife.

11 The turbot can now be cut into steaks.

Shellfish

Crustaceans

Crab – *Crabe (Freshwater and Salt Water)*

Scientific name: Decapod crustaceans in the infraorder Brachyura (from the Greek: *brachy* = "short" + *oura* = "tail")

There are 6,793 known crab species, found in all of the world's oceans, along with freshwater and terrestrial (land) crabs. Varying in size, crabs generally have a very short, projecting "tail." The smallest of the crabs is the pea crab and, as its name would suggest, it is about the size of a pea, although it can grow to the size of a small walnut. The largest of the crabs is the Japanese spider crab, which can grow a leg span of up to 13 feet (4 meters) and weigh about 44 pounds (20 kg).

The crab fishery makes up a significant portion of the crustaceans fished worldwide (estimated at 20 percent), and horse crab accounts for more than one-fifth of the 2 million tons of crab caught annually. Depending on the geographic location of the consumer, there are potentially seven different crab species available either frozen, canned, or fresh.

Horse Crab

Scientific name: *Portunus trituberculatus*

The horse crab is the most heavily fished crab species in the world, with more than 300,000 tons caught annually, 98 percent of it off the coast of China. Horse crabs are found from Hokkaidō, Japan, to southern India and throughout the Malay Archipelago. It is also found as far south as Australia. It lives in shallow water, with sandy or muddy bottoms, usually less than 164 feet (50 meters) deep, and feeds on seaweed, small fish, worms, and mollusks.

Horse crabs have a carapace that can grow as wide as 6 inches (15 cm) and 2.8 inches (7 cm) from front to back. They can be distinguished by the broad teeth located on the front of the carapace.

Flower Crab

Scientific name: *Portunus pelagicus*

The flower crab, also called the blue crab, blue swimmer crab, blue manna crab, or sand crab, is a large crab found in the intertidal estuaries of the Asian coasts of the Indian and Pacific Oceans, and the Middle-Eastern coast of the Mediterranean Sea. The flower crab is mainly used in eastern Africa, Southeast Asia, Japan, Australia, and New Zealand.

Though its meat is considered almost as sweet as the meat of the blue crab, the flower crab is quite a bit larger, with a carapace reaching up to about 8 inches (20 cm) in width. The flower crab mostly stays buried under sand or mud, particularly during the daytime and in the winter.

Purchasing canned crab is a case of buyer beware. Blue crab, for instance, produces a lovely canned meat but marketers have strategically renamed horse crab as *Japanese blue* and a species in Vietnam is likewise being sold as *blue swimmer*. These species are less expensive and tend to produce stringy meat that may not be suitable for all preparations.

In the Indo-Pacific region the flower crab is commercially important, where they are sold either as traditional hard shells or as soft-shell crabs. These are considered a delicacy throughout Asia.

Snow Crab

Scientific name: *Chionoecetes opilio*

The snow crab, also known as a spider crab or queen crab, lives in the cold waters of the Pacific and Atlantic Oceans. It is found as far north as the Arctic Ocean and across the Pacific Ocean, including the Sea of Japan, the Bering Sea, and the Gulf of Alaska.

Blue Crab

Scientific name: *Callinectes sapidus* (from the Greek: *calli* = "beautiful" + *nectes* = "swimmer" and Latin *sapidus* = "savory")

Native to the western edge of the Atlantic Ocean, from Nova Scotia to Argentina, the blue crab has been found in the Baltic, North, Mediterranean, and Black Seas. The blue crab is an omnivore, eating small fish and plants.

In the state of Maryland, Chesapeake Bay yields about US $45 million a year in blue crab harvest, making it famous for its blue crabs. Ironically, due to the lucrative export and declining numbers of the blue crab, consumers in the Chesapeake Bay area rarely get to enjoy their famous crustacean. In fact, most of the whole blue crabs sold in Maryland restaurants are imported from North Carolina, Louisiana, Florida, and Texas. Crab cakes made from blue crab are in such demand that they are frozen and sold via mail order, sometimes even overseas.

The most common way of eating blue crab is directly from the shell. Because of the sharpness of its shell it takes some work for the meat to be extracted—to facilitate this process, an array of tools has been placed at the consumer's disposal. Inside the crab, the equivalent of the liver and pancreas is considered a delicacy by some gourmets, but is generally removed. This is called *tomalley*, but is often referred to as *mustar* or *mustard* in Maryland and Virginia, probably because if its color, which is similar to that of Dijon mustard.

The picked meat, especially from the back fin area, is also used to make crab cakes, crab soups, and other crab dishes. Crabs that are caught just after the molting process are sold as soft-shell crabs.

Edible Crab

Scientific name: *Cancer pagurus*

Edible crabs (also known as the Brown crab) are native to the North Sea, the Mediterranean Sea, and the North Atlantic. The carapace of the mature adult can reach a width of 9.8 inches (25 cm) and it can weigh up to 6.6 pounds (3 kg). The edible crab is distinguished by its characteristic "pie crust" edge and black-tipped claws. This crab is abundant in the northeast Atlantic from Norway to northern Africa. It lives in muddy and sandy shallow water to about 330 feet (100 meters) deep. It can be found living in cracks and holes in rocks and occasionally in open areas.

Dungeness Crab

Scientific name: *Cancer magister*

The Dungeness crab, whose name means "master crab" in Latin, can measure up to 9.8 inches (25 cm), although they are generally under 7.9 inches (20 cm). They are most popular in the Pacific Northwest and the western United States, and are considered a delicacy.

The Dungeness crab is named for Dungeness, Washington, located 15 miles east of Port Angeles. Each October, Port Angeles holds the annual Dungeness Crab and Seafood Festival.

Dungeness crabs may be purchased live or precooked. Live crabs can be steamed or boiled with any number of seasonings added for additional flavor. Because the Dungeness crab will stop eating as soon as it is removed from its habitat, it is best to cook it as soon as it is purchased. This is because the starvation process makes the meat spongy and draws calcium from the shell, which in turn weakens the shell of the crab. This makes it easier to determine the freshness of a crab. When purchasing a Dungeness crab, feel the outer part of the legs; if they bend easily, then the crab is not fresh. These crabs are never sold as soft-shell crab.

Because approximately one-quarter of the crab's weight is meat, the Dungeness crab is one of the meatiest available. The meat has a delicate flavor, often described as slightly sweet.

Mud Crab

Scientific name: *Scylla serrata*

The mud crab, also known as the mangrove crab or black crab, is found in estuaries and mangroves in Africa, Australia, and Asia. Generally, mud crabs have a mottled green to very dark brown shell and can grow up to 9.4 inches (24 cm) in width, weighing 7.7 pounds (3.5 kg). The mud crab is highly cannibalistic in nature—when a fellow crab undergoes the molting process, his hard-shelled companion will attack and devour him. The larger crabs of this species can bite through a wooden handle.

There is a huge demand for mud crabs in South Asia, where they are considered to be the tastiest of the crab species. In northern Australia and Queensland, they arc chosen above other seafood.

Crayfish – *Ecrevisses*

Scientific name: *Procambarus clarkii*

The crayfish is separated into three families: two in the Northern Hemisphere and one in the Southern Hemisphere. The Parastacidae is a freshwater crayfish found in South America, Madagascar, and Australasia and is distinguished by the lack of the first pair of "legs," or pleopods. Also freshwater dwellers, Astacidae crayfish can be found in western Eurasia and western North America. Crayfish in the Cambaridae family inhabit the fresh waters of eastern North America and to a lesser degree those of East Asia.

It is thought that the crayfish and the lobster are closely related and, in fact, the crayfish looks a lot like a small lobster. The name *crayfish* comes from the old French word *escrevisse*, which comes from the Old Frankish *krebitja* from the same root as "crawl." In the eastern United States, the term *crayfish* is more common in the north, whereas *crawdad* is the term more often used in the central and western regions. Further south, *crawfish* is used, although there are overlaps.

In the United States, 98 percent of the crayfish harvested come from Louisiana. In fact, Louisiana produces 90 percent of the world's crayfish and consumes 70 percent locally. The standard culinary terms for crayfish in Louisiana are *crawfish* or *écrevisses*.

In Cajun cuisine crawfish are often are boiled in a large pot with heavy seasoning, usually salt, cayenne pepper, lemon, garlic, and bay leaves. Other items that can be included in the cooking process include potatoes, maize, onions, and sausage. Some other popular Cajun and Creole dishes are crawfish étouffée, crawfish pie, crawfish bread, and crawfish beignets.

Lobster – *Homard (Freshwater and Saltwater)*

Scientific name: From the Nephropidae family; sometimes called Homaridae

The clawed lobster makes up a family of large crustaceans, though there are several different groups of crustaceans known as "lobster," such as the spiny lobster and the slipper lobster, which have no claws and are only distantly related to the clawed lobster. Its closest relatives, however, are the reef lobster and three families of freshwater crayfish.

The lobster is an invertebrate (without a backbone or spinal column) and has a hard, protective exoskeleton. To be able to grow, lobsters must molt, or shed their shells, leaving them quite vulnerable. During the molting process, certain species may change color.

Because lobsters can live as long as 100 years and continue to molt and grow throughout their lifespan, they can reach impressive sizes. The largest lobster recorded was caught in Nova Scotia, weighing in at 44.4 pounds or 20.15 kg! Lobsters live on the bottom of the ocean, on rocky, sandy, or muddy bottoms. They spread from the shoreline to just beyond the edge of the continental shelf, and they live alone in crevices or burrows under rocks. Lobsters are found all over the world.

Lobsters eat live food such as fish, mollusks, plant life, and some crustaceans. When kept in captivity, they may resort to cannibalism, although never in the wild. Lobster skin has been found in the stomachs of lobsters, but only because they will eat their shed skin after they have molted. Because of the murky environment in which they live, lobsters have poor vision and use their antennae as sensors. Lobsters move slowly, but when they are in danger they can swim backward very quickly by curling and uncurling their abdomen—reaching a speed of 11 miles (18 km) per hour! Lobsters come in a variety of colors including red, blue, green, purple, and yellow.

Prior to the mid-19th century, lobsters were so plentiful that their consumption was considered a sign of poverty—a food for servants or lower members of society in Maine, Massachusetts, and the Canadian Maritimes. The advent of modern transportation paved the way for lobsters to be exported live to large urban centers in, for example, Europe and Japan, where lobster remains quite expensive. Fresh lobster became a luxury food and a major tourist attraction for Maine and the Canadian Maritime provinces alike. In Europe, the lobster was mainly eaten by royal and aristocratic families of France and the Netherlands. The European lobster, especially the royal blue Audresselles lobster (from the Nord-Pas-de-Calais region in France), is quite a bit more expensive than American lobster and much rarer.

Most lobster meat is in the tail and two front claws, though meat can be found in smaller quantities in the legs and torso. Lobsters are used in a wide variety of cuisines, from soups or bisques to mixing its meat with salad dressing and serving it as a lobster roll. Best prepared absolutely fresh, it is common procedure to place the live lobster into a pot of boiling water or steam—a process that causes the faint of heart some consternation. Lobster can be baked, grilled, and fried. Note that freezing a lobster will toughen the meat.

Because of its high price, the marketing of "faux lobster" has become quite popular. Faux lobster is often made from pollock or whitefish. Restaurants will sell "langostino lobster" and though *langostino* means "prawn," the meat used is most likely crab.

Langoustine

Scientific name: *Nephrops norvegicus*

The langoustine is a small, slender, orange-pink lobster, growing up to 9.4 inches (24 cm) long. Inhabiting the northeastern Atlantic Ocean and North Sea—as far north as Iceland and northern Norway and as far south as Portugal—langoustine feed primarily on worms and small fish. While known also as the Norway lobster, most menus and recipes favor the term langoustine.

Sixty thousand metric tons of langoustine are caught every year, almost half in the waters of the United Kingdom. Because the lobsters are caught by trawling, lobster boats catch a number of other fish species, including plaice and sole.

The meatiest part of the langoustine is the tail, which is served under the name "scampi" (see sidebar).

Scampi, prawns, and shrimp all suffer from a form of identity disorder: In Europe the term *scampi* generally refers to the tail portion of the smaller species of lobster such as the langoustine. In the United States scampi generally refers to a dish of shrimp or prawns in garlic, butter, and wine. That seems clear enough until one asks the question: What is the difference between prawns and shrimp? In Europe prawns are considered to be quite distinct from shrimp. In fact, not only are shrimp much smaller than prawns, but they have slightly different exoskeletons and gill structures as well. In the United States, the use of the word *prawn* is used interchangeably with *shrimp* or *jumbo shrimp.*

Spiny Lobster – *Langouste (Freshwater and Saltwater)*

Scientific name: *Spiny lobster* refers to about 45 species in the Palinuridae family.

The spiny lobster, also known as the langouste, rock lobster, or Florida lobster (in Florida), is also sometimes mistakenly referred to as a crayfish or crawfish. Although they resemble the American lobster in shape and have a hard exoskeleton, the two are not closely related. The spiny lobster's closest relatives are the furry lobster and the slipper lobster. Spiny lobsters can be easily distinguished from true lobsters by their long, spiny antennae and the absence of claws.

Like claw lobsters, spiny lobsters are edible. An economically significant food source, the spiny lobster is the Bahamas largest food export.

Shrimp – *Crevette*

Scientific name: Decapod crustaceans in the infraorder Caridea

Living in schools close to the sea bottom, shrimp are an important food source for larger animals such as fish and whales. Shrimp are widely caught for human consumption. While most shrimp breed in a marine habitat, there are a small number of freshwater species. The word *shrimp* comes from the Middle English *shrimpe*, similar to the Middle Low German *schrempen*, meaning "to wrinkle" or "to contract," and the Old Norse *skorpna*, meaning "to shrivel up."

In Europe, particularly the United Kingdom, the word *prawn* is used more than the preferred North American word, *shrimp*. The term *prawn* is also used to describe any large shrimp, like those that come 15 to the pound—these are also called king prawns or jumbo shrimp.

Preparing shrimp usually involves removing the head, shell, tail, and "sand vein."

Packaged shrimp are generally sold in a shrimp-per-pound format. For example, U 10's (also known as colossal shrimp) are so big that it takes 10 or fewer shrimp to make up a pound. On the other extreme, U 100's (miniature shrimp) take approximately 100 shrimp to make up a pound. There are four other size classifications: U 20's, U 30's, U 35's, and U 45's.

Preparing Shrimp

1   Shrimp come in a variety of types and sizes.

2   To shell : Gently pull off the head. The head and shells can be reserved to make a shellfish fumet or sauce.

3   Starting from the belly, pull the shell away. Then remove the feet.

(continues on next page)

Preparing Shrimp

(continued from previous page)

4   Gently pull off the tail.

5   Another way of peeling is to cut down the belly of the shrimp with the tip of a small knife.

6   Gently pull away on both sides.

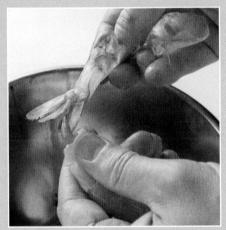

7   Disengage the shell, then gently pull at the tail.

8   To devein: Make a shallow incision along the back of the shrimp.

9   Cut just deep enough to expose the vein. Remove using the tip of a small knife.

10   To devein keeping the shrimp whole, make a small incision on the back, deep enough to expose the vein.

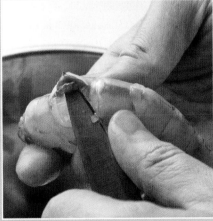

11   With the tip of a small knife, very gently pull the vein out.

12   To butterfly: Place the shrimp on the cutting board and cut deeply down the back of the shrimp being careful not to cut all the way through.

(continues on next page)

Preparing Shrimp

(continued from previous page)

13 Open the shrimp to lay flat.

14 Top row: Whole shrimp with head, without head, peeled. 2nd row: Sliced, chopped, halved, and butterflied.

Mollusks

Clams – *Palourdes*

Scientific name: Family Veneridae

Clams in the Veneridae family make up the better part of the edible bivalve mollusks that burrow in sediment. This distinguishes them from mollusks like mussels that attach themselves to rocks (or pilings if cultivated). *Clam* can be used as a general term for all bivalve mollusks but in cuisine and fisheries it refers mainly to the edible burrowing varieties.

The shell of a clam consists of two, usually equal, valves connected by a hinge joint and ligament. These can be internal or external. The clam has two abductor muscles that contract to close the shell. The clam has no head or eyes (scallops are an exception), but has kidneys, a heart, a mouth, and an anus. They also have an open circulatory system, meaning that their organs are surrounded by watery blood containing oxygen and nutrients. Many edible bivalves have an oval shape, though the razor clam has an elongated, parallel-sided shape, reminiscent of an old-fashioned straight razor.

Because clams live buried in sand or mud, breathing through siphons reaching to the surface, they are collected by digging.

Culinarily, the term *clam* refers to the hard clam, but may also refer occasionally to the soft-shell clam or the ocean quahog. A commercially popular clam on the Atlantic Coast of the United States is the surf clam. Clams may be eaten raw (like oysters), steamed, boiled, baked, or fried, depending on size and species.

Mussels – *Moules*

Scientific name: Order Mytiloida

Mussel is the common name for members of several different families of salt-water and freshwater clams or bivalve mollusks. The mussel shell is longer than it is wide and usually asymmetrical. The outside of the shell is dark blue, black, or brown, and the interior is silvery with a mother of pearl sheen to it. The shell is composed of two hinged halves or "valves." These valves are joined by a ligament and are closed when necessary by strong internal muscles.

Mussel shells are made up of three layers: the inner iridescent layer of nacre (mother of pearl), the prismatic layer, and the periostracum, the outer pigmented layer resembling skin. Marine mussels are eaten by humans, sea stars, and seabirds, whereas freshwater mussels are eaten by otters, raccoons, and some ducks and geese.

Some marine mussels prefer salt marshes or quiet bays, whereas others prefer the pounding surf. Freshwater mussels live in lakes, rivers, canals, and streams throughout the world, except in polar regions. They require cool, clean water with bottoms that are not muddy.

While hand-picked or dragged, the vast majority of mussels on the world market are cultivated. They are either grown on pilings and contained by mesh or, less commonly, are bottom grown in beds.

Like all shellfish, mussels should be checked before cooking to make sure they are still alive; mussels, like oysters, quickly become toxic after they die. Try this simple test: Tap an open mussel with a spoon. If it is alive it will shut tight. If it stays open it is dead and should be discarded. Another way to tell if a mussel is safe to eat is if it opens after steaming. Mussels can be smoked, boiled, steamed, or fried in batter.

Oysters – *Huîtres*

Scientific name: Order Ostreidae

True oysters, belonging to the Ostreidae family, are highly prized as food, and eaten both raw and cooked. Contrary to popular thought, the true oyster is not capable of producing a gem-quality pearl. It was Jonathan Swift who said, "He was a bold man that first ate an oyster." Archaeological evidence shows that the oyster has been an important food source in populated coastal areas around the world well into prehistory. Today, overfishing and pollution have reduced supplies but they remain a popular treat and remain a favorite among the exotic foods.

Oysters grow in beds in shallow and deep water, in cold and temperate zones. Both wild and cultivated, oysters are collected by raking or dredging, depending on the depth of the water. In very deep water, divers are used to collect the oysters.

Oysters have been cultivated for more than a century. Oysters reproduce by releasing their eggs and sperm into the water. They begin their lives as males, release their sperm during their first year, then they become female and release their eggs. After fertilization, the eggs develop into larvae, or *spat*, which then settle themselves onto a reef, rock, or another oyster to continue growing. When cultivating oysters, the spat may be allowed to either settle on the existing oyster bed or hard surface, or they may be allowed to grow into seed oysters then placed in bags or on racks to grow just below the surface. It takes approximately one year for an oyster to fully develop.

Compared to other shellfish, oysters have very long shelf life—up to two weeks—however they should be consumed when fresh because the taste reflects their age. Some "purists" insist on eating oysters raw, with lemon juice, vinegar, or cocktail sauce, but precautions should be taken when eating an oyster raw. Eating a dead, raw oyster can be fatal, so oysters should only be consumed raw if still alive. Depending on the region, raw oysters will have complex flavors, varying from salty to sweet. Their texture is soft and fleshy but crisp to the tooth.

A common food myth is that oysters are not suitable to eat during the summer months and should only be eaten during months containing the letter "R" (in French and English). Although a myth, there is some factual basis: months without "R" (May to August) are warmer months, months when the oyster is breeding, making them less enjoyable. The warmer months make it harder to keep oysters alive on the plate, and because eating a dead, raw oyster can be fatal, you will often see oysters on a bed of ice. Another health issue with oysters is the fact that, during the warmer months, oysters contain high bacterial loads of human pathogens. Because oysters are filter feeders, they will naturally concentrate anything present in their surrounding seawater. One of these pathogens, *Vibrio vulnificus*, is the most deadly seafood pathogen, with a higher death ratio than *Salmonella enterica*, or *E. coli*.

Scallops – *St. Jacques*

Scientific name: Family Pectinidae

Scallops are a marine bivalve mollusk in the Pectinidae family, found in all of the world's oceans and highly prized as a food source. The brightly colored shells of some species of scallops are often valued by shell collectors. Like the true oyster, the scallop has a central abductor muscle. Because scallops are active swimmers, this muscle is quite a bit larger and more developed than the oyster's. The scallop shell tends to have a regular shape, recalling the stereotypical form of a seashell. Because of this shape, the scallop shell is a common decorative motif.

Most scallops are free living, although some species will attach themselves to a substrate (the earthy material in the bottom of a marine habitat). Free-living scallops swim by rapidly opening and closing their shells, which also provides them with a defense mechanism that protects them from predators. Some scallops have been known to make audible popping sounds as they flap their shells, leading some seafood vendors to call them "singing scallops."

Scallops are caught using scallop dredges or bottom trawls, although the market for "diver scallops" (scallops harvested by divers) is growing. These scallops are harvested by divers in scuba gear, as opposed to being dragged, which causes them to collect sand inside the shell. Diver scallops tend to be far less gritty. This

It is important to note the historical symbolism of the scallop. The scallop shell is the emblem of Saint James the Greater and is an evocative symbol among pilgrims on their way to the shrine of St. James the Apostle in Santiago de Compostela, Spain. Medieval pilgrims often wore a scallop shell on their clothes or hat. The pilgrim also carried a shell with him, presenting it at churches, castles, or abbeys, expecting to be given as much sustenance as he could pick up with one scoop.

method is also more ecologically friendly because it does not disturb or cause damage to the undersea flora or fauna. Scallops harvested by machine will experience delays of up to two weeks before arriving at the seafood market, which can cause flesh to break down, resulting in a much shorter life.

Scallops are characterized by having two types of meat: the scallop, which is the white and meaty abductor muscle, and the coral, which is the red or white, soft roe. In Western cuisine, scallops are most often sautéed in butter or breaded and deep-fried. In the United States scallops are usually prepared using only its abductor muscle; outside the United States the scallop is usually sold whole. In European cuisine, scallops are generally prepared in quiche form or as coquilles St. Jacques. The term *scalloped* originally referred to any seafood creamed and served hot in a shell.

Preparing Scallops

1　The scallop shell has a rounded side and a flat side.

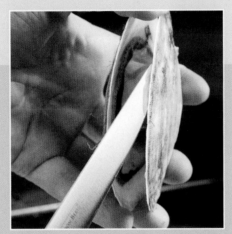

2　Run a thin blade against the flat side of the scallop to disconnect the muscle (scallop).

3　Pull the scallop open.

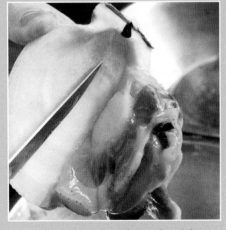

4　Disengage the other side of the scallop from the rounded side.

5　The scallop will need to be trimmed in order to expose the abductor muscle and coral.

6　First remove the gills, being careful not to cut the coral.

(continues on next page)

Preparing Scallops

(continued from previous page)

7   Discard the gills.

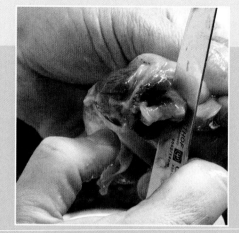

8   Cutting from the base of the coral, remove the digestive gland, cutting along the edge of the scallop.

9   Cut away and discard.

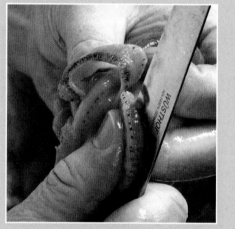

10   Remove the mantle.

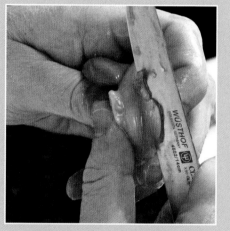

11   Finally cut away the smooth muscle.

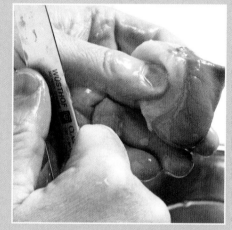

12   The coral should remain attached.

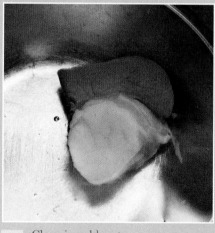

13   Clean in cold water.

Squid – *Calamari*

Scientific name: *Loligo opalescens*

The squid is a marine cephalopod in the order Teuthida, comprising around 300 species. Like all other cephalopods, the squid has a distinct head, mantle, and arms. Squid have eight arms and two tentacles arranged in pairs. Squid cannot survive in freshwater, but are found at all depths of the ocean.

The majority of squid are no more than 2 feet (60 cm) long, although the giant squid may reach about 43 feet (13 meters) in length. In 2007, a colossal squid weighing 1,091 pounds (495 kg) and measuring 33 feet (10 meters) in length was caught by a New Zealand fishing vessel off the coast of Antarctica.

The word *calamari* (singular, *calamaro*), comes from the Italian word for squid and is now used worldwide in the culinary world. In Greece it is called *kalamari*, and in Turkey, *kalamar*. In Spanish, the word *galama* or *calamares* derives from the Latin word *calamarium* for "ink pot," named after the inky fluid that squid secrete. Almost all of the squid is edible. The only parts of the squid not consumed are the beak and gladius (pen).

> Cephalopod is the mollusk class Cephalopoda, characterized by bilateral body symmetry.

Snails – *Escargots*

Scientific name: *Helix pomatia*

The French word for snail, *escargot*, refers to a preparation of cooked snails usually served as an appetizer. Escargot has been eaten since ancient times. In the Mediterranean, a number of archaeological sites have been excavated with findings of physical evidence that several species of snails were eaten as escargot. According to the writings of Pliny the Elder, the Romans considered escargot to be food for the elite classes.

In Western cuisine, snails are most commonly removed from their shells, cooked with garlic butter or chicken stock, and then placed back in their shells for serving. These are generally served on a plate with shell-sized depressions. Snail tongs and forks are usually provided.

Like most mollusks, escargots are high in protein and low in fat—they contain 15 percent protein, 2.4 percent fat, and 80 percent water. A typical snail diet includes decayed matter, carrion, and leaves; therefore, the stomach contents can be toxic to humans. Before they are cooked, snails are purged of the contents of their digestive systems. The snail is deprived of food for three days, living on water alone. After three days, the snail is fed flour and water for one week.

Frogs' Legs – *Cuisses de Grenouilles*

Scientific name: *Pelophylax* kl. *esculentus, Rana esculenta*

Considered a delicacy in French and Chinese cuisines, frogs' legs are also eaten in other regions, like the Caribbean, Portugal, northwest Greece, Spain, and the southern Midwest regions of the United States.

The dry aging of beef is now limited to high-end restaurants and steak houses, as well as gourmet food stores and traditional butchers. It refers to storing a quality cut of beef (USDA Prime or Choice) under very specific conditions—temperature, humidity, and ventilation—from 10 to 21 days. During this time, the flavors begin to concentrate due to evaporation, and the enzymes in the meat begin to break down, resulting in a more tender meat. Because a hard crust forms on the outside, which has to be removed and discarded, and because weight is lost from evaporation, this process is considered too costly for the general consumer market.

More recently, an alternate method of aging, called wet aging, has been developed. With wet aging, the meat is placed in a vacuum-sealed package and stored at a specific temperature. The same enzymatic process that occurs during dry aging takes place, resulting in enhanced tenderness, but there is no loss of humidity, so the flavor lacks the concentration that comes from dry aging.

If you've tasted a dry-aged steak, you will understand the difference, but don't listen to those Web sites that say you can age beef at home. There is a very fine line between aging a piece of beef for 21 days and having it spoil. If it smells bad, it is bad and should be thrown out.

Usually associated with French cuisine, frogs' legs are traditional in the region of Les Dombes and in Lyon, where they are prepared with butter, garlic, and parsley. Only the upper joint of the hind leg is served, which makes them comparable to a chicken wing. Indeed, like chicken wings, frogs' legs are commonly prepared by deep-frying them, breaded or unbreaded.

Indonesia is one of the biggest exporters of frogs' legs and most of Western Europe's supply comes from frog farms there.

MEATS

"It's more useful to have knowledge about cuts of meat than a lot of money."
  ~Jacques Pepin

North American Meat Cuts

The basic sections from which steak and other subdivisions of meat are cut are called *primal cuts*. The toughest cuts of beef are usually the leg and neck, because these areas are the most muscular. The further you go from "hoof and horn" the more tender the meat will be.

Beef – *Boeuf*

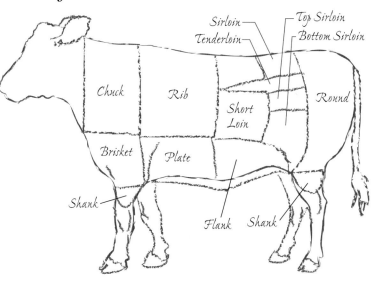

The most commonly known cuts of beef come from the upper half. Chuck, or ground hamburger meat, rib eye steak, short loin, sirloin, tenderloin, and round are all upper half cuts. Because they are closer to the middle of the body, these cuts are tender and used more often than cuts from the lower half. The lower half contains the brisket, shank, plate, and flank cuts, which are all commonly used in stews and soups or with marinades and moist cooking methods, such as braising.

Did you know?
Cows live an average of 7 years. The oldest living cow was "Big Bertha," who lived to be 48 years old. She also holds the record for producing 39 calves!

The best cut will be lustrous and crimson colored, firm to the touch, and have a slight fragrance. The tenderest meat will have streaks of white fat, referred to as marbling, and will have been aged for at least 21 days. The hindquarters provide cuts that can be cooked rather quickly, whereas the forequarters provide cuts that require slow-cooking or boiling methods. Although cooking preferences vary, the general consensus is that beef is best cooked until medium rare—pink on the interior and slightly browned on the exterior.

Trimming a Roast—Denerving a Piece of Meat

1 An untrimmed piece of meat will be covered with long, flat nerves and a layer of fat.

2 Begin by removing the thicker layers of fat. The fat is attached to the nerve by a thin membrane. Slip the knife in between and cut at the membrane while pulling away the fat.

3 Continue to the end.

4 Some of the nerves are attached to the flesh by a thin membrane and are easily removed by cutting the membrane.

5 For thicker nerves, slip the knife in between the nerve and the flesh at one end. Holding the knife at a slight outward angle, slide it along the nerve to disengage.

6 Holding the loose end of the nerve, slide the knife in the other direction using a gentle sawing motion.

(continues on next page)

Trimming a Roast—Denerving a Piece of Meat

(continued from previous page)

7 Depending on the cut of meat, there may be a large internal nerve. This cannot be entirely removed without splitting the piece so you want to remove the largest part. The nerve is pretty tough so you can scrape away the flesh with the tip of the knife until the nerve is exposed.

8 Cut away the thickest part.

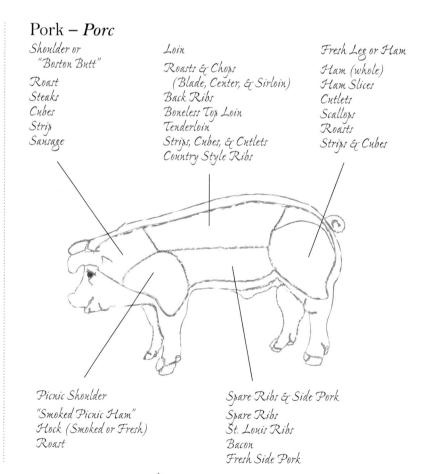

Pork – *Porc*

Shoulder or "Boston Butt"
Roast
Steaks
Cubes
Strip
Sausage

Loin
Roasts & Chops
  (Blade, Center, & Sirloin)
Back Ribs
Boneless Top Loin
Tenderloin
Strips, Cubes, & Cutlets
Country Style Ribs

Fresh Leg or Ham
Ham (whole)
Ham Slices
Cutlets
Scallops
Roasts
Strips & Cubes

Picnic Shoulder
"Smoked Picnic Ham"
Hock (Smoked or Fresh)
Roast

Spare Ribs & Side Pork
Spare Ribs
St. Louis Ribs
Bacon
Fresh Side Pork

The old saying that you can eat every part of the pig but the squeal is almost true. Head, blade shoulder, arm shoulder, loin, spare ribs, belly side, leg, and hock are all cuts of pork used in everyday pork recipes. The head is used for soups and broths, and the ears are sometimes frozen and fried. In fact, many high-end restaurants now include "crispy pork ears" on their menus. The loin is the most versatile section of the pig, providing us with baby back ribs, pork chops, Canadian bacon, pork loin crown roast, and the pork loin itself, which is practically fat free. You get your cured, bone-in picnic ham from the leg, and if you've ever eaten pickled pig's feet or pig's tail, you're eating hock.

The best cut of pork is firm and pink. Pork should not be too red, too white, too fatty or damp.

Lardons

1 Remove the rind from the slab bacon.

2 Cut in smooth strokes and try not to remove any meat.

3 Save the rind for flavoring soups and braises.

4 Place the trimmed slab bacon, fat-side down and cut into even, thick slices.

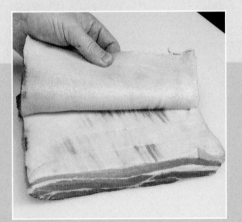

5 Stack the slices and cut horizontally into what is called a lardon.

6 The thickness of the slice can be adjusted depending on the size of the lardons needed.

(continues on next page)

Lardons

(continued from previous page)

7 Two samples of large and small lardons.

8 To blanch lardons: Place the lardons in a saucepan and add enough cold water to cover.

9 Place over medium-high heat and bring to a boil. Impurities will rise to the surface in the form of white foam.

10 Refresh in cold water.

11 Drain through a sieve.

12 Place on paper towel to finish draining. The lardons are ready to be used.

Veal – *Veau*

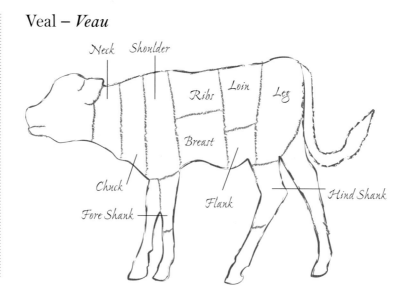

Cows that are slaughtered prior to 12 months of age are utilized within the veal industry. Veal meat is succulent and lean and is considered to be a luxury meat among beef connoisseurs and chefs alike. However, quality can vary considerably, depending on how the calf was raised. About 100 years ago, the highest quality veal was produced from calves that were nourished with milk, eggs, and barley. Today, quality meat producers feed their calves mother's milk, a diet that is naturally rich in phosphorus and iron. Veal is renowned for its tender, creamy, much-sought-after texture.

Veal is well loved in France, and for that reason a multitude of veal dishes have become a part of the culture: stuffed breast of veal, bresolles, and saddle of veal Orloff. In Italy, veal is also a specialized meat that results in celebrated cultural dishes: osso bucco, piccata, and saltimbocca.

An ideal veal cut should appear moist and milky white to slightly rose colored. The primary choice cuts from a veal calf are the rump end of the loin, the loin, the ribs, and the filet. The next best cuts are shoulder, breast, flank, and upper ribs.

Preparing Escalopes

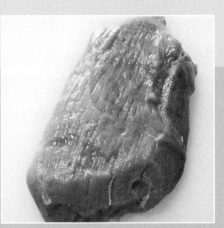

1   Trim the meat of fat and nerves.

2   Using a long slicing knife, cut at an approximately 45° angle, holding the top of the meat to ensure a thin, even slice.

3   Cut along the grain of the meat.

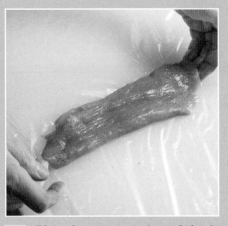

4   Place the meat on a piece of plastic wrap.

5   Cover with a second sheet of plastic wrap and lightly pound using a mallet.

6   Continue until the escalope is the desired thickness.

Lamb and Mutton

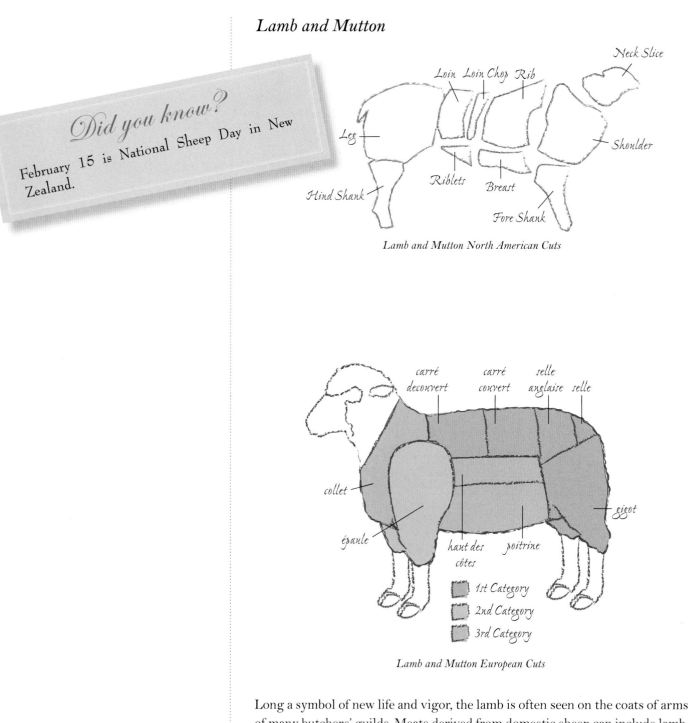

Lamb and Mutton North American Cuts

Lamb and Mutton European Cuts

Long a symbol of new life and vigor, the lamb is often seen on the coats of arms of many butchers' guilds. Meats derived from domestic sheep can include lamb, hogget, and mutton, with lamb being the most expensive of the three varieties. Classification systems are used to discourage mislabeling, which helps ensure that customers are receiving the correct product. The stringent definitions for each variety vary between countries, but are overall quite similar:

Tying a Leg of Lamb for Roasting

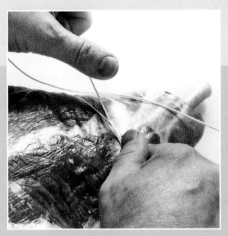

1   Tie a length of string about one-third up from the bone. Tie firmly, but not too tightly. Trim the string.

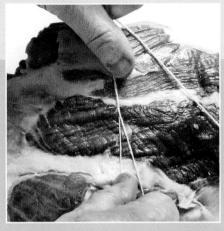

2   Tie a second length of string around the middle of the leg.

3   Tie a third length of string at the top third of the leg. Trim the string after each tie.

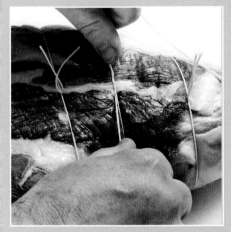

4   Now tie string in between the first three strings, as well as one above and one below, ensuring that the strings are of equal distance. This ensures that the leg is tied evenly.

5   Continue by tying between the strings, working evenly along the leg.

6   The leg is ready for marinating and/or roasting.

Lamb:	Young sheep under 12 months with no permanent incisor teeth in wear
Hogget:	Young male sheep or maiden ewe having no more than two permanent incisors in wear
Mutton:	Ewe or wether (castrated male) having more than two permanent incisors in wear

In Australia, however, these classifications are extended to include ewes and rams, and Australia also uses a stricter definition of lamb:

Lamb:	Female or castrated male ovine 0 to 12 months, no permanent incisors

Other types of lamb classifications include the following:

Baby lamb:	Milk-fed lamb between six and eight weeks old
Spring lamb:	Milk-fed lamb, three to five months old, born in late winter/early spring and sold before July 1
Yearling lamb:	Young sheep between 12 and 24 months old
Milk-fed lamb:	Meat from an unweaned lamb, typically four to six weeks and weighing 5.5 to 8 kg (about 12 to 17 lb) (This type of lamb is almost unavailable in North America and the United Kingdom because it is not considered economically viable).
Sucker lamb:	A term used in Australia; includes young milk-fed lambs and slightly older lambs (up to 7 months) who are still dependent on mother's milk
Salt marsh lamb (presalé):	Young sheep that graze on salt marshes in coastal estuaries that support salt-tolerant grasses such as samphire, Sparta grass, sorrel, and sea lavender

Lamb is used in a multitude of cultural recipes, specifically in the Mediterranean, the Middle East, and India. Lamb is the traditional meat served in France on Easter Sunday.

Lamb should be firm to the touch and range in color from red to dark pink. Tenderness and taste depend on the age of the lamb at the time of slaughter. Older lambs provide meat with a stronger flavor than that of younger animals. A general rule to remember is that as an animal ages, the color of its flesh darkens. Large cuts of lamb are usually roasted; chops and cutlets are often grilled. Lamb also lends itself well to braising.

Boning a Leg of Lamb for Roasting

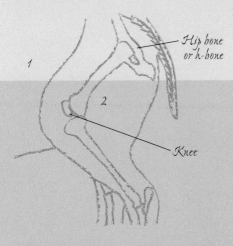

Hip bone or h-bone

1

2

Knee

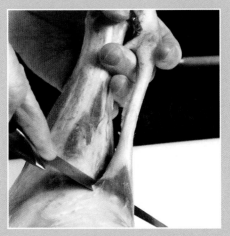

| 1 | Detach the long tendon from where it attaches to the muscle. |

| 2 | Score around the lower part of the shank. |

| 3 | Cut the meat away from the bone. |

| 4 | Using the back of the knife, scrape the bone clean. |

| 5 | Using a saw, cut through the bone just above where the tendons are attached. |

| 6 | Step one has been completed. |

(continues on next page)

Boning a Leg of Lamb for Roasting

(continued from previous page)

7   Feel along the large end of the leg for the hip bone, also known as the h-bone.

8   Using short strokes with the tip of the knife, scrape against the bone. The bone is unusually shaped so it will require some maneuvering.

9   Continue scraping, exposing more of the h-bone.

10   Continue until you can expose the ball of the joint.

11   Cut around the ball of the joint.

12   Continue following the contours of the h-bone until it can be pulled away from the leg.

13   Step two has been completed.

14   Cut around the ball of the joint, to expose the other side.

15   Using the same short strokes, follow the line of the bone to expose it.

(continues on next page)

Boning a Leg of Lamb for Roasting

(continued from previous page)

16 Continue to scrape the meat away from the bone.

17 Continue until you have exposed the other end of the bone, and cut around the joint to be able to remove it completely.

18 There will be a soft bone inside that will need to be removed.

19 This is the cap of the other end of the bone.

20 Trim the edges of excess fat, reserving the scraps.

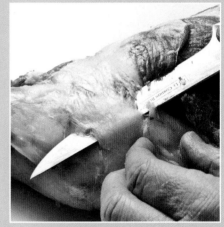

21 Trim the exterior of extra fat and nerves. Reserve all trimmings.

22 Boned Leg of Lamb

Mutton – *Mouton*

As cited earlier, mutton is the meat of adult sheep (ewe or wether) "having two or more incisors in wear." In keeping with the rule "the darker the color, the older the animal," mutton meat is dark red with firm, white fat. Although mutton represents only a fraction of the meat consumed in North America, it is commonly used in England, Scotland, Wales, Australia, and New Zealand. In the Middle East and India, mutton is considered a staple meat.

The cuts are leg, loin (chops and roasts), rack (rib chops and French chops), chuck, breast, and flank. Delicacies include heart, kidneys, and sweetbreads (thymus gland and pancreas).

Goat – *Chèvre, Chabri*

Although not regularly consumed in North America, goat meat is one of the most widely consumed red meats in other countries. It is consumed in parts of the Mediterranean, Southern Europe, the Middle East, East Africa, Southeast Asia, South and Central America, and the Caribbean. It also plays an important role in religious and cultural events in many of these regions.

Goats are the earliest domesticated animal dating back to 9000 BC in India, and pigs were domesticated near 7,000 BC. They were raised for their milk, hair, meat, and skin. Even though goats have a reputation for eating everything and it is true that their systems can digest just about anything, they are actually particular about what they eat. Like deer, they like to eat woody stems, bark, and coarse grass. They are mainly pasture raised due to their grazing preferences.

Considered very close to sheep, goats are raised and slaughtered using the same classifications as sheep. The three age groups are kid, wethers, and chevon or mutton. Kids are raised and slaughtered in the same manner as lamb and veal.

Many people describe goat meat as tasting similar to lamb, veal, or venison, but it is lower in saturated fat, cholesterol, and calories while high in protein and iron, compared to other meats, including chicken. See the accompanying chart for a nutrition comparison.

Nutrition Comparison Chart (3-oz Serving)

Species	Calories (kcal)	Fat (g)	Saturated fat (g)	Cholesterol (mg)	Protein (g)	Iron (mg)
Beef	242	16.3	6.5	73.7	22	2.3
Bison	123	2.1	0.8	70.2	24	2.9
Chicken	162	6.3	1.7	76.3	25	1.0
Goat	**122**	**2.6**	**0.8**	**63.8**	**23**	**3.2**
Lamb	**172**	**8.3**	**2.9**	**74.5**	**24**	**1.4**
Pork	211	12.5	4.6	73.7	23	0.9
Salmon	175	10.5	2.1	53.6	19	0.3

Source: USDA (2001) and "The Bison Connection" (2003).

European Meat Cuts

Because food and health standards vary worldwide, British, French, and North American primal cuts are very different. While the British try to use as many parts of the animal as they can, the French have stricter standards and categories for each animal, using a letter and number grading system.

With the creation of the European Community, certain standards have been implemented by the Common Agricultural Policy (CAP), which has sought to standardize the classification and labeling of meats in Europe. This has not affected the butchery cuts used by different countries and regions.

British Primal Cuts

Although British primal cuts are very similar to those of North America, Britons have different names for their cuts and tend to use more of the cow. This includes the neck and clod, silverside, topside, and shin.

French Primal Cuts

The French have very high standards when it comes to their meat cuts (and all food for that matter) and have devised a grading chart, including letters and numbers.

Beef

Categories
1. surlonge
2. train de côtés découvert
3. train de côtés couvert
4. faux-filet
5. filet
6. arguillette de rumsteak
7. rumsteak
8. gîte noix
9. semelle
10. tranche grasse

aloyau

globe

11. paleron
12. macreuses
13. jumeaux
14. charolaise
15. plat de côtés
16. plat de côtés
17. bavette d'aloyau

18. veine maigre
19. veine grasse
20. gros bout
21. jarret
22. poitrine
23. flanchet
24. gîte de derrière
25. crosse

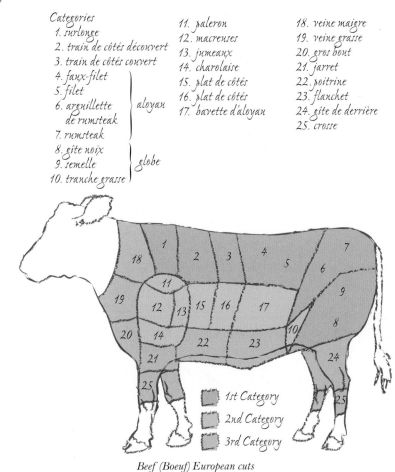

1st Category
2nd Category
3rd Category

Beef (Boeuf) European cuts

Meat Grading System

Letter	Conformation	Number	Fatty state
E	Superior	1	Thin
U	Very good	2	Waxed or little covered
R	Good	3	Covered
O	Good enough	4	Fat
P	Passable	5	Very fatty

Canada also uses a grading system that has three different grades: AAA, AA, and A.

The French have also come up with a category system, breaking down the different cuts and cooking methods for each animal:

1st Category:	Thighs and back	*Cooking method:* roast, sauté, grill
2nd Category:	Shoulder and sides	*Cooking method:* fry, stew, braise
3rd Category:	Chest, neck, bulges, hook	*Cooking method:* poach, stew, braise

Pork

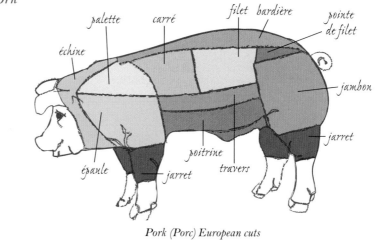

Pork (Porc) European cuts

The meat grading system is used for all meat cuts; however, pork has a more involved grading chart and has no category system.

Additional Grading for Pork

Letter	Content of lean meat expressed as a percentage
E.E or S	Superior at 60%
E	55–60%
U	50–55%
R	45–50%
O	40–45%
P	Less than 40%

For pork, the French use a production types chart, detailing the commercial denomination, and also a detailed uses chart.

Pork Production Types

Commercial denomination	Slaughter date	Weight
Milk-fed pig	3–4 weeks	13.2 lb (6 kg)
Piglet (not separated)	6–8 weeks	17.6–22 lb (8–10 kg)
Pork sausage maker	5–6 months	220.4 lb (100 kg)

Pork Principal Uses Chart

Principal pieces*	Detail And uses
Ham: 38.1 lb (17.3 kg)	~ With or without bone (raw or cooked) ~ Thin and soft fats: pâtés, galantines, sausages, and stuffing
Loin: 51 lb (23.1 kg)	~ Whole loin, backbone, cutlet or chop, roast, bacon, lean sausages, and delicatessen meats
Chest hash shoulder: 41 lb (18.6 kg)	~ Fresh chest, salted, cured, and dried ~ Small salt, delicatessen meats ~ Roasted shoulder or lamb
Fat: 24.5 lb (11.1 kg)	~ Sausages, air-cured sausages, lard, as covering, breakdown
Head: 11.2 lb (5.1 kg)	~ Pâté, hure, muzzle, roulade, breaded ears
Offal: 18 lb (8.2 kg)	~ Brain, tongue, feet, tail, kidney, heart, liver (pâté, sausage) ~ Digestive system: packing sausage and sausage
Blood: 8.8 lb (4 kg)	~ Pudding
Issues: 17 lb (7.8 kg)	~ Not consumed

* Weights represent typical size of the piece of meat from which cuts are taken.

Veal

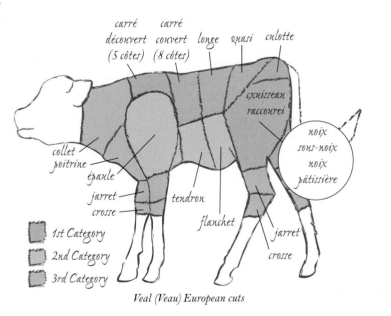

Veal (Veau) European cuts

The French do not use a grading system for veal; however, there are two types of category charts: the side (*le pan*) and animal front.

Veal Grading System: The Side

Category	Principal pieces	Cooking methods
1st	Leg: scallop, dark, outside round, knuckles	Roast, fry, sauté, braise, stew, grill
1st	Loin	Roast, fry, sauté, sous-vide
1st	Covered rib roast	Roast, fry, sauté, sous-vide
3rd	Hook and shank	Poach, braise, stew, sous-vide

Veal: Animal Front

Category	Principal pieces	Cooking methods
2nd	Shoulder	Poach, stew, roast
2nd	Chest: flank, tendon, chest, neck, opened loin rib half	Poach, stew, fry, sous-vide
3rd	Hook and shank	Poach, stew, fry, sous-vide

OFFAL

Kila nyama nyama Tu. (Every meat is meat.)

—Swahili saying

The term *offal*, pronounced *off-fall*, refers to what would fall off the animal carcass as the butcher dressed the animal. Offal includes all internal organs and entrails of the animal, in contrast to the meat, which refers exclusively to the skeletal muscles of an animal. Offal that is not prepared for human consumption is processed into animal feed, fuel, and fertilizer.

Offal is categorized into two groups: white offal (brains, sweetbreads, marrow, tripe) and red offal (liver, heart, kidneys). It also includes the blood (made into sausages), ears, eyes, intestines, spinal cord, the whole head, the snout, and the feet. Offal can also come from poultry, where in addition to liver and gizzards, the cockscombs, kidneys, and testicles are regularly consumed, and from fish, where the liver, stomach, and roe are highly prized in many cultures. What is considered offal and how it is prepared varies by region and culture. In North America offal is referred to as "variety meats."

Because internal organs serve to process nutrients and waste in an animal, they may contain impurities and other matter that requires removal before preparation. This is often done by *degorging* (soaking in cold water) and blanching. These processes remove impurities and excess blood while preserving the flavor and textures for which offal is appreciated. Offal meats are rich in protein and contain many vitamins and minerals that are needed for daily cellular production and function.

As long as man has eaten meat, he has eaten offal. In fact, in the Paleolithic era, when men went hunting, they would celebrate by feasting on the highly perishable organs of their kill on site before bringing the rest of the animal back to their dwelling to share with the rest of their community.

Sweetbreads *Ris de Veau*

The term *sweetbreads* refers to the thymus gland and the pancreas of young animals, particularly veal and lamb. The thymus gland shrinks as the animal ages, which is why you will not see beef or mutton sweetbreads on a menu. The thymus gland extends from the throat down to the chest of the animal. The part of the gland nearest the heart is the most prized for its shape and size. An average veal sweetbread weighs 14 to 21 oz (400 to 600 g). Lamb sweetbreads are much smaller and, therefore, don't offer as many preparation choices as the larger glands.

Veal sweetbreads are a versatile white cooking meat. They can be roasted, fried, poached, grilled, braised, or sautéed. They will stand alone in a main entrée, or they can be made into hot or cold appetizers, salads, stews, terrines, pâtés, and sausages.

Ris de Veau

1 Degorge the ris de veau in cold water, milk, thyme, bay leaf, and lemon, preferably overnight under refrigeration.

2 Drain and rinse under cold running water.

3 Place the degorged ris de veau in a large pot and add enough cold water to completely cover. Add lemon juice, bay leaf, thyme, and black peppercorns.

4 Bring the ris de veau to a low boil. White foam will form on the surface.

5 Skim off the foam which contains the impurities in the ris de veau.

6 After simmering, rinse under cold running water.

(continues on next page)

Ris de Veau

(continued from previous page)

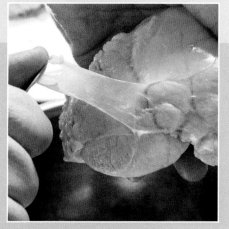

7   Once cooled, peel away the outer membrane.

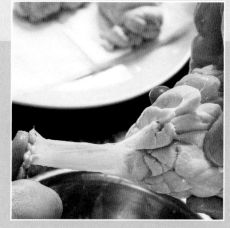

8   The membranes may need to be removed in layers.

9   Remove as much of the membrane as possible.

10   Arrange the cleaned ris de veau in a towel-lined pan in a single layer.

11   Cover with another kitchen towel.

12   Place a weight on top and leave refrigerated overnight to remove any excess water.

Kidneys *Rognons*

Kidneys are a multi-lobed glandular organ. Veal and lamb kidneys are considered among the best because they possess a delicate flavor and are very tender. Pork and beef kidneys are less appreciated due to their stronger flavor and tendency toward toughness when overcooked.

Kidneys should be consumed while still very fresh and thoroughly and properly cleaned. They should be degreased, denerved, and the outer membrane removed. However, certain preparations allow for the entire lobe to be roasted in its fat. Kidney fat is considered to be the best fat for deep frying. Kidneys should be served medium rare to rare; if cooked beyond medium rare, they may become too tough and develop too strong a flavor.

Kidneys are rich in iron, protein, vitamin A, thiamine, phosphorus, and riboflavin. Suggested cooking methods include braising, simmering, and broiling.

Brains *Cervelles*

The brain is the most nutrient-rich organ in the body of a mammal. Brain matter also possesses healthy cholesterol that assists the human body in the development of essential hormones. The brain contains DHA or *docosahexaenoic acid*, an omega-3 fatty acid that is critical to the optimal functioning of the brain. Eating foods that are DHA rich is also thought to reduce the risk of Alzheimer's, age-related macular degeneration, and dementia in the elderly.

Considered a white offal, the brain is one of the most delicate types of offal. Lamb's brains are the most popular. They are light pink in color and weigh around 3.5 oz (100 g) each. Sheep's brains are somewhat larger at about 5 oz (150 g), and veal brains are considerably larger at about 9 to 10.5 oz (250 to 300 g).

Brain has a delicate creamy texture, almost comparable to that of a custard. The brains most commonly available are those of lamb and veal. The brains of adult animals, pigs, or game should not be consumed because of the risk of contracting a disease or infection such as BSE (bovine spongiform encephalopathy), scrapie, or parasites.

To prepare brains for cooking, the outer membrane (meninges) needs to be removed before degorging in cold water with vinegar or lemon juice. Degorging serves to remove any blood and impurities. After degorging, the brains are rinsed until the water runs clear. The brains are then poached in acidulated water before being used in a finished dish. Brains can then be broiled, fried, or baked.

Preparing Brains for Cooking

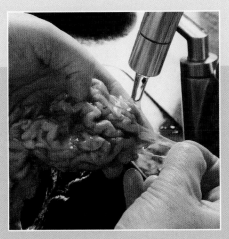

1 Clean brains by removing the meninges.

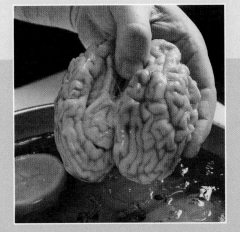

2 Prepare ice water with lemon, thyme, and bay leaf. Soak the brains overnight to degorge.

3 After degorging, rinse the brains in cold running water.

(continues on next page)

Preparing Brains for Cooking

(continued from previous page)

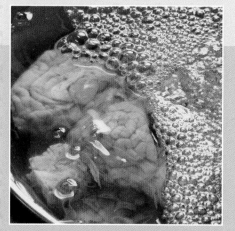

4 Continue to change the water until it runs clear.

5 Remove the brains, pat dry and place on a towel-lined dish.

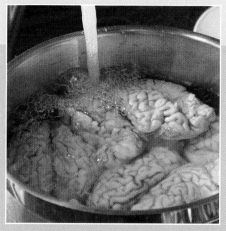

6 Place in a large pot and generously cover with cold water.

7 Add lemon juice, crushed pepper-corns, thyme, and bay leaf.

8 Bring to a boil.

9 Skim off any foam and impurities from the surface.

10 Once blanched, drain off the cooking liquid and transfer the brains to a large bowl.

11 Refresh in cold water.

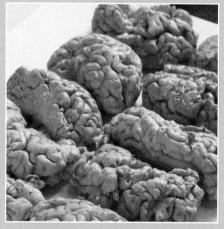

12 Strain and pat dry. Drain on a clean towel.

(continues on next page)

Preparing Brains for Cooking

(continued from previous page)

13   Lightly dredge in flour.

14   Place in a heated clarified butter in a large frying pan over medium heat.

15   Allow to lightly color, then turn over and color the other side. Remove and keep warm.

16   Discard butter and add fresh butter and heat. Add the cubed bread.

17   Toss to evenly coat and cook until golden.

18   Add capers and diced lemon and toss together.

19   Add chopped parsley.

20   Add the brains back into the pan to heat and absorb the flavors of the garnish.

21   Spoon onto a plate accompanied by the garnish.

Liver – *Foie*

The liver is a large organ that plays an important role in distributing nutrients throughout the body. The liver stores vitamins A, D, C, E, K, B_6, and B_{12}. The liver is also high in protein, thiamine, riboflavin, niacin, folate, pantothenic acid, phosphorus, iron, and selenium. In addition, the role of the liver is to neutralize any toxins that are ingested into the body without storing them.

Liver is a delicate organ that requires care while cooking. Unlike other offal, liver has very little connective tissue, so overcooking will result in liver that is dry and crumbly.

Liver from a young animal is preferred because it is milder in flavor and more tender. Liver from goose, duck, chicken, veal, cow, pork, lamb, and fish are all edible.

Foie Gras

Foie gras is the French term for fatty liver. Foie gras is a delicacy that dates back to ancient Egypt where the concept of force feeding poultry was developed after observing the voracious eating habits of migrating birds.

Traditionally foie gras is produced by means of force feeding, or *gavage*. Most birds possess throats that are capable of dilating and expanding, enabling them to consume large amounts of food, which is held in the esophagus pending digestion. Force feeding is done by inserting a large tube into the esophagus. The animals are then confined to a small area that restricts their movement so they are able to increase in weight and size. This practice can result in a fattened liver 10 to 12 times its normal size. The birds are fed several times per day over a period of two to five weeks. Water fowl take best to gavage because they lack the gag reflex present in other birds.

Some countries have banned the practice of *gavage*, considering it to be cruel and unnecessary.

Tongue – *Langue*

Today, we enjoy cooked tongue from beef, veal, sheep, and pork, but throughout history, gastronomes have also dined on pink flamingo and whale tongues.

Fresh tongue should be soaked in cold water for a few hours, with frequent water changes. It should then be trimmed of fat and cartilage before gently cooking in salted water with aromatic vegetables. Tongue requires a lengthy and slow cooking process to properly tenderize. Once cooked, the root and outer skin are removed.

Tongue is high in niacin, protein, iron, and vitamin B_{12}.

Foie Gras's Beginnings

Modern foie gras gained its popularity in the 18th century. This is due in part to the influx of corn that was brought from the New World by the Spanish. The best known story linked to the "rediscovery" of foie gras is attributed to Jean-Pierre Clause, chef to the Maréchal de Contades, military governor of Alsace. In 1789, he created a dish consisting of pâté of goose foie gras on a bed of bacon and veal, wrapped in pastry, which he named "pâté à la Contades." The Maréchal de Contades enjoyed the new dish so much that he had some delivered to King Louis XVI of France. The king was delighted by this exciting new dish and thanked the Maréchal de Contades with an estate in Picardie, and the chef with 20 pistoles.

Bone Marrow — *Moëlle*

Many cultures enjoy bone marrow as food. It is the soft, fatty tissue found in the hollow of long bones, and should not be confused with spinal marrow (*amourettes*). It is often poached and scooped out with a small spoon onto toasted country bread. It is also used to flavor risotto or sauces and can be used as a filling or in forcemeats. It is an important element in the enjoyment of *osso bucco*, braised veal shank.

Feet or Trotters — *Pieds*

Trotters are the feet of four legged animals, primarily those of pig, lamb, and veal. They are considered a white offal meat. Trotters are sold either whole or boned. In either case, they will have been thoroughly cleaned and have had the hair removed. They can be prepared in any manner of ways and served hot or cold.

The classic preparation of pig's trotters is "à la Sainte-Menehould," in which they are breaded and then grilled or roasted and served with mustard.

Veal trotters can be enjoyed in the same manner as pig's trotters, however, they are most often used to provide gelatin in bouillons and stocks.

Trotters are protein rich and possess a high fat content. The other nutrients they supply, such as calcium, zinc, vitamins B_6 and B_{12}, iron, and magnesium, are all overshadowed by the amount of gelatin that they contain.

Tripe — *Tripe*

Tripe is the stomach of an animal. It is a tough meat that requires a long, slow, and moist cooking process. Because it contains bacteria that are harmful to humans, tripe must be thoroughly cleaned before it makes its way into the simmering pot. Tripe is nutritious and contains calcium, niacin, iron, zinc, and protein. The tripe of cow, deer, sheep, goats, and pigs are all consumed. Boiling tripe will result in large amounts of gelatin.

Beef tripe is made from the first three chambers of a cow's stomach: the rumen, the reticulum, and the omasum. The preferred beef tripe is from the reticulum (the second stomach of a ruminating animal) because it is the tenderest and possesses a subtle flavor. The reticulum is also known for its resemblance to honeycomb, and is sometimes called honeycomb tripe.

Green tripe is tripe that contains undigested stomach contents and is most often sold to pet food manufacturers. Despite its name, this tripe is not actually green. Chlorophyll in the undigested grass will turn the stomach contents gray or brown. Green tripe is unwashed, has a foul odor, and is not considered to be safe for human consumption.

GAME – *GIBIER*

Before animals were domesticated for livestock, early man hunted wild animals for sustenance. In ancient Rome the serving of wild game was very popular; it was this popularity in fact that lead to the early domestication of, in particular, game birds. Roman nobleman Lucullus was said to have installed an enclosure in his kitchen so that he could enjoy eating thrush while live thrush flew around him. During the feudal period, hunting was a privilege of the aristocracy and this practice endured in France until the revolution. Herons, swans, and peacocks, all of which were grain fed, were used in medieval cooking.

The commercialization of game began in the 17th century with large game such as wild boar. Today, domestic game includes pheasant, duck, and partridges, as well as hare, venison, and elk. Game has become a refined and deluxe item on the table.

Modern game meat can be separated into two broad categories: ground game (*gibiers à poil*) and winged game (*gibiers à plumes*). Ground game can be further separated into large (*venaison*) and small game (*basse venaison*).

Both wild and domestic game meat is leaner and denser than regular meats, although wild game generally has more flavor than its domestic counterparts due to a more diverse diet and the physical demands of the environments where they live. Wild animals get a great deal more exercise, so their muscles and tendons are far more developed than those of domestic animals.

Winged Game

Pheasant – *Faisan*

Family: *Phasianinae*

Pheasants are a large family of birds comprising some 50 species. They originated from Asia and made their way into Europe around the time of the ancient Greek empire.

The most prevalent species of pheasant is the common pheasant. The male is recognizable by the white ring around his neck, green plumage on his head, and red skin around his eyes. The hen of this species is fairly nondescript compared to the males.

A dressed pheasant weighs between 2 and 2.25 pounds (about 1 kg). Pheasant meat has been described as having the flavor of poultry and venison. Most culinary experts agree that wild pheasants should be hung prior to being eaten; additional flavor will be obtained if the feathers are left on during this process because the oil from the feathers will absorb into the flesh. Pheasant meat is tender and highly flavored, and because of its "wild" flavor should not be overseasoned. Pheasant can be poached and stewed, but it is most often roasted, with or without stuffing.

The myth goes that on their quest for the golden fleece, Jason and the Argonauts stumbled across a beautiful species of birds by the Phasis River, so they named it after the location where they had first sighted it, calling it the bird of the Phasis River, hence, the pheasant.

Due to the vast array of pheasant, partridge, and pigeon species, in the following text all three will be identified by their scientific family, their French and their common names only.

Partridge – *Perdrix*

Family: *Phasianinae*

The partridge is a nonmigratory bird in the pheasant family *Phasianidae*, native to Europe, Asia, Africa, and the Middle East. Partridges were introduced to North America toward the end of the 19th century, before finally adapting to their new environs at the beginning of the 20th century. They can now be found from Canada down to Central America.

Partridges are much smaller than pheasants, weighing on average 8 to 10 ounces (220 to 280 g), but are larger than their other cousin, the quail.

Young partridge under one year of age, are known as *perdreaux*. Perdreaux are still young enough that they do not need much cooking and can in fact be served medium rare. Their meat is highly prized for the delicacy of its texture and flavor.

Mature partridges, called *perdrix* in French, are much tougher and will generally be braised or barded and slow roasted. The flavor of adult partridges is much more pronounced and gamey than that of young partridges.

Pigeon – *Pigeon*

Family: *Cocumbidae*

Pigeons come from the same family as doves. In fact, it is believed that all the pigeons and doves that roam the earth today, including our city friends the rock pigeons, descend from the Brittany rock dove. The rock pigeon is the world's most domesticated bird—evidence suggests that the domestication of pigeons began between 5,000 and 10,000 years ago.

All species of pigeons are edible and they are not really differentiated between once they are on the table. However, there is a distinction between wild and domesticated pigeon, the former having a denser, more flavorful flesh than the latter. The term squab (*pigeonneaux* in French) designates a pigeon that is too young to fly.

Even though wild pigeon can be more flavorful, consumers tend to prefer the tender and relatively mild tasting meat of young (28 days old) domestic pigeon. Domestig pigeon is also more readily available thatn its wild counterpart. Pigeon can be prepared in any number of ways, including roasted, grilled, or braised.

Guinea Fowl – *Pintade*

Numida meleagris

The first guinea fowls originated from western Africa (previously known as Guinea) and even today, they are still hunted in the African bush. They were eaten in ancient Egypt and appeared in Roman banquets under the name of *meleagris*. The bird found its way into Europe in the 15th and 16th centuries through the Strait of Gibraltar by way of the Portuguese conquerors who brought back with them the *pintada* (painted) fowl, so named because of their brightly colored heads and little white spots that cover their bodies.

Guinea fowls are now reared worldwide. The birds are about the same size as roasting chickens, weighing 2.75 to 3.25 pounds (1.2 to 1.5 kg). Guinea fowl have rose-colored flesh with a delicately gamey taste that is richer than that of other game birds. Guinea fowl also tend to stay moist during cooking and have lighter bones providing more meat by weight than chicken.

The young birds, known as *pintadeau*, can be roasted or treated like chicken, but older birds should be cooked longer, just to ensure succulence.

Quail – *Caille*

Coturnix

The quail is a smaller member of the pheasant family. It is a migratory bird found in Europe from April to October. In antiquity, quails were so plentiful that their migrations used to blacken the sky, but sadly they have been driven to the brink of extinction by the spread of pastures and hunting. Today, quails are mostly farmed worldwide. These birds are the smallest of domestic fowl and very delicate to handle. They are generally served boned and stuffed or *en crapaudine*.

Quail eggs are about 2 cm long and white spotted with black and are popular for use on canapés.

Ground Game

Hare – *Lièvre*

Lepus

A larger, darker fleshed relative of the rabbit, hare has played an important role in human survival since the dawn of civilization. Hares are native to Africa, North and Central America and Eurasia, however, through migration and introduction by humans, hares can now be found almost worldwide.

The hare's preferred habitat is the plains just on the edge of the woods, often just on the edge of human settlements. For some reason, throughout history all over the world, they have been made central to mythical and religious beliefs. For example, the idea of there being a hare on the moon is so common that the myth is found in Japan, China, India, England, and many other countries.

The male hare is known as a buck (*capucin*) and the female as a doe (*hase*).

Young hares are called leverets (*levraut*).

Hare meat is extremely flavorful and so tender that only the flesh of older animals requires marinating. Hare is very popular for use in terrines and galantines.

Wild Boar – *Sanglier*

Sus scrofa

The domestic pig appeared about 10,000 years ago in the area now known as Turkey, but its ancestor still roams the wild. The wild boar is an imposing animal, weighing up to 330 pounds (150 kg). It is covered in a dark, bristly coat of fur and has enormous tusks.

The diet of wild boars consists mainly of acorns, larvae, chestnuts, roots and young shoots, and the occasional small rodent. They are social animals and

In 1950, a French veterinarian, who was fed up with the local rabbits digging up his lawn, infected them with myxomatosis. The disease spread rapidly and within two years had all but exterminated the rabbits and hares of France. Extensive breeding programs have been put into place and have been successful in restoring the populations of wild rabbits and hares.

usually travel in packs, with the exception of females when they are in heat and older males, known as hermits (*ermites*).

The meat of the young boar (*marcassin*) is very tender and delicately flavored but as the animal ages, its flesh becomes tougher and gamier in flavor. The meat of boars more than five years of age is not desirable because it is extremely pungent and tough. Marcassin, however, have such succulent flesh that it can be prepared like other red meats, with or without marinating. As for adult animals, they generally need long marinating times, traditionally in red wine, followed by slow, moist cooking, depending on their age and which cut is being prepared. Wild boar is an extremely popular meat for use in charcuterie and can be found in dry sausages, pâtés, rillettes, and terrines.

Venison – *Chevreuil, cerf, biche*

Male: *deer / cerf*

Female: *doe / biche*

Cervidae

The term *venison* once referred to the meat of all large game, but today it refers to the various species of deer that are hunted for their meat. The three main species of deer that are hunted are the red deer, the fallow deer, and the roe deer.

Venison is incredibly lean, containing as little as 3.5 percent fat. Therefore, it is often necessary to add fat when preparing it. Large cuts lend themselves well to slow cooking methods such as braising to prevent the meat from drying out. Other cuts of venison can be prepared in the same manner as equivalent cuts of beef: roasting, grilling, and braising. It can also be dried as jerky or used in making sausages.

The word *venison* comes from the Latin *venari*, which refers to the act of hunting.

POULTRY – *VOLAILLE*

Not to be mistaken for *fowl*, which refers to *all* edible birds, *poultry* is the designation used for farmyard or domesticated breeds. Although it is true that in Roman times peacocks were bred because their great external beauty was mistakenly equated with great flavor, for our purposes we will keep to birds used in modern culinary practices. While not exhaustive, this list includes chicken (including capons and Cornish game hens), duck, goose, and turkey.

Poultry figures largely in our diets as well as in our collective history. Poultry is often the centerpiece on our tables at holiday meals. For example, the Chinese New Year can be celebrated with duck stuffed with sweet rice, a roast goose may be the focal point of a table at a British Christmas dinner, and a turkey at Thanksgiving is almost an American constitutional right!

It is difficult to generalize about the history of the domestication of edible birds because different birds evolved in different parts of the world at different times. Archeologists place the domesticated chicken at 3000 BC in Southeast Asia, the goose was first being domesticated before the rise of the Roman Empire in Gaulish territory (modern-day France), and the turkey was domesticated much later in Mexico around 200 BC.

Modern poultry-farming practices have largely become an industrial endeavor. The mass production of chickens, for example, has led to an emphasis on breeds that develop the most possible meat in the least possible time. Not only has this reduced the varieties of chickens on the market, but the delicacy of the meat texture and flavor has been somewhat degraded as a result. These mass production practices have led to a revival of smaller farms as well as "free-range" and *appellation contrôlée* poultry breeds.

Some popular methods for cooking poultry include roasting, braising, sautéing, steaming, and poaching. The quandary faced by chefs as they prepare whole poultry is the tendency for the white meat to cook faster than the dark meat. This is sometimes controlled by basting, by braising, or by covering the breast meat with tin foil or fat.

In addition to the muscle meat, poultry offal is also extensively prepared and served. *Foie gras* (fattened goose liver) is a delicacy that jumps to everyone's mind, but a host of culinary preparations is used for kidneys and gizzards, as well as rendered poultry fat.

Chicken – *Poulet*

Scientific name: *Gallus gallus domesticus*

Female: Hen

Male: Cock, rooster

The common domestic chicken is a mixture of several breeds that were all originally descendants of the notoriously cranky red jungle fowl of Southeast Asia. Eventually making its way through the Mediterranean to Europe, the chicken remained a meal for the wealthy well into the 20th century. In 1594 to garner popular support, King Henry IX promised the French masses "a chicken in every pot." This, like most political promises, did not pan out, making today's mass production of chickens a strange kind of wish fulfillment for the French king.

It is likely, however, that old Henry would have been disappointed in the plain taste of today's battery (mass produced) chicken and would have insisted on a "Label Rouge" approved or "French Bresse" chicken. These *appèlation contrôlée* chickens are of a higher quality than the standard factory chicken because of the purity of their feed and the number of weeks they are allowed to mature before being slaughtered. The French Bresse, for instance, is raised for at least 32 weeks, whereas a factory chicken is raised for as little as 6 weeks. Also, the Bresse is given space to exercise, which gives the muscle meat a more complex flavor.

The terms *free range* and *grain fed* are also used to imply a better grade of chicken and, although not fully standardized, can mean that the bird has had some access to the outdoors and is allowed to mature a little longer. Depending on what is on the label, *free range* might also mean that the animal has not been fed antibiotics or growth hormones either—all of which are modern concerns that would have left King Henry scratching his head.

In addition to considering the industry standards under which a chicken has been raised, the North American chef can choose between roasters, with a high fat content, and stewing chickens, which are leaner.

One preparatory concern regarding poultry is the need to protect against salmonella. Perhaps because of a general public awareness of the existence of this bacterium on raw chicken, only 4 or 5 percent of salmonella poisonings comes from mishandled chicken. It is nonetheless important to emphasize the need for extreme care in the sanitization of surfaces and tools to avoid cross contamination while working with raw chicken and all other raw poultry.

Trimming (Habiller) a Chicken

1 Hold the head of the chicken face down.

2 Slice the skin of the back of the neck.

3 Cut the length of the skin to expose the neck.

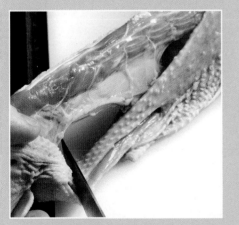

4 Pull the skin away, exposing the neck.

5 Cut off the head.

6 Cut at the base of the neck where it connects to the body. Reserve the neck for making stock.

(continues on next page)

Trimming (Habiller) a Chicken

(continued from previous page)

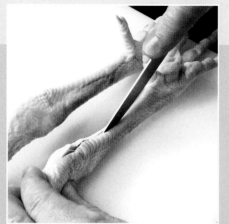

7   Make an incision along the back of the legs.

8   Open up the skin, and slip your thumb under the exposed tendons.

9   Slip the tip of a sharpening steel underneath.

10   Twist the sharpening steel to wind the tendons around. Then pull to disengage the tendons.

11   Pull the tendons loose.

12   Trim off using a pair of scissors.

13   Trim the feet for presentation. With a large knife, cut off the side claws.

14   Cut as closely to the joint as possible.

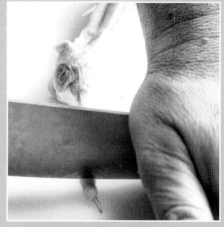

15   Cut off the tip.

(continues on next page)

Trimming (Habiller) a Chicken

(continued from previous page)

16 Place the trimmed feet over an open flame to remove the outer skin.

17 Once the skin has blistered, remove from the heat.

18 Break off the larger pieces with your fingers.

19 Use the tip of a small knife to remove any remaining skin.

20 Trim off the tip of the wing. Reserve for making stock.

21 Cut the lower part of the wing at the joint. Reserve for making stock.

22 Cut around the base of the "drumstick" of the wing.

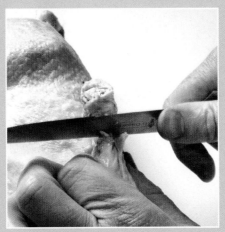

23 Use the back of the knife to scrape the bone clean.

24 With a pair of kitchen scissors, cut off the end.

(continues on next page)

Trimming (Habiller) a Chicken

(continued from previous page)

25 Be sure the cut is clean, remove any splinters of bone.

26 Remove the wishbone: Lift the flap of skin at the shoulders of the chicken and feel for the outline of the wishbone.

27 Use the tip of a small knife, scrape the bone to disengage it from the flesh.

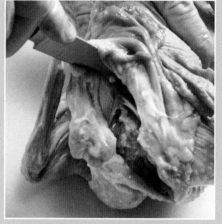

28 Continue scraping until the wishbone is completely exposed.

29 The wishbone is held in place by cartilage, so hook your finger under the prong and gently break away and pull out.

Trussing (Bridage) a Chicken

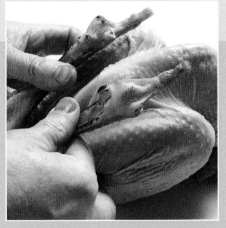

1 Lay the chicken on its back and fold the feet up against the body.

2 Prepare a trussing needle with butcher's string. Pierce the chicken where the leg and thigh meet.

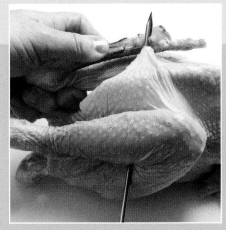

3 Point the needle at a slight diagonal, passing the needle over the opposite foot.

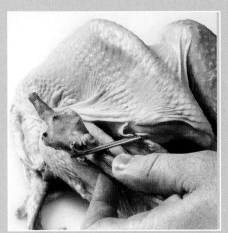

4 The needle should come out just at the bottom of the breast.

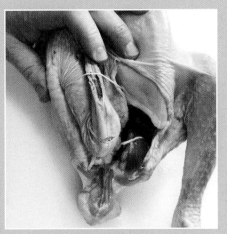

5 In order for the leg to fit snugly against the body, make a shallow incision at the joint to cut the tendon. Tighten the string to hold the foot down.

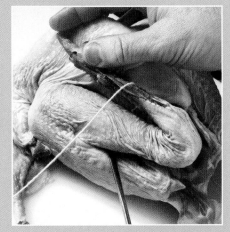

6 Pull the string through, leaving at least 6 inches of the loose end. Perform the same step on the other side, but pointing the needle at a diagonal toward the opposite wing.

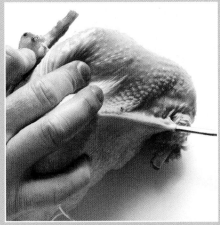

7 The needle should come out just below where the wing joins the body.

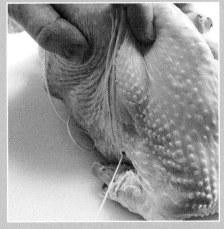

8 Pull the string through loosely.

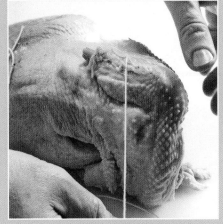

9 Turn the chicken on its side and pass the string over the wing.

(continues on next page)

Trussing (Bridage) a Chicken

(continued from previous page)

10 Pull the flap of neck skin to cover the opening. Pass the needle into one side, as if sewing the flap down.

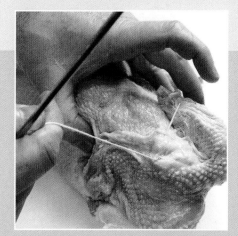

11 Come out on the other side, making sure the wing is secured by the string.

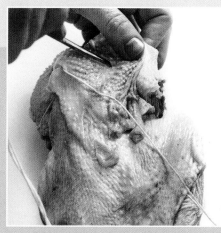

12 Pass the needle into the other side of the flap.

13 Pull the string so that it is on top of the wing.

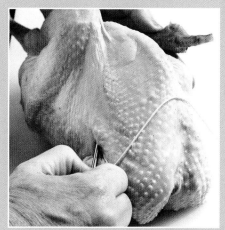

14 Pass the needle at the joint of the wing toward the opposite leg.

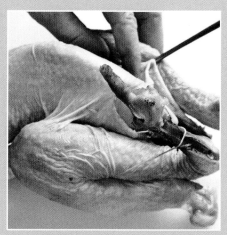

15 Pass the needle at the joint where the thigh connects to the body, pointing it at a diagonal toward the end of the opposite breast.

16 The string should come out just at the bottom of the breast inside the untied leg.

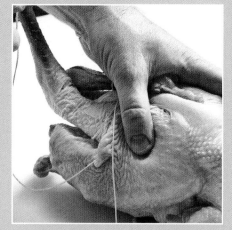

17 Both loose ends should be on the same side, one below and one above the leg.

18 Pull both ends of the string tightly.

(continues on next page)

Trussing (Bridage) a Chicken

Trussing (Bridage) a Chicken

(continued from previous page)

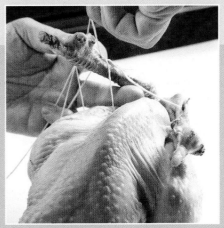

19 Bring both ends above the leg and tie with a butcher's knot.

20 The chicken is now ready for roasting.

Deboning (Désossage) a Chicken

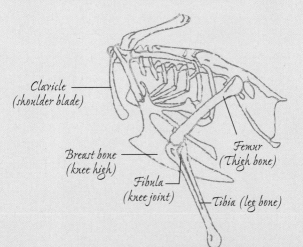

Clavicle
(shoulder blade)

Breast bone
(knee high)

Femur
(Thigh bone)

Fibula
(knee joint)

Tibia (leg bone)

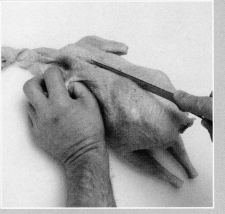

1 Lay the chicken breast-side down. Cut down along the center of the back.

2 Using short strokes with the tip of the knife, scrape along the bone, following the contours of the chicken. Pull the skin and flesh away as you go.

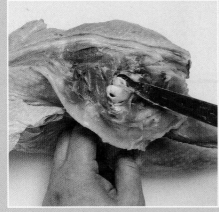

3 Continue down the chicken, until the thigh joint is exposed. Scrape the joint clean.

(continues on next page)

Deboning (Désossage) a Chicken

(continued from previous page)

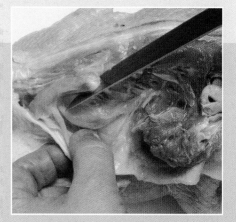

4   When the shoulder blade is exposed, slip the knife underneath to disengage it.

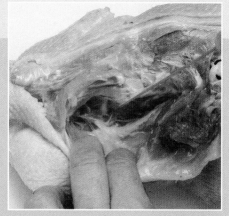

5   Continue down along the ribcage, all the way to the thigh joint.

6   Cut around the thigh joint to disengage it from the socket.

7   Once the joint is disengaged, scrape along the thigh bone toward the knee joint.

8   Once the flesh has been scraped from the bone, pull the thigh loose, exposing a thin membrane. Cut away the membrane to expose the breast meat.

9   Scrape off any flesh from the shoulder blade.

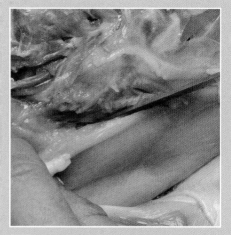

10   Starting at the ribcage, begin to separate the breast meat.

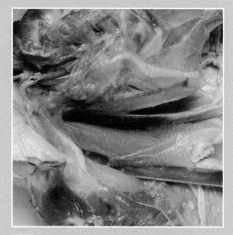

11   Scrape down, following the curve of the breast bone.

12   Cut the joint at the base of the shoulder blade.

(continues on next page)

Deboning (Désossage) a Chicken

(continued from previous page)

13. Cut through the cartilage to remove the shoulder blade.

14. Hold the wing drumstick and push up to expose the joint. Cut through the cartilage to free the wing and continue freeing the breast meat.

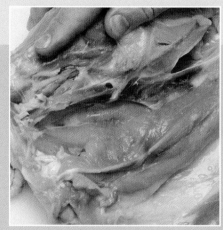

15. Scrape all the way down until the breast meat is attached only at the sternum.

16. Now turn the chicken over and repeat on the other side.

17. Gently scrape away the flesh to expose the cartilage that runs along the edge of the sternum.

18. Carefully cut the flesh, being very careful not to cut through the skin.

19. Once one end is cut, follow along the sternum until it is completely freed.

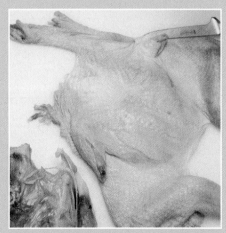

20. The skin should be completely intact.

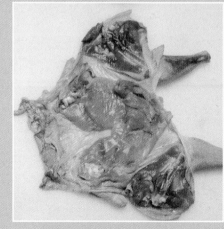

21. The final step is to remove the leg bones.

(continues on next page)

Deboning (Désossage) a Chicken

(continued from previous page)

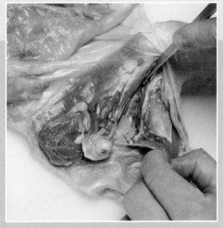

22 Cut through the flesh along the length of the thigh bone.

23 Following the length of the bone, continue around scraping it clean.

24 Locate the knee joint and cut through the cartilage.

25 Pull the bone back to "break" the joint.

26 Finish cutting any remaining attached cartilage.

27 Cut around the "knee" joint to expose it.

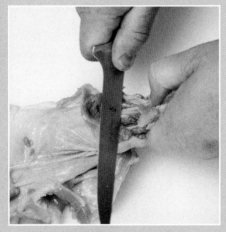

28 Using the back of the knife, start scraping the flesh off following the length of the bone.

29 As the flesh is disengaged, fold the meat inside out to expose the bone and gently pull.

30 Cut to disengage.

(continues on next page)

Deboning (Désossage) a Chicken

(continued from previous page)

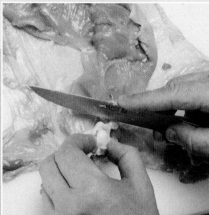

31 Find the end of the wing bone, and as with the leg, cut around the joint.

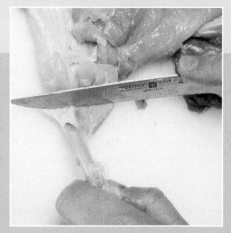

32 Scrape along the length of the bone and cut free.

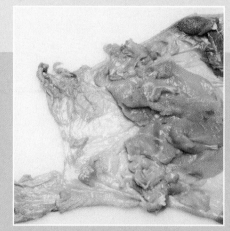

33 Now remove the leg meat.

34 Separate the flesh from the skin using the tip of the knife.

35 The leg and thigh meat will have a thin silvery skin which will need to be removed.

36 Holding the knife at a very shallow angle, scrape the flesh off of the "skin." Reserve the meat for the filling.

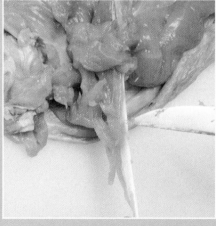

37 Trim the white meat of any nerves, sinew, and any remaining bits of cartilage.

38 The chicken is ready to be filled.

Capon – *Chapon*

To produce a capon, a rooster not more than 8 weeks old is castrated (causing hormonal changes) and fed a diet high in fat; the end result is a succulent and tender bird ideal for roasting. By one account, the capon was invented by Roman breeders who, due to a grain shortage, were forbidden to raise fattened hens. Snubbing the law, they fattened male birds instead.

Cornish Game Hen – *Poussin*

While *poussin* is simply the French word for a young chicken (under 28 days old), in the United States it is used as an alternative name for the Cornish game hen. As a cross between a Cornish and a White Rock chicken, weighing approximately 2.5 pounds (1 kg), it is the perfect size to be plated as a single serving. Common cooking methods include roasting and broiling.

Duck – *Canard*

Scientific name: *Anas domesticus*

Alternate name: White Peking duck

Female: Cane

Male: Drake

The history of the domestication of ducks spans continents and epochs: In China they have been domesticated for more than 2,000 years; in Medieval Europe, duck farming became a necessity as the result of a wildfowl scarcity; whereas in New York the arrival of a ship in 1873 containing a family of Peking ducks from China signaled the beginning of the American duck industry. The Long Island duck (a not too distant relative of those four Peking ducks) is now widely enjoyed in the United States for its moist, dark meat. Equally popular in Europe, the Rouen duck (from Rouen, France) has its own distinct flavor because of the method by which it is slaughtered—it is either strangled or suffocated to retain the blood in the muscle. The Aylesbury, Gressingham, and Norfolk ducks from Britain and the Barbary and Nantes ducks from France all have their respective qualities in terms of color, texture, and flavor.

Ducks are generally considered ready for slaughter between 8 and 16 weeks of age, or when they have reached a weight of between 3 and 5.5 pounds (1.4 and 2.5 kg). *Fryers* are younger, whereas *roasters* are better left to mature a little longer before slaughter. Because they do not keep well, ducks are either slaughtered and frozen immediately or cooked within 2 days.

Depending on how naturally tender the bird is, duck can be braised or roasted on a spit. In one famous dish the carcass of a Rouen is crushed in a press (duck-press) to extract its juices and blood, which are then made into a sauce for the rest of the broiled meat. A recipe that has stood the test of time is "duck à l'orange," which is an example of how perfectly duck meat is paired with acidic fruits. In addition, rendered duck fat is used to condition, preserve, and flavor duck meat for *confit*.

Goose – *Oie*

Scientific name: *Anser anser domesticus*

Female: Goose

Male: Gander

The story goes that it was the honking of penned geese that woke up Roman soldiers just in time to ready themselves for an attack by the Gauls. While its usefulness in modern warfare has yet to be proven, the goose is still loved today as a sumptuous meal.

In many parts of Europe, goose is readily available as a table bird and for *confit*. In France the majority of goose offal is used in *confit*, including the heart, liver, and gizzard, thus making the production of *foie gras* a less wasteful practice. The production of *foie gras* accounts for a significant portion of goose farming in Europe and even more so in the United States where demand for whole birds is limited. Goose *foie gras* is considered by some to be superior to that made from duck; in the seminal *Dictionnaire du Gastronome* it is even referred to as "devine."

Generally slaughtered between 6 and 16 weeks, a goose on the younger side of this range will be more tender for roasting than an older goose. The flavor of goose meat can be described as being fatty but delicate.

Turkey – *Dinde, Dindonneau* (young turkey)

Scientific name: *Meleagris gallopavo*

Female: Hen

Male: Tom

Considering its history, the turkey must surely suffer from cultural confusion. Native to the New World, the turkey was transported to Europe by Spanish explorers in the 16th century. In Europe, the turkey made guest appearances at royal feasts and on the tables of the wealthy. It was then brought back to the New World where it was bred with its wild ancestors. To early North American colonists, however, the turkey was no luxury—often it was the one thing standing between themselves and starvation. This, of course, gives rise to the turkey's place of honor at Thanksgiving meals in the United States and Canada alike.

In parts of Europe the turkey has made considerable gains over the goose as a holiday bird. Also, the introduction of smaller varieties and the sale of individual turkey parts has diversified the consumption of turkey in both the United States and Europe.

Meat Nutrition Chart
(Based on 85-gram servings)

Meat Source	Total Calories (g)	Total Fat (g)	Saturated Fat (g)	Protein (g)	Sodium (mg)	Cholesterol (mg)
Roast turkey	128	2	1	25	57	83
Roast chicken	162	6	2	25	73	76
Roast beef (trimmed)	144	4	1	25	32	53
Roast pork	179	8	3	25	54	80
Ground turkey	200	11	3	23	91	87
Ground beef	230	15	6	22	64	77
Ground pork	253	18	7	22	62	80

Source: U.S. Department of Agriculture, 2006.

Similar to the chicken industry, the quality of turkey has suffered from mechanization. As a reaction to this, American consumers have started to show an interest in paying a little more for "heritage" turkeys. Resembling older varieties in size and proportion, these birds tend to be free-range birds and consequently are more moist and flavorful.

Cooking methods for the turkey are generally similar to those used with other poultry. Recently, however, the trend in roasting turkey is to avoid stuffing it. The rationale is that because stuffing increases cooking time it also increases the risk of drying out the white meat. Also, turkey has become popular among calorie watchers as an alternative to red meat—the nutritional chart on the previous page gives you a good indication as to why.

BASIC MIXED PREPARATIONS – *LES FARCES*

Definition

In the broadest possible sense of the term, a farce can be any savory ingredient that is used as a filling. For example, the rice, tapioca, mushroom, and salmon mixture in the *petit coulibiac* (recipe featured in *Classic Recipes*) is a farce, just as the pork and veal mixture in *petits farcis niçois* (recipe featured in *Classic Recipe*) is also. The nuances of the word *farce* go beyond "fillings" when we consider that *farce à gratin* (recipe featured in *Classic Recipe*) does not technically fill anything, but is rather designed to be finished under a broiler as a garnish for a canapé.

What's in a word?

The closest English translation for *farce* is "forcemeat." In fact, the word *forcemeat* evolved from the French verb *farcir*, which means "to stuff." In many English cookbooks though, the term *forcemeat* is limited to meat fillings and excludes others such as vegetable- and grain-based fillings. *Farce*, in the French usage employed in this book, includes a wider culinary range.

Farce à Gratin

1   Prepare the ingredients.

2   Melt butter over medium heat and add chicken livers.

3   Add the shallots.

(continues on next page)

Farce à Gratin

(continued from previous page)

4   When the shallots begin to soften, stir in the parsley, then add the cognac.

5   Flambé to remove the alcohol.

6   Add the cream and butter. Stir well and reduce.

7   Transfer cooked livers to a drum sieve (tamis).

(continues on next page)

Farce à Gratin

(continued from previous page)

8   Using a corne, press the livers through the drum sieve.

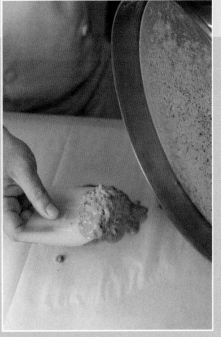

9   Scrape the puréed mixture from the bottom.

10   The farce à gratin is ready to be used.

The term *les farces* refers to fillings that are made from vegetables, grains, and ground proteins. The protein-based farces that fall under the more limited term *forcemeat* are made from meat (chicken, pork, veal, hare, etc.), offal (liver, brains, etc.), or fish (salmon, whiting, langoustine, etc.). Generally these farces are held together with a binder and lightened with either cream or butter and are used with great versatility in ballotines, galantines, paupiettes, croquettes, and rissoles and as an ingredient in terrines and pâtés. Another type of farce is a mousseline de poisson, or, in English, a fish mousse. *Terrine chaude de poisson* (p. 206 *Classic Recipes*) is a good example of how this mousseline can give body and substance to a preparation. The combination of finely puréed white fish bound with egg whites and lightened with cream is used in roulades, to form quenelles as well as in a number of other preparations. The same method can be applied to white chicken meat to make a mousseline de viande that is used in, among other preparations, *croquettes de poulet et jambon* (p. 73 *Classic Recipes*).

Binding

One objective in making a farce is to ensure that the ground proteins and other added ingredients (such as parsley or shallots) form a mass that holds together. This is where binding ingredients come into play. In *mousseline de poisson* (p. 349), the binder is egg whites; in *paupiettes de veau* (recipe featured in *Classic Recipes*), it is a whole egg that binds the *farce simple*; and in other preparations, the farce is kept together with a bread mixture or a panade. A *panade* (also called *panada*) is a cooked paste that is folded into a farce to bind it and provide a uniform consistency. There are five types of panade based on their binding ingredient: flour, bread, eggs, potatoes, and rice.

Mousseline de Poisson

1   Cut the trimmed fillets into large pieces.

2   Cut into smaller pieces.

3   Once small enough, start chopping using a rocking motion.

4   Transfer to a drum sieve (tamis).

5   Using a corne, begin pressing the fish through the sieve.

6   The drum sieve will remove any nerves or bones.

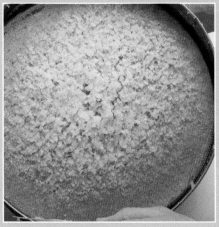

7   Turn the tamis over to scrape away the fish purée.

8   Place into a bowl set in ice.

9   The flesh should be very fine.

(continues on next page)

Mousseline de Poisson

(continued from previous page)

10 Add egg white and beat well.

11 Make sure egg is completely incorporated.

12 Mix in the cream.

13 Once the cream is mixed in, season with salt and pepper.

14 Spread the mousseline up onto the sides of the bowl to ensure that it chills properly.

15 The mousseline can now be seasoned and garnished for various preparations.

The word *panade* comes from the French word for "bread," which is *pain*. This usage goes back to the 16th century when stale bread was mixed with a liquid and used as a thickener. As French cuisine evolved, certain processes were refined and streamlined. For example, instead of waiting for bread to go stale, chefs started making panade by boiling flour in water. This process transformed the flour into a palatable and effective binder for amending farces and other preparations.

Quenelles

1   First dip the spoons in cold water. They should be the same size. Make a large scoop of the mousseline.

2   With the second spoon, scrape the mousseline, following the shape of the bowl of the spoon as tightly as possible.

3   Dip the first spoon in cold water, and repeat the process, scooping in one fluid movement.

4   Repeat again with the second spoon, each time dipping in cold water first. Scrape off any excess.

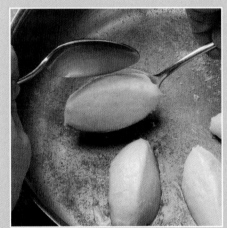

5   Carefully transfer the quenelle to a buttered and seasoned pan. The quenelle should have three sides with clean ridges.

6   Pour in fish stock about halfway up the height of the quenelles.

7   Cover the quenelles with a round of buttered parchment.

8   The quenelles are now ready to be cooked.

Fat Content

An aspect of farces that needs to be mentioned is their fat content. The fat content is pivotal in making a farce. For instance, in a farce made with fish, heavy cream is added both to increase the fat content and, as paradoxical as it sounds, to lighten the texture of the preparation. In a farce made with veal (a lean meat), pork fat will be added to the same effect.

Keep in mind that the desired percentage of fat is based on what the farce is being made for. In the *ballotine de vollaille* (recipe featured in *Classic Recipes*) for example, the fat content of the farce is adjusted in accordance with the fat content of the chicken. To keep the preparation moist, the desired fat content for the entire preparation (the farce and the chicken collectively) is approximately 30%. Although some preparations weigh in at 50% fat, 30% is a generally accepted standard that applies to many preparations.

Pairing

Fat content is not the only place where the composition of the farce must be judiciously chosen. The interplay between the taste of the farce and the taste of the ingredient it is paired with is vital. For example, when making a farce for stuffing game, a mild veal farce is chosen to complement the stronger taste of the meat. By contrast, in the recipe for *cromesquis de langoustines* (recipe featured in *Classic Recipes*), the farce *mousseline de langoustines* that is wrapped in crêpe is itself the prominent flavor in the preparation.

Farce Simple

1 Prepare the ingredients.

2 Finely chop the barding fat, by first cutting into strips.

3 Cut crosswise into a small dice.

(continues on next page)

Farce Simple

(continued from previous page)

4 Continue chopping using a rocking motion until fine.

5 Cut the meat using the same method by first cutting strips.

6 Cut crosswise.

7 Continue chopping until fine.

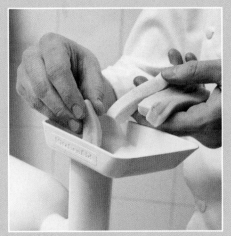

8 One can also use a meat grinder. Cut the fat into large strips and feed into the grinder.

9 Use the pestle for safety reasons. Never put your fingers down the tube with the machine running.

10 Cut the meat into large strips and feed into the grinder.

11 Transfer the ground or chopped fat and meat to a bowl set in ice.

12 Mix together.

(continues on next page)

Farce Simple

(continued from previous page)

13 Add the whole egg and mix completely.

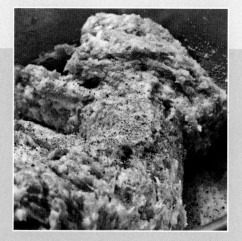

14 Mix in the cream and season with salt and pepper.

15 Spread the farce simple up the sides of the bowl to ensure it cools properly.

16 The farce simple can now be seasoned according to what it will be used for.

DAIRY

One of the main differences between mammals and other living creatures is that mammals produce milk for the sole purpose of nourishing their young. Milk is a nutrient-filled liquid that helps young mammals adapt to life outside the womb. Humans, however, have developed a liking and a dependence on milk that goes beyond infancy, and in many cultures today, milk is considered an essential part of a balanced diet.

The main source of milk for human consumption is the cow. The most common dairy-producing breed in North America is the Holstein, which has been bred specifically for the dairy market. The Holstein reaches maturity earlier than other breeds and has a longer milk-producing life. It also produces more milk in proportion to the amount of food ingested than other breeds. Other common breeds of dairy cows are Jerseys, Guernseys, and Brown Swiss.

The milk of other animals is also used in the dairy industry. The water buffalo, for example, produces a rich milk that is used in true mozzarella (*mozzarella di bufala*). Goat's and sheep's milk are common in many cultures. Also, because they are lower in fat and easier to digest, goat's and sheep's milk have gained popularity.

The commercial production of milk is not limited to providing milk for drinking, but also a wide variety of derivative products. The term *dairy* includes milk, cream, yogurt, and cheese, as discussed later in this section.

Liquid or Drinking Milk

Prior to the Industrial Revolution, most Europeans had access to local dairies where they could buy fresh raw milk. In the late 1800s and early 1900s, however, commercial farming methods were developed to accommodate the growing number of city-dwelling factory workers. The raw milk that was being carted or trained into

Lactose Intolerance

Lactose is a type of sugar contained in milk that requires the enzyme lactase in order to be processed by the intestines. After weaning, most mammals, including humans, either lose their ability to produce lactase or experience much lower production of the enzyme. While reduced lactase production in adult mammals is universal, the degree of this reduction depends upon individual physiology but also genetic differences between groups of people. For example, people with a northern heritage (such as Scandinavians) tend to have a higher tolerance for lactose. Because milk has been an integral part of their diet for centuries, their systems have adapted to produce enough lactase to process a certain amount of milk and milk products. People with a southern heritage, where there was little dependence on dairy for sustenance, tend to have higher rates of lactose intolerance.

the cities was not as fresh as it once was. Even worse, the milk was highly prone to transmitting disease. The process of *pasteurization* was invented to control this risk. With modern refrigeration and sanitation, raw milk is again available (except in much of North America), but its sale is strictly controlled through legislated guidelines.

Pasteurization

First discovered by French chemist Louis Pasteur in the mid-1800s, pasteurization serves two main purposes: (1) to protect public health and (2) to increase the shelf life of the product. By quickly heating the milk and then cooling it, pasteurization kills harmful bacteria such as *E. coli, Listeria,* and *Salmonella.* To further ensure food safety, the milk is dated at the time of pasteurization and is kept refrigerated from farm to store to the consumer's refrigerator.

As successful as pasteurization is at making milk safe, it does have the negative effect of removing some bacteria and enzymes that are potentially (the debate rages on in the United States) beneficial to the digestive process. To help make up the losses incurred by pasteurization, producers add vitamins and minerals to their finished milk.

Depending on the destined use of the milk and its derivative products, it may go through several pasteurization processes.

When purchasing milk, you should always look at the expiration date. These dates are intentionally conservative and, under refrigeration, pasteurized milk will normally keep for about a week after purchase. It should be refrigerated as soon as possible because its storage life is greatly reduced when left out at room temperature for more than 30 minutes.

Homogenization

If left undisturbed raw milk will naturally separate into two distinct layers: The fat globules, which are less dense, will float to the top forming a layer of cream, and the remaining skim milk will remain on the bottom. After pasteurization, the milk is processed in order to prevent these layers from forming. The milk is pressed through miniscule tubes at high pressure, which breaks the fat into such small globules that it is prevented from clustering back together and floating to the top. This process is called homogenization.

Types of Milk

Raw Milk

Raw milk is milk that is unpasteurized. Vitamins and enzymes that would normally be removed during the pasteurization process remain. Outlets that are certified to sell raw milk must adhere to strict guidelines, respect hygiene standards, and have their livestock inspected regularly. Raw milk acquired from unlicensed farms may contain contaminants that are harmful to both children and adults.

HTST Pasteurization

HTST stands for *high temperature, short time*. In this method of pasteurization, the milk is heated to a temperature between 162° and 171°F (72° to 77°C) for 15 seconds. The milk is then rapidly cooled to 39°F (4°C). HTST milk has a characteristic cooked flavor. It can be stored refrigerated for 2 to 3 weeks.

UHT Pasteurization

UHT stands for *ultra-high temperature*. This method of pasteurization depletes the vitamin and mineral count of milk even more than the standard pasteurization processe. In UHT pasteurization, milk is heated instantly from between 265° and 300°F (130° to 150°C) for 1 to 3 seconds before being flash chilled to under 39°F (4°C). Most often packaged in aseptic boxes, UHT milk can be stored up to 6 months without refrigeration. Once opened, it can last several weeks in the refrigerator.

Milk Fat

Milk is made up of 87.3 percent water, 3.9 percent milk fat, and 8.8 percent nonfat solids such as proteins, lactose, minerals, acids, enzymes, gases, and vitamins.

Milk is sold at various percentages of milk fat: 3.25 percent (whole or homogenized), 2 percent, 1 percent, and skim (nonfat). Before mechanization, fresh milk was left to separate naturally, taking 12 to 24 hours. The cream was then "skimmed" from the surface and the remaining milk was referred to as the skim. Today, dairies use centrifugal cream separators to save time. The cream is then packaged or used to make butter or it is added back to the skimmed milk to achieve the desired milk fat percentages. Milk with 3.25 percent milk fat is often referred to as whole milk because practically almost all of the natural milk fat is present. It is also called homogenized, referring to the process to keep the milk from separating.

Concentrated Dairy Products

Evaporated Milk

Evaporated milk is a canned product in which 60 percent of the water has been removed from whole milk. The process of evaporation, sterilization, and canning produces a slightly thicker milk with a light brown color.

It was created more than 100 years ago as a substitute for fresh milk and allowed for the transport and storage of milk without refrigeration. It can be consumed like regular milk by adding an equal amount of water. Evaporated milk can be stored for up to 1 year.

Sweetened Condensed Milk

While evaporated milk uses sterilization to extend its shelf life, sweetened condensed milk uses sugar. Sugar can be added before or after evaporation, but the final product should be 45 percent sugar. Like evaporated milk, it was created as a canned milk substitute for regions that did not have access to dairies. Due to the high concentration of sugar, condensed milk can be stored for up to 2 years without refrigeration.

People often confuse condensed and evaporated milk, but they have different properties and, thus, different uses. In the United States, evaporated milk does not contain any sugar, whereas evaporated milk produced elsewhere may have some sugar added. Due to the sugar content of condensed milk, recipes calling for it will take this into account. Always use the type of milk called for to ensure your recipe achieves the desired sweetness.

Milk Powder

The use of dried milk is cited by Marco Polo during the 13th century, but the commercial production of milk powder dates back to the mid-1800s. After pasteurization, the milk is sprayed into a heated container where its water immediately evaporates, leaving a fine powder. In this process the milk is exposed to heat much higher than that of normal pasteurization and not only kills any pathogens, but also eliminates the enzyme that would cause the milk fat to become rancid.

After being rendered into powder form, it is packaged to protect it from moisture, air, and light. It can be stored up to 6 months at room temperature. Depending on the process used for drying, milk powder is used commercially in the preparation of baby formula, candy, and baked goods. It is also used for international food aid, because it is easy to transport and store and is considered a nonperishable item.

Fermented Dairy Products

Buttermilk

Buttermilk does not contain butter as the name implies, but refers to the liquid remaining after churning. Traditionally, the liquid was strained and left to ferment, giving it a thicker texture and slightly sour taste. It was in fact much lower in fat than other milks. Commercial buttermilk is made by adding lactic acid bacteria to 1 percent or skim milk that is left to ferment at a low temperature for 12 to 14 hours. This is called cultured buttermilk and is sold salted or unsalted.

Yogurt

Yogurt is milk that has been allowed to ferment until thick and slightly acidic in flavor. The word has Turkish origins and roughly translated means "thick" and would have originally been applied to goat's milk. Today, yogurt is made by introducing live bacteria, *Lactobacillus bulgaricus* and *Streptococcus thermophilus*. These bacteria are most often used together to convert the natural sugars into lactic acid. The increased acid causes the milk to thicken and take on a tart flavor.

Consumed by different cultures for centuries, yogurt gained popularity in Europe at the turn of the 20th century. In the commercial production of yogurt,

Fermentation versus Spoilage

Fermentation is not to be confused with spoilage. The difference is between the work of good bacteria and of bad bacteria. Fermentation takes place under very controlled circumstances. The presence of bacteria that converts lactose into lactic acid naturally results in a thickened milk product with a distinct tanginess. Milk that has spoiled due to poor storage or age may exhibit the same thickened appearance, but it will not provide the same gustatory or olfactory pleasure as a serving of yogurt or cheese. In fact, it may result in fever, vomiting, diarrhea, or abdominal pain. The process of pasteurization often removes both good and bad bacteria, thus requiring the reintroduction of the desirable bacteria to ferment the milk. Fermentation not only thickens the milk product, it impedes spoilage as well.

milk is first separated in order to achieve the desired milk fat content. Next, it is pasteurized at higher temperatures or for a long period of time in order to kill any pathogens and to encourage the coagulation of the whey proteins. Then it is homogenized and cooled before cultures are added. Finally, it is left to ferment for 4 to 6 hours at 43°C (109°F) before it is stirred and cooled to stop the fermentation process. At this point it is flavored and packaged. Most commercial yogurts in North America have gelatin or pectin added for thickness.

The recent introduction of *L. acidophilus bifidus* in yogurt has become quite popular because it is considered to assist in maintaining a healthy digestive system. Those who are slightly lactose tolerant can consume yogurt with little or no discomfort due to the reduction of lactose in the product.

L. acidophilus bifidus is a naturally occurring bacteria within the digestive tract that maintains the natural balance of the intestinal wall to aid in digestion and stave off illness.

Cream

Once the milk has been separated, the milk fat is removed and sold separately as cream. Treated in the same manner as milk, cream is pasteurized and packaged for a longer shelf-life. The fat content of cream will vary depending on its intended use and its country of origin.

Crème Fraîche

Crème fraîche is a fermented cream that is thick and slightly tart tasting. In France, where it originated, it is made from unpasteurized heavy cream that is allowed to ferment naturally. In countries where unpasteurized cream is unavailable, bacteria cultures are added to the cream to make crème fraîche. It is preferred by many for cooking in place of regular heavy cream because it will not break or become unstable. It can be used just like heavy cream in both hot and cold preparations.

Sour Cream

Sour cream is the North American counterpart to crème fraîche, however, it is lower in fat and it has a more distinctive tartness. Because it is made by adding

Table 3–2 Cream Fat Content and Uses by Country of Origin

North America	Europe	Fat content (%)	Use
Half-and-half		10.5–18	Coffee, pouring
	Crème légère	12–30	Coffee, pouring, enriching sauces, soups, etc., whipping
	Single cream	18+	Coffee, pouring
Light cream		20 (18–30)	Coffee, pouring
	Coffee cream	25	Coffee, pouring
Light whipping cream		30–36	Pouring, enriching, whipping
	Crème fraîche (fleurette or épaisse)	30–40	Pouring, enriching, whipping (if rich, spreading)
Whipping cream		35+	Pouring, enriching, whipping
Heavy whipping cream		38 (36+)	Pouring, enriching, whipping
	Double cream	48+	Spreading
	Clotted cream	55+	Spreading

Source: *On Food and Cooking,* by Harold McGee p29.

lactic acid to a mixture of cream and milk, it is not as stable as crème fraîche when heated. In a pinch, it can be used to replace crème fraîche, but it should be added at the end of cooking and served immediately, otherwise the sauce has a tendency to develop a grainy appearance.

Clotted Cream

Closely associated with England, clotted cream is also known as Devonshire or Devon cream, which is an appellation that refers to its origins in Southwest England. It is a rich, thick, and yellow cream made by gently heating whole milk in shallow pans and then allowing it to stand for up to 12 hours. The cream floats to the top in "clots," which are then skimmed off.

Butter

The origins of butter are obscure, but one can imagine that since cows have been milked, there has been butter; in fact, the oldest traces of butter making date back to 3500 BC.

The process for making butter starts by separating the cream from the skim after pasteurization. The cream is then pasteurized a second time to ensure the elimination of any remaining pathogens. It is then left to age, with or without the addition of cultures. After aging, the cream is churned, or agitated, forcing the butterfat in the cream to coagulate into grains. The buttermilk is drained off and the butter is worked until the grains form a single mass. At this point, the butter can be salted (or left unsalted) and packaged for sale.

International food standards dictate that butter must contain a minimum of 80 percent butterfat, 2 percent milk solids, and no more than 16 percent water.

Margarine

Margarine was developed in 1869 as a cheap butter substitute for the poor and for the French navy. It was originally made from beef tallow and skim milk, and was an instant hit in the dairy industry since it made use of the skim milk, which at the time was merely a by-product of butter making. Today, the beef tallow has been replaced by vegetable oils.

Cheese

The famous 18th-century gastronome Jean Brillat-Savarin once said, "A meal without cheese is like a young girl who is missing an eye." Quips such as these are meant as exaggerations . . . or are they? Like wine, cheese plays a central role in our culinary repertoire and has its share of experts, connoisseurs, and, yes, even fanatics!

Cheese also has a history that goes back 5,000 years to Central Asia and the Middle East where the basic principle of curdling milk to make cheese was already being used. Today, however, cheese making has evolved into an art and a science, employing different curdling procedures, a vast selection of edible bacterial additives, and numerous ripening or aging techniques. The variety of cheese flavors and consistencies is further expanded by the availability of different types of milk (cow's, goat's, sheep, and buffalo) as well as the particular breed and diet of each of these milk-producing ruminant mammals.

Cheese Making

Cheese is made using three basic steps, as briefly described next.

Production of Cheese Curd

The first step in the process is to acidify the milk by adding lactic acid bacteria. In the same way yogurt is processed, lactic acid bacteria transform lactose into lactic acid, which thickens the milk and prepares it for curdling. The second step is the addition of rennet. Rennet causes the casein proteins in the milk to come together and form curds. In this process the liquids in the milk separate from the solids. The solids clump together into curds and the remaining cloudy liquid is called "whey."

Concentrating the Curd

Because some residual liquid (whey) is left in the newly formed curd, the cheese can be further dried out. Depending on the cheese that is being made, some drying methods are used on their own, whereas other drying methods are used

What Is Rennet?

Up until the 19th century, the rennet used in cheese production was made from the stomach lining of a young calf. Traditional European cheeses still require the use of pure animal rennet, whereas more than 75 percent of cheese produced in the United States uses a genetically modified version based on calf genes. Vegetarians take heart! In your local health food store, you can also find cheese made with plant-based coagulants.

in conjunction with other methods. The following methods are used for concentrating curd:

1. *Draining:* The curds are left to drain in special colanders.

2. *Cutting:* The curds are cut into smaller pieces. This encourages a more profuse drainage.

3. *Spinning:* The curds are put in a spinner and drained using centrifugal force.

4. *Pressing:* The curds are put under pressure to force out the desired amount of liquid.

5. *Cooking:* The curds are heated. This has the combined effect of evaporating moisture and transforming the consistency and flavor of the finished cheese.

6. *Salting:* The freshly formed curds are salted. The addition of salt draws away moisture just as in the culinary practice of *dégorger* (see the Glossary). Salt is also a preservative and has the effect of adding its own flavor.

Although further concentration occurs through the ripening stage, this more intense period of concentration is complete when the curds have reached the desired moisture content and are put into molds or are hand shaped.

Ripening the Curd

In French this stage is called *affinage,* which refers to finishing the cheese. Some fresh cheeses like cottage cheese are ready to eat as soon as the curd is formed, whereas harder cheeses like Parmesan can take a year to come to full maturity.

Ripening methods vary depending on the cheese being produced. Some factors involved in ripening include humidity and temperature control, and the application of salt, edible molds, or specific herb combinations. There is more to ripening cheese than following recipes and set schedules; this stage depends on the cheese maker's blend of science and intuition to determine when exactly a cheese is ready for distribution.

Types of Cheese
Fresh Cheeses

Cheeses in this group are considered either unripened or slightly ripened. What makes cottage cheese an example of an unripe cheese is that it is edible as soon as it forms curds. Feta is "slightly ripened" in that it is edible within a week of forming curds. Cheeses in this category also tend to be soft and have a high water content. Some examples of fresh cheeses are mascarpone, paneer, cottage cheese, and fromage blanc.

Bloomy Rind Cheeses

What bloomy rind cheeses all have in common is a thin velvety rind encasing soft, often creamy cheese. In addition, these cheeses are all surface ripened for

When Is a Cheese Too Smelly?

In cartoons the smell of Limburger is the cause of much comedic swooning and fainting. In reality, Limburger, and other odiferous cheeses, are widely enjoyed. But how do you know when these smelly cheeses are beyond their prime? Even a faint smell of ammonia (think window cleaner) is a surefire sign that unwanted enzymes and molds are finally attacking the lactic acid that otherwise keeps the cheese from spoiling.

approximately 1 month before they are eaten. Surface ripening means that after being shaped they are sprayed with molds that flavor and ripen the cheese from the outside in. Camembert, Brie, and triple cream cheeses are all examples of bloomy rind cheeses.

Wash-Rind Cheeses

Wash-rind cheeses are semi-soft cheeses that are aged between 1 and 3 months and have their rind periodically washed in brine, beer, brandy, or wine. This process encourages desirable molds to flavor the cheese. Wash-rind cheeses tend to have a distinctive, almost musty perfume. Examples in this group include Pont l'Évêque, Livarot, a number of monastery and Trappist cheeses, caboc (a Scottish creation), and Limburger.

Blue-Veined (Persillé) Cheeses

Distinctive for their blue-green edible molds, persillé cheeses are similar to wash-rind and bloomy rind cheeses except that the molds are injected rather than cultured on the surface. The process of introducing the mold is called *needling*. Blue-veined cheeses rely specifically on *Penicillium* molds (simple bread molds), which have the ability to grow in low-oxygen zones such as at the center of a cheese. Examples of these cheeses include Roquefort, Gorgonzola, Stilton, and Cabrales.

Pressed, Uncooked Cheeses

Cheeses in this group are semi-hard and rely on the pressing method for removing liquid (whey). Depending on the desired moisture level of the cheese, more or less pressure is applied to the curds. Semi-hard cheeses are subject to less pressure than are harder cheeses. Cantal, Cheshire, Saint Nectaire, and Tommes all belong to this group.

Pressed, Cooked Cheeses

Also subject to pressing, cheeses in this group are further transformed by cooking. Emmental (known generically as Swiss) cheese, for instance, owes its distinctive holes to the gas bubbles that are formed when its bacteria are heated. Cooking also contributes to the evaporation of whey. This effect is most evident in hard cheeses like Romano and Parmesan, which are both cooked and very firmly pressed. Semi-hard cheeses in the pressed and cooked category include Gruyère, Fontina, and Asiago.

Stretched-Curd Cheeses

Stretched, kneaded, and hand formed, the cheeses in this category often have a stringy texture. This is obvious in Armenian string cheese, which can be pulled apart into tasty threads. Other stretched-curd cheeses include mozzarella, provolone, and Oaxaca.

Cheddar is also a pressed, semi-hard cheese; however, it undergoes a process called *cheddaring*. Cheddaring means that the curds are milled into pea-sized bits and stirred to remove the whey before being pressed. This process accounts for the crumbly texture most noticeable in an aged cheddar.

Processed Cheeses

In North America, processed cheese calls to mind those orange cheese-like slices that are, against all odds, pretty good in a grilled cheese sandwich. The category of processed cheeses, however, relates to a broader range of products. *La vache qui rit* (the laughing cow), for instance, is a mixture of Comté cheese, cream, flavoring, and preservatives. A number of the spreadable processed cheeses are usually based on a specific cheese (cheddar or Emmental, for instance) that has been heated and augmented with cream and various flavorings.

BASIC DOUGHS –
LES PÂTES DE BASE

What's in a word?

The French word *pâte* translates into English as both "dough" and "paste." This borrowing of language is evident when we think of the English for *pâte à choux*, which is *choux pastry*. Among the French words that will be encountered in pâtisserie are *détrempe* and *pâton*. As early as 1100 BC, the definition of the word *pâte* was *farine détrempée*, or "flour mixed with water." In modern French pastry the term *détrempe* is often used in the production of *pâte feuilletée* and *pâte à croissants* and describes the dough before the butter is added, whereas *pâton* is dough that has had its butter added and is ready to be rolled out.

The first question one might ask in trying to understand the parameters of basic doughs is: "What sets pastry dough apart from other dough preparations?" The quick answer is that "doughs" can be broken down into two flexible categories: (1) yeast-risen doughs that have relatively long gluten strands and (2) pastry doughs that have a higher fat content and shorter gluten strands. Yeast-risen doughs, prepared for various breads, are worked or kneaded to stretch out the gluten strands to form a baked product that is both elastic and tender. Pastry doughs range from "flaky" to "crumbly," textures that reflect, to one degree or another, a higher fat content, minimal mixing or kneading, and a shorter gluten strand.

In terms of the mouth feel of finished doughs, shorter gluten molecules contribute to the crumbly (or friable) texture of, for instance, a pâte sablée. A major ingredient at play in achieving this texture is fat. Depending on the mixing method of a specific dough preparation, fat can be made to surround dough particles and create different sizes of crumb. Fat also has the effect of producing and trapping humidity between layers of dough. This is evident in pâte feuilletée with its light flaky texture. Trapped humidity also helps pastry dough rise; the "puffy" quality of a finished pâte à choux is a result of this.

Pastry dough (as opposed to bread dough) is commonly defined as a preparation made with flour, fat, and water (or milk) that is formed into dough and is used as a base or an encasement for a filling. Like French grammar, however, French pâtisserie also has its exceptions. Brioche, beignets, and croissants, for example, can all be served with or without a filling. Pâte à crêpe is also exceptional in that it is not a malleable dough, but is instead a liquid batter.

The definition of pastry can be further stretched by including ingredients such as leavening agents, eggs, salt, and even beer. Basic doughs can be used for sweet and savory preparations and can be baked, boiled, deep-fried, or, as is the case with pâte à crêpe, cooked on the stovetop.

Shortcrust Pastry – *Pâte Brisée*

The word *brisée* translates into English as "broken" and refers to the friable or crumbly nature of the dough. Pâte brisée gets its texture largely from its high percentage of butter, which has the effect of limiting gluten growth. The relatively minimal mixing and kneading of the dough also contributes to its friability. Pâte brisée is used mainly as a base for tarts, pies, and quiches.

Lining Pastry – *Pâte à Foncer*

Pâte à foncer is essentially pâte brisée without the addition of eggs; it is unsweetened and is used exclusively for savory preparations that call for a drier pastry. Historically, pâte à foncer was used more often in the poorer regions of France, in the preparation of a *tourte de campagne*, for example. This heritage explains the elimination or reduction of relatively expensive ingredients such as butter and eggs in pâte à foncer.

Sweet Shortcrust Pastry – *Pâte Sucrée*

Like other doughs used as the base for tartes, pâte sucrée also has a high fat content. However, in this case the friability of the dough is increased by the addition of sugar. Because higher concentrations of sugar can make a dough fall apart, pâte sucrée compensates by adding whole eggs for structure as well as moisture. As in all pastry, a balance is struck between taste, texture, and structure.

Pâte Sucrée: Crèmer Method

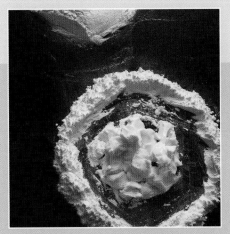

1 Place the flour and powdered sugar on the work surface. Make a large well in the powdered sugar and add the butter.

2 Work the butter with your fingertips until smooth.

3 Using the corne, begin to incorporate the sugar and butter.

(continues on next page)

Pâte Sucrée: Crèmer Method

(continued from previous page)

4 Mix the sugar into the butter until creamy.

5 Add the egg yolks and mix well. It will not be smooth.

6 Add the vanilla and mix well.

7 Mix together until completely incorporated.

8 Gradually add the flour.

9 Once the flour has been incorporated, use the corne to cut the flour into the wet ingredients.

(continues on next page)

Pâte Sucrée: Crèmer Method

(continued from previous page)

10 Cut and turn the mixture onto it-self until it begins to form a dough.

11 Once the dough forms, continue cutting the dough.

12 Eventually the white traces of the flour will disappear and the dough will hold together.

13 *Fraiser* the dough by smearing it on the work surface, using the ball of the hand. Scrape up the dough with the corne and repeat several times.

14 Form the dough into a smooth ball and wrap in plastic. Chill and rest for at least 30 minutes, or overnight.

Sabler Method

1 Make a large well in the center of the flour. Add the butter and flavoring.

2 Begin by cutting the butter into the flour and incorporating the flour into the butter with your fingertips.

3 Begin rubbing between your hands.

4 Continue to work the larger pieces with your fingertips.

4 Continue rubbing until the mixture resembles evenly colored sand.

6 Make a well in the center.

7 Add the egg and water.

8 Mix together with your fingertips.

9 Gradually incorporate the dry ingredients.

(continues on next page)

Sabler Method

(continued from previous page)

10   Continue until a paste begins to form.

11   If the dough appears dry, add a little cold water.

12   Using a corne, begin to cut in the remaining dry ingredients. This minimizes the formation of gluten.

13   Continue to gather the dough as it forms and cut it.

14   It will begin to hold together.

15   *Fraisage* is the final step and is done to ensure that the butter is fully incorporated. Using the heel of your hand, smear the dough away from you.

16   Scrape up the dough until it forms a rough ball. Wrap in plastic and allow to rest at least 30 minutes or overnight.

Lining a Tart Pan

1 Flatten the dough on a floured surface.

2 Begin rolling applying pressure evenly.

3 Lift the dough and give it a quarter turn.

4 Continue rolling evenly.

5 Continue to give the dough a quarter turn. This ensures an even shape and thickness.

6 Roll out to about 2 mm thick.

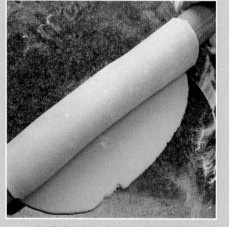

7 Roll the dough onto the rolling pin.

8 Gently drape the dough over the buttered mold.

9 Ensure that there is at least 1 to 2 inches of dough extending over the edge of the mold.

(continues on next page)

Lining a Tart Pan

(continued from previous page)

10 Lift the dough and lightly press into the corners of the mold.

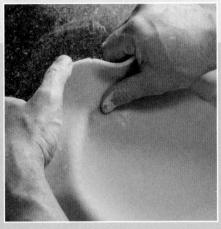

11 Press well to ensure there isn't any air.

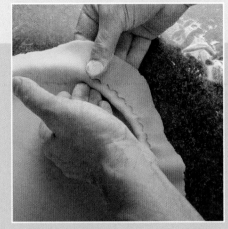

12 Lift the dough and make a small fold toward the inner edge.

13 Roll the rolling pin over to cut any excess dough and reserve the scraps for another use.

14 Pinch the dough between the thumb and forefinger.

15 Create a rim that extends about 1/8 inch above the edge of the mold.

16 Supporting the inner edge with one hand, use the pastry tweezers and lightly pinch to form a decorative border.

17 Once finished, run a finger around the edge to make sure the border is straight.

18 Prick the bottom with a fork and refrigerate the tart base for at least 30 minutes.

(continues on next page)

Lining a Tart Pan

(continued from previous page)

19 After resting, remove the tart base and make a cartouche out of parchment paper, measuring from the center of the mold to about 1 inch beyond the edge.

20 Unfold the cartouche and press it into the corners of the mold.

21 Fill the mold with baking beads and place in a preheated oven.

22 Once the edges are nicely browned, remove the beads by lifting the paper. Be careful, the beads are hot.

23 Prebaked

Pâte Sablée – Shortbread Pastry

In the same family as pâte sucrée, pâte sablée is a degree more friable, and, due to the inclusion of baking powder, slightly lighter and easier to break with the teeth. This texture makes it function on its own (for instance, as shortbread biscuits) or as a base for petits fours. The word *sablée* translates as "sandy," which refers to the sandy texture of the flour once the fat is rubbed into it (*sablage*).

Pâte à Choux – Choux Pastry

In terms of method and chemical process, pâte à choux is a bit of a maverick. Because the flour is added directly to a solution of boiling milk, or water, and melted butter, the fat element is dispersed evenly throughout the flour particles. Not unlike laminated pastry (such as pâte feuilletée; see next entry), pâte à choux rises when trapped humidity expands as it turns to steam. The high proportion of egg in the preparation stabilizes and binds it. Éclairs, religieuses, gâteau St. Honoré, and Paris-Brest are all examples of how pâte à choux is used.

Pâte à Choux

1 Heat the liquid in a saucepan with the butter and seasoning.

2 Just as it comes to a boil, add the flour all at once.

3 Stir vigorously over the heat.

4 Once the dough comes cleanly away from the sides of the pan, remove from the heat.

5 Continue stirring until the dough forms a smooth ball.

6 Transfer to a bowl.

(continues on next page)

Pâte à Choux

(continued from previous page)

7 Incorporate the eggs a few at a time.

8 Mix well.

9 Make sure the eggs are well incorporated before adding more.

10 Once most of the eggs are incorporated, check the texture before adding more.

11 Dough should be soft and elastic.

Pâte Feuilletée – Puff Pastry

Of all the pastry doughs, pâte feuilletée wins the prize for the most laborious (and perhaps the most satisfying) methodology. This is a laminated pastry in which layers of butter (*beurrage*) are sandwiched between layers of détrempe (a dough mixture made of water, flour, salt, and vinegar). This is achieved by successively folding and rolling out the beurrage and détrempe.

When pâte feuilletée is baked, the butter melts and releases humidity in the form of steam that is then trapped between the layers of détrempe. This causes the dough to rise and develop its characteristic flaky quality. Millefeuille, palmier, and the savory *vol-au-vent* are examples of preparations that use pâte feuilletée.

Détrempe

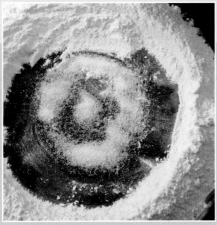

1 After incorporating the butter into the flour, make a large well in the center and add the salt. Add some of the water and mix until dissolved.

2 Begin to incorporate the flour into the water.

3 Using the corne, combine mixing and cutting to incorporate the remaining flour.

4 Once a dough begins to form, continue cutting. If the dough appears dry, add additional cold water.

5 The dough should hold together loosely.

(continues on next page)

Détrempe

(continued from previous page)

6   Cut until there are barely any traces of flour left.

7   Form into a coarse ball.

8   Using a large knife, score the top of the dough with a cross.

9   Cut deep enough that it opens slightly.

10   Wrap loosely in plastic and allow to rest at least 30 minutes.

Pâte Feuilletée Tourage

1   The détrempe will be rolled out in the shape of a cross, the center being large enough to accommodate the butter.

2   Place the détrempe on the floured surface.

3   Starting with one of the corners, roll outward leaving the center thick.

4   Continue with the other corner.

5   Leave the center thicker than the outer arms of the cross.

6   Place the square of butter in the middle.

7   Fold the opposite sides over, then turn.

8   Fold the other two sides like an envelope, pressing well to seal the butter in.

9   Lightly tap the dough to even.

(continues on next page)

Pâte Feuilletée Tourage

(continued from previous page)

10 Turn and repeat the same process. Tap the sides with the length of the rolling pin to keep a straight edge.

11 Measure out twice the length of the dough.

12 Begin rolling out the dough using even strokes. Roll only up and down.

13 Once the proper length, brush off any excess flour.

14 Fold the top third down, and brush off excess flour.

15 Fold the bottom third over the first fold.

16 Give the folded dough a quarter turn to the right.

17 Repeat the same rolling as before.

18 Roll the dough out to form a 1 cm thick rectangle.

(continues on next page)

Pâte Feuilletée Tourage

(continued from previous page)

19 Fold in thirds again and give it a quarter turn to the right.

20 Mark the dough with two fingers.

21 The two indentations indicate that two turns have been made to the dough. It can now be placed in the refrigerator to rest until the next two turns.

Bande Tarte

1   Roll the dough out to 3 mm in thickness and trim off rounded edges.

2   Using a corne as a guide, cut a long strip.

3   Lay the strip onto an ungreased baking sheet.

4   Allow the dough to hang over both edges of the baking sheet.

5   Fold the remaining dough in half, and then in half again. Do not press.

6   Firmly cut the folded dough into 2.5-cm-wide strips.

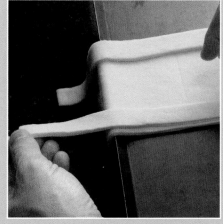

7   Brush the outer edges of the band with egg wash.

8   Unfold the strips on top of the egg wash, lining the edges up evenly.

9   Allow the strips to hang over as well.

(continues on next page)

Bande Tarte

(continued from previous page)

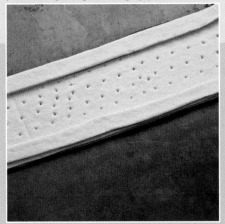

10 Prick the bottom.

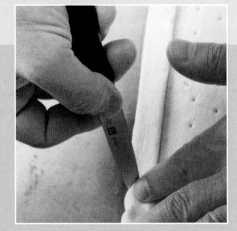

11 *Chiqueter* the outer edge using the back of a small knife.

12 Lift the baking sheet and with one stroke, trim the overhang even with the edge of the baking sheet.

13 Brush the raised edges with egg wash.

14 The bande is ready to be filled and baked.

Bouchées et Fleurons

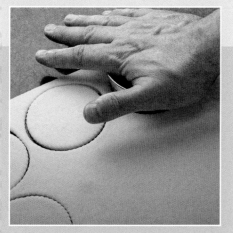

1 Bouchées: Cut an even number of small rounds.

2 Cut rings using a smaller cutter from half of the rounds.

3 Place the whole rounds on an un-greased baking sheet.

4 Brush rounds with egg wash.

5 Carefully place a ring on top of each round.

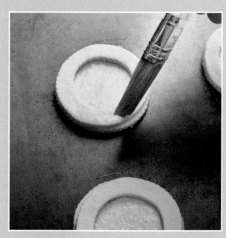

6 Brush the edges with egg wash.

7 Score inside of the rings using the tip of a small knife.

8 Repeat with the remaining rounds and rings.

9 Using metal ring molds of equal height, place one in each corner of the baking sheet and cover with a wire rack. This will ensure that the bouchées will be even.

(continues on next page)

Bouchées et Fleurons

(continued from previous page)

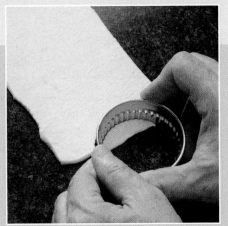

10   Fleurons: Start by cutting a half circle. Reserve the scraps for other uses.

11   Continue to cut half circles.

12   Try to make them of equal size. Arrange them on a clean baking sheet.

13   Brush with egg wash.

14   Score with a criss-cross pattern with the tip of a small knife. They are now ready for baking.

Vol-au-Vent

1   Assemble the equipment needed.

2   Lay the larger round on the dough.

3   Use the tip of a sharp knife and cut cleanly around the circle.

4   Repeat, cutting out three large rounds of the same size.

5   Place a smaller round in the center.

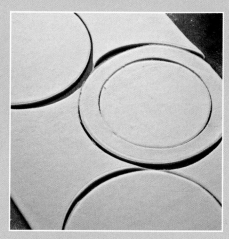

6   Cut cleanly around.

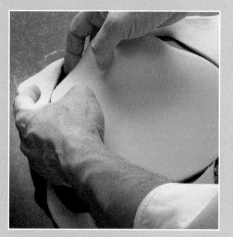

7   Lift a large circle and transfer to a clean baking sheet.

8   Brush the surface with water.

9   Lift the second round and carefully place on top of the first round.

(continues on next page)

Vol-au-Vent

(continued from previous page)

10 Make sure that the edges are even.

11 Smooth out any air bubbles.

12 Brush the edges with water.

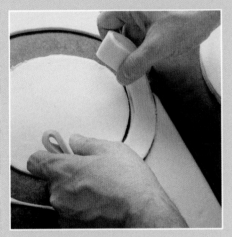

13 Fold in half and carefully lift up the ring of dough.

14 Lay on top of the stack.

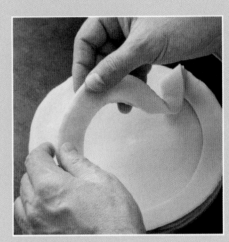

15 Be careful not to stretch the dough.

16 Make sure the edges are even.

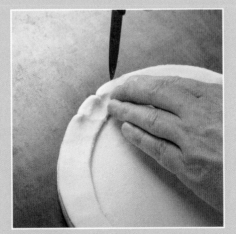

17 *Chiqueter* the edges using the back of a small knife. Push the back edge of the knife at an angle into the dough.

18 Continue all the way around.

(continues on next page)

Vol-au-Vent

(continued from previous page)

19   Press well against the edges.

20   The result should be an even scalloped edge.

21   Brush raised edge with egg wash.

22   Brush the center with egg wash.

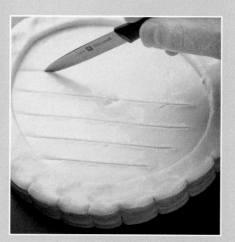

23   With the tip of a small knife, score across the top.

24   Turn, and score in the opposite direction.

25   Using a toothpick, pierce the dough at the inner points of the edge.

26   Once finished, the vol-au-vent is ready for baking.

Pâte Levée – Risen Dough

Doughs included under the heading of pâte levée (yeast doughs) are as numerous as there are different styles of yeast breads, pizza doughs, savarins, and viennoiseries. Within this group, textures ranging from the density of pumpernickel bread to the air-filled and buttery characteristics of a croissant can be found. *Pissaladière* (recipe featured in *Classic Recipes*) and *tarte au sucre* (recipe featured in *Classic Recipes*) are, respectively, examples of savory and sweet pâte levée preparations.

Pâte à Croissant – Croissant Pastry

The risen and bready consistency of this viennoiserie is why it is referred to as a pastry–bread hybrid. It is a type of pâte levée and is, therefore, yeast risen. Aside from differences in ingredients, pâte à croissant uses the same fundamental methodology as pâte feuilletée. The folding and rolling of *détrempe* and *beurrage* are identical, which is why a croissant is considered a laminated pastry.

　　The finished pastry is a traditional French breakfast food that is often eaten plain but can be filled with almond paste, chocolate, or, less frequently, with savory fillings such as ham, cheese, or mushrooms.

Pâte à Brioche – Brioche Pastry

Pâte à brioche is another viennoiserie that is a type of pâte levée and, therefore, falls into the category of pastry–bread hybrid. Like pâte à croissant, pâte à brioche is a yeast dough but it differs from its cousin in fundamental ways: Unlike croissants, brioche is not laminated and it has a finished texture that can be described as being slightly more resistant than that of a croissant—a resistance or "plasticity" that is due mainly to the coagulation of egg proteins and the binding of flour proteins. Brioches come in a variety of shapes with or without fillings. *Brioche à tête, brioche coulante,* and braided brioche are examples of this diversity.

Brioche

1　Lightly dust the work surface with flour.

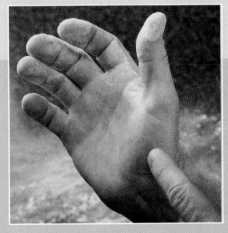

2　You will be using the meaty portion of your hand.

3　Flatten the rested dough on the work surface.

(continues on next page)

Brioche

(continued from previous page)

4   Fold the upper third down onto itself.

5   Using the lower portion of your hand, press and seal. Turn around and repeat.

6   Press well to seal.

7   Roll the dough into an even cylinder.

8   Fold in half and score at the midpoint.

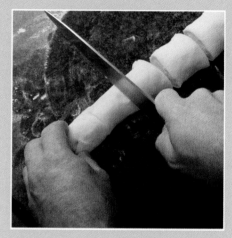

9   Cut in half, and score each half into even-sized pieces. Cut.

10   Dip a piece into some flour.

11   Cup your hand around the dough and move the dough in a circular motion.

12   Continue until the dough is smooth and tight.

(continues on next page)

Brioche

(continued from previous page)

13 Then roll each ball back and forth.

14 Continue rolling the other balls into oblongs.

15 Dip the side of your hand in flour.

16 Hold the oblong with the other hand, roll the floured hand about one-third down from the end.

17 Continue rolling until the dough resembles a bowling pin.

18 Repeat with remaining dough.

19 Dip the tips of your thumb, index, and middle fingers in flour.

20 Take the dough and hold it by its "head."

21 Place the dough in the buttered mold.

(continues on next page)

Brioche

(continued from previous page)

22 Press the head into the "body" of the dough.

23 Carefully remove your fingers.

24 Flour your index finger, and press it in between the head and the body.

25 Press down deeply.

26 Ensure that the heads are secure.

27 To make large brioche. Remove one-fouth of the dough and set aside. Flatten the larger piece of dough into a disk.

28 Take an edge and fold it into the middle of the round.

29 Press and seal with the meaty part of your hand.

30 Turn the dough and continue all the way around.

(continues on next page)

Brioche

(continued from previous page)

31 Turn the dough over.

32 Cup your hands around the dough, and roll it in a circular motion on the work surface.

33 Make a depression in the center.

34 Place the dough in the buttered mold.

35 Cup your hand around the smaller piece, and roll it in a circular motion on the work surface until smooth and tight.

36 Roll back and forth at one end of the ball.

37 The dough should be in the shape of a teardrop.

38 With fingers dipped in flour, hold the larger end of the teardrop and press your fingers deeply into the center of the dough.

39 Dip a finger in flour, and press it in between the "head" and "body" of the brioche.

(continues on next page)

Brioche

(continued from previous page)

40 Be sure to press all the way to the bottom all the way around.

41 To make a braid, measure out three pieces of dough of the same weight.

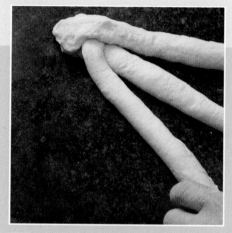

42 Attach the three pieces at one end. Pieces 1, 2, and 3.

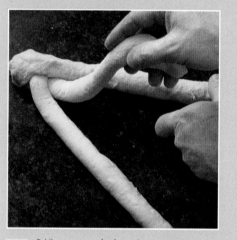

43 Lift up 2 and place it over 3.

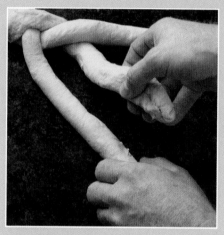

44 Then lift 3 and place it over 1.

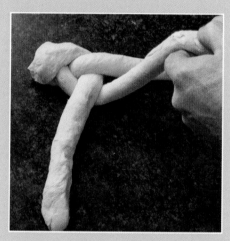

45 Lift 1 and place over 2.

46 Continue with the pattern until the end, then tuck the ends in underneath.

47 Allow to rise in a warm place, then brush with egg wash before baking.

Pâte à Crêpe – Crêpe Batter

Composed of flour, milk, and butter, pâtes à crêpe share basic ingredients with other pastry mixtures. On a chemical level, however, the pâte à crêpe comes by its tender texture in a process that is exclusive to thin-batter preparations. The tenderness of a crêpe is mainly due to the high ratio of liquid that keeps the flour gluten dispersed and unable to form bonds. Furthermore, the crêpe does not get its structure from flour proteins, but rather from the starches that stick together once they have been saturated with milk. The coagulation of egg protein also contributes to this structure.

Although crêpes are distinct in that they are cooked on a stovetop, they have a place in the pastry repertoire as a casement for both sweet and savory ingredients.

Pâte à Crêpe

1 Savory crêpes with herbs.

2 Sweet crêpes with vanilla, lemon, and chopped mint.

3 Equipment needed includes a crêpe pan and small ladle for measuring out the correct amount of batter.

4 Sift the flour into a bowl and make a well in the center. Add sugar or salt according to whether you are making sweet or savory crêpes. Add the eggs.

5 Whisk the eggs, while gradually incorporating the flour.

6 When half the flour is incorporated, add the melted butter.

(continues on next page)

Pâte à Crêpe

(continued from previous page)

7 Stir well until smooth.

8 For sweet crêpes: split a vanilla bean lengthwise.

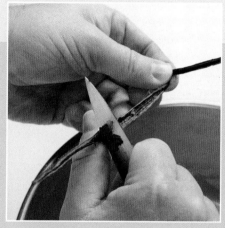

9 Scrape out the interior seeds.

10 Add to the batter with any other flavorings. For sweet crepes pictured here, we have added the zests and chopped mint.

11 Gradually incorporate the milk.

12 Allow to rest at least one hour before using. The batter can be prepared a day ahead of time.

13 Preheat a crêpe pan and brush with melted butter.

14 Pour a ladleful of batter in the center of the pan.

15 Turn the pan so the batter spreads evenly.

(continues on next page)

Pâte à Crêpe

(continued from previous page)

16 Place on the heat to cook.

17 When the edges begin to brown, slip a spatula beneath and flip over.

18 Cook the other side for about 30 seconds, then transfer to a plate.

19 Crêpes can be served folded in half or in quarters or rolled with or without filling.

Pâte à Beignet – Fritter Batter

Pâte à beignet is leavened batter used specifically for deep-frying. Among some standard dough ingredients such as milk, flour, butter, salt, and egg whites, beer is also an active ingredient. The yeast and the beer add to the "puffy" quality of this dough. In recipes such as *beignets de pommes* (recipe featured in *Classic Recipes*), pâte à beignet provides a watertight pastry casement that seals in the juices of the product.

Pâte à Beignet

1 This batter is leavened with baking powder.

2 Mix all of the dry ingredients in a large bowl and stir in the water.

3 Continue mixing until smooth.

4 Add the oil and mix well.

5 The batter should be fairly thick.

6 This batter is leavened with yeast.

7 Mix all the dry ingredients together including the yeast. Add the eggs.

8 Gradually incorporate the flour into the eggs.

9 When a dough begins to form, begin to add the cider or beer.

(continues on next page)

Pâte à Beignet

(continued from previous page)

10   Continue mixing until homogenous.

11   Beat the egg whites to stiff peaks.

12   Fold the egg whites into the batter.

13   Add the melted butter.

14   Pâte à Beignet

Pâte à Savarin – Savarin Pastry

This yeast risen dough is designed specifically for savarin pastry, which is served soaked in rum syrup. To be effective for this purpose, the baked dough must be both porous enough to take in the syrup (*imbibage*) and firm enough to not get soggy. Its high egg-to-flour ratio is what gives this preparation the ideal structure.

Pâte à Pâtes – Pasta Dough

Knowing that the French term for pasta is *pâtes alimentaires* should help to clarify the potentially confusing sound of *pâte à pâtes* (which simply means "pasta dough"). This dough is almost always boiled in water and served in an exclusively savory context. For those who might not have considered pasta a pastry dough, in terms of ingredients (flour, water, fat [olive oil], and eggs) and purpose (it can be used on its own or as a casement for a filling), pasta dough can be defined as pastry.

Pâte à pâtes is incredibly versatile in terms of its shapes and uses. The neutrality of flavor in the dough and its workable consistency make it the perfect vehicle for a wide range of sauces and fillings.

Pâte à Pâtes

1   Prepare the ingredients.

2   Place the flour on the work surface and make a well in the center and add the salt. Beat the eggs and oil together.

3   Pour the eggs into the well and, using your fingertips, gradually begin incorporating the flour.

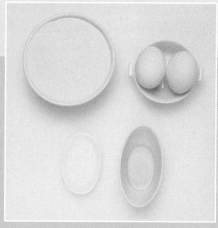

4   Use the corne or a dough cutter to help form the dough.

5   Add a little cold water at a time until the dough just begins to hold together.

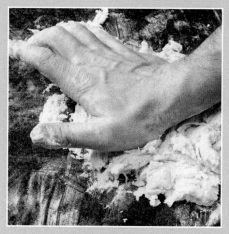

6   Using the heel of your hand, begin kneading the dough, adding more water if needed. It should be a fairly hard, tight dough.

(continues on next page)

Pâte à Pâtes

(continued from previous page)

7   Continue kneading until the dough is smooth. It should not be sticky. If it is, add a little flour.

8   Once the dough has formed, wrap tightly in plastic wrap and allow to rest before rolling out.

LES BISCUITS – BASIC MIXTURES

The term *biscuit* translates as "twice" (*bis*) "cooked" (*cuit*). Originally, it described a dough that was dried by baking it a second time. In modern terms, biscuit describes a variety of preparations, but no longer requires the second cooking time. The English use of the term biscuit tends to be specific, but its meaning varies between different English-speaking countries; depending on the country, cookies, sponge cake, and crackers may be described as biscuits. In French cooking, or more specifically, pâtisserie, the term *biscuit* covers all of the above, but is used primarily for sweet preparations.

Biscuit Cuillère – Ladyfinger

Cuillère is French for spoon, referring to how this biscuit or sponge was originally spooned out prior to baking. Somewhat akin to the North American drop cookie, it is a soft, light, and spongy preparation that relies on the air in beaten egg whites as a leavening agent. Today, biscuit cuillère are referred to in English as ladyfinger biscuits, because they are often piped out in short, narrow shapes. The mixture lends itself well to being piped in decorative swirls and shapes and is an easy sponge to handle. It is used in preparing Bavarian creams (charlotte aux poires) and other cakes and pastries.

The earliest form of biscuit-like preparations dates back to Roman times when a dry pastry that kept well was used as a provision for Roman soldiers.

Biscuit Cuillère

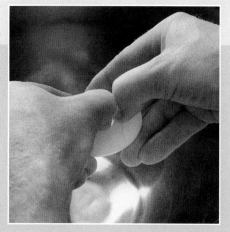

1   Separate the eggs.

2   Carefully pass the yolk from one shell to the other.

3   Be sure not to break the egg yolk as this can inhibit the development of the whites when beaten.

4   Wipe off the egg with a fingertip and transfer the yolk to another bowl.

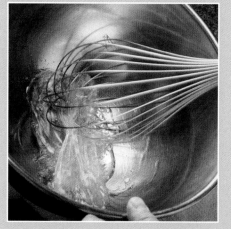

5   Vigorously beat the egg whites using a balloon whisk.

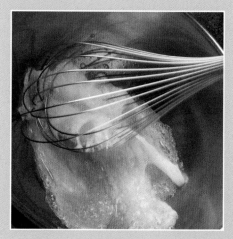

6   Beat until frothy.

7   Set aside.

8   Add the sugar to the egg yolks.

9   Begin whisking immediately.

(continues on next page)

Biscuit Cuillère

(continued from previous page)

10 Continue whisking until thick and light yellow in color.

11 Finish whisking the egg whites to soft peaks.

12 Gradually beat in the sugar.

13 Once all the sugar has been added, continue beating until stiff and glossy.

14 Add one-third of the sifted flour to the egg yolks.

15 Fold in with a rubber spatula.

16 When just about incorporated, add one-third of the meringue.

17 Fold in until just incorporated, you should still be able to see streaks of egg white.

18 Add the remaining egg whites.

(continues on next page)

Biscuit Cuillère

(continued from previous page)

19   Fold in the meringue gently.

20   The batter is ready for piping and/or baking.

Biscuit Dacquoise

The origins of dacquoise can be traced to the town of Dax in southwestern France (its inhabitants are known as *dacquois*). It is a meringue-based pastry in which ground almonds and sugar have been incorporated into an uncooked meringue. It can be baked in a mold or piped in different shapes. The result is a pastry that is light and crunchy on the surface, with a tender, slightly chewy center. It is used as a base for mousse cakes or for layering with butter cream (gâteau succès).

Biscuit Génoise – Genoese Sponge

Biscuit génoise literally translated means "Genoa cake" so one can assume that its origins are from Genoa, a port city in Italy. The modern génoise is made from whole eggs beaten with sugar over a bain marie to the ribbon stage (122° to 131°F [50° to 55°C]). The dry ingredients are then folded in along with melted butter. According to Pierre Lacam, the process of heating the eggs was introduced in 1850. Before that time, Carême made a cake similar to the génoise using whole eggs, but was reliant on beaten egg whites to leaven the cake. In *Le memorial de la pâtisserie*, Lacam implies that a sort of génoise that was beaten without heat existed before 1850.

Biscuit Génoise

1   Prepare a bain marie.

2   Place the eggs in a large bowl and add the sugar.

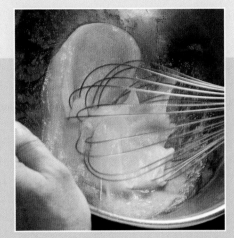

3   Whisk with a balloon whisk.

4   Place over the bain marie and continue whisking until hot to the touch.

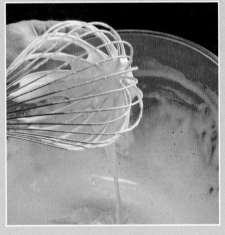

5   Remove from the bain marie and continue whisking until cooled. The mixture will be thick and light yellow in color.

6   Gradually fold in the sifted dry ingredients.

7   Fold until just incorporated.

8   Mixture should remain thick and light.

9   Spoon into the prepared mold being careful not to work the batter too much.

(continues on next page)

Biscuit Génoise

(continued from previous page)

10 Bake until golden and the top springs back when pressed and the surface feels dry.

11 Allow to cool a few minutes, before unmolding.

12 Allow to finish cooling on a wire rack.

CRÈMES, MERINGUES, AND OTHER FINISHINGS

The word *crème* (cream) is used in so many ways in classic French cuisine that it can cause confusion, particularly if you are new to the terminology. As is evident in the section on dairy, crème refers to a number of dairy products (everything from clotted cream to crème fraîche). Crème can refer to soups (crème de potage) and even to alcoholic beverages like crème de menthe. The term *les crèmes* also refers to a number of preparations that share a similar creamy texture and are almost exclusively used in pâtisserie. It is to these that we will now turn our attention.

Les crèmes range from stirred (like crème Anglaise), which are pourable, to baked (like crème caramel), which are firm and gelatinous. The consistency of these egg/milk crèmes can be understood as a continuum in terms of the degree to which the egg coagulates and binds the preparation. The longer an egg/milk mixture is cooked and the higher the temperature to which it is exposed, the more it will coagulate and the firmer it will be. The lower the temperature and the sooner the coagulation process is halted, the thinner the mixture will be (see the Coagulation entry in the Eggs section, p. 244). An aspect to consider in this process is that whole eggs and egg whites coagulate at a lower temperature than do egg yolks. Crème Anglaise, for example, is made with egg yolks, which help the crème retain its liquid form. Conversely, crème caramel uses both the whites and the yolks, which help the crème (along with baking) set to a firmer consistency.

Another consistency in the continuum can be found in crème pâtissière, which is neither set nor pourable. The addition of flour or cornstarch to what is essentially a crème Anglaise has the effect of adding body while, at the same time, allowing the mixture to be brought to higher temperatures without coagulating.

Within the category of les crèmes are some preparations that are not egg/milk preparations, but share similarities in consistency. These are brought to a similar consistency by the incorporation of air into either cream or egg whites.

In trying to understand les crèmes as a whole it is perhaps best to consider that the original meaning of the word *crème* (in old French, *cresme*) simply meant to "blend." The word subsequently came to be understood as the part of milk that rises to the surface (that is, cream). The following preparations all share, to one degree or another, the action of creaming in the old sense of the term (that is, some form of blending, stirring, or whipping) and, likewise, they all share similarities with the new sense of the term *cream* in that they have a creamy texture.

Baked Creams

Baked creams (also known as set custard creams) are egg/milk preparations that are first cooked on the stove top and then baked until set. Although they share elements of method and ingredients with pourable creams, baked creams do not accompany other desserts but are instead desserts unto themselves. Crème brûlée, crème renversée au caramel, and flan are all examples of baked creams that have their own particular recipes.

Crème Anglaise

Crème Anglaise is a cream sauce (also known as a pouring custard) that is made with egg yolks, milk, and sugar. Although vanilla bean is most commonly infused in this sauce, crème Anglaise is suited to a number of other flavorings as well. Served hot or cold with various desserts, crème Anglaise is also the foundation for many preparations, including ice creams, Bavarian creams (*bavarois*), and baked custards.

Crème Anglaise

1 Add sugar to the egg yolks.

2 Whisk immediately until the yolks begin to lighten in color.

3 Add some of the hot milk to temper.

(continues on next page)

Crème Anglaise

(continued from previous page)

4 Whisk well.

5 Add the tempered yolks back into the remaining hot milk.

6 Stir with a wooden spatula over low heat. The mixture should be foamy on the surface.

7 As the crème cooks, the foam will begin to disappear and the liquid will begin to move like oil.

8 Keep cooking until it coats the back of a spoon, and when you run a finger through it, it leaves a trail. Remove from the heat immediately and strain into a clean recipient.

Buttercream – *Crème au Beurre*

Crème au beurre can be made using three different methods: (1) with butter incorporated into a pâte à bombe base (syrup cooked to the softball stage that is added to egg yolks), (2) with butter incorporated into cooked meringue (Italian or Swiss), and (3) with butter incorporated into a base of crème Anglaise. The defining feature of these preparations—if it isn't abundantly clear already!—is the supremacy of butter. Used as a filling between layers of a cake or as an icing, crème au beurre is often flavored with chocolate, coffee, or pralines.

Crème au Beurre

1   Place the sugar syrup on the heat to cook.

2   Whisk the remaining sugar into the egg yolks until light yellow in color.

3   When the sugar reaches the soft-ball stage, gradually incorporate the hot syrup into the egg yolks.

4   Continue whisking, until the mixture has cooled.

5   The mixture should be light yellow in color and flow smoothly from the whisk.

6   Begin incorporating the butter.

7   The mixture will first appear curdled, but continue whisking.

8   Once the butter is incorporated and is aerated, the crème will be smooth and glossy. For a whiter crème au beurre, continue beating.

Masquage

1   Place the cake on a cake board and trim off the excess.

2   Start with the sides.

3   Hold the palette knife at a narrow angle and follow the contour of the cake.

4   Continue all the way around.

5   Place a mound of buttercream on top.

6   Spread evenly to cover the top.

7   Allow the excess frosting to extend over the edges.

8   With the palette at a shallow angle, move it toward you.

9   Switch the angle of the palette knife and move it away, maintaining even pressure.

(continues on next page)

Masquage

(continued from previous page)

10 Once smooth, lift the cake and remove the excess buttercream.

11 Move the palette around and down at the same time.

12 Continue around the cake.

13 Place the masked cake onto another cake board, or plate.

14 Allow to drop onto the cake board.

15 The cake is now ready to be decorated.

Whipped Cream – *Crème Chantilly*

Crème Chantilly is a basic crème in terms of ingredients and method. In this preparation, cream with at least a 30 percent fat content is whipped, sweetened, and flavored with vanilla. Unlike egg/milk mixtures that are stabilized by linking proteins (coagulation), crème Chantilly owes its texture to the incorporation of air. In this process the action of the whisk does two things: (1) It adds air to the cream and (2) it breaks down the fat globules which in turn trap the air bubbles and stabilize the cream.

Chantilly accompanies desserts such as charlottes and bavaroises and goes particularly well with strawberries and raspberries. The phrase "à la Chantilly" refers to preparations in which sweetened whipped cream is an element.

Crème Chantilly

1 Place the cream in a round-bottomed bowl set in ice.

2 Whisk in a circular motion following the contours of the bowl.

3 Beat to soft peaks.

4 Add sugar based on what you are using the crème Chantilly for.

5 Mix in the sugar then continue beating to stiff peaks. Keep chilled until ready to use.

Almond Cream – *Crème d'Amande*

Crème d'amande is made with equal quantities of butter, sugar, almond powder, and eggs. Flour is sometimes added to make the crème firmer, and vanilla extract or rum may be used as a flavoring. Crème d'amande is the traditional filling for Pithiviers, and can be found in croissants and tartes amandines.

Crème d'Amande

1 Whisk the butter and sugar together.

2 Whisk until fluffy and light in color.

3 Split the vanilla beans lengthwise and scrape out the seeds.

4 Stir the vanilla seeds into the sugar and butter mixture.

5 Add one-third of the almond powder and one-third of the egg. Whisk well.

6 Continue adding the almond powder and egg in two more increments, stirring well after each addition.

7 Add the rum and stir well.

8 The final crème should be smooth and creamy in appearance.

Crème Frangipane

Crème Frangipane is made by mixing two-thirds crème d'amande with one-third crème pâtissière. It is the traditional filling for galette des rois but can also be used in many of the same preparations as crème d'amande.

Pastry Cream – *Crème Pâtissière*

Crème pâtissière is very similar to crème Anglaise in terms of ingredients and method. The major differences are that in crème pâtissière (1) the milk is boiled, (2) half the amount of egg yolks is used, and (3) flour (or cornstarch) makes up part of the ingredients list. This combination produces a stable cream that is perfect for filling pastries such as éclairs, choux, and religieuse. Crème pâtissière can be flavored in a number of ways including with vanilla, chocolate, or coffee.

Crème Pâtissière

1   Split a vanilla bean lengthwise.

2   Scrape out the seeds from the inside.

3   Add the seeds to the milk.

4   Stir until incorporated, and place on the heat.

5   Add about three-quarters of the sugar to the egg yolks.

6   Add the remaining sugar to the heating milk. Stir to dissolve.

(continues on next page)

412

Crème Pâtissière

(continued from previous page)

7 Whisk the sugar into the egg yolks.

8 Keep whisking until homogenous and the yolks take on a light yellow color.

9 Add the flan powder, or mixture of flour and cornstarch.

10 Stir until well combined.

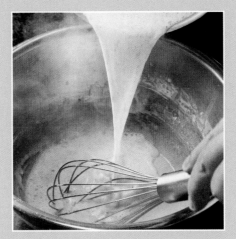

11 Temper the mixture by adding some hot milk.

12 Stir well.

13 Pour the tempered yolks into the remaining milk.

14 Place back on the heat and bring to a boil. Cook 1 minute whisking constantly.

15 Transfer to a clean bowl.

Crème Chiboust

Crème Chiboust is a derivative that involves the addition of Italian meringue and gelatin to crème pâtissière. Chiboust is the traditional filling for gâteau St. Honoré.

Crème Mousseline

Another derivative, crème mousseline is made by adding butter and praline to crème pâtissière and is the traditional filling for Paris-Brest.

As a final note on crème pâtissière, most modern recipes use egg yolks exclusively; however, Lacam's recipe for *crème pâtissière à l'ancienne* in *Le Mémoriale Historique de la Pâtisserie* (1892) calls for whole eggs.

Meringue

Although the origins of the term are unknown, the earliest use of the word appeared in the *Nouveau Cuisinier Royal et Bourgeois*, by François Massialot in 1691. The term was kept when the book was translated into English in 1706. However, a mixture similar to meringue is included in François La Varenne's *Le Pâtissier François*, first published in 1653, but it is called *biscuit sucre en neige*.

Meringue is beaten egg whites to which sugar has been added. There are three types of meringue: French, Italian, and Swiss. French meringue is the easiest to make, but is considered a raw meringue and thus requires cooking before serving. Egg whites are beaten to soft peaks after which granulated sugar is gradually incorporated. The egg whites are beaten until the sugar granules can no longer be detected when the meringue is rubbed between two fingers. As a result of this process, the whites take on a smoother, tighter consistency. The meringue should be used immediately. It can be piped into shapes and baked in a low oven, or poached in sugar syrup.

Italian meringue is egg whites beaten to soft peaks to which hot syrup cooked to the soft ball stage (100°F [38°C]) is gradually incorporated. The meringue is then beaten until completely cooled. The result is a very stable meringue that is smooth and glossy and maintains its volume for some time. It can be used to mask cakes or as a topping to a tart (*tarte au citron*). Italian buttercream is Italian meringue to which butter has been incorporated.

Swiss meringue is egg whites that are mixed with sugar, then gently whisked in a bain marie until hot to the touch (100°F [38°C]). It is then beaten until completely cooled. Like Italian meringue, it is a stable meringue that is tight, smooth, and glossy and will maintain its volume. It is usually piped into shapes, then baked in a low oven. Swiss buttercream is Swiss meringue to which butter has been incorporated.

Fondant

Fondant is a creamy and opaque sugar paste that is used as a finishing glaze on pastries. Its name orginates from the French word fondre, meaning "to melt." Fondant is the result of sugar and liquid glucose that is heated to 244°F (118°C) then cooled to 110°F (43°C) then stirred until it crystallizes into a semi-liquid state. The consistency of this paste largely depends upon the degree of cooking allowed by the cook, a consistency which is determined by its intended usage. Fondant is used in classic preparations like Millefeuille, Religieuse, and Éclairs.

Meringue Italienne

1 Prepare the ingredients and equipment needed.

2 Put sugar and water in a small pan.

3 Bring to a boil and prepare a bowl of cold water.

4 Skim off any white foam, and brush the sides of the pan down with cold water.

5 When the syrup thickens, dip your fingertips in cold water.

6 Quickly pinch some of the syrup and immediately put fingers back in the cold water.

7 Keep your fingers and the syrup in the water for a few seconds.

8 Sugar should form a soft ball.

9 It should be easy to squeeze.

(continues on next page)

Meringue Italienne

(continued from previous page)

10 Immediately pour the hot syrup in a thin steady stream into the beaten egg whites while whisking.

11 Once the syrup has been incorporated, continue beating until cool.

12 Italian meringue will be supple and glossy.

Millefeuille Glaçage

1 Glazing and cutting a millefeuille.

2 Once the millefeuille is filled and trimmed, brush the top with a simple syrup.

3 Prepare the fondant by gently heating until barely warm and thinning with sugar syrup if needed.

4 Pour the fondant over the top.

5 Spread the fondant evenly over the top. Work quickly before the fondant begins to dry.

6 Using a cornet, pipe thin lines of chocolate along the length of the millefeuille.

(continues on next page)

Millefeuille Glaçage

(continued from previous page)

7   Using the back of a small knife, or toothpick, pull the tip through the fondant at an angle at 2-inch intervals.

8   Pull the knife in the opposite direction. In between the first lines.

9   Allow to set and dry.

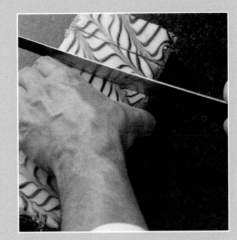

10   To cut the millefeuille you will need a serrated knife, a large palette, and a small, thin knife.

11   First score the top using the serrated knife. Cut through the top layer of pastry only.

12   Place the large palette along the edge of the millefeuille closest to you. Place the small knife where the millefeuille was scored and pull it toward the palette knife in one single stroke.

13   Edges should be clean.

Chapter 4

CHIBOUSTÉ DOUILLE ST HONORÉ

L'EAU
LAIT
BEURRE
SEL
SUCRE
FARINE
OEUFS
MAIZENA
GOUSSE DE VAN
...ZON

DESSÉCH...
...MISE...

PÂTE À CHOUX

...S UNE GRANDE CASSEROLE, FAIRE CHAUFFE...
...U, BEURRE, SUCRÉ ET SEL. FAIRE BOUILLIR...
...UN FEU MOYEN. UNE FOIS LE BEURRE EST...
...DU. RETIRER LE CASSEROLE DE FEU ET AJOUT...
...ARINE.

vanille bean

...MERCL...
...CHE PÂTE B...
...INCEAU...
...FOUET.
OEUFS

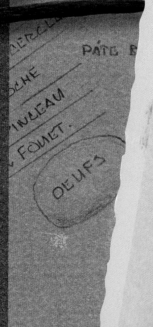

INTRODUCTION

Since man first discovered fire and applied it to food, the act of cooking has come a long way. Instead of fire, we now use electric stoves, microwaves, induction, and so on, but the idea remains the same: the application of heat to a food to transform it into something easier to chew and digest. Modern man also strives to meet another goal—to make our food taste absolutely wonderful—a goal that wasn't a priority for our ancestors back when food was harder to obtain and all of their efforts went into hunting and gathering the basics.

Over the centuries and especially during the 20th century, many people have tried to redefine the cooking process, but that's like reinventing the wheel. You can't really reinvent something, but you can make it better. By understanding the processes and the resources at hand, you can not just cook: you can create.

L'art culinaire literally translates from French into English as "culinary art," and, like any art form, you should begin with the basic fundamentals and build from there. In music, those are the notes of the scale; for painters, the color palette. All beginning students of music learn their scales and practice their études—seemingly boring stuff, but as they practice and master these, they can confidently go on to play any type of music that inspires them, whether it's jazz, classical, or pop. Painters go to school to learn about balance and symmetry, and with a color palette based on three primary colors—red, blue, and yellow—they can create infinite shades and nuances of color.

Learning to cook is very much like learning an art. All students of the culinary arts, whether in school or on the job, will be exposed to the same basic techniques and principles of cooking on which they can build. They also learn a basic, common language that can be shared and understood in any kitchen.

LES CUISSONS

In classic French cooking technique, seven standard cooking methods are universally recognized. The cooking methods, commonly referred to as *les cuissons*, were not invented by any one person. They describe the physical process that takes place when a food is exposed to heat. When a food is heated, its physical chemistry or **organoleptic** properties change, including the food's appearance, color, aroma, flavor, texture, volume, and weight. The heat source varies from hot air to boiling liquid to hot fat and even microwaves. Depending on the protein being prepared, selecting the proper cooking technique will maximize its flavor, consistency, and digestibility, as well as its hygiene and preparation.

The cooking process is broken down into three categories: type, humidity, and color. The following section introduces you to the categories, describes each cooking method and the techniques involved, explains how to use and apply this information, and introduces the French culinary terms associated with these cooking methods as well as all techniques in general.

What's in a word?

Organoleptic is often used to describe the changes that take place when a food is cooked. It incorporates all of the factors that can be affected, including taste, color, odor, and texture.

THE CATEGORIES

The system of categorizing the types of cooking allows you to select a cooking method that is best adapted to the quality and size of the product to be cooked and the desired result. For instance, you would not cook a large piece of meat, such as a whole leg of lamb, the same way you would cook a small steak. By understanding the classification system, different criteria can be used to select the ideal cooking method for the product at hand.

The following categories should be considered when selecting the proper cooking method:

Type: refers to the application of heat and how the heat develops the flavor.

Humidity: refers to the amount of moisture or liquid used during the cooking process.

Color: refers to the change in appearance of the product once exposed to heat.

Type

Type refers to how the flavor develops during the cooking process. Flavor can be developed by applying heat in any of three ways: by concentration, by expansion, or by mixed, a combination of concentration and expansion.

Concentration

The two types of concentration are direct and indirect. Direct concentration refers to the exposure of a food to direct heat, such as an open flame. This type of heating is closest to the process used by primitive man. The product is seared on the outside to preserve the cooking juices and flavor within. Searing quickly exposes the piece to high heat that causes surface proteins to coagulate, thus creating a thickened "crust" that concentrates the flavors within the interior of the piece. When this takes place in a dry atmosphere, this results in the "caramelization" or browning of glucides, a process that is often referred to as the *Maillard reaction.*

The second type of concentration is indirect concentration, in which the food is placed in a recipient or covered by a layer of fat.

Illustration of Concentration application

The Maillard Reaction

The Maillard reaction describes the chemical reaction that occurs between amino acids and sugar, usually when heat is applied. Like caramelization, the Maillard Reaction is a browning process. Elements of the sugar react with the amino acids to change the odor and flavors of the product. During the process hundreds of new flavors are created. Each product will produce different sets of flavors.

This reaction was first discovered at the turn of the 20th century by French physician and chemist, Louis Camille Maillard (1878–1936). Maillard joined the army during World War I. After the war, he left Paris for Algeria where he practically stopped his research. Maillard received several awards for his work, including one from the French Academy of Medicine in 1914.

Aromates

You will often hear reference to *garniture aromatique* or aromates. These are vegetables that are used to add flavor and moisture during the cooking process. One of the most common is the *mirepoix*, which consists of onion, carrot, and celery. Added to that would be a *bouquet garni*, which consists of thyme, bay leaf, parsley stems, and celery stalk or leaves, wrapped in the green of a leek.

When using aromates, such as a *mirepoix*, they should be cut based on the length of the cooking time and size of the product with which they are being cooked. Thus, longer cooking times would require the aromates to be cut into larger pieces so that they cook completely without disintegrating. Shorter cooking times for smaller pieces require the aromates to be cut smaller so they cook completely and release their full flavor.

Of the seven classic cooking methods, six use concentration:

Rôtir (to roast)

Griller (to grill)

Poêler (to pan roast)

Sauter (to pan-fry)

Frire (to deep-fry)

Pocher (to poach).

These cooking methods will be explained in more detail later in this chapter.

Expansion

Illustration of Expansion application

In contrast to concentration, expansion uses indirect heat that is usually created by a liquid or steam. Expansion is gentler than concentration because the liquid or steam does not exceed 100°C (212°F).

When using a liquid, the product is placed in the cold liquid and brought to the boiling point. Any impurities, excess salt, and nutritive and flavor elements will appear as a foam on the surface of the liquid, and an exchange of flavors will take place. If the liquid contains aromates, such as carrots, onion, or celery, the flavors will be absorbed by the product as the flavor elements of the aromates are released.

Cooking methods that use expansion are *pocher* (to poach), *blanchir* (to blanch), and *mouillage* (adding cold liquid when making a stock).

Mixed

Illustration of Mixed application

The term *mixed* describes the application of both concentration and expansion principles to the product. For example, a piece may first be seared using the concentration method to cause the Maillard reaction to occur. Then, utilizing the expansion method, the piece is finished in an aromatic liquid in order to soften the connective tissues. During this step the nutritive and flavor elements of the product go into the sauce, while absorbing the flavors in the liquid and/or aromates.

Two cooking methods that take advantage of the mixed category are *sauter en ragoût* and *braiser* (see pages 431 and 432).

Humidity

Humidity refers to the amount of liquid that is used during the cooking process. Humidity is supplied by the addition of either a liquid such as water or stock or by the introduction of aromatic vegetables that release steam as they cook. This affects the final texture and flavor of the product.

Dry and humid environments have different cooking requirements:

- *Dry environment:* In a dry environment, no additional liquid is added or accumulated other than a small amount of fat such as butter or oil. Cooking is usually done with the pot or pan uncovered.

- *Humid environment:* To create this type of environment, a small or large amount of liquid is added. Cooking is usually done with the pot or pan covered to maintain a humid environment or to control the rate of evaporation of the liquid.

Illustration of Dry Environment

Illustration of Humid Environment

Color

The term *color* refers to the process of giving the product color through the application of direct heat. This relates to the "type" category because color is a consequence of concentration or expansion. The browning process is usually applied to meats (both red and white) because it changes the color of the meat as a direct result of the proteins and sugars coagulating.

The degree of coloring depends on the cooking technique, the product, the intensity of the heat being applied, and the length of exposure. Products can take on three degrees of coloring:

- *Brun* (Brown)
- *Blond* (Blond)
- *Blanc* (White).

Now that you have been introduced to the three categories of type, humidity, and color, you can choose the best cooking method for almost any dish by keeping these three categories in mind.

THE SEVEN CLASSIC COOKING METHODS

The seven classic cooking methods are as follows:

- Rôtir (to roast)
- Griller (to grill)
- Poêler (to pan roast)
- Sauter (to pan-fry, sauté)
- Braiser (to braise)
- Frire (to deep-fry)
- Pocher (to poach).

The wonderful thing about French culinary terms is that a single word describes most processes. We will be using these terms throughout the book when logically possible. These terms will be highlighted the first time they appear and will also be included in the glossary at the end of this book.

Sucs

Sucs is a French term that describes the browned cooking juices on the bottom of the pan from the use of dry cooking methods. *Suc* is an old French word for *juice*.

When to Season?

A good rule of thumb is to season just before cooking. Be aware, however, that even though salt will assist in the cooking process by promoting coloration of the product's exterior, it can also cause a loss of moisture if applied too early.

To Roast (*Rôtir*)

Roasting is used to cook large tender pieces in a dry atmosphere (no added liquid or vegetables), in the oven or on a spit. One of the finished goals of a roast is to create a crust through the Maillard reaction, which adds color and aroma and ensures a moist and juicy interior. A roast would be prepared by the *rôtisseur* in a traditional Escoffier brigade or the *grillardin* in a smaller brigade.

The roasting process is categorized as follows:

Type: concentration because the product is seared to keep the natural juices within.

Humidity: dry because no liquid or aromate is used in the cooking.

Color: brown *(à brun)* because exposure to high heat results in coloration of the product.

The Roasting Process

- Prepare the piece by trimming and, if needed, tying with butcher's twine.
- Place on a rack in a roasting pan, season and generously cover with pieces of butter.
- Place directly into a hot oven.
- Turn, baste with fat or oil, and cook to desired doneness. For larger pieces, the heat would be reduced to allow the heat to penetrate without overcooking the outside, whereas smaller pieces would be cooked quickly to prevent overcooking by prolonged exposure to high heat.
- Allow to rest.
- Make a jus from the sucs, or browned cooking juices, left in the pan.

Service

A roast is traditionally served with a *jus* on the side, always uncovered, and sliced tableside. Roasts are traditionally accompanied by fresh watercress. If portioned in the kitchen, the *jus* is poured onto the plate with the meat placed on top.

Applications

Roasting is applied to:

- Large pieces of tender butchery meats such as beef tenderloin, pork loin, and veal rack
- Poultry, usually whole
- Game, such as venison
- Large fish, usually whole
- Vegetables, such as onions, potatoes.

Variations

Poêler, one of the other seven cooking methods, shares some of the same criteria of roasting.

To Grill (*Griller*)

Grilling is the process of cooking a tender piece of meat by exposing it directly to a heat source in the open air or in a well-ventilated space. Grilling was present at the birth of the culinary arts because it was the first step toward cooking when early man instinctively wanted to eat better.

The goal in grilling is the formation of a crust through the Maillard reaction (coloration and formation of traditional aromas). The piece is traditionally *quadriller* (see Culinary French 101 to the right). Never pierce red meat during

Jus

Jus translates into English as *juice*, and in many ways it resembles the natural cooking juices of a product. *Jus* is very difficult to make properly even though it does not require any special ingredients or equipment. A traditional *jus* is made by dissolving the browned cooking juices *(sucs)* that remain on the bottom of the pan with water, and then reducing. This process is then repeated four to five times. It is then finished with *beurre noisette* (browned butter).

Quadriller

Ever notice the crisscross pattern on your steak? This technique is called *quadriller* and literally translated it means "to square." If your grill is heated properly, it should leave a mark when the product is placed on it. The principle of *quadrillage* is to turn the piece only four times, each time changing the direction in order to create the crisscross pattern.

Determining Doneness by Touch

Rare: Form a loose fist and with your index finger of the other hand, touch the meaty area between the thumb and forefinger.

Medium: Tighten the fist and press in the same area.

Well-done: Press the area at the base of the thumb.

culinary french 101

Lustrer

Similar to *luster*, its English equivalent, *lustrer* means just that: to give the product a shiny finish. Especially when grilling, the product can have a tendency to dry out during the cooking process. Thus, brushing it with some sort of fat not only makes the product look more attractive, it also prevents further drying. In fact, with other cooking processes such as *sauter* and *poêler*, brushing the product (fish, poultry, meat) with some fat will not only prevent it from drying, but will enhance the flavor.

the cooking process because a break in the outer crust will allow juices to escape and dry out the product. Doneness can be determined by using the finger test. In a classic Escoffier brigade, grilling is done by the *grillardin*, or in a small brigade by the *rôtisseur*.

The grilling process is categorized as follows:

Type: concentration because the product is seared to keep the natural juices within.

Humidity: dry because the product is cooked without the addition of aromates or liquids.

Color: brown (*à brun*) because the product will color as a result of its exposure to a direct heat source.

The Grilling Process

- Heat and clean the grill.
- Prepare the piece by drying and, if needed, tying with butcher's twine.
- Season or marinate in advance.
- Sear.

- Cook and mark *(quadriller)* the piece.
- Leave to rest.
- *Lustrer* with a cold composed butter or other fat or oil.

Service

Grilled foods are traditionally served with a hot emulsion sauce or cold compound butter. A sauce is served on the side, never on the meat, whereas butter is served on the meat or on the side. Meat and poultry are traditionally decorated with watercress, and fish with parsley.

Applications

Grilling is applied to:

- Small tender cuts of meat such as steaks, chops, cutlets, scallops, medallions
- Fish, whole or in pieces
- Vegetables (may be blanched first).

Variations

There are no variations for the grilling process, but a surface other than the traditional grill could be used, such as a flat stone or griddle. The heat source for grilling varies and includes natural gas, propane, electricity, or a charcoal or wood fire.

To Pan Roast (*Poêler*)

Poêler is considered a variation of roasting, but differs from the traditional roasting process in that after searing, the product is roasted covered, creating a moist cooking environment. Also, some aromatics, traditionally a *matignon* garnish (Classic Garnishes above), are added at the end of the cooking time to add additional moisture and flavors. *Poêler* combines the advantages of braising, which creates a tender, juicy product, with the flavor of roasting. During the cooking process, there is an exchange of flavors between the different elements, which are then fixed by the fat present in the meat. Cooking with a cover prevents the steam from escaping, thus

Classic Garnishes

Matignon

Like a *mirepoix*, the *matignon* is an aromatic preparation used to cook certain large pieces of meat or poultry. It is traditionally made up of carrots, onions, and celery that have been finely diced (a *brunoise* or *paysanne*), to which raw ham, cut in the same manner, is added along with some thyme and bay leaf. It is cooked in butter and finished with some Madeira. The matignon can be served with the product with which it was cooked.

What's in a word?

Poêler – There is no true English equivalent to the poêler cooking method, and it should not be confused with the verb *poêler*, which refers to the use of a specific type of frying pan, a *poêle*. The cooking method term poêler is more closely related to *sauter*.

What's in a word?

Why is it called *matignon*? The name comes from Jacques François Léonor Goyon de Matignon, the Count of Thorigny and Jacques I of Monaco. A colorful figure from the 18th century, his former Paris home is currently used as the residence for the French prime minister. The residence changed owners many times, but it was always referred to as the Hôtel Matignon. One of those owners included the famous Talleyrand (1754–1838), who gave dinners four times a week for 36 guests, prepared by his chef, the celebrated Boucher. Note, too, that Talleyrand once employed Carême as his chef. As was the custom of the time, new dishes were often named after the chef's patron or the person for whom the dish was created.

Classic Garnishes

Twenty classic garnishes are used for various preparations. The *garniture financière* for example is used for large pieces of meat or poultry. It is made of truffles, cockscombs, cock's testicles, and veal sweetbreads in a Perigord sauce (*demi-glace* with Port wine). It also includes channeled mushrooms, turned blanched olives, and veal or chicken *quenelles*, depending on whether it is accompanying meat or poultry.

creating a flavorful, humid atmosphere. A *glaçage* (glaze) is applied at the end of cooking to replace the crust that would have resulted from straight roasting. This dish would usually be executed by the *rôtisseur* or *saucier* in a traditional Escoffier brigade.

The pan-roasting process is categorized as follows:

Type: mixed because the piece is usually seared, then covered while it finishes cooking.

Humidity: humid in the form of liquid and aromates.

Color: brown (*à brun*) because the initial searing results in the coloration of the piece.

The Pan-Roasting Process

- Prepare the piece by trimming and, if needed, tying with butcher's twine.
- Season.
- Sear in a small amount of fat or oil.
- Cook covered in a medium oven [190°C (375°F)], turning and basting the piece.
- Add aromatic garnish, traditionally a *matignon grasse*.

- Finish cooking.

- Leave to rest covered.

- Make a sauce (infuse the *matignon* for 20 minutes) by adding a jus or a fonds.

- Glaze *(glacer)*.

This last step of glazing is very important to the *poêler* and it is one of the steps that differentiates it from a *rôtir*. At the end of the cooking, the product is glazed with a reduction on all sides. This step is usually performed at the open door of the oven, so the heat helps the glaze coat evenly. The finished piece should be evenly colored with a glossy finish all around.

Service

Pan-roasted items are traditionally served with the sauce on the side and accompanied by an elaborate garnish such as a *garniture financière* (see Classic Garnishes on page 428).

Applications

Poêler is applied to large pieces of meat that are too tough for roasting but too tender for braising, such as contre filet, noix de veau, and large lamb roasts.

Poêler is applied most often to red meats using the technique *poêler à l'ancienne*. It is also applied to duck or other large birds.

Variations

Poêler en casserole: cooked in butter, covered, then deglazed with stock.

Poêler en cocotte: like *en casserole*, but the aromatic garnish is served with the finished meat; often served with a *garniture grand-mère* (potatoes, mushrooms, and bacon).

Poêler à l'ancienne: The *matignon* is sweated in butter then covered with a slice of pork fat. The seared meat is wrapped with the fat, enfolded in parchment, and then roasted in the oven. The sauce is made with the *matignon*, Madeira, and *demi-glace*.

To Sauté (*Sauter*)

The sauter cooking method is used to sauté or pan-fry small, tender pieces in a small amount of hot fat. The goal of sauter is to create a crust through the

Décanter

Décanter literally translated means "to decant," as with a bottle of wine. In cooking, décanter describes the process of removing the cooked product from the cooking liquid so the liquid can be strained and finished for the sauce.

Mouiller

Mouiller literally translated means "to make wet." The term refers to the addition of stock or other liquid to a preparation. The noun *mouillage* refers to the liquid itself.

Luter

The term *luter* refers to the technique of sealing a covered casserole, or cocotte with a dough made of flour and water. This provides an almost airtight seal that prevents moisture from escaping during cooking.

Maillard reaction that will maintain the natural juices of the piece. In a traditional brigade, sauter is normally executed by the *saucier* for meat and poultry, the *poissonier* for fish, and the *entremétier* for eggs and vegetables.

The sautéing process is categorized as follows:

Type: concentration because the product is seared to keep the natural juices within.

Humidity: dry because no liquid or aromate is used in the cooking.

Color: brown *(à brun)* because searing results in coloration of the piece.

What's in a word?

Sauter - Similar to *poêler*, the word *sauter* as a cooking method should not be confused with the verb *sauter*, which is used with an accent, *sauté*. The verb *sauter* in English means "to jump" and is used in reference to cooking small pieces that are shaken about in the pan. It is also commonly used in English as *sauté* in the same spirit as the French.

The Sautéing Process

- Prepare the piece by trimming and drying.
- Season.
- Sear in a small amount of fat, usually clarified butter.
- Cook the piece by turning and basting.
- Allow to rest.
- Prepare the garniture.
- Make the sauce.

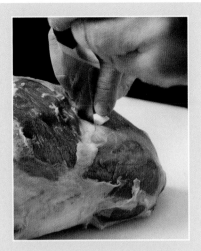

Piquer, Larder, and Barder

Piquer means "to pick" or "to stick," and refers to the addition of small pieces of fat or flavor elements to a piece for cooking, usually with poultry or smaller pieces of meat.

Larder means to lard, and refers to the introduction of long strips of pork fat under the surface of large pieces in order to ensure that the piece stays moist during its long cooking process.

Barder refers to partially covering a large piece of meat or whole bird with a thin layer of pork fat (barding fat) in order to prevent the crust from over-coloring and drying out.

Service

Sautéed items are traditionally served uncovered, with all of the elements together. Due to the size of the product, the doneness of the product ranges between rare to well done. For more information on proper doneness, see the Determining Doneness by Touch feature on page 426.

Applications

Sautéing can be applied to small, tender cuts of meat:

- Poultry
- Offal
- Game
- Fish
- Vegetables

Variations

Meunière: dredged in flour and cooked in clarified butter only.

Sauter en ragoût: sautéed mixed with roasted flour, then finished in a stock in the oven.

The Sauter en Ragoût Process

- Prepare the product by cutting it into small pieces.
- Sear the meat until nicely colored.
- Sprinkle with flour and allow to roast in the oven *(singer)*, then stir.
- Add the *garniture aromatique* sautéed with some color.
- Deglaze, reduce, then add white or brown stock to just cover *(mouiller)*.
- Cover and seal *(luter)* if needed, place in the oven to cook.
- Separate the product from the cooking liquid *(décanter)*.
- Finish the sauce.
- Add pieces back into the sauce, not to cook, but to bring back to temperature.

To Braise (*Braiser*)

Braising is defined as slowly cooking a large piece in a liquid over low consistent heat in a covered cooking vessel with an aromatic garnish. The finished goals of braising are to transform the connective tissues of tougher cuts of meat into gelatin, and to impart a particular flavor to a product. Braiser is performed by the *saucier*, or *rôtisseur* on a traditional Escoffier brigade.

The braising process is categorized as follows:

Type: mixed because the product is seared to keep the natural juices within and finished by cooking in a liquid.

Humidity: humid because a small amount of liquid is added along with aromates

Color: white (*à blanc*) or **brown** (*à brun*) because the searing is dependent on the product

The Braising Process

- Marinate larger pieces in either a raw or cooked marinade.
- Prepare the piece by larding and, if needed, tying with butcher's twine.
- Season (ground pepper and sea salt) and sear the piece white or brown.
- Add the aromates.
- Deglaze (*déglacer*) and add the liquid (*mouiller*) just to the height of the solids.
- Cover, seal (*luter*), and cook slowly in a medium oven. If available, use a *braisière*—an extra deep pan with a tight-fitting cover.
- Remove the product and strain cooking liquid through a large *chinois*.
- Finish the sauce.

Service

A braise is served with its sauce, without the aromatic garnish, and is finished with a glaze to give it a glossy finish.

Applications

This technique is usually applied to large pieces of meat from older animals that require longer cooking times. These pieces should be seared before the liquid is added. This technique can also be applied to whole fish and some vegetables; however, they would not require searing as a first step.

The chart following this section shows the different cuts of meat that can be braised and the different braising methods that would be used with each cut.

Variations

Based on the product being prepared, five braising techniques are used:

Braisage à blanc: white braising; primarily for white meats (veal, pork, and poultry) and white offal.

Braisage à blond: blond braising; used for white meats such as veal, pork, and poultry.

Braisage à brun: brown braising; used for red meats, poultry, game, and certain offal (often marinated beforehand).

Braisage des poissons: braising of fish; for large whole fish, with the skin usually stuffed or *piquer*.

Braisage des légumes: braising of vegetables.

The Braisage à Blanc Process

- Prepare the piece by larding and, if needed, tying with butcher's twine.
- Season.

- Sear the meat without coloration *(raidir)*.
- Add the *braisière* sweated in butter.
- Deglaze and add white stock to three-quarters the height of the solids.
- Cook and seal *(luter)*, if needed. Place in the oven.
- Remove pieces from the cooking liquid *(décanter)*.
- Finish the sauce with *demi-glace*.
- Glaze whole or individual pieces or slices.

The Braisage à Blond Process

- Prepare the piece by larding and, if needed, tying with butcher's twine.
- Season.
- Sear the meat until lightly colored.
- Add the *garniture aromatique*, sautéed with some color.
- Deglaze and add white stock to three-quarters the height of the solids.
- Cover and seal *(luter)*, if needed. Place in the oven.
- Remove piece from cooking liquid *(décanter)*.
- Finish the sauce.
- Glaze whole, or individual pieces or slices.

The Braisage à Brun Process

- Prepare the piece: cut and larder, tie, if needed.
- Sear the meat until nicely and evenly browned.
- Add the *garniture aromatique*, sautéed with some color.
- Deglaze and add brown stock to three-quarters the height of the solids.
- Cover and seal *(luter)*. Place in the oven.
- Remove piece from cooking liquid *(décanter)*.
- Finish the sauce.
- Glaze whole or individual pieces or slices.

Braisage des Poissons

- Clean and scale the whole fish, can be stuffed if desired.
- Prepare butter and seasoning.
- Deglaze and add enough stock to three-quarters its height.
- Cook covered basting regularly.
- Glaze the piece with or without the skin.

Braisage des Légumes

- Prepare the vegetables by cleaning and blanching, can be filled if desired.
- Prepare butter and seasoning.
- Deglaze and add enough stock to three-quarters the height of the vegetables.
- Cook covered.
- Glaze piece to desired color.

Table 4-1 Braising Meat Cuts

	Brown braising	White braising	Blond braising	Ragoût
Cut of Meat	Second or third category	Young animal, large whole fish, blanched vegetables	"White" meats such as veal, poultry, and pork	Second or third category
Examples	Beef: leg			Beef: leg
	Veal: shoulder	Veal loin, noix (thigh), shoulder pork	Veal: shoulder pork	Veal: shoulder, neck
	Lamb: shoulder			Lamb: shoulder, neck
	Game: hare, wild boar, and venison (shoulder, neck)			
		Vegetables: lettuce, celery, endive		
		Fish: salmon, turbot, sea bass, carp		
	Poultry: hen		Poultry: hen, guinea fowl	Poultry: rooster, capon

To Deep-Fry (*Frire*)

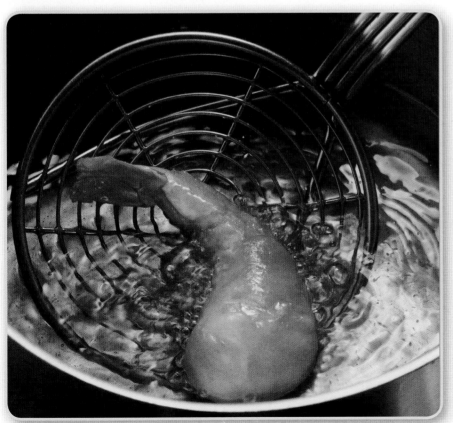

Frire describes the cooking of a tender piece in a large amount of hot fat or oil. The English equivalent would be deep-frying. The goal of deep-frying is the formation of a crust through the Maillard reaction. The interior of the piece however should be moist and not oily. There are six types of fat or oil to choose from, depending on what is being cooked: melted butter (clarified), lard or pork fat, beef or veal fat, goose or poultry fat, coco oil, and vegetable oil. The great chefs from the 19th century into the 20th century considered the rendered fat from beef kidneys to be the best medium for deep-frying.

The deep-frying process is categorized as follows:

Type: concentration because the product is surrounded by hot fat to keep the natural juices within.

Humidity: dry because the piece is cooked without the addition of aromates or liquid.

Color: brown *(à brun)* because the meat will color as a result of its exposure to the hot fat.

The Deep-Frying Process

- Prepare the piece by seasoning or marinating, breading or coating in batter.
- Cook.
- Drain on paper.
- Season while hot, serve immediately.

Service

Deep-fried pieces are traditionally served with an emulsion sauce, served on the side, never on the pieces. It is served on a white napkin, *papier gauffré* or a paper doily to absorb excess oil, and is always served uncovered.

Applications

Deep-frying can be applied to small pieces that are plain or have been dredged, breaded, or battered:

- *Fish:* smelt, whiting, sole, strips *(goujonnettes)*
- *Shellfish:* shrimp, oysters, squid
- *Meat:* small tender cuts such as beef fondue, chicken pieces, boneless chicken, or offal
- *Eggs*
- *Vegetables:* potatoes, zucchini, herbs (*Note:* Most vegetables either cooked or raw are always coated before cooking with the exception of potatoes and herbs.)
- *Beignets:* raw ingredient coated in a batter.

Variations

Deep-frying can vary by the temperature of the fat or oil:

- Low temperature: 140°C (285°F)
- Medium temperature: 160°C (320°F)
- High temperature: 180°C (355°F).

To Poach (*Pocher*)

Equipment Check

A *poissonière* is a fish poacher, a long, deep pan fitted with a rack on which the whole fish may rest. The rack makes it easy to remove the fish from the cooking liquid once it is cooked. The aromatic garnish can be arranged beneath the rack before cooking.

A *turbotière* is less common be-cause it is specifically designed for cooking a whole turbot or *barbue* (sea bream), which is a large, flat fish. It is diamond shaped and fitted with a rack as well.

Escoffier defines *pocher* as "boiled without boiling." While his statement is a bit of a riddle, what he is saying is that the poached ingredient is cooked in hot liquid that is not quite at the boiling point. (The English equivalent of *pocher* is *poaching* or *simmering*.) Pocher refers to gentle, slow cooking that requires the piece to be completely covered by a hot liquid. The goal of poaching is to tenderize a tough piece of meat, or to use liquid to impart flavor to an ingredient during cooking. It also is used to hydrate certain dry ingredients that require liquid for cooking such as rice and pasta. Poaching is performed by a *poissonier, saucier* or *entremétier* in a traditional Escoffier brigade.

Traditionally, poaching starts with a cold liquid and the liquid is brought to the desired temperature as quickly as possible. The poaching liquid is normally flavored by aromates such as a *court bouillon* (used for fish). The liquid is brought to a temperature that can gently cook the piece, but the one constant is that the liquid is never brought above the boiling point during the cooking process. However, the poaching liquid itself can be brought to a boil before the product is added.

The poaching process is categorized as follows:

Type: expansion for *pocher à froid* (starting in a cold liquid), because there is always an exchange of flavors between the piece and the poaching liquid when a *garniture aromatique* is used. This is used for cooking large pieces such as whole fish.

Concentration: concentration for *pocher à chaud* (starting in a hot liquid), because the heat seals the outer surface of the product. This is used for cooking small pieces such as eggs.

Humidity: humid because the piece is cooked in a large amount of liquid.

Color: white *(à blanc)* because the meat is indirectly exposed to a heat source, so it does not take on any color.

The Poaching Process

* Prepare the piece.
* Prepare the liquid for cooking (flavor, temperature).
* Immerse the piece and cook.
* Remove from liquid and keep covered.
* Finish the sauce.

Service

Poached foods can be served hot or cold, and are usually served with a sauce, either covered by the sauce or if whole, the sauce can also be served in a sauce boat.

Equipment used for poaching includes the following pieces:

* *Sauce pan Russe* or *dutch oven cocotte* (for fish, a *poissonière* or *turbotière*)
* Wire skimmer *(araignée)*
* Thermometer or finger test
* Pan with fitted lid for keeping the piece warm and moist.

Applications

* Meat or poultry (blanched before poaching to remove impurities)
* Fish
* Vegetables
* Eggs
* Grains
* Pasta.

Variations

Poaching can vary by temperature:

* *Pocher à chaud:* start in a boiling liquid
* *Pocher à l'anglaise:* using water and salt only
* *Pocher à froid:* start in a cold liquid.

> ### NOTE
>
> *Blanchir* (to blanch) is not a cooking technique but a preparation.

ADDITIONAL COOKING TERMS
Vacuum Cooking (*Sous-Vide*)

Sous-vide, or vacuum cooking, is defined as cooking an ingredient in a closed or controlled atmosphere. This is the modern adaptation of cooking in a paper packet *(en papillote)*, but the *sous-vide* process accommodates larger pieces and quantities. This cooking method prevents the loss of product weight by minimizing any loss of humidity, transforms collagen into gelatin, and preserves nutrients and flavor. This interesting technique offers nutritional, hygienic, and organoleptic advantages and also extends the storage life of prepared foods.

The *sous-vide* process is categorized as follows:

Type: concentration because the product is in a sealed packet.

Humidity: humid because the piece is cooked in an enclosed atmosphere, with or without aromates.

Color: white *(à blanc)* because the piece does not take on any color, or brown *(à brun)* because pieces can be browned before cooking.

> ### NOTE
> The process of *sous-vide* is highly controlled and should respect the regulations of individual countries and/or states.

The Vacuum Cooking Process

* Prepare the piece.
* Precook or color if needed.
* Combine ingredients for flavoring.
* Place in the special bag, apply the vacuum, and seal.
* Cook under 100°C (212°F).
* Cool to less than 10°C (50°F) in less than 2 hours.
* Store at 3°C (37°F) for up to 21 days.
* Bring back to more than 65°C (149°F) in less than 1 hour.

Service

The service for *sous-vide* varies depending on the recipes utilized.

Steam Cooking (*Cuisine à la Vapeur*)

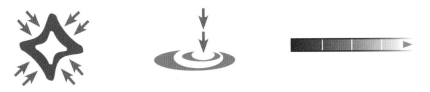

Cuisine à la vapeur, or steam cooking, is defined as cooking an ingredient indirectly with steam produced by boiling a liquid, such as water or stock. Steam cooking has been used in Chinese and Arabic cuisine for many centuries and has long been considered to be a healthy manner of preparing food that also offers hygienic and organoleptic advantages. This cooking method prevents the loss of product weight by minimizing any loss of humidity, transforms collagen into gelatin, and preserves nutrients and flavor.

The steam cooking process is categorized as follows:

Type: concentration because the product does not come into direct contact with the liquid and thus maintains its properties.

Humidity: humid because the piece is cooked in an enclosed atmosphere, over a boiling or simmering liquid.

Color: white *(à blanc)* because the piece is cooked without coloring.

The Steam Cooking Process

* Prepare the piece.
* Prepare liquid.
* Place in the special steamer or a pan fitted with a basket or grill that will hold the piece above the liquid.
* Bring liquid to a boil.
* Place piece in steamer and close tightly with the lid.

Variations

Pressure cooking is one variation of steam cooking. Pressure cooking confines steam in a specially designed pot that is used to generate high pressure. As the pressure rises, so does the boiling point, thus allowing the liquid in the pan to reach a higher temperature than normally required for boiling. For example, the standard boiling point for water is 100°C (212°F). With a pressure cooker the boiling point is raised to 120°C (257°F). Being able to use liquids at a higher temperature speeds up the cooking process. Pressure cookers are fitted with a valve to allow steam to escape in order to prevent the closed cookers from exploding.

Smoking (*Fumage/Fumaison*)

The Pressure Cooker

We think of the pressure cooker as an invention of the 20th century, but it was actually invented in 1679 by a French physicist named Denis Papin. It was originally used to remove fat from animal bones, making the bones brittle enough to be ground into bonemeal, but the autoclave, used in hospitals to sterilize instruments, resulted from Papin's invention. Originally called the steam digester, it led to the invention of the steam engine!

One of the oldest ways of cooking and preserving food, *fumaison*, or smoking, was used to preserve foods without refrigeration through a process of brining or salting and exposure to smoke, either cold or warm.

The smoking process is categorized as follows:

Type: concentration because, after salting, the product is left to form an outer crust.

Humidity: dry because the piece is cured or smoked without any liquid.

Color: brown *(à brun)* because the piece will naturally color from exposure to smoke.

To Preserve (*Confire*)

A very old method of preparing food, there are two types of *confire*, one savory and one sweet. The savory method is the slow or gentle cooking of an ingredient immersed in its own fat. A classic example would be duck confit *(confit de canard)*.

A sweet confit is not a cooking process, but the finishing of a precooked ingredient by submersing it in a sugar syrup and allowing it to slowly "candy" over low heat or over a period of time.

The savory preserving method is categorized as follows:

Type: concentration because the ingredient is immersed in a hot fat.

Humidity: dry because the piece is cooked without aromates or liquid.

Color: white *(à blanc)* because the piece is cooked without coloring.

Microwave Cooking

Advances in technology have had their influence in the kitchen and have made the process of cooking more efficient in terms of time, energy, and manpower. This is evident in the equipment in today's kitchens both commercially and at home.

The most popular technology to come out of the 20th century is microwave cooking. Microwave ovens use radio-frequency electromagnetic energy to heat food. The energy causes the water molecules in food to rotate, causing friction that results in a rapid rise in temperature. Thus, cooking in a microwave oven is faster than conventional methods. It can also be used to defrost frozen foods quickly and to reheat foods more efficiently. Some cooking techniques adapt well to the microwave, such as steaming.

FINISHING TECHNIQUES
To Brown, Broil (*Gratiner*)

Gratiner, or browning or broiling, is not considered a cooking method; it is more of a finishing technique. Its purpose is not to cook the piece to a specific doneness, but to give it a final touch of color or a top crust.

Technical and Fabrication Sheets
for Classic French Preparations

Chapter 5

black pepper

Fonds blanc de volaille
—White Stock
(*Chicken*)

Fonds brun de veau
—Brown Stock
(*Veal*)

Fumet de poisson —
Fish Stock

FONDS BLANC DE VOLAILLE

Learning Outcomes

Basic white stock
(*fonds blanc*)
Blanchir
Abattis
Écumer
Dégraisser
Passer

Equipment

Knives:
Vegetable peeler (*économe*), paring knife (*office*), slicing knife (*éminceur*), scissors (*ciseaux*)

Tools:
Ladle, chinois, wooden spoon

Pans:
Stock pot (*marmite*)

Yield

1 ½–2 gallons or 6-8 liters

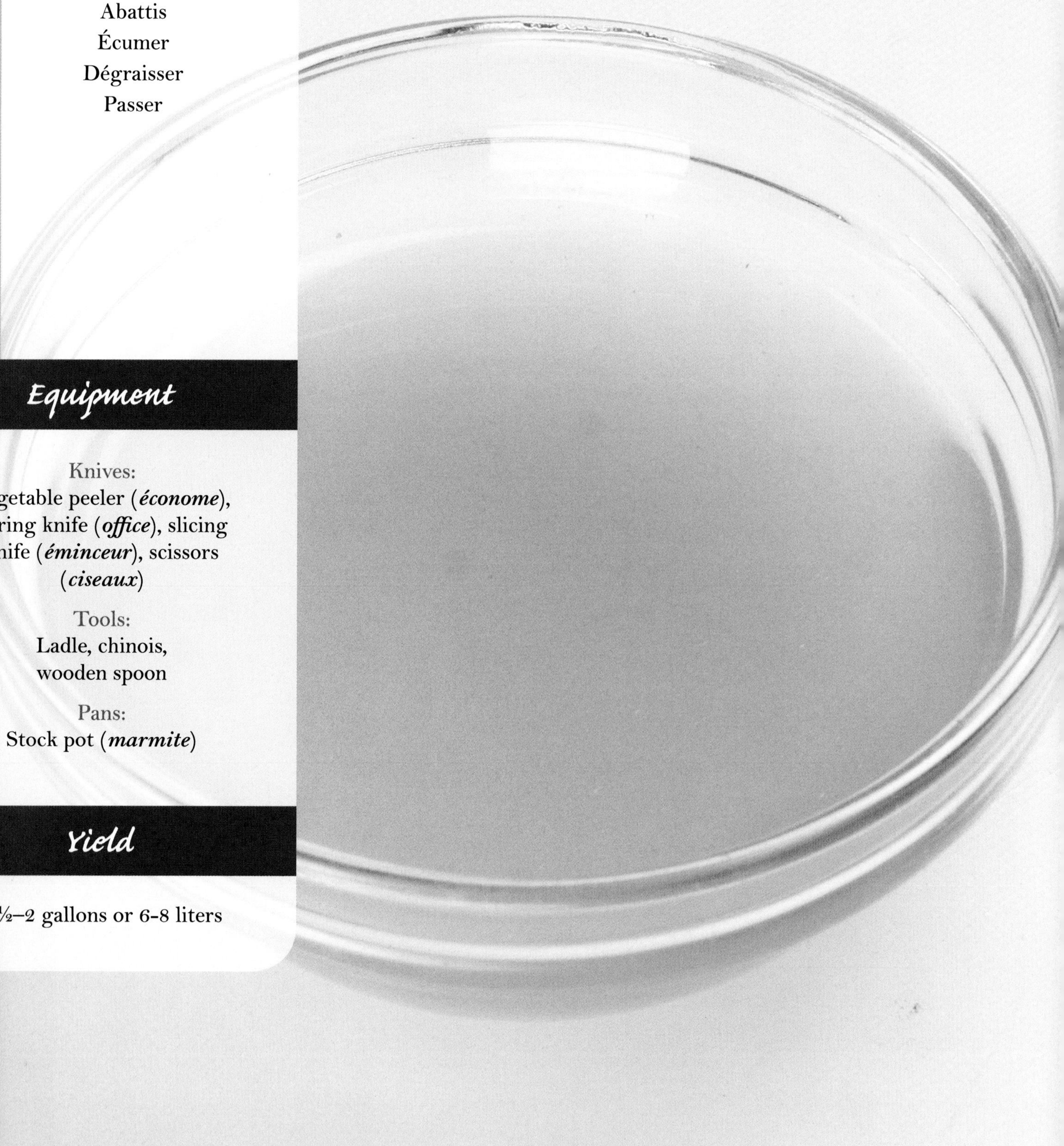

FONDS BLANC DE VOLAILLE
White Stock (Chicken)

Method

1. Rinse the chicken pieces under cold running water. Place in a stock pot and add enough cold water to generously cover. Place over high heat and bring to a boil. Reduce the heat to medium low and simmer for 5–10 minutes (**blanchir**). Skim (**écumer**) the surface of the impurities that rise to the surface in the form of a dirty foam. Skim off any fat as well (**dégraisser**).
2. Rinse under cold running water until water runs clear. Drain.
3. Add the carrot, leek, onion (studded with the clove), celery, **bouquet garni**, mushroom trimmings, white peppercorn, and garlic to the pot. Add enough fresh water to cover. Simmer the stock gently until the liquid is strongly scented (2 to 4 hours). Skim and degrease the pot regularly during the cooking process.
4. Strain the finished stock through a fine mesh sieve (**chinois**) and discard the chicken pieces and **garniture aromatique**.
5. Let the stock cool to room temperature before covering it and placing it in the refrigerator.

Note

The same technique is applied for making fonds blanc de veau (white veal stock).

Quantity		Ingredient
U.S.	**Metric**	
6 lbs	3 kg	Chicken wings, carcasses, giblets (**abattis**)
1 pc	1 pc	Carrot, whole
1 pc	1 pc	Leek, white, whole
1 pc	1 pc	Onion, peeled
3 pcs	3 pcs	Clove
1 pc	1 pc	Celery, stalks, halved
1 pc	1 pc	**Bouquet garni,** large
		Mushroom trimmings
2 ½ gallons	10 L	Water
1 pc	1 pc	Garlic head, cut in half
¼ oz	5 g	White peppercorn

The French word *fonds* is a derivative of the Latin *fondus,* which translates as the base element of things. In English, the word *stock* is used synonymously with *fonds* to describe this clarified and flavored liquid that is the base of many sauces, soups, and stews.

Basic brown stock
(*fonds brun*)
Cutting a mirepoix
for long cooking
Pincer les os
Pincer la tomate
Bouquet garni
Mouiller
Pincer les sucs
Déglacer

Equipment

Knives:
Vegetable peeler (*économe*),
paring knife (*office*), slicing
or chef knife (*éminceur* or
couteau chef),
scissors (*ciseaux*)

Tools:
Ladle (*louche*), chinois,
wooden spatula,
skimmer (*écumoire*)

Pans:
Stock pot (*marmite*),
roasting pan (*plaque à
rôtir*)

Yield

1 ½–2 gallons or 6-8 liters

FONDS BRUN DE VEAU
Brown Stock (Veal)

Method

1. Preheat the oven to 400°F to 450°F (205°C to 230°C).
2. Cut two onions in half horizontally and burn the cut sides directly on the stovetop. Set aside. Heat a small sauté pan over medium heat. Cut the garlic head in half and brown the cut sides in the sauté pan. Set aside.
3. Place the veal bones in a large roasting pan and transfer them to the oven to roast until very dark but not burnt (*pincer les os*).
4. When the bones are dark, add the carrots, onions, leeks, and celery and roast them until they brown. Spread with the tomato paste and roast for 5 minutes (*pincer la tomate*). Transfer all the ingredients to a large stock pot and add the *bouquet garni*, veal feet, burnt onions, and garlic head. Pour in enough water to completely cover the ingredients.
5. Pour the fat out of the roasting pan.
6. Place the roasting pan over medium-high heat to concentrate the roasting residues (*pincer les sucs*) then deglaze the pan with 500 mL of water. Scrape the bottom of the pan with a wooden spatula to dislodge the *sucs* and pour the resulting liquid into the stock pot.
7. Bring the contents of the stock pot to a boil over high heat. Skim (*écumer*) the surface to remove any impurities or fat (*dégraisser*). Reduce the temperature to a gentle simmer and let the *fonds* simmer until deep brown and strongly scented (for at least 4 to 6 hours but not more than 8). Skim and degrease the pot regularly during the cooking process.
8. Strain the finished stock through a fine mesh sieve (*chinois*) and discard the bones and *garniture aromatique*.
9. Let the stock cool to room temperature before covering it and placing it in the refrigerator.

Tip

To make a **glace de viande**, reduce a **fonds brun** approximately by half.

Quantity		Ingredient
U.S.	Metric	
2 pcs	2 pcs	Onions, burnt (*optional*)
1 pc	1 pc	Garlic head, browned
10 lbs	5 kg	Veal bones
4 pcs	4 pcs	Carrots, peeled, cut into *mirepoix*
2 pcs	2 pcs	Onions, peeled, cut into *mirepoix*
3 pcs	3 pcs	Leeks, preferably greens, quartered
3 pcs	3 pcs	Celery, stalk, halved
1 oz	30 g	Tomato paste
2 pcs	2 pcs	Veal feet
2 ½ gallons	10 L	Water
1 pc	1 pc	*Bouquet garni*

In *fonds brun de veau*, as with other stocks, it is important to start the process with cold water because this causes the soluble proteins on the bones to form larger clumps that are easier to skim off.

FYI...

Learning Outcomes

Fish fumet
(*fumet de poisson*)
Dégorger
Suer
Raidir
Écumer
Dépouiller
Dégraisser
Passer

Equipment

Knives:
Cleaver (*couteau à batte*),
chef knife (*couteau chef*),
paring knife (*office*)

Tools:
Wooden spatula, chinois,
colander, skimmer
(*écumoire*), bowls,
cheesecloth or paper filter
(optional)

Pans:
Medium stockpot
(*marmite*)

Yield

1 quart or 1 liter

FUMET DE POISSON
Fish Stock

Method

1. Degorge the fish bones: Cut the bones into large pieces (**concasser**) and place them in a large bowl or pot of cold water. Refrigerate (preferably overnight), changing the water as frequently as possible to draw out the blood and impurities (**dégorger**).
2. Melt the butter in a medium stock pot (**marmite**) over low heat and sweat (**suer**) the onions and shallots until they are soft. Add the celery and leek and sweat for 5 minutes, then add the **bouquet garni**. Drain the fish bones, add them to the marmite, and cook them gently until they stiffen and turn opaque (**raidir**).
3. Pour in the wine, turn the heat up to medium-high, and bring it to a low boil. Reduce the wine by half.
4. Pour in the water and stir well. Add the peppercorns and mushrooms and bring the liquid to a low boil. Skim (**écumer**) the surface of any impurities and fat and reduce the heat to a gentle simmer. Allow the fumet to simmer for 20 minutes.
5. Strain the finished fumet through a fine mesh sieve (**chinois**); tap the sieve with a ladle to recuperate the maximum amount of liquid without pressing.
6. Allow the fumet to cool completely before covering and refrigerating it.

Tip

For a clearer **fumet***, the* **chinois** *can be lined with a piece of damp cloth or coffee filter.*

Quantity		Ingredient
U.S.	Metric	
2 lbs	1 kg	Fish bones from white fish such as sole or whiting
1 oz	30 g	Butter
2 pcs	2 pcs	Onion, thinly sliced (*émincer*)
3 pcs	3 pcs	Shallots, thinly sliced (*émincer*)
1 pc	1 pc	Celery stalk, sliced (*émincer*)
1 pc	1 pc	Leek, white part, sliced (*émincer*)
1 pc	1 pc	*Bouquet garni*
10 fl oz	300 mL	White wine
1 qt	1 L	Water
10 pcs	10 pcs	Whole peppercorns
2 oz	60 g	Mushrooms, thinly sliced (*émincer*)

The etymology of the word *fumet* in *fumet de poisson* is difficult to reconcile. Translating as *aroma* in relation to savory ingredients and *bouquet* when describing wine, there is little history to match fumet with fish more than to any other aromatic ingredient. In terms of technique, *fumet de poisson* follows quite a different set of preparation rules than do meat-based stocks. While meat stocks improve with prolonged simmering, a fumet, if let to simmer too long, will become cloudy and develop undesirable flavors. This is because the calcium in fish bones dissolves and infiltrates the liquid after a relatively short period of time

FYI...

Beurre manié

Roux blanc, blond,
et brun

Jaunes d'oeufs
Egg yolks

Learning Outcomes

Making a beurre manié
Beurre pommade
Liaison instantanée

Equipment

Tools:
Sieve, wooden spoon,
mixing bowl

Yield

4 ounces or 120 grams of
beurre manié will thicken
1 quart or liter of liquid.

Quantity		Ingredient
U.S.	Metric	
2 oz	60 g	Flour
2 oz	60 g	Butter

Method

1. Sift the flour (*tamiser*).
2. Soften the butter (**beurre pommade**).
3. Work the flour and butter together until they form a homogenous paste.
4. Reserve in the refrigerator.

Tip

Beurre manié *is used as a last minute liaison as well as to amend existing sauces that have the right taste but are too thin in consistency. Add* **beurre manié,** *piece by piece, to a hot liquid while stirring vigorously with a whisk (making sure the first piece has dissolved before adding the next). To complete the* **liaison,** *bring the liquid to a boil, stirring, until it has reached the desired thickness.*

Beurre manié can be loosely translated from the French as "worked butter." In fact, the act of making this liaison is just that—equal amounts of butter and flour are worked together until each flour particle is coated in butter.

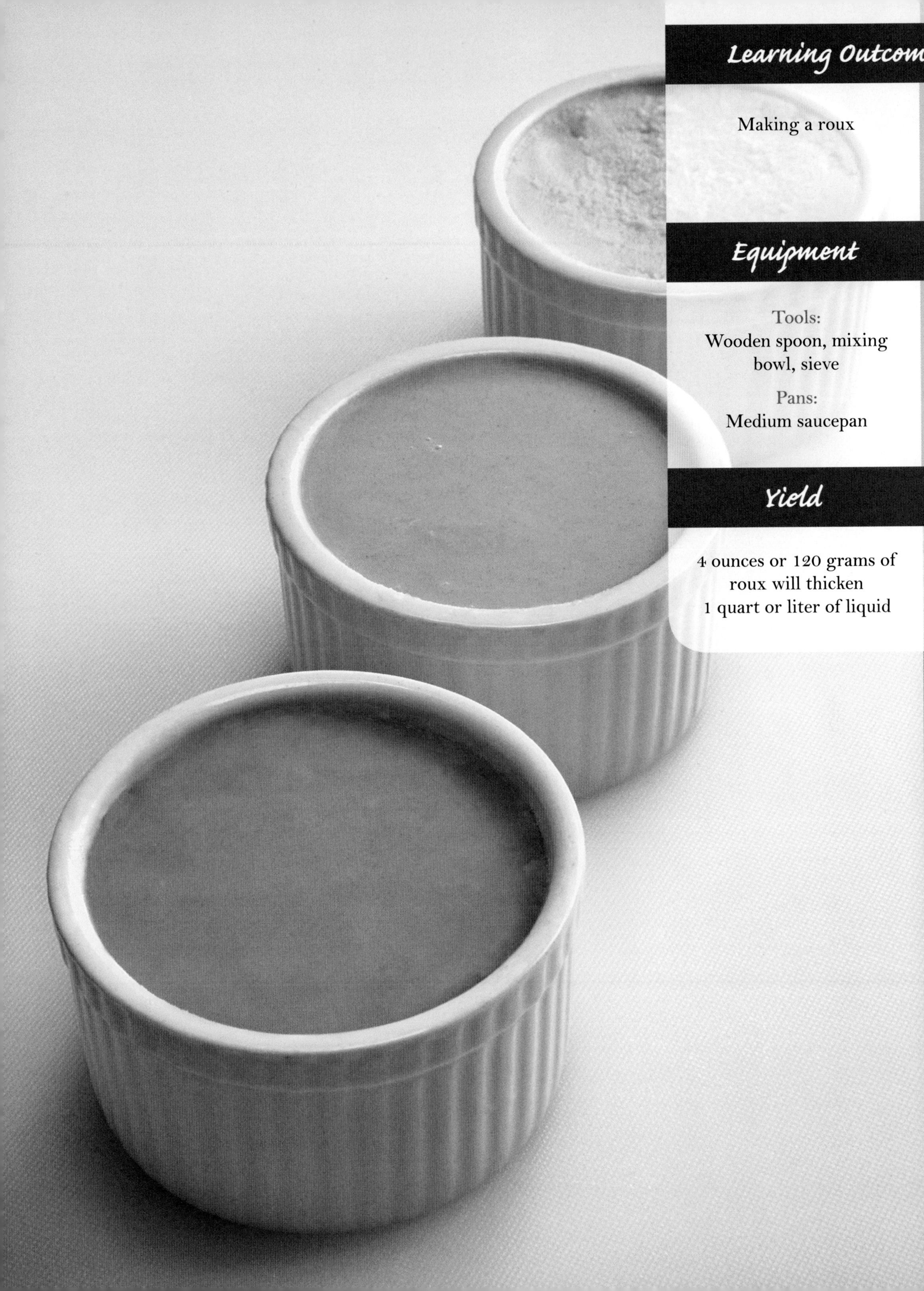

Learning Outcomes

Making a roux

Equipment

Tools:
Wooden spoon, mixing bowl, sieve

Pans:
Medium saucepan

Yield

4 ounces or 120 grams of roux will thicken 1 quart or liter of liquid

Quantity		Ingredient
U.S.	Metric	
2 oz	60 g	Flour
2 oz	60 g	Butter

Method

Roux Blanc

1. Sift the flour (**tamiser**).
2. Melt the butter in a medium pan over medium heat. When the butter begins to foam, add the flour and stir well until the mixture begins to bubble. Cook for 1 or 2 minutes to obtain a white roux (be careful not to let it color). Transfer the roux to a clean container and set it aside to cool.

Tip

The **roux blanc** is used primarily for the preparation of **sauce béchamel.**

Roux Blond

1. Proceed as for the **roux blanc** but cook the roux 4 to 5 minutes, or until it starts to take on a golden hue.

Tip

The roux blond is used to thicken **velouté** sauces

Roux Brun

1. Proceed as above but cook the **roux** until it reaches a deep golden color.

Tip

Do not rush cooking the roux as it can burn very easily. **Roux brun** is used to thicken brown sauces.

In order for it to work as a **liaison,** the cold **roux** is stirred into a hot liquid, piece by piece; or, conversely, cold liquid is added to the hot **roux.** Once the **roux** is incorporated into a sauce-base, let the preparation cook a little while; while long cooking can adversely affect a **beurre manié, roux** benefits from it. A **roux** must be sufficiently cooked; otherwise, an undesirable flour taste will persist.

Learning Outcomes

Liaison instantanée
Thickening with egg yolks
Tempering

Equipment

Tools:
Mixing bowl, whisk, chinois

Pans:
Saucepans

Yield

1.8 quarts or liters
thickened soup
or sauce

Method

1. Whisk the egg yolks with the cream.
2. Add some stock to warm the mixture *(tempérer)*.
3. Off the heat, add the tempered mixture to the remaining sauce and mix well.
4. Place over low heat and cook until thickened and unctuous. Do not allow it to come to a simmer or boil.
5. Strain into a clean pan and keep warm in a bain marie.

Tip

Egg yolks are the thickening agents (liaisons) in veloutés. Literally translated, velouté means "velvety" and egg yolks and the cream provide a rich, smooth finish to certain soups and sauces. The quantities provided above are based on a liter of sauce, and can be adjusted depending on the desired outcome of the sauce.

Quantity		Ingredient
U.S.	**Metric**	
4-6	4-6	Egg yolks
3 ½ oz	100 mL	Cream
1 qt	1 L	Sauce

Les Sauces de base
(Basic Sauces)

. . . .

Mayonnaise and
derivatives

. . . .

Sauce nantaise —
Nantaise Sauce

. . . .

Sauce hollandaise —
Hollandaise Sauce

. . . .

Sauce béarnaise —
Béarnaise Sauce

. . . .

Sauce béchamel —
Béchamel Sauce

. . . .

Sauce mornay —
Mornay Sauce

. . . .

Sauce velouté and
derivatives —
Velouté Sauce

. . . .

Sauce tomate —
Tomato Sauce

. . . .

Fondue de tomate

. . . .

Learning Outcomes

Making a cold
emulsion sauce

Equipment

Knives:
Chef knife (*couteau chef*)

Tools:
Mixing bowl, whisk, sieve

Yield

1 ½ pounds or 750 grams

HISTORY

In 1756, the Duke of Richelieu held a celebratory dinner after the French capture of Mahon on the Spanish island of Minorca. It is said that the presiding chef was out of cream for his sauce and added a substitution of olive oil—the resulting sauce was purportedly the first cold emulsion using eggs, oil, and vinegar. Named *mahonnaise* after the town of Mahon, the sauce, through successive misspellings, became known as mayonnaise.

MAYONNAISE AND DERIVATIVES

Method

Sauce Mayonnaise

1. Whisk together the mustard and vinegar in a large mixing bowl and season with salt and pepper.
2. Whisk in the egg yolks until well-combined.
3. Place the bowl on a cloth to keep it from slipping and gradually whisk in the oil in a steady stream.
4. Continue whisking until the mayonnaise is thick and light in color.
5. Reserve in a covered container in the refrigerator until needed.

Sauce Chantilly

1. Prepare a **sauce mayonnaise** using lemon juice instead of vinegar.
2. Fold in the whipped cream.
3. Reserve in a covered container in the refrigerator until needed.

Sauce Rémoulade

1. Prepare a **sauce mayonnaise**.
2. Mix in all the ingredients.
3. Reserve in a covered container in the refrigerator until needed.

Sauce Gribiche

1. Separate the cooked yolks from the boiled eggs. Press the yolks through a drum sieve (**tamis**) and reserve. Cut the cooked whites into a **julienne**.
2. Prepare a **sauce mayonnaise** using the puréed egg yolks in place of the raw egg yolks.
3. Mix in the julienned whites with the other ingredients and reserve in a covered container in the refrigerator until needed.

Note

As is often the case with emulsion sauce, the oil may separate. To fix a cold emulsion, place a small amount into a clean bowl. Whisk in enough hot water until re-emulsified, then gradually whisk in the remaining mayonnaise.

Quantity		Ingredient
U.S.	**Metric**	**Sauce Mayonnaise**
½ fl oz	10 mL	White wine vinegar
½ oz	10 g	Dijon mustard
2 pcs	2 pcs	Egg yolks
1 pint	0.5 L	Vegetable oil
		Salt and white pepper
		Sauce Chantilly
½ fl oz	10 mL	Lemon juice
½ oz	10 g	Dijon mustard
2 pcs	2 pcs	Egg yolks
1 pint	0.5 L	Vegetable oil
1 ¾ fl oz	50 mL	Cream, whipped, stiff peaks
		Salt and white pepper
		Sauce Rémoulade
8 ¾ fl oz	250 mL	Sauce mayonnaise
¾ oz	25 g	Capers, finely chopped (**hacher**)
¾ oz	25 g	Gherkins, finely chopped (**hacher**)
2 brs	2 brs	Parsley, finely chopped (**hacher**)
2 brs	2 brs	Chervil, finely chopped (**hacher**)
2 brs	2 brs	Tarragon, finely chopped (**hacher**)
¼ oz	5 g	Dijon mustard
		Anchovy essence
		Salt and white pepper
		Sauce Gribiche
¼ fl oz	10 mL	White wine vinegar
¼ oz	10 g	Dijon mustard
2 pcs	2 pcs	Eggs, hard boiled
1 pint	0.5 L	Vegetable oil
½ oz	15 g	Gherkins, finely chopped (**hacher**)
½ oz	15 g	Capers, finely chopped (**hacher**)
2 brs	2 brs	Parsley, finely chopped (**hacher**)
2 brs	2 brs	Chervil, finely chopped (**hacher**)
2 brs	2 brs	Tarragon, finely chopped (**hacher**)
		Salt and white pepper

Learning Outcomes

Sauce au beurre
Réduction
Monter au beurre

Equipment

Knives:
Paring knife (*office*)

Tools:
Whisk, chinois, bain marie

Pans:
Medium saucepan

Servings

4 servings

SAUCE NANTAISE
Nantaise Sauce

Method

1. Reduce the red wine vinegar and shallots in a medium saucepan over medium heat. Reduce by three-quarters.
2. Remove the pan from the heat and whisk in half of the butter until melted and well emulsified. Add the remaining butter and repeat. Season to taste.
3. Reserve the sauce in a ***bain marie*** until needed.

Quantity		Ingredient
U.S.	**Metric**	
10 oz	300 g	Red wine vinegar
2	2	Shallots, finely chopped (**hacher**)
7 oz	200 g	Butter, cold, diced
		Salt and pepper

FYI...

Sauce nantaise takes its name from the city of Nantes in the Brittany region of France. As to the inception of this sauce, one popular story occurs in a restaurant outside of Nantes in 1890 when chef Clémance Lefeuvre is said to have run out of eggs while making a sauce béarnaise. He found that the emulsion without eggs was pleasing to the palette and he served it to his customers, who also approved. A variation of this sauce is *beurre blanc*.

463

SAUCE HOLLANDAISE

Learning Outcomes

Making a hot emulsion
Stable emulsion
Sabayon

Equipment

Tools:
Bain marie, sieve, whisk

Pans:
Small saucepan, large saucepan

Yield

12 oz or 350 grams
4-6 servings

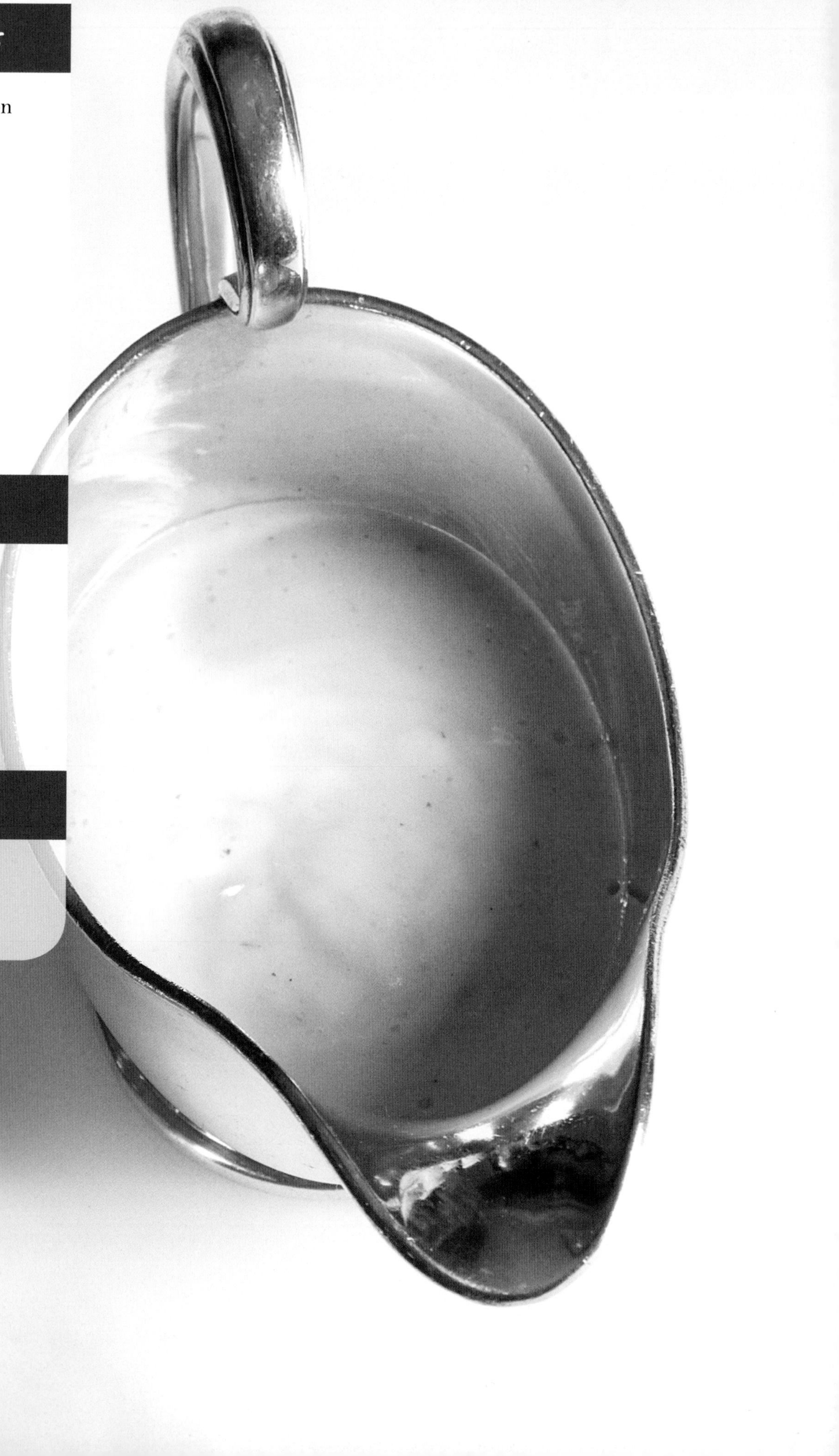

SAUCE HOLLANDAISE

Method

1. Bring the water and peppercorns to a boil in a small saucepan over medium-high heat and reduce by one-quarter.

2. Strain the water into a clean saucepan through a sieve and mix the egg yolks into the water with a whisk. Place the saucepan over a simmering bain marie and whisk the egg yolks and water until thick. At first the egg mixture will become light and frothy, then as the egg yolks cook, it will become dense (*sabayon*).

3. When the whisk leaves traces in the mixture when lifted, remove the pan from the bain marie. Place the pan on a cloth to keep it from slipping and gradually whisk in the clarified butter in a steady stream. The finished sauce should have the texture of a thick mayonnaise. Season to taste with the lemon juice, salt, and cayenne pepper. Reserve the Hollandaise in a bain marie until ready to use.

Tip

If the sauce splits, transfer a little of it to another bowl, then add a little cold water and whisk until it re-emulsifies. Slowly whisk the broken sauce into the amended sauce.

Quantity		Ingredient
U.S.	Metric	
2 oz	60 mL	Water
8 to 10 pcs	8 to 10 pcs	Black peppercorns, crushed (*mignonette*)
4 pcs	4 pcs	Egg yolks
8 oz	250 g	Butter, clarified
		Salt
		Cayenne pepper
		Lemon juice

FYI...

There is evidence to suggest that sauce hollandaise was originally named sauce d'Isigny. Isigny is a part of Normandy historically famous for its excellent dairy products and eggs (both of which are ingredients central to this sauce). However, due to the increasing import of dairy and eggs from Holland into France in the 17th century, the name hollandaise stuck. Sauce hollandaise accompanies many fish and vegetable preparations, and it is also the foundation for a number of other sauces—mousseline and mustard sauce are examples. Hollandaise makes up one of the five mother sauces as set out by Carême in the mid-1800s.

Learning Outcomes

Making a hot emulsion
Making a réduction
Stable emulsion
Sabayon

Equipment

Knives:
Chef knife (*couteau chef*)

Tools:
Bain marie, whisk,
chinois, ladle (*louche*)

Pans:
Small saucepans,
large saucepan

Servings

4 servings

SAUCE BÉARNAISE

Method

Sauce Béarnaise

1. Place the peppercorns, chopped shallots, and one-half of the chopped chervil and tarragon into a small saucepan. Add the white wine vinegar and water and season lightly with salt. Bring the liquid to a boil over medium-high heat and reduce it by two-thirds (*réduction*).

2. Remove the pan from the heat and mix the egg yolks into the réduction with a whisk. Place the pan over a bain marie and beat the mixture to increase the volume of the sauce; this process also serves to cook the eggs and, in so doing, thicken the sauce (*sabayon*).

3. When the whisk leaves traces in the mixture when lifted, remove the pan from the bain marie. At this point, the temperature should have reached a minimum of 65°C (149°F) to ensure that the eggs are cooked. *Note While the sauce has to be brought to 65°C (149°F), the sauce cannot be heated beyond 75°C (167°F) or else the yolks will coagulate to the consistency of scrambled eggs.*

4. Place the pan on a cloth to prevent it from slipping and whisk in one-third of the butter in small pieces. When completely incorporated, gradually mix in the rest of the butter. The finished sauce should have the texture of a mayonnaise and be light in color.

Finishing

1. Strain the mixture through a fine mesh sieve (*chinois*) into a clean pan, pressing well with a ladle (*fouler*).

2. Stir in the tarragon, taste the sauce, and adjust the seasoning. Although the sauce should be used immediately, it can be reserved in a gentle bain marie.

Quantity		Ingredient
U.S.	**Metric**	*Sauce Béarnaise*
5 pcs	5 pcs	Black peppercorns, crushed (*mignonette*)
¾ oz	25 g	Shallots, finely chopped (*hacher*)
2 brs	2 brs	Chervil, finely chopped (*hacher*)
2 brs	2 brs	Tarragon, finely chopped (*hacher*)
3 ½ oz	100 g	White wine vinegar
1 ¾ oz	50 g	Water
2 pcs	2 pcs	Egg yolks
6 oz	170 g	Butter
		Salt
		Finishing
¾ oz	20 g	Tarragon, finely chopped (*hacher*)
		Salt and white pepper

Unlike preparations "à la béarnaise," which are directly inspired by the cuisine of the Basses-Pyrénées (ancient Béarn), sauce béarnaise itself appears to have no obvious historical association to this region of France. Created in approximately 1813 for Barron Brisse at the Pavillon Henri IV (a restaurant on the outskirts of Paris), this sauce has similar features to the hollandaise. While Carême classified the béarnaise as "une petite sauce" and not a mother sauce it is, nevertheless, the base for a number of sauces such as Choron and Valois.

FYI...

Learning Outcomes

Preparing a béchamel
Preparing a roux
Tamponner
Lining a pan with bard
(*chemiser*)
Tamiser
Dégraisser

Equipment

Knives:
Paring knife (*office*),
chef knife (*couteau chef*)

Tools:
Wooden spoon, fork,
chinois, whisk, sieve,
bain marie

Pans:
Large saucepans (*russes*)

Yield

3.4 quarts or liters

It is ironic that such a lovely tasting sauce was named after such a distasteful man. Through opportunistic and sometimes fraudulent means, Louis de Béchameil (Marquis) made his fortune profiting from the chaos surrounding France's civil war (1643–1653). While the Marquis Béchameil is sometimes attributed with inventing the sauce himself, it is more likely that a chef under his supervision was responsible. Despite the controversy, this simple combination of roux and seasoned milk rightly deserves its place as one of Carême's five mother sauces. Due to its long cooking process, béchamel à l'ancienne was often prepared in advance like a stock.

SAUCE BÉCHAMEL
Béchamel Sauce

Method

Sauce Béchamel à l'ancienne

1. Preheat the oven to 175°C (350°F)
2. *Prepare a white roux:* Sift the flour (*tamiser*). Melt the butter in a medium pan over medium heat. When the butter begins to foam, add the flour and stir well until the mixture begins to bubble. Cook for 1 or 2 minutes to obtain a white roux (*be careful not to let it color*). Set aside to cool.
3. Line a 4 liter / 4 quart ovenproof saucepan with barding fat. Add white peppercorns and an onion studded with a clove and a bay leaf to the pan. Refrigerate the saucepan to harden the barding fat.
4. Meanwhile, heat the milk and an onion studded with a clove and bay leaf in a large saucepan over medium heat and let it infuse for 30 minutes.

Note
To produce a stronger onion flavor, finely slice the onion before adding it to the milk.

5. Strain half the hot milk onto the cold roux through a fine mesh sieve (*chinois*) and whisk well to combine the ingredients. Continue whisking the mixture over medium heat until smooth. Strain the remaining milk into the pan and whisk well to combine the ingredients. Season the contents of the pan with grated nutmeg and increase the heat to medium-high. Bring the liquid to a low boil, stirring constantly. Continue to simmer it while gently stirring until it thickly coats the back of a spoon (*à la nappe*). Strain the sauce through a fine mesh sieve (*chinois*) into the prepared saucepan. *Optional: Add the mushroom trimmings and the veal foot (cut into small enough pieces to fit into the pan).* Cover the pan and transfer to the oven to cook for 1½ hours.

Finishing

1. Remove the béchamel from the oven. The sauce should be very thick and coated in a layer of melted fat. Remove (*décanter*) the onion and *bouquet garni* and let the sauce cool to room temperature. Once cooled, cover and refrigerate overnight to set.
2. The cold sauce should be nearly solid. Unmold it into a clean saucepan and peel off all the barding fat. Melt the sauce over medium heat, stirring it occasionally. Then strain it through a fine mesh sieve (*chinois*) into a clean saucepan. Pat (*tamponner*) with a piece of butter held on the end of a fork, to cover it in a film of fat that will prevent the sauce from developing a skin.
3. Reserve in a *bain marie* until needed.

Sauce Béchamel Moderne

1. Heat the milk and an onion studded with a clove and bay leaf in a large saucepan over medium heat and let it infuse for 30 minutes. Next, strain half the hot milk onto the cold roux through a fine mesh sieve (*chinois*) and whisk well to combine the ingredients. Continue whisking the mixture over medium heat until smooth. Strain the remaining milk into the pan and whisk well to combine the ingredients. Add the *bouquet garni* and season the sauce lightly with salt, pepper, and nutmeg. Bring the liquid to a low boil, stirring constantly, and continue to simmer it while gently stirring until it coats the back of a spoon (*à la nappe*). Strain the sauce through a fine mesh sieve (*chinois*) into a clean saucepan. Pat (*tamponner*) with a piece of butter held on the end of a fork, to cover it in a film of fat that will prevent the sauce from developing a skin.
2. Reserve in a *bain marie* until needed.

Quantity		Ingredient
U.S.	**Metric**	*Sauce Béchamel à l'ancienne*
6 oz	180 g	Butter
6 oz	180 g	Flour
1 lb	500 g	Barding fat
2 pcs	2 pcs	Onions (halved)
4 pcs	4 pcs	Cloves
2 pcs	2 pcs	Bay leaves
¼ oz	5 g	White peppercorns, crushed (*mignonette*)
1 pc	1 pc	*Bouquet garni*
3 qt	3 L	Milk
½ pc	½ pc	Veal foot, degorged, blanched (*optional*)
3 ½ oz	100 g	Mushroom peelings (*optional*)
½ oz	10 g	Salt
		Nutmeg, grated
		Sauce Béchamel Moderne
4 oz	120 g	White *roux*, cold
1 qt	1 L	Milk
1 pc	1 pc	Onion, studded (*clouter*)
1 pc	1 pc	*Bouquet garni*
		Salt
		Pepper
		Nutmeg

Learning Outcomes

Making a sauce Mornay
Sauce béchamel
Tempering egg yolks

Equipment

Tools:
Wooden spoon, ladle
(*louche*), fork, chinois,
whisk, grater

Pans:
Large saucepan (*russe*)

Yield

1 ⅓ pounds or 600 grams
4-6 servings

SAUCE MORNAY
Mornay Sauce

Quantity		Ingredient
U.S.	Metric	
1 pint	0.5 L	*Sauce béchamel*
1 pc	1 pc	Egg yolk
3 ½ oz	100 g	Gruyère cheese, grated
1 oz	30 g	Butter

Method

1. Temper the egg yolk: Whisk a small quantity of hot *sauce béchamel* into a bowl with the egg yolk, then stir the tempered yolk back into the *sauce béchamel*.
2. Strain the mixture through a fine mesh sieve (*chinois*), add the gruyère cheese and mix until melted, then finish by mixing in the butter (*monter au beurre*).
3. Serve immediately.

Note

Sauce Mornay can be kept warm in a bain marie over very low heat; however, if the bain marie is too hot, the yolks can curdle.

HISTORY

A derivative of sauce béchamel, sauce Mornay is characterized by the addition of egg yolks and gruyère cheese. Invented by Joseph Voiron in the 19th century and named after his son Mornay (who was himself a cook), this sauce accompanies preparations destined to be grilled or baked.

Learning Outcomes

Making sauce velouté
Roux blond
Tamiser
Liaison with egg yolks
Tamponner

Equipment

Knives:
Paring knife (*office*)

Tools:
Wooden spatula, whisk, fork, bain marie, bowls, chinois, sieve

Pans:
Medium saucepans

Yield

1.120 quarts or liters

HISTORY

Velouté translates as "velvety" or "silky," adjectives that describe the texture of this sauce very well. Used as a base for a number of other derivative sauces (sauce suprême and sauce allemande, among others), velouté is also used to describe soups. Sauce velouté makes up one of the five mother sauces as set out by Carême in the mid-1800s.

Quantity		Ingredient
U.S.	*Metric*	*Sauce Velouté*
2 oz	60 g	Butter
2 oz	60 g	Flour
1 qt	1 L	Chicken stock
1 pc	1 pc	*Bouquet garni*
		Mushroom peels and stems
		Salt
		Pepper
		Sauce Suprême
1 pint	500 mL	*Sauce velouté*
1 pc	1 pc	Skin from poached poultry
3 ½ oz	100 mL	Cream
1 pc	1 pc	Lemon, juice of
		Salt and pepper
		Sauce Allemande ou Parisienne
1 pint	500 mL	*Sauce velouté*
3 ½ oz	100 mL	Cream
2 pcs	2 pcs	Egg yolks
		Salt and pepper

Method

Sauce Velouté

1. Prepare a blond *roux*: Sift the flour (*tamiser*). Melt the butter in a medium pan over medium heat. When the butter begins to foam, add the flour and stir well until the mixture begins to bubble. Cook for 4 to 5 minutes, or until the mixture starts to take on a golden hue.
2. Remove the pan from the heat. Add the cold chicken stock all at once and whisk. Whisking continuously, raise the heat to medium-high and bring the sauce to a boil. Add the *bouquet garni* and mushroom trimmings and season lightly with salt and pepper. Reduce the heat to medium-low and let the sauce simmer gently for 20 minutes.
3. Strain the sauce through a fine mesh sieve (*chinois*) into a clean pan. Taste and adjust seasoning.
4. Pat (*tamponner*) the sauce with a knob of butter held on the end of a fork. This will cover it in a film of fat and prevent the sauce from developing a skin. Reserve the sauce in a warm bain marie until needed.

Sauce Suprême

1. Mix the cream and poultry skin into the *sauce velouté* and simmer it gently for a further 20 minutes over medium-low heat.
2. Strain the sauce through a fine mesh sieve (*chinois*) into a clean pan. Taste and adjust the seasoning and finish the sauce with lemon juice to taste.
3. Pat (*tamponner*) the sauce with a knob of butter held on the end of a fork. Reserve the sauce in a warm bain marie until needed.

Sauce Allemande ou Parisienne

1. Whisk the yolks and cream together.
2. *Temper egg yolk mixture:* Remove the *sauce velouté* from the heat. Stir in a ladle or two of the hot liquid into the yolk and cream mixture. Mix well, then turn off the heat, stir the tempered yolks into the pan. Taste and adjust the seasoning.
3. Pat (*tamponner*) the sauce with a knob of butter held on the end of a fork to prevent a skin from forming. Reserve the sauce in a bain marie until needed.

Tip

Once the yolks have been incorporated, the mixture should never be brought to a temperature above 85 °C (185 °F) or it will curdle.

Learning Outcomes

Preparing sauce tomate
Écumer
Dégraisser
Singer
Tamponner, using a
food mill

Equipment

Knives:
Chef knife (*couteau chef*),
vegetable peeler (*économe*),
paring knife (*office*)

Tools:
Twine, wooden spatula,
écumoire, food mill (*moulin
de légumes*), chinois, ladle,
carving fork

Pans:
Dutch oven (*cocotte*),
small saucepan,
large saucepan (*russe*)

Yield

3.5 quarts or liters

Although the tomato was introduced to Europe in the 16th century, its culinary strengths were not recognized in France until the 1800s. This time lag had much to do with the fruit's botanical connection with another plant, the deadly Belladonna; however, once this fear was debunked, the tomato became a cause célèbre—to the extent that *sauce tomate* was designated by Carême as one of the five mother sauces.

SAUCE TOMATE
Tomato Sauce

Quantity		Ingredient
U.S.	**Metric**	
2 fl oz	60 mL	Vegetable oil
2 ½ oz	75 g	Smoked pork belly, cut into lardons and blanched (reserve rind)
3 ½ oz	100 g	Carrot, cut into *mirepoix*
2 ½ oz	75 g	Onion, cut into *mirepoix*
3 ½ oz	100 g	White leeks cut into *mirepoix*
1 ½ oz	50 g	Celery cut into *mirepoix*
1 oz	30 g	Tomato paste (*optional*)
2 ½ oz	75 g	Flour
6 lbs	3 kg	Tomatoes, quartered
1 pc	1 pc	***Bouquet garni***
4-6 pcs	4-6 pcs	Garlic clove, finely chopped (*hacher*)
½ oz	15 g	Salt
½ oz	15 g	Sugar
20 pcs	20 pcs	Peppercorns
1 qt	1 L	White stock (*chicken or veal*)
1 oz	30 g	Butter
		Salt and pepper

Method

1. Preheat the oven to 175°C (350°F).
2. Heat the oil in a large Dutch oven (*cocotte*) over high heat and sauté the *lardons* until they are lightly colored (*blond*). Add the carrot, onion, and garlic, and sauté until they begin to lightly color (*blond*). Then add the celery, then the leek, stirring after each addition.
3. Stir in the tomato paste and cook for 1 to 2 minutes *(pincer la tomate).* Add the tomatoes, salt, and sugar then stir until combined.
4. Stir in the flour and cook it for 1 to 2 minutes, stirring well (*singer*). Place the *bouquet garni* and bacon rind on top, fit the cover on the *cocotte* and transfer to the hot oven. Cook for 25 to 30 minutes. This will concentrate the tomatoes and further cook the flour (*singer*).
5. Remove the *cocotte* from the oven and pour in the white stock. Stir well, replace the cover and place back in the oven to cook for 1 ½ to 2 hours.
6. Remove the *cocotte* from the oven and discard the bacon rind and *bouquet garni*. Purée the contents of the *cocotte* in a food mill, then strain the purée through a fine mesh sieve (*chinois*) into a clean saucepan. Bring the sauce to a boil over medium-high heat and skim (*écumer*) the surface if needed. Taste the sauce, adjust the seasoning, and mount with cold butter.
7. Remove the pan from the heat and pat (*tamponner*) the surface of the sauce with a knob of butter held on the end of a fork. This will cover the sauce in a film of fat that will prevent it from developing a skin. Reserve the sauce in a bain marie until needed.

Tip

Sauce tomate *made as a base for other sauces can also be made without flour, instead being reduced to the desired thickness.*

Method

1. Preheat the oven to 175°C (350°F).
2. Melt the butter in a medium saucepan over medium heat and cook the tomato paste for 2–3 minutes (*pincer la tomate*).
3. Add the diced tomatoes, the *bouquet garni*, and season with salt and pepper. Stirring continuously, cook the ingredients for 5 minutes then cover with a parchment paper lid (*cartouche*). Transfer the saucepan to the oven for 25 to 30 minutes or until the tomatoes have thickened.
4. Remove the *bouquet garni*, adjust the seasoning and add a pinch of sugar if necessary. Allow to come to room temperature and reserve the finished fondue de tomate in a covered recipient in the refrigerator until needed.

Learning Outcomes

Fondue de tomate
Tomates concassée
Making a cartouche

Equipment

Knives:
Chef knife (*couteau chef*), paring knife (*office*)

Tools:
Wooden spatula, parchment paper

Pans:
Medium saucepan

Yield

1 cup or 250 grams

Quantity		Ingredient
U.S.	Metric	
2 oz	60 g	Butter
1 oz	30 g	Tomato paste
8 pcs	8 pcs	Tomatoes *concassée*
1 pc	1 pc	*Bouquet garni*
		Salt and pepper
		Pinch of sugar (optional)

Les Preparations de base
(Basic Preparations)

Farce à gratin

Farce simple —
Simple Stuffing

Farce mousseline —
Fish Mousse

Légumes glacés —
Glazed Vegetables

Riz Créole —
Creole Rice

Riz Pilaf —
Rice Pilaf

FARCE À GRATIN

Learning Outcomes

Making a farce à gratin
Flambage
Puréeing using a tamis

Equipment

Knives:
Slicing knife (*éminceur*),
paring knife (**office**)

Tools:
Tamis, mixing bowl,
spatula, corne

Pans:
Sauté pan

Yield

Approximately 1 pound or
500 grams

FARCE À GRATIN

Method

1. Melt half of the butter in a sauté pan over medium heat. When the butter is hot (but not turning brown) add the livers and lightly sear on both sides making sure they do not color too much. The livers should still be soft when touched.
2. Add the shallots and sweat (**suer**), then add the chopped parsley. Stir to combine.
3. Add the cognac, flambé, and allow the flames to die down.
4. Add the cream and the remaining butter and reduce for one minute.
5. Transfer the cooked livers to a drum sieve (**tamis**) placed over a sheet of parchment paper. Using a plastic scraper (**corne**), press the ingredients through the **tamis**. Scrape the farce from the underside of the tamis along with any on the parchment and transfer to a clean bowl.
6. Before storing it in the refrigerator, lay a sheet of plastic wrap in direct contact with the farce.

Optional: *To give the farce a little more flavor, cook some finely chopped smoked pork belly with the chicken livers.*

Quantity		Ingredient
U.S.	**Metric**	
12 oz	350 g	Chicken liver (*cleaned and de-nerved*)
3 ½ oz	100 g	Butter
2 pcs	2 pcs	Shallots, finely chopped (**hacher**)
1 oz	30 mL	Cognac
2 oz	60 mL	Cream
1 ¾ oz	50 g	Lardons (*optional*)

This farce is traditionally spread on a slice of toasted bread (canapé) that will serve as a bed to present a small roasted bird. Ideally this farce is made from the liver of the bird it is served with.

Learning Outcomes

Preparing a farce simple
Chopping or grinding meat
Monter la farce

Equipment

Knives:
Chef knife (*couteau chef*)

Tools:
Meat grinder (optional), mixing bowl, ice bath, rubber spatula

Yield

1 ¾ pound or 800 grams

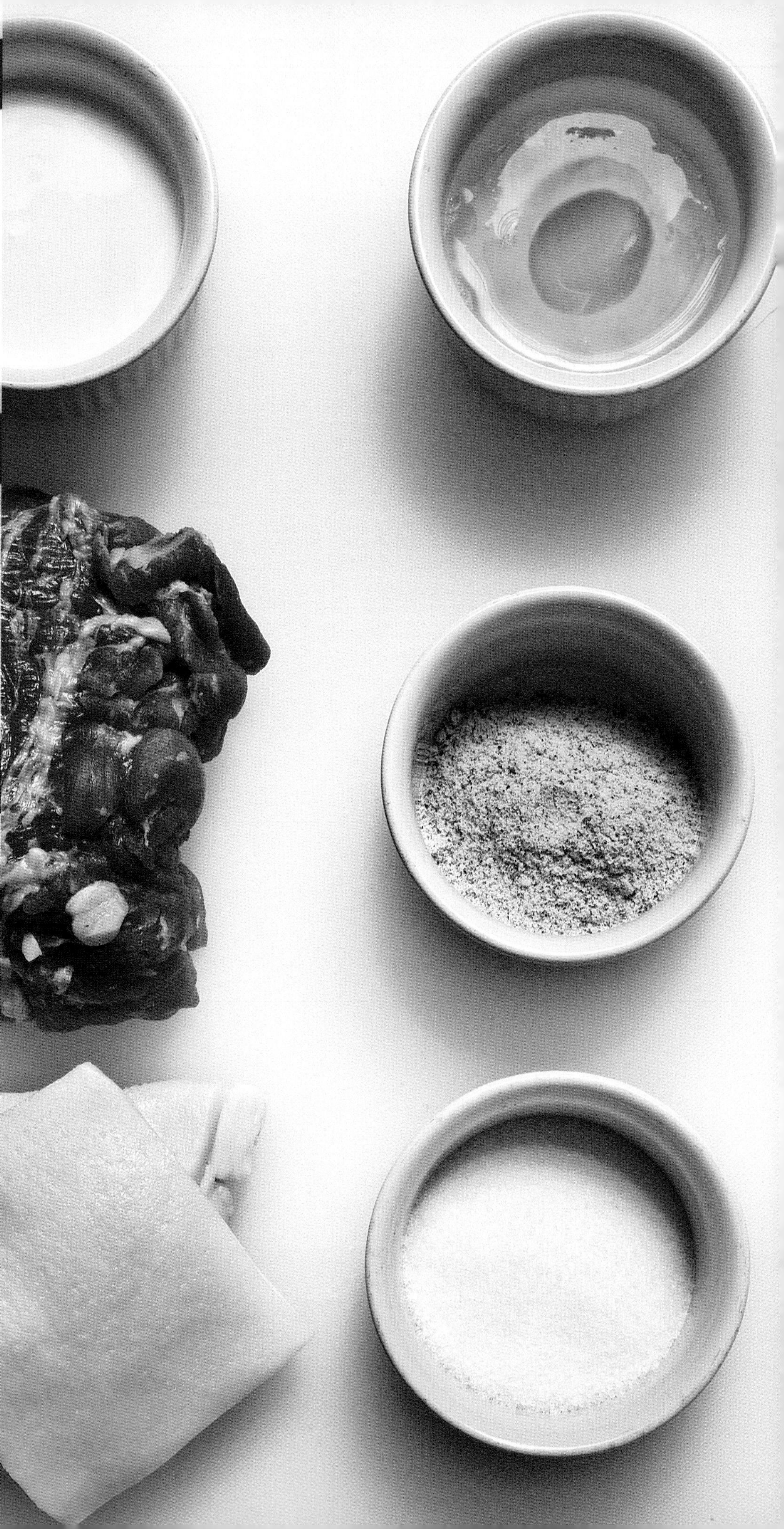

FARCE SIMPLE
Simple Stuffing

Method

1. Finely chop (**hacher**) the pork fat and meat or grind them through a meat grinder fitted with the large grind plate.
2. Using a rubber spatula, combine the ground or chopped meat and pork fat in a large mixing bowl set in an ice bath.
3. Once combined, add the egg into the mixture, mixing well.
4. Mix in the cream little by little (**monter la farce**) again mixing well after each addition. Keep mixing until the mixture is thick and pale. Season the farce with salt and white pepper and spread the finished farce up the side of the bowl to ensure it cools properly.

Tip

If preparing the farce for a later use, cover it in plastic wrap (in direct contact with the farce) and reserve it in the refrigerator.

Never conserve a farce for more than a day as it is very fragile and prone to contamination.

To check the seasoning, poach a small amount of farce in boiling water and taste.

Quantity		Ingredient
U.S.	Metric	
1 lb	500 g	Meat (veal or pork)
5 oz	150 g	Pork fat
1 pc	1 pc	Egg
3 ½ fl oz	100 mL	Cream
		Salt and white pepper

Generally, farce simple is made up of 70 to 75% lean meat, and 25 to 30% fatty meat or, as is the case in this recipe, pure fat. The fat percentage of a farce will depend on its application; if the farce accompanies another meat that is low in fat then the farce will compensate with a higher fat content—the fat content acts to keep the farce moist. Egg whites, also a component in farce simple, add volume and serve to bind the ingredients. Distinguishing it from the mousseline in texture, the meat in a farce simple is not passed through a tamis nor is the use of cream obligatory. While an over-cooked mousseline will become rubbery, the farce simple is a little more lenient in this regard and can be cooked at a slightly higher temperature. The basic recipe featured above can be enhanced with other ingredients including herbs, shallots, and various spices. In terms of application, the farce simple is often used in *terrines de viande,* sausages, or as a stuffing in meat preparations such as ballotines.

Learning Outcomes

Farce mousseline
or farce fine
Tamiser
Monter la farce

Equipment

Knives:
Chef knife (*couteau chef*)

Tools:
Tamis, corne, food processor, ice bath, mixing bowl, spatula

Yield

2 pounds or 900 grams

FARCE MOUSSELINE
Fish Mousse

Quantity		Ingredient
U.S.	Metric	
1 lb	500 g	White fish fillets, boned and skinned (or white meat such as chicken)
2 pcs	2 pcs	Egg whites
12 fl oz	350 mL	Cream
		Salt and white pepper

Method

1. Chop the fish very finely (**hacher**) or purée it in a food processor using quick bursts. Using a plastic scraper (**corne**), press the puréed fish (pulp) through a drum sieve (**tamis**) into a bowl sitting in an ice bath.
2. Using a rubber spatula, work the egg whites into the fish one by one, mixing well after each addition. Keeping the bowl over the ice bath, mix in the cream little by little (**monter la farce**). Continue mixing until the mixture is thick and pale.
3. Season the mousseline with salt and white pepper then spread the mousseline around the edges of the bowl to help it chill thoroughly.

Tip

If preparing the mousseline for a later use, cover it in plastic wrap (in direct contact with the mousseline) and reserve it in the refrigerator.

Never conserve a mousseline for more than a day as it is very fragile and prone to contamination.

To check the seasoning, poach a small amount of mousseline in boiling water and taste.

FYI...

The operative word in *mousseline* is *mousse*, which indicates a lighter, more voluminous end result to a preparation. The primary uses for mousseline de poisson are as a stuffing for fish and in the preparation of fish terrines. Mousseline de poisson can also be used in roulades as well as in a number of other preparations including quenelles.

Learning Outcomes

Glaçage à blanc, à blond,
à brun
Tourner, blanchir
Étuver
Cartouche

Equipment

Knives:
Paring knife (*office*) or
turning knife

Tools:
Parchment paper

Pans:
Small pan

Yield

2-4 servings

Method

1. Blanch (**blanchir**) the vegetables and refresh them under cold running water.
2. Place the blanched vegetables in a small saucepan that is wide enough to fit them in a single layer.
3. Add the water, salt, sugar, and butter.
4. Cover the vegetables with a parchment-paper lid (**cartouche**). Place the pan over low heat and gently cook the vegetables (**étuver**), gently shaking the pan from time to time to turn the vegetables over. Continue to cook the vegetables over low heat until the water has evaporated and a glaze forms. Toss the vegetables to evenly coat them in the glaze.

Légumes Glacés à Blond

1. Proceed as above.
2. Once the liquid has reduced to a glaze, cook it a little longer until it begins to lightly color.
3. Toss the vegetables to evenly color and coat them in the glaze.

Légumes Glacés à Brun

1. Proceed as above.
2. Once the liquid has reduced to a glaze, continue cooking until it begins to color.
3. Continue to cook, tossing the vegetables to coat them in glaze and evenly color them a dark caramel color.

Note

The vegetables listed in this recipe should always be glazed separately. The quantities of water, salt, sugar and butter are indicated for one vegetable type only, not a combination of all three.

Quantity		Ingredient
U.S.	**Metric**	
10 oz	300 g	Carrots, turned
10 oz	300 g	Turnips, turned
10 oz	300 g	Pearl onions, peeled
8 fl oz	250 mL	Water
Pinch	Pinch	Salt
½ oz	15 g	Sugar
1 oz	30 g	Butter

FYI...

Methods for glazing are numerous. Pastry may be glazed with a beaten egg or a glacé royale. A glaze can also be obtained by reducing stock to the consistency of a syrup, or in the case of the above, by cooking a vegetable in a sugar–water–butter solution that is itself simultaneously being reduced into a glaze.

RIZ CRÉOLE
Creole Rice

Quantity		Ingredient
U.S.	**Metric**	
8 oz	250 g	Rice, long grain
1.5 qt	1.5 L	Water
5 oz	150 g	Butter (for reheating)
		Salt

Method

1. Rinse the rice in a large amount of cold water and drain it in a sieve.
2. Place the rice in a large pan and add the water.
3. Place the pan over medium-high heat and once the rice comes to a boil, cook the rice for 14 minutes. Remove from the heat, strain the rice and refresh with cold water. Drain well then transfer the rice to a colander lined with a cloth. Allow to drain completely.

Note

*Riz créole is often used for cold preparations such as salads, or in a farce. To reheat: place in a buttered dish and dot the surface with butter and season with salt and pepper. Place in a hot oven. Once the rice is hot, remove it from the oven and separate the grains with a fork (**égrener**). Delicately mix in the rest of the butter until it is completely melted (**lier au beurre**).*

Learning Outcomes

Cooking rice créole
Égrener
Lier au beurre

Equipment

Tools:
Strainer, carving fork, colander

Pans:
Medium saucepan

Servings

6 servings

Rice is the grain produced from a variety of grasses in the *Oryza sativa* family. Reaching between 2 and 6 feet in height, rice plants can be found growing from the North American prairie wetlands to the terraced rice fields of Indonesia. Free of sodium, cholesterol, and fat, rice is a healthy grain that over half of the global community relies upon for sustenance. *Riz Créole* refers to a simple but effective method for boiling rice that

Making riz pilaf
Nacrer
Lier au beurre
Égrener

Equipment

Knives:
Chef knife (*couteau chef*),
paring knife (*office*)

Tools:
Wooden spatula, twine,
scissors (*ciseaux*), fork or
carving fork

Pans:
Medium saucepan with
cover (optional)

Servings

4 servings

RIZ PILAF
Rice Pilaf

Method

1. Preheat the oven to 180°C (350°F).
2. Melt the butter in a medium saucepan over low heat and sweat (**suer**) the onion until translucent. Add the rice and stir gently until it turns opaque and shiny (**nacrer**). Pour in the cold water and add the **bouquet garni.** Bring the water to a boil, then remove the pan from the heat. Cover the saucepan with a parchment-paper lid (**cartouche**) or cover with a lid. Transfer the rice to the oven to cook for 18 minutes (or until **al-dente**).
3. Remove the rice from the oven, lift the cartouche or the lid, and dot the surface with pieces of butter. Replace the cartouche and allow the butter to melt (**lier au beurre**).
4. Once the butter has melted, gently separate the grains of rice with the prongs of a carving fork (**égrener**).

Quantity		Ingredient
U.S.	**Metric**	
1 ½ oz	40 g	Butter
3 ½ oz	100 g	Onion, finely chopped (**hacher**)
8 oz	250 g	Rice, long grain
12 ½ fl oz	375 mL	Water
3 oz	90 g	Butter
		Salt and white ground pepper
1 pc	1 pc	**Bouquet garni**

A derivative of the Persian word *pilaou,* which means boiled rice, pilaf in the modern context indicates a method that involves cooking the rice in fat (**nacrer**) before adding the liquid element (usually stock). Pilaf can be flavored with onion and **bouquet garni,** but has a whole host of variations. This includes the much loved paella, which is garnished with chicken, vegetables, and shellfish.

La Pâtisserie
(Kitchen Doughs and Mixtures)

Pâte à pâtes —
Pasta Dough

Pâte brisée

Pâte feuilletée —
Puff Pastry

Pâte sucrée —
Sweet Dough

Pâte sablée

Biscuit cuillère —
Ladyfinger Biscuit

Biscuit dacquoise

Biscuit génoise

Learning Outcomes

Making pâte à pâtes
(pasta dough)
Tamiser
Making a fontaine
Kneading

Equipment

Tools:
Tamis, corne, fork

Yield

1 pound or 500 grams
4-6 servings

Quantity		Ingredient
U.S.	Metric	
14 oz	400 g	Flour
2 pcs	2 pcs	Eggs
Pinch	Pinch	Salt
1 fl oz	30 mL	Olive oil
¼ fl oz	10 mL	Water

Method

1. Sift (*tamiser*) the flour onto a clean work surface and, using a plastic scraper (*corne*), make a large well (*fontaine*) in the center.
2. Whisk the eggs and salt together in a small bowl until the salt is completely dissolved. Pour these ingredients into the well, add the olive oil and water, and stir them together with your fingertips.
3. While incorporating these ingredients, slowly add flour from the sides of the well using the *corne*. When the mixture resembles a thick paste, add the remaining dry ingredients and cut them with the *corne* until a dough forms. Knead the dough until it is smooth (5 minutes) and no longer sticky.
4. Form the dough into a disk and wrap in plastic, then place it in the refrigerator to rest for a minimum of 20 minutes (preferably overnight) before rolling it out.

FYI...

Generally when people think pasta they think Italian—and well they should. In European cuisine, the vast array of pasta shapes, stuffings, and sauces are certainly a gift from Italian cuisine. The origin of pasta, however, is less certain. According to 16th century travel writer Giovanni Ramusio, Marco Polo brought wheat noodles back to Venice from China in the 13th century. If, however, Italians contest the origins of pasta, they are not alone; in Asia, the same dispute is unresolved, with the Koreans challenging the Chinese for the patent rights of this versatile food.

PÂTE BRISÉE

Quantity		Ingredient
U.S.	Metric	
7 oz	200 g	Flour
3 ½ oz	100 g	Butter, cold, diced
1 pc	1 pc	Egg
¼ oz	5 g	Salt
¼ fl oz	10 mL	Water, cold

Method

1. Sift (**tamiser**) the flour onto a clean work surface and make a large well (**fontaine**) in the center using a plastic scraper (**corne**).
2. Place the cold, diced butter in the center of the well. Work the butter into the flour using your fingertips while simultaneously cutting through the mixture with the plastic scraper. Continue cutting until the butter is crumbly and coated in flour.
3. Rub the mixture between the palms of your hands until it resembles fine sand (**sabler**).
4. Gather the flour–butter mixture into a neat pile and make a well in the center using the **corne**. Add the salt, water and the egg to the center of the well. Stir these ingredients together using your fingertips until combined, then gradually incorporate the dry ingredients from the sides until the mixture in the center of the well resembles a paste.
5. Using the corne, incorporate the remaining dry ingredients with a cutting motion. Scoop and turn the mixture onto itself and continue cutting until a loose dough forms. Using the heel of your palm, firmly smear the dough away from yourself to ensure that no lumps are left (**fraiser**). Scrape up the dough and repeat until the dough becomes uniform.
6. Shape the dough into a ball, wrap it in plastic, and flatten it into a disk. Let the dough rest in the refrigerator for at least 30 minutes (preferably overnight).

Note

Kneading a shortcrust dough as if it were bread will encourage the formation of gluten molecules that will make it elastic, resulting in a hard, tough pastry. That is why using a cutting motion will provide a superior result.

Learning Outcomes

Making a pâte brisée
(shortcrust dough)
Sabler (sanding method)
Tamiser
Fraiser

Equipment

Tools:
Tamis, corne

Servings

One 8-10 inches (20-22 centimeters) tarte mold

Commenting on the production of pâte brisée (translated as broken dough—referring to the dough's crumbly nature) in the 1913 edition of *La Pâtisserie Pratique*, Henri Pellaprat suggests that to lose unwanted elasticity, let this pastry dough rest as long as possible. He warns that if the dough is tough before it is cooked it will be like *"carton"* (cardboard) afterwards. Furthermore, if the dough is tough, it could shrink and cause the filling to overflow.

Learning Outcomes

Making pâte feuilletée
(puff pastry)
Détrempe
Enveloppe
Tourer
Fleurer
Abaisser
Pâton

Equipment

Knives:
Chef knife (*couteau chef*)

Tools:
Tamis, corne, rolling pin,
baking brush

Yield

2 ½ pounds or
1.2 kilograms

HISTORY

There are many theories on the origins of pâte feuilletée, however, historians agree that the preparation was being developed during the Renaissance (circa 1400) in Europe. By the 16th century, the pastry had gained in popularity to the degree that a convent in Paris developed the *feuillantine pastry*, which was a word play on the name of their order, *Les Feuillantines*. The remarkable feature of pâte feuilletée (known also as *feuilletage* and, in English, puff pastry) is its many flaky and aerated layers, an effect caused by the steam from butter trapped in the layers of dough.

PÂTE FEUILLETÉE
Puff Pastry

Quantity		Ingredient
U.S.	**Metric**	**Pâte Feuilletée**
1 lb	500 g	Flour
7 oz	225 mL	Water
7 oz	200 g	Butter, room temperature
1 ¾ tsp	10 g	Salt
7 oz	200 g	Butter

Method

Détrempe

1. Sift (**tamiser**) the flour onto a clean work surface and make a well in the center using a plastic scraper (**corne**). Add the salt and water to the well. Stir with your fingertips until the salt is dissolved.
2. Add the butter, cut into pieces and begin to incorporate the flour using your fingertips. As the flour, butter, and water begin to combine, use the corne to cut the ingredients together, until it resembles a coarse dough. Sprinkle with additional water if the dough is too dry.
3. Once there are barely any traces of flour left, gather the dough into a ball and score the top of it with a deep cross using a large knife.
4. Loosely wrap the finished **détrempe** in plastic and transfer it to the refrigerator to rest for a minimum of 1 hour (preferably overnight).

Note Détrempe refers to the dough before the layer of butter (**beurrage**) is added.

Beurrage and Tourage

1. Place the cold butter between two sheets of parchment paper and pound it with a rolling pin until it is similar to the **détrempe** in consistency.
2. Using the **corne,** shape the butter into a flat square about 1cm/ ½ inch thick. Set the butter aside, if the kitchen is warm, place it in the refrigerator.
3. Lightly dust a clean work surface with flour (**fleurer**) then unwrap the **détrempe** and place it on the floured surface.
4. Using the scored marks as a guide, roll out (**abaisser**) the corners of the **détrempe** into a cross shape. Be careful to keep the center of the cross thicker than its outer arms (this will be important when rolling out the dough and the butter). Place the square of butter in the center of the cross and fold the two side arms over it so that they overlap slightly in the center (in the process be careful not to trap any air bubbles). Give the dough a quarter turn and fold the two remaining arms over the butter so that the butter is completely enclosed. Press the seams well to seal.
5. Lightly tap the dough with the length of the rolling pin to even out the distribution of the butter inside. Give the dough a quarter turn and repeat the tapping process. This is called the **enveloppe.**

Tourage, 6 Turns (6 tours simples)

1. Turns 1 and 2: Roll out (**abaisser**) the dough in long even strokes to form a rectangle that is three times the original length of the **enveloppe** or 1 cm thick. Brush off any excess flour.
2. Fold the bottom third of the dough up; then fold the top third down over the first fold. Make sure the edges are even. Give the dough a quarter turn to the right and repeat the same rolling process. Make sure to always brush away any excess flour.
3. Repeat the folding process (top third up, top third down over first fold) and give the dough a quarter turn to the right. Make two finger impressions in the top left corner of the dough.

Note These marks are a reminder of the number of turns that the dough has received; they also indicate the position for subsequent turns. Wrap the dough in plastic and transfer it to the refrigerator to rest for a minimum of 20 minutes. With two turns, the dough is now referred to as the *pâton*.

4. Turns 3 and 4: Lightly dust the work surface with flour (**fleurer**). Remove the dough from the refrigerator and unwrap it onto the floured surface (with the 2 indents in the top left corner). Proceed to give the dough a third and fourth turn (rolling and folding in the same manner as the first and second turns). Mark the dough with 4 imprints in the top left corner before wrapping it in plastic and returning it to the refrigerator to rest for a minimum of 20 minutes.
5. Turns 5 and 6: Lightly dust the work surface with flour (**fleurer**). Remove the dough from the refrigerator and unwrap it onto the floured surface (with the 4 indents in the top left corner). Proceed to give the dough its final 2 turns, folding and rolling as in previous turns. Wrap it in plastic and return it to the refrigerator to rest for a minimum of 20 minutes before rolling it out (the longer the dough rests the better it will perform).

Tip

Because the détrempe and the butter are at the same consistency, it is necessary to complete the turns as explained above. Allowing the dough to over-chill between turns, the butter may become too hard and crack when rolled out. Make sure you have allotted the necessary time to complete the turns.

Learning Outcomes

Making a pâte sucrée
Crémer (creaming method)
Tamiser
Fraiser

Equipment

Knives:
Paring knife (*office*)

Tools:
Sieve, corne

Yield

Approximately 15 ounces or
450 grams of dough
Two 8 inch /
20 centimeter tartes

PÂTE SUCRÉE
Sweet Dough

Quantity		Ingredient
U.S.	*Metric*	
7 oz	200 g	Flour
3 ½ oz	100 g	Powdered sugar
pinch	pinch	Salt
3 ½	100 g	Butter, diced
3 pcs	3 pcs	Egg yolks
1 tsp	1 tsp	Vanilla extract

Method

1. Sift the flour (**tamiser**) onto a clean work surface and gather it into a neat pile. Sift the powdered sugar in a separate pile in front of the flour. Sprinkle the salt over the sugar and, using a plastic scraper (**corne**), make a large well in the center of these ingredients.

Note *In the following steps, keep one hand clean and dry (for the plastic scraper) and use the other to stir in the wet ingredients.*

2. Add the butter to the center of the sugar and work it with your fingertips until it is soft. Using the **corne,** gradually add the powdered sugar from the edge of the well while simultaneously working it into the butter with your hands. Continue to mix the butter and sugar together until they are fully incorporated and creamy (**crémer**).

3. Add the egg yolk to the butter and sugar and mix it in with your fingertips. The result will be slightly lumpy. Add the vanilla extract to the mixture and work it in with your fingers until it is completely incorporated.

4. With your clean hand, use the **corne** to gradually add some flour to the creamed ingredients while simultaneously mixing with your fingertips. Continue until the mixture resembles a thick paste. Using the **corne**, cut in the remaining flour until a loose dough is formed.

5. Using the heel of your palm, firmly smear the dough away from yourself to ensure that no lumps are left (**fraiser**). Scrape up the dough and repeat until a smooth dough forms. Form the dough into a smooth ball, wrap it in plastic, and flatten it into a disk. Let it rest in the refrigerator for a minimum of 30 minutes (preferably overnight).

FYI... Like pâte sablée, pâte sucrée owes its crumbly, or friable, texture to its high concentration of butter as well as to the technique of creaming (*crémage*). This dough is primarily used as a shell for tarts.

PÂTE SABLÉE

Quantity		Ingredient
U.S.	Metric	
14 oz	400 g	Flour
¼ oz	4 g	Baking powder
pinch	pinch	Salt
7 oz	200 g	Butter, cold, diced
7 oz	200 g	Powdered sugar
4 pcs	4 pcs	Egg yolks
1 pc	1 pc	Vanilla bean

Method

1. Sift (*tamiser*) the flour and baking powder together onto a clean work surface.
2. Sprinkle the salt on top of the sifted ingredients and make a large well in the center using a plastic scraper (*corne*). Place the cold, diced butter in the center of the well. Work the butter into the flour using your fingertips while simultaneously cutting through the mixture with the *corne*. Continue cutting until the butter is crumbly and coated in flour.
3. Rub the mixture between the palms of your hands until it resembles fine sand (*sabler*).
4. Gather the flour–butter mixture into a neat pile and make a well (*fontaine*) in the center using the *corne*.
5. Cut the vanilla pod in half lengthwise, scrape the seeds out, and put in the well. Add the powdered sugar and egg yolks. Stir these ingredients together using your fingertips while simultaneously using the *corne* to gradually incorporate the dry ingredients from the sides.
6. Continue this process until the mixture in the center of the well resembles a paste.
7. Gather all the ingredients together and cut through them repeatedly with the *corne.* Continue this process until the mixture forms a homogenous dough.
8. Using the heel of your palm, firmly smear the dough away from yourself to ensure that no lumps are left (*fraiser*). Scrape the dough up and repeat until it is completely smooth. Shape the dough into a ball, wrap it in plastic, and flatten it out into a thick disc. Let it rest in the refrigerator for at least 30 minutes (preferably overnight).

Learning Outcomes

Making a pâte sablée
Tamiser
Fontaine
Sabler
Fraiser

Equipment

Knives:
Paring knife (*office*)
Tools:
Sieve, corne

Yield

2 pounds or 900 grams

Though it is known in English as "short-crust pastry," *pâte sablée* can be literally translated as "sandy pastry." The reason for the reference to "sandy" is because the first step in making this pastry is to mix the flour and butter together until they develop a sand-like appearance. The result of this procedure is that each flour granule becomes isolated by a coating of fat. This isolation of the flour crumb inhibits the development of glutinous bonds and gives the finished dough its crumbly texture. The presence of baking powder makes this dough more appropriate for making tea biscuits (cookies) than as a pastry liner.

FYI...

Learning Outcomes

Making a biscuit cuillère
Mounting egg whites
Meringue
Folding dry ingredients
Using a pastry bag

Equipment

Tools:
Mixing bowl, balloon
whisk, rubber spatula,
piping bag, plain tip,
parchment paper
or silicone mat

Pans:
Baking sheet

Yield

Enough for two 10 inch /
22 centimeter
entremets

BISCUIT CUILLÈRE
Ladyfinger Biscuit

Method

1. Preheat oven to 190°C (375°F).
2. Line a heavy baking sheet with a silicone mat or parchment paper.
3. Whisk the egg yolks and sugar together until pale and creamy (**blanchir**).
4. In a separate bowl, whisk the egg whites to soft peaks. Gradually add the sugar and continue whisking until the sugar is dissolved and the whites are stiff and glossy (**meringue**).
5. Fold about one-third of the whites into the yolk mixture to lighten the texture (**délayer**), then fold in the remainder. Before the whites are completely combined, fold in the sifted flour until just incorporated.
6. Fill a piping bag fitted with a large plain tip with the mixture. Pipe the biscuit onto the prepared baking sheet, into the appropriate shapes for the recipe and dust generously with powdered sugar. Alternatively, spread out evenly on lined baking sheet (in this case dusting with powdered sugar is not necessary).
7. Bake until lightly golden and the biscuit feels dry and springs back when touched (8 to 10 minutes).
8. Transfer the parchment immediately to a rack to cool.

Quantity		Ingredient
U.S.	Metric	
8 pcs	8 pcs	Egg yolks
5 ½ oz	160 g	Sugar
7 oz	200 g	Flour, sifted (**tamiser**)
8 pcs	8 pcs	Egg whites
2 ½ oz	80 g	Sugar
		Powdered sugar, for dusting

The name for this biscuit appears to come from an earlier, recipe that did not use a piping bag but rather a *cuillère* (spoon) to form the elongated biscuit. Recipes for "biscuits à la cuiller" show up in French cookbooks as old as *La Science du Maître d'Hôtel*, published in 1750. In Pellaprat's 1913 *La Pâtisserie Pratique*, the 1750 recipe remains largely unchanged, except of course for the use of the ever-practical piping bag.

Learning Outcomes

Making a dacquoise
Mounting egg whites
Making a meringue
Folding in dry ingredients
Using a piping bag

Equipment

Tools:
Sieve, mixing bowl, whisk,
rubber spatula, pastry bag,
plain tip, metal spatula,
parchment paper
or silicone mat

Pans:
Baking sheet

Yield

Two 10-12 inch /
22-24 centimeter rounds

BISCUIT DACQUOISE

Quantity		Ingredient
U.S.	Metric	
5 oz	150 g	Almond powder
7 ½ oz	225 g	Powdered sugar
¼ oz	3 g	Vanilla
1 ½ oz	50 g	Flour
6 pcs	6 pcs	Egg whites
2 ½ oz	75 g	Sugar

Method

1. Preheat the oven to 190°C (375°F).
2. Prepare a baking sheet by lining it with parchment paper or a silicone mat.
3. Sift the almond powder, sugar, flour, and vanilla together. Set aside.
4. Make a meringue: Beat the egg whites to soft peaks. Gradually incorporate the sugar until the meringue is firm and glossy, and the sugar granules cannot be felt when the meringue is rubbed between two fingers.
5. Fold in the sifted ingredients until just combined.
6. Transfer the mixture to a pastry bag fitted with a plain tip and pipe the shapes required for the recipe onto a prepared baking sheet. Alternatively, spread the mixture into a prepared mold.
7. Dust the piped shapes with powdered sugar. Bake them until they are lightly golden (approximately 20 to 25 minutes). Remove the baking sheet from the oven and transfer the parchment paper with the dacquoise to a rack to cool. Reserve at room temperature.

HISTORY

Used as a base or for layered gâteaux, dacquoise is a traditional preparation from the region surrounding the town of Dax in southwestern France. Due to the high sugar content of dacquoise, sometimes the paper is difficult to remove. To fix this problem turn the cooked dacquoise over and moisten the parchment paper with simple syrup until it is easily peeled off.

BISCUIT GÉNOISE

Quantity		Ingredient
U.S.	**Metric**	*Chemisage*
1 oz	30 g	Flour
1 oz	30 g	Butter
		Biscuit Génoise
4 oz	125 g	Flour, sifted (*tamiser*)
4 pcs	4 pcs	Eggs
4 oz	125 g	Sugar
¾ oz	25 g	Butter

Method

Chemisage

1. Preheat the oven to 205°C (400°F).
2. Butter an eight inch round cake pan/mold (*moule à manqué*) and place it in the freezer for 5 minutes to set the butter. Butter the mold a second time then coat it in flour (*chemiser*). Tap off any excess flour and reserve the mold in the refrigerator.

Génoise

1. Melt the butter in a small saucepan over low heat and set it aside.
2. Sift (*tamiser*) the flour onto a sheet of parchment paper.
3. Fill a saucepan one-quarter full of water and bring it to a simmer over medium-high heat (*bain marie*).
4. Break the eggs into a large mixing bowl, add the sugar and whisk together until combined. Place the bowl on the simmering bain marie and continue whisking until the mixture lightens in color and feels hot to the touch (45°C / 110°F).
5. At this point the mixture should form a ribbon when the whisk is lifted from the bowl. Remove the bowl from the bain marie and continue to whisk until it reaches room temperature.
6. Add the flour and gently fold it into the egg mixture with a rubber spatula until the flour is just incorporated. Fold in the melted butter then transfer the finished batter into the prepared cake mold and place it in the oven to bake.
7. Once the oven door is closed, reduce the heat to 350°F/185°C and bake the génoise for 18-20 minutes (test by inserting a knife into the center; if it comes out clean the cake is fully baked). Remove the génoise from the oven and let it cool in the mold for two to three minutes. Turn the cake out of the mold and finish cooling it upside down on a wire rack.

Learning Outcomes

Making a génoise
Mounting eggs
in a bain marie
Folding dry ingredients

Equipment

Tools:
Pastry brush, sieve, mixing bowl, balloon whisk, rubber spatula

Pans:
8 inch / 20 cm cake mold, medium saucepan

Yield

One 8 inch /
20 centimeter round

Generally translated into English as Genoese spongecake, it is said that the modern version of this biscuit was first adopted into French pâtisserie in 1852 when pastry chef Auguste Julien was intrigued to see a Genoese employee preparing the batter over a low heat.

FYI...

Les préprations de base
de la pâtisserie—
(Basic Pastry Preparations)

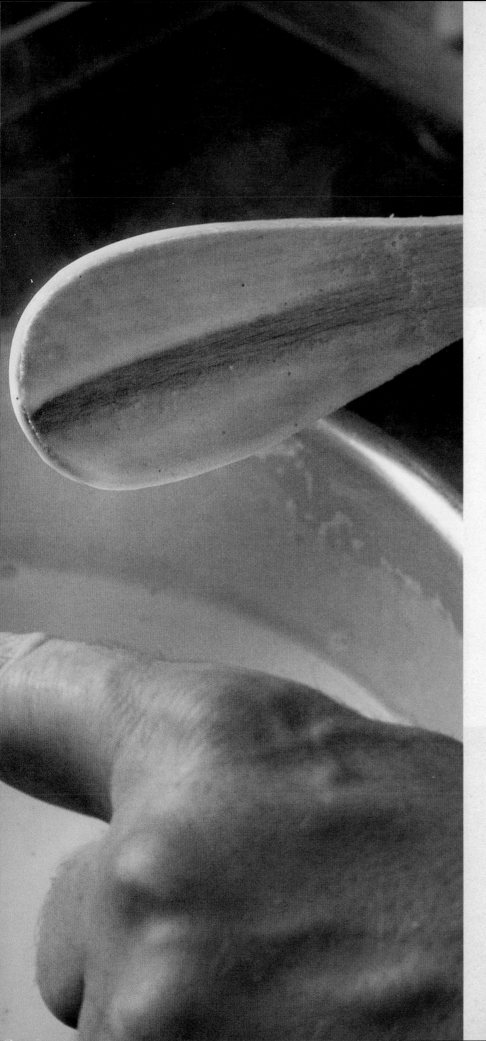

Les préprations de base de la pâtisserie—
(Basic Pastry Preparations)

. . . .

Crème anglaise —
Custard

. . . .

Crème d'amandes —
Almond Cream

. . . .

Crème pâtissière —
Pastry Cream

. . . .

Learning Outcomes

Cooked pouring custard
Blanchir
À la nappe
Vanner

Equipment

Knives:
Paring knife (*office*)

Tools:
Whisk, mixing bowls,
wooden spatula, chinois

Pans:
Medium saucepan

Yield

Approximately 12 ounces
or 350 mL
4-6 servings

CRÈME ANGLAISE
Custard

Quantity		Ingredient
U.S.	Metric	
8 fl oz	250 mL	Milk
3 pcs	3 pcs	Egg yolks
2 oz	60 g	Sugar
1 pc	1 pc	Vanilla bean, split and seeded (*optional*)

Method

1. Place the milk in a medium saucepan and bring to a low boil over medium high heat. Using a small knife, split the vanilla bean lengthwise. Scrape the seeds from both sides and add to the milk along with the pod. Whisk well.
2. Place the egg yolks in a mixing bowl, add the sugar and immediately begin to whisk it into the yolks. Continue whisking until the sugar is completely dissolved and the mixture is pale in color (**blanchir**).
3. Once the milk is scalded whisk about one-third of the hot milk into the yolks to temper them. Whisk until the mixture is well-combined and evenly heated.
4. Stir the tempered egg yolks into the pan of remaining hot milk and stir with a wooden spatula. Place the pan over low heat and stir in a figure 8 pattern. As you stir, the foam on the surface will disappear; at the same time, the liquid will begin to thicken and become oil-like in resistance. Continue cooking until the mixture is thick enough to coat the back of a wooden spatula and when your finger leaves a clean trail (**à la nappe**).
5. Remove the pan from the heat and strain the crème Anglaise through a fine mesh sieve (**chinois**) into a clean bowl set in a bowl of ice. Stir it back and forth (**vanner**) with the spatula until cooled.
6. Cover the bowl in plastic wrap and reserve the bowl in the refrigerator until needed.

Tip

Crème anglaise should be cooked to between 75°C and 85°C (167°F and 185 °F) and it is suggested that beginners use a digital thermometer.

FYL...

Apart from the omission of flour and cornstarch for thickening, crème anglaise is similar to crème pâtissière in terms of method and ingredients. The consistency and application, however, are very different. This pouring custard has a vast array of uses such as an accompaniment for desserts (charlottes are one example) and as a base in ice cream. In *L'Art Culinaire Moderne*, Pellaprat offers the generous advice " . . . that if by misfortune your crème anglaise separates from overcooking, try vigorously whisking-in small quantities of cold milk or cream." He adds that this will bring back the crème anglaise only partially.

CRÈME D'AMANDES
Almond Cream

Quantity		Ingredient
U.S.	**Metric**	
2 oz	60 g	Butter, *pommade*
2 oz	60 g	Sugar
2 oz	60 g	Almond powder
1 pc	1 pc	Egg
½ fl oz	10 mL	Rum
1 pc	1 pc	Vanilla bean

Method

1. Cream the butter and sugar together until light and fluffy (*crémer*).
2. Beat in the egg until well-combined.
3. Using a small knife, split the vanilla bean in half lengthwise and scrape out the seeds. Whisk into the mixture.
4. Add the rum and finish by mixing in the almond powder.
5. Reserve the crème d'amandes in a covered bowl in the refrigerator until ready to use.

Learning Outcomes

Making a crème d'amandes
Creaming

Equipment

Knives:
Paring knife (*office*)

Tools:
Whisk, mixing bowl

Yield

1 tarte

The almond powder in crème d'amandes serves the dual function of being a thickener as well as a flavor agent. In a very similar recipe for crème d'amandes in the *Mémorial Historique de la Pâtisserie*, Lacam quips, "There are plenty of other recipes for crème d'amandes, I simply prefer the best."

FYI...

Learning Outcomes

Cooked cream
Blanchir
Tamponner

Equipment

Knives:
Paring knife (*office*)

Tools:
Whisk, mixing bowl, rubber spatula, fork, serving tray or platter

Pans:
Medium saucepan

Yield

13 ounces or 375 grams

CRÈME PÂTISSIÈRE
Pastry Cream

Quantity		Ingredient
U.S.	**Metric**	
8 fl oz	250 mL	Milk
1 pc	1 pc	Vanilla bean
2 pcs	2 pcs	Egg yolks
2 oz	60 g	Sugar
1 oz	30 g	Flour (or cornstarch)

Method

1. Line a small serving tray or platter with plastic wrap.
2. Pour the milk into a medium saucepan. Split the vanilla bean in half lengthwise and scrape out the seeds. Stir the seeds into the milk and bring it to a boil over medium-high heat. Add about one-quarter of the sugar to the milk and stir to dissolve it.
3. Meanwhile, place the egg yolks in a small mixing bowl and add remaining sugar. Whisk the sugar into the eggs until it completely dissolves and the yolks lighten in color (**blanchir**). Add the flour or cornstarch to the yolks and stir until well-combined.
4. When the milk begins to come to a boil, remove it from the stove and pour one-third of it into the egg yolks. Stir well to temper the yolks, then whisk the tempered mixture into the remaining hot milk. Place back onto the heat and cook until the crème pâtissière begins to bubble. Continue whisking (being sure to press the whisk around the corners of the pan) and allow to cook for 1 minute in order to cook the starch. The crème pâtissière will become very thick. Immediately transfer the finished crème pâtissière to the plastic-lined serving tray. Pat (**tamponner**) the surface with a piece of cold butter held on the end of a fork to create a protective film. Completely cover with a second piece of plastic wrap, pressing out any air bubbles. Let the crème pâtissière cool to room temperature before refrigerating it.

Crème pâtissière is a thick custard used for filling pastries such as choux à la crème and éclairs as well as a variety of other pastry applications. It is translated into English as "pastry cream." The recipe dates back to La Varenne (1653), who called it crème de pâtissier.

CONVERSION CHART

A Note about Conversions

For cooking and baking, the metric system is probably the easiest to manage and an electronic scale can become your most valued tool in the kitchen! When making conversions, we took the liberty to sometimes round off the measurements as long as the proportions in the recipe were still respected.

Volume

U.S.	METRIC
1/4 fl oz	5 ml
1/2 fl oz	15 ml
3/4 fl oz	25 ml
1 fl oz	30 ml
2 fl oz	60 ml
3 fl oz	90 ml
4 fl oz	120 ml
5 fl oz	150 ml
6 fl oz	180 ml
7 fl oz	210 ml
8 fl oz	240 ml
9 fl oz	270 ml
10 fl oz	300 ml
11 fl oz	330 ml
12 fl oz	360 ml
13 fl oz	390 ml
14 fl oz	420 ml
15 fl oz	450 ml
1 pint (16 fl oz)	500 ml
1 quart (2 pints)	1L (1000 ml)
2 quarts	2 L (2000 ml)
3 quarts	3 L (3000 ml)
1 gallon (4 quarts)	4 L (4000 ml)

Weight

U.S.	METRIC
1/4 oz	5 g
1/2 oz	15 g
3/4 oz	20 g
1 oz	30 g
2 oz	60 g
3 oz	90 g
4 oz	120 g
5 oz	150 g
6 oz	180 g
7 oz	200 g
1/2 lb (8 oz)	250 g
9 oz	270 g
10 oz	300 g
11 oz	330 g
12 oz	360 g
13 oz	390 g
14 oz	420 g
15 oz	450 g
1 lb (16 oz)	500 g
1 1/2 lb	750 g
2 lb	1 kg

Common Household Equivalents

U.S.	METRIC
1/4 tsp	1 ml
1/2 tsp	3 ml
3/4 tsp	4 ml
1 tsp	5 ml
1 tbsp	15 ml
1/4 cup	60 ml
1/2 cup	120 ml
3/4 cup	180 ml
1 cup	250 ml
1/4 lb	120 g
1/2 lb	230 g
1 lb	450 g
1 pint	500 ml
1 quart	1 L
1 gallon	4 L

U.S. Measure Equivalents

3 tsp	1 tbsp	1/2 fl oz
2 tbsp	1/8 cup	1 fl oz
4 tbsp	1/4 cup	2 fl oz
5 tbsp + 1 tsp	1/3 cup	2 2/3 fl oz
8 tbsp	1/2 cup	4 fl oz
10 tbsp +2 tsp	2/3 cup	5 1/3 fl oz
12 tbsp	3/4 cup	6 fl oz
14 tbsp	7/8 cup	7 fl oz
16 tbsp	1 cup	8 fl oz
2 cups	1 pint	16 fl oz
2 pints	1 quart	32 fl oz
4 quarts	1 gallon	128 fl oz

GLOSSARY

Abaisser (**AH bay say**). *(lit: to lower)* to roll a dough out with the aid of a rolling pin to the desired thickness.

Abats (**AH bah**). *(lit: offal)* internal organs of butchered animals sold mainly by stores specializing in this called "triperies."
White offal: sweetbreads, feet, brains.
Red offal: heart, lungs, liver.

Abattis (**AH bah tee**). *(lit: giblets)* feet, neck, heads, wingtips, liver, gizzard, and heart of poultry.

Abricoter (**ah BREE coh tay**). *(lit: to abricot)* to cover a pastry with apricot glaze in order to give it a shiny appearance (see Nappage, Napper).

Accommoder (**ah COH moh day**). *(lit: to accommodate)* to prepare and season a dish for cooking.

Acidifier (**ah SEE deef yay**). *(lit: to acidify)* to add lemon juice or vinegar to fruits, vegetables, and fish to prevent oxidation.

Aciduler (**ah SEE doo lay**). *(lit: to acidulate)* to make a preparation slightly acidic, tart or tangy by adding a little lemon juice or vinegar.

Affûter (**AH foo tay**). *(lit: to hone)* to refine the cutting edge of a knife blade using a sharpening stone.

Aiguillette (**AY gwee yet**). *(lit: small needle)*
1. Long and narrow strip of meat cut from the breast of poultry (especially that of duck) and game birds.
2. A beef cut taken from the top of the thigh.

Aiguiser (**AY ghee zay**). *(lit: to sharpen)* to maintain the cutting edge of a knife through the use of a steel (fusil).

Allumettes (**AH loo met**). *(lit: matchstick)*
1. A type of savory petits fours (long rectangles of puff pastry). Covered with cheese or filled with anchovy.
2. Very thin sticks of potatoes that are deep-fried.
E.g. pommes allumettes.

Angélique (**ON jay leek**). the green stalk of an aromatic plant, most often candied in sugar. Used for decoration in pastry making.

Anglaise (**on GLEZ**). *(lit: English)*
1. Mixture made up of whole egg, oil, water, salt, and pepper; used to help coat in flour and breadcrumbs (paner à l'anglaise).
2. To cook in boiling water (potatoes, vegetables, rice, pasta).

Aplatir (**AH plah teer**). *(lit: to flatten)* flattening a piece of meat or fish in order to make it more tender and facilitate cooking or stuffing.

Appareil (**AH pah ray**). *(lit: apparatus)* mixture of the principal elements of a final recipe (usually egg based).

Aromate (**AH roh mat**). *(lit: aromatic)* a condiment or vegetable that has a characteristic smell or taste (spices and herbs).

Arroser (**AH roh zay**). *(lit: to baste)* the wetting of meat or fish with a liquid or fat during or after cooking.

Aspic (**ASS peek**). 1. Dish composed of meat, vegetables, and or fish, cooked, chilled, and then molded in gelatin.
2. A savory jelly made from clarified stock, used for molding terrines and glazing cold preparations.

Assaisonner (**ah SAY zoh nay**). *(lit: to season)* seasoning a preparation with certain ingredients that bring out the flavor of the food.

Attendrir (**AH ton dreer**). *(lit: to tenderize)* to pound a piece of meat in order to tenderize it.

Au jus (**oh JOO**). *(lit: with juice)* preparation served with its natural cooking juices.

Bain marie (au) (**BAN marie (oh)**). *(lit: Marie's bath)* a hot water bath; a way of cooking or warming food by placing a container in a larger recipient of very hot or simmering water, such as preparations that must not cook over direct heat, for keeping delicate sauces hot, and for melting chocolate. Bain marie is said to be named after an alchemist by the name of Marie la Juive dating back to around 300 BC.

Barder (**BAR day**). *(lit: to bard)* to cover or wrap a piece of meat, poultry, or occasionally fish with a very thin piece of pork fat (barding fat) in order to protect it and keep it moist during cooking, in order to prevent it from drying out.

Barquette (**bar KET**). *(lit: little boat)* small, long, oval pastry mold.

Bâtonnet (**BEH toh nay**). *(lit: little stick)* cut into sticks, generally 5 mm x 5 mm x 5 cm long (e.g., vegetables).

Bavarois (**bah var WAH**). *(lit: Bavarian)* cold dessert made from crème anglaise or fruit purée, set with gelatin and whipped cream.

Béchamel (**BEH shah mel**). white sauce made from milk and white roux. One of the mother sauces of classic cuisine. Named after Louis XIV's maître d'hôtel Marquis de Béchamel.

Beurre (**burr**). *(lit: butter)* product obtained by churning milk or cream. There are several different types of butter:
beurre demi-sel (**duh mee SELL**) lightly salted butter; contains up to 5% salt.
beurre déshydraté (**dez EE drah tay**) butter fat or butter-oil, contains up to 99.3% fat and 0.7% water.
beurre fermier (**FAIRM yay**) farm-fresh butter.

beurre laitier (**LET yay**) dairy-made butter.

beurre pasteurisé (**PAST urr ee zay**) factory produced and pasturized.

beurre salé (**SAH lay**) salted butter, contains up to 10% salt.

beurre sec (**sek**) dry butter; minimum water content; the percentage of water can vary 5–8% depending on the quality of the butter.

Beurre blanc (burr BLON). *(lit: white butter)* a sauce made by whisking large amounts of cold butter into a hot pan with a little lemon juice or reduction to create an emulsion. Served with poached or grilled fish.

Beurre clarifié (burr CLAH reef yay). *(lit: clarified butter)* butter that has been gently heated until it melts and the pure butterfat can be extracted.

Beurre composé (burr COM poh zay). *(lit: composed butter)* butter that is mixed with one or more aromatic ingredients (e.g., anchovy butter: butter + crushed anchovies).

Beurre en pommade (BURR on poh mad). *(lit: creamed butter)* softened butter (not melted). The name is derived from its face cream-like texture.

Beurre manié (BURR man yay). *(lit: handled butter)* butter mixed with an equal weight of flour. Used to thicken sauces.

Beurre noisette (BURR nwah ZET). *(lit: hazelnut butter)* butter that is cooked to a light brown color and nutty flavor.

Beurrer (BURR ay). *(lit: to butter)*
1. To lightly coat a container with butter in order to prevent sticking.
2. To add butter to a sauce or dough.

Biscuit (BEE skwee). *(lit: twice cooked)*
1. Type of small cake or cookie.
2. A specific type of sponge cake mostly used in making entremets.

Bisque (beesk). type of potage usually made from a shellfish base and traditionally thickened with rice.

Blanc (un) (blon (an)). *(lit: white)* mixture of water, flour, and lemon juice used to prevent vegetables such as artichokes, celery root, or salsify from discoloring during cooking.

Blanchir (BLON sheer). *(lit: to whiten, to blanch)*
1. To place vegetables or meats in cold water and then bring to a boil (or to plunge in boiling water) in order to precook, soften, or remove an excess of flavor (acidity, saltiness, bitterness) or remove impurities.
2. The process of incorporating sugar and eggs together until lightened in color.

Blondir (blon DEER). *(lit: to make blond)* to cook in hot fat in order to lightly color.

Bouchée (BOO shay). *(lit: a mouthful)* a small round of puff pastry that can be filled with different savory mixtures. Served as an appetizer.

Bouillir (BOO yeer). *(lit: to boil)* to bring a liquid to the boiling point.

Bouquet garni (boo kay GAR nee). *(lit: garnished bouquet)* a mixture of herbs (thyme, bay leaf, celery stalk, and parsley stems) enclosed and tied in the green portion of a leek used to flavor dishes during cooking.

Braiser (BRAY zay). *(lit: to braise)* to slowly cook a food in a covered and sometimes sealed dutch oven with vegetables and jus, in the oven.

Brider (BREE day). *(lit: to truss)* to tie a bird into a compact shape to ensure even cooking and maintain its shape, using a trussing needle.

Brochette (BROH shett). *(lit: little roasting spit)*
1. A skewer, a long piece of wood or metal onto which pieces of food are skewered before being grilled.
2. Food that has been cooked on skewers over a grill.

Broyer (BRWA yay). *(lit: to grind)* to finely crush or grind.

Brunoise (BROON wahz). vegetables cut into very small regular cubes, 2 to 4 mm per side.

Cacao (KAH kah oh). *(lit: cocoa)* by-product of the processing of cocoa beans. Available as a dark, bitter powder (poudre de cacao) or as a solid block (liqueur de cacao).

Calvados (KAHL vah dos). an alcohol made from distilled cider exclusively in the Normandy region.

Canapés (KAH na pay). *(lit: sofa)*
1. A small slice or piece of bread that is toasted in the oven or in butter.
2. Bread cut into bite-size shapes and topped with a number of varying garnishes. Can be served hot or cold at buffets or to accompany aperitifs.

Canneller (KAH nuh lay). *(lit: to channel)* a way of cutting small grooves in fruit or vegetables in order to give them a decorative edge when sliced.

Caraméliser (kah RAH meh lee zay). *(lit: to caramelize)*
1. To coat a mold with cooked sugar.
2. To cook sugar until caramelized.

Chantilly (SHON tee yee). whipped cream to which sugar and vanilla have been added. Named after the château of Chantilly where Vatel headed the kitchens in the 1600s (see Monter).

Chapelure (SHAH puh loor). dried breadcrumbs; made from both the crust and center of dried bread. Used for breading or as a topping.

Chaud-froid (SHOW frwah). *(lit: hot-cold)* a dish that is prepared hot but served cold, covered with a specific sauce (sauce chaud-froid, made from 1/3 velouté, 1/3 gelatin, and 1/3 cream).

Chemiser (SHEH mee zay). *(lit: to shirt)* to line or coat the interior sides and/or bottom of a mold before adding a filling or to prevent the finished product from sticking to the mold.

Chiffonnade (SHEE foh nad). leafy vegetables or herbs that have been rolled together and then sliced crosswise into thin strips. From the French verb, chiffoner meaning to crumple.

Chinois (SHEE nwah). *(lit: Chinese)* china cap sieve; a conical strainer.

Chiqueter (SHEEK tay). to lightly score the cut edges of puff pastry to help ensure that it rises straight and evenly.

Ciseler (SEE zuh lay). *(lit: to engrave)*
1. To shred; (old French term) to finely slice leaves of green vegetables (lettuce, sorrel).
2. To finely chop or mince; a manner of finely cutting onions, shallots, and garlic.

Citronner (**SEE troh nay**). *(lit: to lemonize)*
1. To rub certain foods with lemon to prevent them from discoloring.
2. To add lemon juice to a dish.

Clarifier (**KLAH reef yay**). *(lit: to clarify, to make clear)*
1. To clear a cloudy liquid (by straining, heating, and then gently simmering with egg whites).
2. Process of separating the milk solids from butter.
3. Separating the white and yolk of an egg.

Clouter (**CLOO tay**). *(lit: to stud)*
1. To pierce an onion with a whole clove.

Coller (**KOH lay**). *(lit: to stick, to glue)* to thicken or set using gelatin (e.g., jelly, fruit mousse).

Concasser (**KON kah say**). *(lit: to crush)* to break up coarsely with a knife or a pestle in a mortar.

Confit (**KON fee**). a long cooking method where the food is slowly cooked in animal fat or syrup until saturated. (fruits), fat (poultry) to allow cooking or conservation.

Consommé (**KON soh may**). *(lit: consummated)* clear bouillon made from meat, fish, or vegetables, served hot or cold, usually clarified (consommé double).

Corne (**korn**). *(lit: horn)* plastic tool used for scraping out recipients.

Corser (**KOR say**). *(lit: to coarsen)* to intensify the flavor of a preparation.

Coucher (**KOO shay**). *(lit: to lay out)*
1. To place a rolled-out piece of dough onto a baking sheet.
2. To spread a layer of cream or other garnish.
3. To force a mixture from a piping bag onto a baking sheet.

Coulis (**KOO lee**). a smooth purée of fruits or vegetables, used as a sauce.

Couper (**KOO pay**). *(lit: to cut)* to separate food items into pieces using the sharp edge of a knife.

Court-bouillon (**koor boo YON**). *(lit: short broth)* a cooking liquid composed of water, aromatic vegetables, and sometimes white wine or vinegar in which fish and shellfish are cooked or certain dishes using meat.

Crème anglaise (**krem on GLEZ**). *(lit: English cream)* a sweet sauce made from eggs, sugar, and milk that is cooked to 85°C.

Crème de riz (**krem duh REE**). *(lit: cream of rice)* a powder made from finely ground rice, used in pastry or to thicken sauces.

Crème fouettée (**KREM fway tay**). *(lit: whipped cream)* cream that has been whisked in order to incorporate air.

Crème fraîche (**krem FRESH**). *(lit: fresh cream)*
1. Cream that has been lightly soured to thicken it and develop its flavor.
2. French liquid cream.

Crème pâtissière (**krem pah teess YAIR**). *(lit: pastry cream)* cream thickened with flour, cornstarch, or flan powder, used for making pastry.

Crémer (**KREM ay**). *(lit: to cream)*
1. To beat butter and sugar together until they lighten in color and texture.
2. To add cream.

Croquette (**kroh KET**). *(lit: little bite)* a bite-sized mixture savory or sweet, that is fried in oil after being breaded. Can be in any shape or form. From the French verb croquer meaning to crunch.

Croustade (**kroos TAD**). a case made from any type of dough, that is cooked and filled with a savory mixture just before serving.

Croûte (**kroot**). *(lit: crust)*
1. The browned outer covering of bread.
2. En croûte: to cook a meat or fish wrapped in a crust.

Croûton (**KRU toenh**). a slice or piece of bread that is toasted with or without butter usually served with a dish in sauce, or as a bed to soak up any juices that might dilute the sauce (Tournedos Rossini)

Crudités (**KROO dee tay**). raw vegetables, sliced or cut and served with a vinaigrette or mayonnaise, as a first course.

Cuisson (**KWEE son**). *(lit: cooking)*
1. The action and manner of cooking a food.
2. The degree to which meat is cooked (rare, medium, etc.)

Darne (**darn**). thick bone-in steak cut from whole round fish before cooking.

Décanter (**DAY con tay**). *(lit: to decant)*
1. The liquid.
2. To separate the meat and aromatic garnish from the cooking liquid in order to finish the sauce.

Décortiquer (**DAY kor tee kay**). *(lit: to husk)*
1. To shell; to remove the outer covering from shellfish and crustaceans.
2. Remove the shell from nuts.

Découper (**DAY koo pay**). *(lit: to cut)* to cut using scissors, a knife, or pastry cutter. Used mainly in the dining room to describe the act of carving at tableside.

Déglacer (**DAY glah say**). *(lit: to deglaze)* to dissolve the substance attached to the bottom of a pan with liquid.

Dégorger (**DAY gor jay**). *(lit: to degorge)*
1. To soak an ingredient in cold water in order to remove blood, salt, or impurities.
2. To lightly salt vegetables in order to extract the maximum amount of water.

Dégraisser (**DAY gray say**). *(lit: to degrease)* to trim or remove excess fat from a food or the surface of a preparation.

Délayer (**DAY leh yay**). *(lit: to mix with)* to mix with a liquid, to thin out with water; to dissolve a powder in liquid.

Demi-glace (**duh mee GLASS**). *(lit: half-glaze)* traditionally referred to as a derivative of sauce espagnole. Modern demi-glace is a reduced brown stock.

Démouler (**DEH moo lay**). *(lit: to unmold)* to carefully remove a set preparation from the mold in which it was chilled or cooked.

Dénerver (**DAY nair vay**). *(lit: to denerve)* to remove the nerves or tendons from meat and fowl.

Dénoyauter (**day NWAH yoh tay**). *(lit: to pit, to stone)* to remove the seed or pit of stone fruits and olives.

Dés (**day**). *(lit: dice)* cubes; small regular squares.

Désosser (**DEH zoh say**). *(lit: to debone)* to remove the bones from meat and fowl.

Dessécher (**DUH say shay**). *(lit: to dry out)* to remove moisture through heat.

Détailler (**DEH tah yay**). *(lit: to size)* to cut into pieces. Applies mostly to meat, fowl, fish, and crustaceans.

Détendre (**day TON druh**). *(lit: to relax)* to thin a preparation by adding liquid.

Détremper (**DAY trom pay**). *(lit: to soak, to moisten)*
  1. To add water to flour to make a paste.
  2. To soak something in a liquid.

Dorer (**DOH ray**). *(lit: to gild)* to brush with beaten egg or egg yolk in order to give a deep color and shine during baking.

Dorure (**doh ROOR**). *(lit: gilding)* egg wash; beaten egg or egg yolk, with water and/or salt added, applied to dough before baking, to provide color.

Douille (**DOO-yee**). *(lit: socket)* pastry tip; a conical piece made of metal or plastic used for piping with a pastry bag.

Dresser (**DREH say**). *(lit: to dress)* to arrange prepared food on a plate or platter for serving.

Duxelles (**dook SELL**). finely chopped mushrooms cooked in butter with finely chopped shallots; can be used as a garnish or filling.

Ébarber (**ay BAR bay**). *(lit: to debeard)*
  1. To remove the beards from shellfish, e.g., mussels, scallops.
  2. To remove the filaments from poached or fried eggs.

Ébouillanter (**ay BOO yon tay**). *(lit: to scald)* to dip fruit, vegetable, or fish in boiling water for a few seconds.

Ébullition (**AY boo leess yon**). *(lit: boiling point)* the appearance of bubbles in a hot liquid (98° to 100°C).

Écailler (**AY kah yay**). *(lit: to scale)* to remove the scales from fish.

Écaler (**AY kah lay**). *(lit: to shell (eggs))* to remove the shell from soft- and hard-boiled eggs.

Écumer (**AY koo may**). *(lit: to skim)* to remove the foam from the surface of a boiling liquid.

Effiler (**AY fee lay**). *(lit: to flake)* to slice very thinly (almonds).

Égoutter (**AY goo tay**). *(lit: to strain)* to remove the liquid from a cooked preparation by pouring it into a strainer.

Émietter (**aym YAY tay**). *(lit: to crumble)* to break into small pieces.

Émincer (**AY man say**). *(lit: to slice)* to cut into thin slices.

Émonder or monder (**AY mon day**). *(lit: to prune)* to remove the skin of certain fruits or vegetables (peaches, tomatoes) by plunging into boiling water, cooling them in an ice bath, and pulling the loosened skin off.

Enrober (**ON rob ay**). *(lit: to enrobe, to coat)* used in pastry, to completely cover with setting liquid such as chocolate.

Entremets (**ON truh may**). *(lit.: "between courses")* originally a course served between the roast and the dessert. Modern usage is limited to patisserie and refers to a whole cake.

Éplucher (**AY ploo shay**). *(lit: to peel)* to remove the skin of vegetables.

Éponger (**AY pon jay**). *(lit: to sponge)* to remove excess liquid or fat by absorbing with a kitchen or paper towel.

Escaloper (**es KAH loh pay**). *(lit: escalope)* to slice meat or fish on the bias.

Essence (**ESS onss**). *(lit: essence)*
  1. A concentrated extract used as a flavoring (e.g., coffee essence).
  2. A stock with concentrated flavor. Can also be a stock made from a single ingredient such as mushroom or tomato.

Étuver (**AY too vay**). *(lit: to steam)* to slowly cook over low heat in a covered pot or pan with some fat.

Évider (**AY vee day**). *(lit: to empty)* to gut; to hollow out the center of an ingredient (poultry, fruit, vegetables).

Farce (**FARSS**). *(lit: forcemeat stuffing)* a mixture of various ground ingredients (meat, herbs, vegetables) used to fill poultry, fish, vegetables, etc.

Farcir (**FAR seer**). *(lit: to stuff)* to fill poultry, fish, meat, fruits, or vegetables with a forcemeat stuffing.

Fariner (**FAH ree nay**). *(lit: to flour)* to dredge; to sprinkle flour on fish or meat; to sprinkle a mold and tap out the excess.

Ficeler (**FEESS lay**). *(lit: to tie up)* to tie with string, without a trussing needle.

Fines herbes (**feen ZAIRB**). *(lit: delicate herbs)* a mixture of parsley, chives, tarragon, and thyme. A classic seasoning.

Flamber (**flon BAY**). *(lit: to flame)*
  1. To use a flame in order to remove the down from poultry.
  2. To burn off alcohol by lighting it in a preparation (e.g., crêpes suzette).

Fleurons (**FLUH ron**). *(lit: florets)* pieces of puff pastry cut into crescent shapes, served as a classic decoration with fish dishes.

Foncer (**FON say**). *(lit: to line)* to line the bottom and sides of a mold or pan with dough.

Fond (**fon**). *(lit: base)* stock; flavored bouillon. Made from veal, beef, chicken, vegetables, and aromates.

Fondant (**FON don**). *(lit: melting)* a sugar preparation used for glazing pastries, and used in candy making.

Fondre (**FON druh**). *(lit: to melt)* to turn a solid into liquid by heating (e.g., butter).

Fontaine (**FON ten**). *(lit: a well)* to form a deep impression in flour in order to add other ingredients for making a dough.

Fraiser (**FRAY zay**). *(lit: to mill)* to crush dough with the heel of the palm in order to ensure a smooth texture and even mixing

Fraser (**FRAH zay**). see Fraiser.

Frémir (**FREH meer**). *(lit: to simmer)* to bring a liquid just to the boiling point, the bubbles being barely perceptible.

Frire (**freer**). *(lit: to deep-fry)* to cook foods by plunging in a recipient hot oil.

Friture (**free TOOR**). deep-fried foods.

Fumet (**FOO may**). *(lit: scent)*
  1. Cooking aromas.
  2. Sauce made from cooking juices.
  3. Basic stock made from fish (Fumet de poisson) and used to make sauces.

Fusil (**FOO zee**). sharpening steel; rounded, metal or ceramic rod used to maintain the cutting edge of a knife (see Aiguiser).

Galantine (**GALL on teen**). 1. The old French word for jelly. Meat that has been stuffed, larded, and poached. Served cold, it is coated with aspic made from the poaching liquid. 2. Knife holder—a soft knife holder that can be rolled up.

Ganache (gah NASH). a mixture made from chopped chocolate and boiling cream.

Garniture (GAR nee toor). *(lit: garnish)* an accompaniment to a dish.

Gastrique (GAS treek). *(lit: gastric)* a caramel deglazed with vinegar; used as a base for sweet and sour sauces (duck à l'orange).

Gelée (je LAY). *(lit: jelly)*
1. Gelatin, aspic; meat or fish stock that has been clarified and then set with gelatin. Used in various preparations "en gelée" or to give shine to foods as well as protect them from drying out.
2. Fruit juice plus gelatin used in pastry to add sheen to cakes and desserts.
3. Preserve made by boiling together fruit juice (from fruit rich in pectin such as quinces, red currants, apples, blueberries, blackberries, raspberries, or black currants) and sugar then set in jars like jams.

Génoise (JEHN waz). yellow sponge cake; made from sugar, flour, and eggs named after the town of Genoa.

Glaçage (GLAH saj). *(lit: glaze)* mixture of ingredients with a syrupy consistency, sweet or savory, used to coat pastries, candies, and certain savory foods.

Glace (glass). *(lit: ice, glaze)*
1. Ice cream; crème anglaise, which is turned and frozen.
2. Glaze; stock reduced until thick and syrupy.

Glacer (GLASS ay). *(lit: to glaze)* to cover a finished product with a coating such as a reduction or sugar, to give a smooth, shiny final appearance, and add extra flavor.

Glace royale (glass RWO yahl). *(lit: royal glaze)* mixture of icing sugar, egg whites, and lemon juice used to decorate pastries. Dries hard.

Glace à l'eau (GLASS ah loh). *(lit: glaze with water)* mixture of sugar or powdered sugar and water, used to glaze pastries.

Glucose (GLOO coze). thick, clear syrup made from vegetable starch. Half as sweet as sugar, it is mostly used to stop sugar-based preparations from crystalizing.

Graisser (GRAY say). *(lit: to grease)* to coat or cover with fat before baking or roasting in the oven.

Griller (GREE yay). *(lit: to grill)* to cook on a grill.

Habiller (ah bee yay). *(lit: to dress)* to prepare an item for cooking (fish, meat usually by cleaning and trimming).

Hacher (AH shay). *(lit: to chop)* to chop evenly with a knife.

Imbiber (AM bee bay). *(lit: to imbibe)* to wet or soak an element with stock or syrup.

Inciser (AN see zay). *(lit: to incise)* to score a food more or less deeply before cooking in order to encourage even cooking (e.g. whole fish filet) or create a decorative pattern (e.g. pastry).

Incorporer (AN kor poh ray). *(lit: to incorporate)* to fold an ingredient into a batter.

Infuser (AN foo zay). *(lit: to infuse)* to place an element into simmering liquid and allow it to sit in order for the element to flavor the liquid (e.g., tea).

Jardinière (JAR deen yair). *(lit: gardener)* a mixture of carrots and turnips cut into sticks and green beans and green peas. Cooked separately and then served as an accompaniment.

Julienne (JOOL yen). cut into very fine strips (e.g., vegetables). Generally 3–5 cm long, 1–2 mm thick.

Jus (joo). *(lit: juice).*
1. Liquid made from pressing a fruit or vegetable.
2. De cuisson: mixture of fats and juices released from meats during cooking (e.g., roast).

Kirsch (keersh). a spirit made by distilling fermented cherry juice.

Lard (larr). solid fat from pork. Lard gras contains only fat; lard maigre (bacon) contains some meat.

Larder (LAR day). *(lit: to lard)* to insert strips of lard into tough or inexpensive meats using a larding needle in order to prevent the meat from drying out during the cooking.

Lardons (LAR don). a specific way of cutting slab bacon into small pieces; used to garnish both meat and fish.

Levain (LUH van). *(lit: leaven)* a dough starter made from live yeast and flour used to make breads.

Lever (LUH vay). *(lit: to rise)* to leave a dough to rise or proof (brioche, bread, croissants).

Lever les filets (luh VAY lay fee lay). *(lit: to lift the fillets)* to remove the fillet of a fish using a knife.

Levure (luh VOOR). *(lit: yeast)* a live bacteria. When mixed with flour and warm water it ferments and produces a carbonic gas (the bubbles of gas which in trying to escape make a bread rise).

Levure chimique (luh VOOR shee meek). *(lit: chemical yeast)* baking powder; odorless and flavorless rising agent made from bicarbonate of soda and cream of tartar.

Liaison (lee ay zon). *(lit: a connection, a bond)* thickener; element or mixture used to thicken a liquid or sauce.

Lier (LEE ay). *(lit: to bind)* to change the consistency of a liquid by adding a liaison, such as a roux, starch, egg, flour, or beurre manié.

Macédoine (mah SAY dwan). *(lit: Macedonia)*
1. A mixture of vegetables or fruit cut into small cubes, generally 4–5 mm square.
2. A classic salad made of small cubes of carrot, turnip, and green beans, with peas, tossed in mayonnaise. The dimensions would be based on the size of the peas.

Macérer (mah SAY ray). *(lit: to macerate)* patisserie term, to soak fruit and dried fruit in alcohol in order to flavor and soften it.

Manchonner (MON shoh nay). *(lit: to cuff)* to remove the meat that covers the end of a bone such as a chicken leg or a rack of meat in order to achieve a clean presentation.

Mandoline (MON doh leen). *(lit: mandolin)* a long rectangular kitchen tool made of stainless steel with two blades, one straight, the other wavy. The mandoline is used to slice vegetables very finely and to make gaufrettes.

Margarine (MAR gah reen). margarine. emulsion made of vegetable oil and milk or whey. Used as an inexpensive replacement for butter.

Mariner (MAH ree nay). *(lit: to marinate)* to soak a piece of meat or fish in a liquid and aromats in order to tenderize, flavor, and conserve. Can also be used to tame the flavor of strong-flavored game.

Médaillon (MAY dah yon). *(lit: medallion)* round slice of meat, fowl, fish, or crustacean, served hot or cold.

Meringue (muh RAN g). mixture of beaten egg whites and sugar. There are three types of meringues:
French meringue: mounted egg whites with granulated sugar beaten in.

Italian meringue: mounted egg whites with cooked sugar. Swiss meringue: egg whites and sugar beaten over a hot water bath, then beaten until cooled.

Mijoter (faire) (mee JO tay). *(lit: to simmer)* to cook several elements over gentle heat or in the oven over a given time.

Mirepoix (MEER pwah). vegetables cut into cubes, the size depending on the length of cooking. Also refers to a certain blend of aromatic vegetables (onion, carrot, and celery).

Monder (MON day). *(lit: to hull)* see Émonder.

Monter (MON tay). *(lit: to rise, to go up)*
1. To incorporate air and increase the volume using a wire whisk (egg whites, cream).
2. Au beurre: to add butter to a sauce in small pieces.

Mouiller (MOO yay). *(lit: to wet)* to add a liquid to a preparation during cooking.

Mouler (MOO lay). *(lit: to mold)* to fill a mold before or after cooking.

Nappage (nah PAJ). *(lit: a coating)* apricot glaze (jelly) used to finish pastries by giving it a shiny coating. Also serves to protect from drying out.

Napper (nah PAY). *(lit: to coat)* to cover a food, savory or sweet, with a light layer of sauce, aspic, or jelly.

Noircir (NWAR seer). *(lit: to blacken)* the darkening or discoloring of certain fruits and vegetables when left in contact with air for too long (e.g. artichokes, apples).

Panade (Pah nad). a mixture made from milk, water or stock and a starch such as flour, eggs, bread, rice or potato. Used as a binder for mousses, terrines, quenelles and gnocchi.

Paner (pa NAY). *(lit: to bread)* to coat a food with fresh or dry breadcrumbs after dipping in flour and beaten egg (see Anglaise) and then cooking in butter or oil.

Panier (PAN yay). *(lit: basket)*
1. A frying basket, used with a deep fryer in order to easily plunge and remove foods from hot oil.
A steam basket; used for placing foods to be steamed.
2. Nestling baskets; a frying tool in the form of two ladle-shaped baskets, one being slightly smaller than the other used in order to form "nests" out of shredded potatoes to decorate certain platters.

Papillote (PAH pee yot). 1. Paper frill used to decorate the ends of bones of certain poultry and meats.
2. En papillotte: an envelope made of parchment paper or foil in which ingredients are baked in order for them to cook gently in their own steam and not lose any flavor.

Parer (PAH ray). *(lit: to pare, to trim)* to remove the nerves or excess fat from meat or fish or to remove the damaged or inedible portions of fruit and vegetables before cooking or serving.

Passer (PAH say). *(lit: to pass)* to strain; generally using a wire strainer or china cap sieve.

Pâte (pat). *(lit: paste)* dough, a hard or soft paste based on flour that is mixed with a combination of water, eggs, sugar, milk, butter, etc., then cooked or baked. Used in both savory and sweet preparations with different combinations resulting in different textures.

Pâté en croûte (pah TAY on kroot). *(lit: pâté in a crust)* chopped meat, poultry, fish, etc., cooked in a dough.

Pâton (PAH ton). a ball of finished dough or pastry waiting to be formed into a loaf or rolled out.

Paupiette (pawp yet). thin piece of meat or fish that is stuffed, rolled, tied, and braised.

Peler (PEH lay). *(lit: to peel)* to remove the peel or skin of fruits.

Peler à vif. *(lit: to peel open)* to remove the peel and outer membrane of citrus using a knife. Then cutting out the segments.

Persillade (PAIR see yad). a mixture made from parsley and chopped garlic.

Pétrir (pet REER). *(lit: to knead)* to work or knead a dough.

Piler (PEE lay). *(lit: to crush or pound)* to crush or blend using a mortar and pestle.

Pilon (PEE lon). *(lit: a pestle)*
1. A pestle; a tool used for crushing and grinding.
2. The drumstick of a chicken leg.

Pincée (PAN say). *(lit: a pinch)* a small quantity of a dry ingredient measured by pinching with the thumb and index finger.

Pincer (PAN say). *(lit: to pinch)*
1. To use a pastry crimper to give a decorative finish to the edges of a dough before cooking.
2. Pincer la tomate (PAN say lah toh matt): to cook tomato paste in order to remove excess humidity and acidity.
3. Pincer les os (PAN say lay zohs): to well color bones in a very hot oven. The first step in making a fond brun.
4. Pincer les sucs (PAN say lay sook): to darken the browned cooking juices in a pan in order to reinforce the flavor when deglazing.

Piquer (PEE kay). *(lit: to sting, to prick)*
1. Term used when larding a piece of meat using a larding needle in order to keep the meat from drying out during the cooking.
2. To make small holes in a dough using a fork in order to prevent it from rising during cooking.

Pluches (ploosh). *(lit: sprigs)* small leaves picked off the larger stems of herbs, e.g., sprigs of chervil.

Pocher (POH shay). *(lit: to poach)* to cook in barely simmering water or other liquid.

Poêler (PWAH lay). *(lit: to pan roast)* to cook large pieces of meat in a covered cocotte over a garniture aromatique that has been sweated in butter. Finished with a glaze.

Pointe (pwant). *(lit: point (knife)*
1. A small quantity measured out using the point of a knife (e.g., point of ground vanilla).
2. The tip of something; the tip of asparagus.

Pousser (POO say). *(lit: to grow, to push)*
1. To leave a yeast-leavened dough to increase in volume.
2. The action of feeding meat into a meat grinder.

Praliné (PRAH lee nay). invented by Clément Juluzot (1598t–1675), cook to Marshal Plessis-Pralin. Caramelized sugar with almonds or hazelnuts that is then ground to a smooth paste, used to flavor and decorate pastries.

Quadriller (KAH dree yay). *(lit: to criss-cross)*
1. To mark squares or diamonds on meat with a hot grill.
2. To mark squares using a knife.

Quatre-épices (**KAT rah peess**). *(lit: four spices)* a mixture of ground spices made up of pepper, cinnamon, nutmeg, and cloves. Often used to flavor meat stuffings.

Quenelles (**KUH nell**). *(lit: dumplings)*
1. Oval or egg shape made out of a mousse or other mixture using two spoons.
2. Preparation made of panade mixed with finely minced meat or fish which is then poached and served in a sauce.

Quiche (**keesh**). savory tart garnished with a rich custard base (e.g., quiche lorraine: bacon and cheese custard tart).

Rafraîchir (**RAH fray sheer**). *(lit: to refresh)* to plunge a food into an ice bath after cooking in order to halt the cooking process and cool the food (for greens, to preserve the chlorophyl). Liquids are placed in a bowl over an ice bath and stirred.

Raidir (**RED eer**). *(lit: to stiffen)* to cook a meat or fish in hot fat just enough to stiffen the fibers but without coloring it. Used mostly for fish bones when making fumet.

Râper (**RAH pay**). *(lit: to grate)* to shred using a grating tool (e.g., cheese).

Rassir (**RAH seer**). *(lit: to go stale)* to let bread sit out until stale to make breadcrumbs (see Chapelure).

Rassis (**RAH see**). *(lit: stale)* something that is no longer fresh (bread).

Rectifier (**REK teef yay**). *(lit: to rectify)* to correct the seasoning of a dish.

Réduire (**RED weer**). *(lit: to reduce)* to heat a liquid in or to reduce it in volume by boiling. As the liquid evaporates, the sauce becomes thicker.

Relever (**RUH luh vay**). *(lit: to lift)* to reinforce flavor through the use of spices.

Revenir (faire) (**RUH vuh neer (fair)**). *(lit: to make come back)* to quickly color a food in hot fat or oil.

Rissoler (**REE soh lay**). *(lit: to brown)* to cook a food until well colored in hot fat or oil.

Roux (**roo**). used for thickening sauces. A cooked mixture of equal weights of flour and butter that is used as a thickening agent. There are three types of roux that vary in color depending on how long they cook: white, blond, and brown. Roux is a thickening agent (see Liaison).

Saisir (**SEZ eer**). *(lit: to seize)* to sear, to quickly color over very high heat at the start of cooking.

Salamandre (**sah lah MON drh**). *(lit: salamander)* a broiler; the upper heating element in an oven or a professional appliance used to brown foods.

Saupoudrer (**soh POO dray**). *(lit: to powder)* to evenly distribute a topping (sugar, breadcrumbs) over the surface of a dish or dessert.

Sauter (**SOH tay**). *(lit: to jump)* to sauté; to cook small pieces with coloring over high heat, stirring or tossing often in order to prevent sticking.

Singer (**SAN jay**). to sprinkle with flour at the start of cooking in order to cook and eventually thicken the sauce.

Siroper (see **ROH pay**). to add syrup to a pastry (see Imbiber).

Suer (**SOO ay**). *(lit: to sweat)* to gently cook vegetables in a little fat without coloring in order to bring out their flavor.

Suprême (**soo PREM**).
1. Segments cut out of a citrus that has been peler à vif.
2. Boneless chicken breast with the drumstick of the wing still attached.

Tailler (**tah YAY**). *(lit: to size)* to cut in a precise fashion.

Tamis (**Tah MEE**). drum sieve. Large cylinder with a wire mesh covering one side.
Passer au tamis: press a puréed solid such as chicken or veal by through a tamis resulting in a finer texture while removing any remaining nerves or sinew.

Tamiser (**TAH mee zay**). *(lit: to sift)* to sift a dry ingredient using a wire strainer or sifter in order to remove lumps or foreign matter.

Tamponner (**TOM poh nay**). *(lit: to stamp)* to dot the surface of a cream or sauce with butter to prevent the formation of a skin on the surface.

Timbale (**TAM bahl**). *(lit: metal cup)*
1. Mold in the shape of a large thimble.
2. Recipient made of dough, baked and filled with different elements. Served as a hot appetizer.

Tourer (**TOO ray**). *(lit: to turn)* term used to refer to the process of rolling and folding butter into a dough (puff pastry, croissants).

Tourner (**TOOR nay**). *(lit: to turn)*
1. To give certain vegetables a regular barrel shape using a knife.
2. To mix ingredients together by stirring in a circular motion.

Travailler (**trah VAH yay**). *(lit: to work)* to knead, mix, soften.

Tremper (**TRAHM pay**). *(lit: to soak; to dip; to wet)*
1. To leave an item to soak in liquid, such as dried beans.
2. To quickly dip an item in a coating such as chocolate, to cover it.
3. To saturate an item with liquid.

Truffer (**TRUE fay**). *(lit: to garnish with truffles)* to add chopped truffles to a dish, stuffing, or foie gras. To slide a thin slice of truffle under the skin of poultry.

Turban (**TOOR bon**). *(lit: turban)* usually used with fish, a way of rolling a small fillet with or without a filling, the final result resembling a turban.

Vanner (**VAH nay**). *(lit: to winnow.)* to stir a hot liquid over an ice bath in order to stop the cooking process and to cool it down.

Vapeur (**vah PURR**). *(lit: steam)* the vapor that rises from boiling. When confined the heat is hot enough to cook foods. A method of cooking without using fat.

Velouté (**vuh LOO tay**). *(lit: velvety)* a thickened soup; made from a stock and a roux to which egg yolk and cream is added.
1. One of the five mother sauces, it is a white stock thickened with a roux.
2. A soup or potage made from a velouté to which egg yolk and cream have been added, and served with an accompanying garnish.

Zester (**ZESS tay**). *(lit: to zest)* to remove the colored part or zest of citrus fruit (e.g., oranges, lemons) by grating or peeling with a small knife.

RECIPE INDEX

A

Almond Cream, 503
Almond powder, 503

B

Béarnaise Sauce, 466–467
Béchamel Sauce, 468–469
Beurre Manié, 454
Biscuit Cuillère, 496–497
Biscuit Dacquoise, 498
Biscuit Génoise, 499
Brown Stock (Veal), 448–449
Butter
   Beurre Manié, 454
   Biscuit Génoise, 499
   Crème d'Amandes, 503
   Crème Pâtissière, 504
   Farce à Gratin, 478–479
   Fondue de Tomate, 475
   Fumet de Poisson, 450–451
   Légumes Glacés, 483–484
   Pâte Brisée, 491
   Pâte Feuilletée, 492–493
   Pâte Sablée, 495
   Pâte Sucrée, 494
   Riz Créole, 485
   Riz Pilaf, 486–487
   Roux Blanc, 456
   Roux Blond, 456
   Roux Brun, 456
   Sauce Béarnaise (Béarnaise Sauce), 466–467
   Sauce Béchamel, 468–469
   Sauce Hollandaise (Hollandaise Sauce), 464–465
   Sauce Mornay, 470
   Sauce Nantaise, 462–463
   Sauce Tomate, 473–474
   Sauce Velouté, 471–472

C

Cheese
   Sauce Mornay (Mornay Sauce), 470
Chicken
   Fond Blanc de Volaille (White Stock, Chicken), 446–447
Chicken livers
   Farce à Gratin, 478–479
Chicken stock
   Sauce Allemande ou Parisienne, 472
   Sauce Suprême, 472
   Sauce Velouté (Velouté Sauce), 472

Cream

Cream
   Sauce Chantilly, 461
Crème Anglaise, 502
Crème d'Amandes (Almond Creme), 503
Crème Pâtissière, 504
Creole Rice, 485
Custard, 502

E

Egg Yolks
   Crème Anglaise, 502
   Crème Pâtissière, 504
   Mayonnaise and Derivatives, 460–461
   Sauce Béarnaise, 466–467
   Sauce Hollandaise, 464–465
   Sauce Velouté, 471–472
Eggs
   Biscuit Cuillère, 497
   Biscuit Génoise, 499
   Crème d'Amandes, 503
   Crème Pâtissière, 504
   Jaunes d'Oeufs (Egg Yolks), 457
   Mayonnaise and Derivatives, 460–461
   Pâte à Pâtes, 490
   Pâte Brisée, 491
   Pâte Sablée, 495
   Pâte Sucrée, 494
Egg Whites
   Bisquit Dacquoise, 498
   Farce Mousseline, 482
   Farce Simple, 480

F

Farce à Gratin, 478–479
Farce Mousseline, 482
Farce Simple, 480–481
Fish
   Farce Mousseline (Fish Mousse), 482
   Fumet de Poisson (Fish Stock), 450–451
Fish Mousse, 482
Fish Stock, 450–451
Flour
   Beurre Maníe 454
   Biscuit Cuillère (Ladyfinger Biscuit), 496–497
   Biscuit Dacquoise, 498
   Biscuit Génoise (Genoese Sponge), 499
   Crème Pâtissière, 504
   Derivatives, 471–472
   Pâte à Pâtes (Pasta Dough), 490

Pâte Brisée, 491
Pâte Feuilletée (Puff Pastry), 492–493
Pâte Sablée, 495
Pâte Sucre (Sweet Dough), 494
Roux Blanc, 456
Roux Blond, 456
Roux Brun, 456
Sauce Béchamel, 458–469
Sauce Tomate, 473–474
Sauce Velouté, 471–472
Fond Blanc de Volaille, 446–447
Fond Brun de Veau, 448–449
Fondue de Tomate, 475
Fumet de Poisson, 450–451

G

Genoese Sponge, 499
Glazed Vegetables, 484

H

Hollandaise Sauce, 464–465

J

Jaunes d'Oeufs, 457

L

Ladyfinger Biscuit, 497
Beurre Manié, 454
Jaunes D'Oeufs, 457
Liasons, 453–457
Roux, 455–456
Légumes Glacés, 483–484

M

Milk
Crème Anglaise (Custard), 502
Crème Pâtissière (Pastry Cream), 504
Sauce Béchamel (Bechamel Sauce), 468–469
Mornay Sauce, 470

N

Nantaise Sauce, 462–463

P

Pasta Dough, 490
Pastry Cream, 504
Pâte à Pâtes, 490
Pâte Brisée, 491
Pâte Feuilletée, 492–493
Pâte Sablée, 495
Pâte Sucrée, 494
Pork
Farce Simple (Simple Stuffing), 480–481
Puff Pastry, 492–493

R

Red wine vinegar
Sauce Nantaise (Nantaise Sauce), 462–463
Rice
Riz Créole (Creole Rice), 485
Riz Pilaf (Rice Pilaf), 487
Rice Pilaf, 487
Riz Créole, 485
Riz Pilaf, 485
Roux Blanc, 456
Roux Blond, 456
Roux Brun, 456

S

Sauce Allemande or Parisienne, 472
Sauce Béarnaise, 466–467
Sauce Béchamel, 468–469
Sauce Chantilly, 461
Sauce Gribiche, 461
Sauce Hollandaise, 464–465
Sauce Mayonnaise, 460–461
Sauce Mornay, 470
Sauce Nantaise, 462–463
Sauce Rémoulade, 461
Sauce Suprême, 472
Sauce Tomate, 473–474
Sauce Velouté, 471–472
Shortcrust Dough, 491
Simple Stuffing, 481
Sweet Dough, 494

T

Tomato Sauce, 473–474
Tomatoes
Fondue de Tomate, 475
Sauce Tomate (Tomato Sauce), 473–474

V

Veal
Farce Simple (Simple Stuffing), 480–481
Fonds Brun de Veau (Brown Stock, Veal), 448–449
Vegetable oil
Sauce Gribiche, 461
Sauce Mayonnaise (Mayonnaise Sauce), 461
Sauce Rémoulade, 461
Vegetables
Légumes Glacés (Glazed Vegetables), 483–484
Velouté Sauce, 471–472

W

White Stock (Chicken), 446–447

SUBJECT INDEX

A

Aboyeur. *See* Announcer/expediter
Abricot. *See* Apricot
Accessory fruit, 182
Accompanying garnish (garniture de caisson), 40, 41
Acorn squash (courge), 109
Affinage. *See* Ripening curd
Aging, of beef, 304
Aiglefin. *See* Haddock
Aigulle à brider. *See* Trussing needle
Ail. *See* Garlic
Alaska plaice, 277
Albacore tuna, 273
Allmouth, 261
Allspice (piment de la Jamaïque), 194
Allumette, 42, 144
Almond cream (crème d'amande), 410–411
Amarelle cherry, 190
American cranberry, 185
American plaice, 277
Anchovy (anchois), 257
Aneth. *See* Dill
Anglerfish, 261
Anise (anis), 194–195
Anjou pears, 173
Announcer/expediter (aboyeur), 23
Apicius, Marcus Gavius, 6
Appellation contrôlée, 332
Apple (pomme), 173, 174
Apprentice (apprenti/apprentie), 4, 16, 17, 27–28
Apricot (abricot), 189
Aprons, 29
Aromates (garniture aromatique), 422
Aromatic garnish (garniture de cuisson), 40, 41
Art de Cuisinier, L' (Beauvilliers), 9
Art de la Cuisine Française, L' (Carême), 9
Artichoke (artichaut), 159–165
    about, 159
    blanc de cuisson, 165
    turning, 160–164
Asparagus (asperges), 167–168
Atlantic salmon, 267
Aubergine. *See* Eggplant
Avocado (avocat), 101–102

B

Badianne. *See* Star anise
Baie de Genièvre. *See* Juniper berry
Baked creams, 405
Baker (boulanger), 29
Bande de tarte, 380–381
Bar. *See* Sea bass
Barbue. *See* Brill
Barder, 431
Bartlett pears, 173
Basil (basilic), 195
Basilic. *See* Basil
Basket (panier), 177
Bâtonnet, 42–44
Bay leaf (feuille de laurier), 195–196
Bearberry, 185
Béarnaise sauce (sauce béarnaise), 237, 238–239
Bearss lime, 178
Beauvilliers, Antoine, 9
Béchamel sauce (sauce béchamel), 230–231
Beef (boeuf)
    aging, 304
    British primal cuts, 317
    French cuts, 317–318
    North American cuts, 304–305
Beef tripe, 327
Beetroot (betteraves), 136
Belgian endive (endive), 169–170
Bell peppers (poivrons), 102–103
Bergamot orange (bergamote), 179
Berries. *See* Grapes and berries
Betteraves. *See* Beetroot
Beurre composé. *See* Composed butter
Beurre manié, 225
Biche. *See* Venison
Big heart artichoke, 159
Bigarade orange, 179
Bigeye tuna, 275
Bilberry (myrtille), 183
Binding, 348
Birds, consumption of chili peppers, 102
Biscuit cuillère. *See* Ladyfinger
Biscuit dacquoise, 402
Biscuit Génoise. *See* Genoese sponge

Biscuits, 399–404
  about, 399
  dacquoise, 402
  Genoese sponge, 402–404
  ladyfinger, 399–402
Black crab, 293
Black currant (cassis), 183
Black mustard, 204
Black pepper, 207
Black raspberry (framboise noire), 183–184
Black sea bass, 269–270
Blackberry (mûre), 183
Blackfin tuna, 273–274
Blanching (blanchir), 119–120, 437
Blanching lettuce, 119–120
Bleuet. *See* Blueberry
Block, cutting a, 40–41, 141
Blond braising (braisage à blond), 433, 434, 435
Blood, as thickening agent, 226
Blood orange (orange sanguine), 180–181
Bloomy rind cheeses, 362–363
Blue crab, 291–292
Blue manna crab, 291–292
Blue swimmer crab, 291–292
Blue-veined cheeses (fromage persillé), 363
Blueberry (bleuet), 184
Boeuf. *See* Beef
Boiling potatoes, 141
Bon d'économat. *See* Ingredient list
Bon récapitulatif, 35–36
Bone marrow (moelle), 327
Bosc pears, 173–174
Bouchées et fleurons, 382–383
Boucher. *See* Butcher
Boulanger. *See* Baker
Bouquet garni, 92–93, 422
Boysenberry (mûre de Boysen), 184
Brains (cervelles), 323–325
Braisage à blanc. *See* White braising
Braisage à blond. *See* Blond braising
Braisage à brun. *See* Brown braising
Braising (braiser), 432–435
Brassicas, 79–89. *See also specific types*
Bridage. *See* Trussing
Brill (barbue), 276
Brioche pastry (pâte à brioche), 387–392
British primal cuts, 317
Broad beans (fèves), 135
Broccoli, 79–80
Broiling (gratiner), 441
Brouillé. *See* Scrambled eggs
Brown braising (braisage à brun), 433, 434, 435
Brown game stocks (fonds brun de gibier), 216
Brown mustard, 204
Brown poultry stocks (fonds brun de volaille), 216
Brown stocks (fonds brun), 215–217
Brown veal stocks (fonds brun de veau), 215–216
Browning (gratiner), 441
Brugnon. *See* Nectarine

Brunoise, 44–46, 125
Brunoisette, 47
Brussels sprouts (choux de Bruxelles), 81
Bulb vegetables, 135
Bulbs, 90–100. *See also specific types*
Butcher (boucher), 25
Butcher knife (couteau à batte), 30
Butter, 360
Butter sauce (sauce au beurre), 240
Buttercream (crème au beurre), 406–409
  about, 406
  masquage, 408–409
  preparing, 407
Butterhead lettuce, 117
Buttermilk, 358
Butternut squash (courge musquée), 109

C

Cabbage (choux), 82–87
  about, 82–83
  cooking, 84
  cooking leaves, 85–86
  head, 83
  nutrition, 83
  red, 87
  savoy, 87
  trimming white cabbage, 82–83
  white, 82–83, 87
Cabillaud. *See* Fresh cod
Caille. *See* Quail
Calamari. *See* Squid
California sole, 282
Canard. *See* Duck
Candy-maker (confiseur), 28
Canneberge. *See* Cranberry
Canneler—mushroom
  left handed, 132–133
  right handed, 130–131
Canneler émincer—mushroom, 110–111
Canneleur. *See* Channeler
Cannelle. *See* Cinnamon
Cantaloupe (melon), 188
Capon (chapon), 344
Capsaicin, 102
Capsicums. *See* Bell peppers
Caramelization, 421
Caraway (carvi), 196, 200
Cardamom (cardamome), 196–197
Careers in the kitchen, 12–37
  discipline and the kitchen brigade, 16–20
  equipment, 33
  hygiene and sanitation, 29–30
  kitchen brigade, 20–29
  menu, 35–37
  personal hygiene and appearance, 31–32
  safety precautions, 33–34
  tools, 30–31
  work area preparations, 34–35
  work habits, 32–33

Carême, Antonin, 9, 10, 227
Carrots (carottes)
    about, 136
    bâtonnet, 42
    cuts, classic, 40, 42, 57, 62, 63, 68, 137
    cutting a block, 40
    julienne, 57
    macédoine, 62
    mirepoix, 63
    paysanne, 68
Cartouche, 166
Carvi. See Caraway
Cassia, 198
Cassis. See Black currant
Cauliflower (choux fleur), 87–89
Cédrat. See Citron
Céleri branche. See Celery
Céleri rave. See Celery root
Celery (céleri branche)
    about, 170
    bâtonnet, 44
    brunoise, 44
    cuts, classic, 44, 58, 65, 69, 72, 75, 172
    julienne, 58
    mirepoix, 65
    paysanne, 69
    preparation, 171
    sifflet, 72
    tournés, 75
Celery root (céleri rave), 138
Celery seed (graines de céleri), 197
Cèpe, See Porcini mushroom
Cephalopod, 303
Cerf. See Venison
Cerfeuil. See Chervil
Cerise. See Cherry
Cervelles. See Brains
Chabri. See Goat
Champagne grapes, 187
Champignon cannelé. See Channeled mushroom
Champignon de Paris. See White button mushroom
Champignon tourné, 75
Champignons. See Mushrooms
Channeled mushroom (champignon
    cannelé), 75
Channeler (canneleur), 31
Chanterelle mushroom (girolles), 121
Chapon. See Capon
Charcutier, 25
Cheese, 361–364
    making, 361–362
    odor of, 362
    types, 362–364
Chef de partie. See Station chef
Chef entrepreneurs, 14
Chefs. See also Careers in the kitchen
    corporate executive, 20–21
    female, 18
    international, 18–19
    teaching, 15–16, 17–18
    uniform for, 29–30
Chef's knife (couteau chef), 30
Cherry (cerise), 190–191
Chervil (cerfeuil), 197–198
Cheveux, 42, 142
Chèvre. See Goat
Chevreuil. See Venison
Chicken eggs. See Eggs
Chicken (poulet), 332–344
    about, 332–333
    deboning (désossage), 339–343
    salmonella and, 333
    trimming (habillage), 333–336
    trussing (bridage), 337–339
    types, 344
Chicory (frisée), 117, 118
Chiffonade, 47
Chilean sea bass, 270–271
Chili peppers, bird consumption of, 102
Chinese cinnamon, 198
Chinook salmon, 267
Chives (ciboulette), 198
Cholesterol, 243
Choux blanc. See White cabbage
Choux de Savoie. See Savoy cabbage
Choux rouge. See Red cabbage
Choux. See Cabbage
Choux de Bruxelles. See Brussels sprouts
Choux fleur. See Cauliflower
Choux pastry (pâte à choux), 373–374
Chum salmon, 268
Ciboulette, See Chives
Cinnamon (cannelle), 198–199
Cinq épices. See Five-spice powder
Ciseaux. See Scissors
Ciseler, 47–50
Citron, See Lemon
Citron (cédrat), 175
Citron vert, See Lime
Citrouille, See Pumpkin
Citrus fruits, 175–182. See also specific types
Clams (palourdes), 298
Clarification, with egg whites, 244
Clause, Jean-Pierre, 326
Cleaver (couteau à batte), 30
Clementine, 180
Clingstone peach, 192
Clotted cream, 360
Cloves (clou de girofle), 199
Coagulation, 244
Cod (salted, morue) (fresh, cabillaud), 260
Coho salmon, 267
Cole crops, 79
Color, in cooking methods, 423
Commis. See Junior cook
Common cranberry, 185
Communard, 20
Compagnons, 16

Companion planting, 109

Competitions, culinary, 20

Composed butter (beurre composé), 241

Concasser, 51, 97

Concentration, in cooking methods, 421–422

Concombre. *See* Cucumber

Confire. *See* Preserving

Confiseur. *See* Candy-maker

Confit, 345

Consommé, 244

Cookbooks, history of, 5, 6–10

Cooking careers. *See* Careers in the kitchen

Cooking methods (les cuissons)
    about, 420
    braising, 432–435
    categories by color, 423
    categories by humidity, 423
    categories by type, 421–422
    deep-frying (frire), 435–436
    grilling (griller), 425–427
    pan roasting (poêler), 427–429
    poaching (pocher), 437–438
    roasting (rôtir), 424–425
    sautéing (sauter), 429–431

Cooking school, 4

Coriander (coriandre), 199–200

Corn (maïs), 134

Corn salad. *See* Lamb's lettuce

Corne. *See* Dough scraper

Cornish game hen (poussin), 344

Cornstarch, 226

Corporate executive chefs, 20–21

Costing, food, 35–37

Coupe de légume classique. *See* Vegetable cuts, classic

Courge. *See* Acorn squash

Courge musquée. *See* Butternut squash

Courge spaghetti. *See* Spaghetti squash

Courgette. *See* Zucchini

Couteau à batte. *See* Butcher knife; Cleaver

Couteau à scie. *See* Serrated knife

Couteau chef. *See* Chef's knife

Couteau désosseur. *See* Deboning knife

Couteau d'office. *See* Paring knife

Couteau émincer. *See* Slicing knife

Couteau filet de sole. *See* Sole filet knife

Crab (crabe), 291–293

Cranberry (canneberge), 184–185

Crayfish (écrevisses), 293–294

Cream, 226, 359–360

Crème, as term, 404, 405

Crème Anglaise. *See* Custard

Crème au beurre. *See* Buttercream

Crème brûlée, 6, 8

Crème Chantilly. *See* Whipped cream

Crème Chiboust, 414

Crème d'amande. *See* Almond cream

Crème fraîche, 359, 360

Crème Frangipane, 411

Crème mousseline, 414

Crème pâtissière. *See* Pastry cream

Crèmer method, 365–367

Crèmes, meringues, and other finishings, 404–417
    about, 404–405
    almond cream, 410–411
    baked creams, 405
    buttercream, 406–409
    crème Anglaise, 405–406
    crème Chiboust, 414
    crème Frangipane, 411
    crème mousseline, 414
    fondant, 414, 416–417
    meringue, 414, 415–416
    pastry cream, 412–413
    whipped cream, 409–410

Crenshaw, 189

Crêpe batter (pâte à crêpe), 393–395

Cresson. *See* Watercress

Crisphead lettuce, 117

Croakers, 270

Croissant pastry (pâte à croissant), 387

Crustaceans, 291–298. *See also specific types*

Cucumber (concombre), 104–106
    dégorger, 106
    dépépiner, 105

Cuisine à la vapeur. *See* Steam cooking

Cuisine Classique, La (Dubois), 10

Cuisinier François, Le (La Varenne), 6

Cuisiniere Bourgeoisie, La (Menon), 9

Cuisses de grenouilles. *See* Frogs' legs

Cuissons, les. *See* Cooking methods

Culinary school, 4

Cultured buttermilk, 358

Cumin, 200

Curcuma. *See* Turmeric

Curd, 361–362

Curdling, 251

Curly endive (frisée), 117

Curly parsley, 206

Curry powder, 214

Custard (crème Anglaise), 405–406

Cuts. *See* Primal cuts; Vegetable cuts, classic

Cutting a block, 40–41, 141

D

Dacquoise, 402

Dairy, 355–364. *See also specific types*
    butter, 360–361
    cheese, 361–364
    cream, 359–360
    fermented dairy products, 358–359
    margarine, 361
    milk, 355–358

De-germing garlic, 91

Deboning (désossage), 339–343

Deboning knife (couteau désosseur), 30

Décanter, 429
Decorator (décorateur), 29
Deep-fried eggs (oeufs frits), 247
Deep-frying (frire), 435–436
Degorging (dégorger), 106, 107, 320
Demi-glace, 227
Denerving meats, 305–306
Dents de loup. *See* Wolves teeth
Deputy kitchen chef (sous chef de cuisine), 22–23
Dés, 52
Desert globe artichoke, 159
Désossage. *See* Deboning
Destemming mushrooms, 126
Détrempe, 364, 375–376
Devonshire cream, 360
Dill (aneth), 200
Dinde. *See* Turkey
Dindonneau. *See* Turkey
Direct concentration, 421
Directeur de cuisine. *See* Executive chef
Dishwasher (plongeur), 28
Diver scallops, 300–301
Dog salmon, 268
Doneness, determining by touch, 426
Dorade. *See* Sea bream
Dough scraper (corne), 31
Doughs, basic (pâtes de base), 364–399
    about, 364
    brioche pastry, 387–392
    choux pastry, 373–374
    crêpe batter, 393–395
    croissant pastry, 387
    fritter batter, 395–397
    lining pastry, 365
    pasta dough, 398–399
    puff pastry, 374–386
    risen dough, 387
    savarin pastry, 397
    shortbread pastry, 372
    shortcrust pastry, 365
    sweet shortcrust pastry, 365–372
Dover sole, 278
Dried currants (raisins de Corinthe), 187
Dried mushrooms, 133
Drupes, 189
Dry aging, of beef, 304
Dry environment, 423
Dubois, Felix Urbain, 10
Duck (canard), 344
Dungeness crab, 293

E

Échalote. *See* Shallots
Économe. *See* Vegetable peeler
Ecrevisses. *See* Crayfish
Edible crab, 292–293
Egg whites, 244, 251
Egg yolks, 226, 245
Eggplant (aubergine), 106–108

Eggs, 241–254
    about, 241–242
    adding starch to, 251
    basic cooking techniques, 244–253
    biological function, 242
    cholesterol and, 243
    coagulation, 244
    cooking in their shell, 251
    cooking out of their shell, 251–253
    curdling, 251
    deep-fried, 247
    foaming, 251
    from fowl other than chicken, 244
    grades/freshness, 243
    liquid, frozen, and powdered, 243
    nutrient value, 242
    Oeufs au plat, 245
    omelettes, 248–250
    overheating, 251
    poached, 252
    questions, frequently asked, 254
    salmonella and, 253
    scrambled, 246
    sizes, 242–243
    specialty, 244
    tips, 243
Émincer, 53, 123
Emu eggs, 244
Emulsified sauces, cold and hot (sauces émulsifiée, froide et chaude), 235–241
Endive. *See* Belgian endive
English peas, 134
English sole, 282
English whiting, 275–276
Entrée and hot appetizer cook (entremetier), 26–27
Epinard. *See* Spinach
Equipment, 33
Escalopes, 309
Escargots. *See* Snails
Escoffier, Auguste, 5, 10, 16–17, 227
Essences, 222
Estouffades. *See* Brown stocks
Estragon. *See* Tarragon
European meat cuts, 317–320
European plaice, 277–278
European plum, 193
Evaporated milk, 357
Executive chef (directeur de cuisine), 21
Expansion, in cooking methods, 422

F

Fairly firm potatoes, 142
Faisan. *See* Pheasant
False berry, 182
Farces, 346–354
    à gratin, 346–348
    binding, 348
    fat content, 352
    mousseline de poisson, 349–350

pairing, 352
quenelles, 351
simple, 352–354
as term, 346, 348
Fat content
doughs, 364
farces, 352
milk, 357
Fava beans (fèves), 135
Favism, 135
Feet (pieds), 327
Female chefs, 18
Fennel (fenouil), 201
Fennel root (fenouil), 171
Fenouil. *See* Fennel; Fennel root
Fermentation, 359
Fermented dairy products, 358–359
Feuille de chêne. *See* Oakleaf
Feuille de laurier. *See* Bay leaf
Fiche technique de fabrication, 36–37
Filleting
round fish, 264–266
sole, 282–285
Fines herbes, 198, 213
Firm-fleshed ware potatoes, 141
Firm potatoes, 141
Fish, 254–290. *See also specific types*
about, 254
body shape, 255
braising, 433, 434
cleaning, 256
fat content, 255
flatfish, 276–290
habitat, 254–255
round fish, 257–276
Fish cook (poissonier), 26
Fish fumet (fumet de poisson), 220–221
Five-spice powder (cinq épices), 213–214
Fixed work area, 34
Flat-leaf parsley, 206
Flatfish, 255, 276–290. *See also specific types*
Flavonoids, 175
Flétan. *See* Halibut
Fleur de sel, 210
Florida lobster, 296
Flower crab, 291–292
Foaming, with egg whites, 251
Foie. *See* Liver
Foie gras, 326, 345
Fonds de légumes. *See* Vegetable stock
Fondant, 414, 416–417
Fonds. *See* Stocks, basic
Fonds blanc. *See* White stock
Fonds blanc de veau. *See* White veal stocks
Fonds blanc de volaille. *See* White poultry stocks
Fonds brun. *See* Brown stocks
Fonds brun de gibier. *See* Brown game stocks
Fonds brun de veau. *See* Brown veal stocks
Fonds brun de volaille. *See* Brown poultry stocks

Fondue de tomate, 234–235
Food costing, 35–37
Force feeding (gavage), 326
Forcemeat, 346, 348
Fourchette. *See* Roasting fork
Fowl vs. poultry, 331
Fraise. *See* Strawberry
Framboise. *See* Raspberry
Framboise noire. *See* Black raspberry
Free range chicken, 332
Free range eggs, 244
Free run eggs, 244
Freestone peach, 192
French Bresse chicken, 332
French meringue, 414
French primal cuts, 317–320
Fresh cheeses, 362
Fresh cod (cabillaud), 260
Freshwater fish, 254–255
Frire. *See* Deep-frying
Frisée. *See* Curly endive
Fritter batter (pâte à beignet), 395–397
Friturier. *See* Fry cook
Frogs' legs (cuisses de grenouille), 303–304
Frozen eggs, 243
Fruit vegetables. *See also specific types*
Fruits, 173–193. *See also specific fruits*
citrus, 175–182
grapes and berries, 182–187
melon, 187–189
pears and apples, 173–174
stone, 189–193
as term, 78–79
Fry cook (friturier), 26
Full-blood orange, 181
Fumage. *See* Smoking
Fumaison. *See* Smoking
Fumet de crustacés. *See* Shellfish fumet
Fumet de poisson. *See* Fish fumet
Fumets, 220–222
Fusil. *See* Steel

G

Gagnaire, Pierre, 11
Game (gibier), 328–331. *See also specific types*
brown stocks, 216
ground, 330–331
winged, 328–330
Garam masala, 214
Garçon de cuisine, 28
Garde manger. *See* Pantry supervisor
Garden peas, 134
Garlic (ail)
about, 90
ciseler, 50
de-germing, 91
hacher, 56
peeling, 90
Garnishes, 40, 41, 427, 428

Garniture aromatique. *See* Aromates

Garniture de caisson. *See* Accompanying garnish

Garniture de cuisson. *See* Aromatic garnish

Garniture financière, 428

Gavage. *See* Force feeding

Genoese sponge (biscuit Génoise), 402–404

Gerard, John, 113

Giant bluefin tuna, 274

Gibier. *See* Game

Gibiers à plumes. *See* Winged game

Gibiers à poil. *See* Ground game

Ginger (gingembre), 201

Girolles. *See* Chanterelle mushroom

Glacier. *See* Ice-cream maker

Goat (chèvre, chabri), 316

Golden celery, 170

Golden Delicious apple, 174

Goose (oie), 344–345

Goosefish, 261

Gouffé, Jules, 9–10

Grain fed chicken, 332

Graine de moutarde. *See* Mustard seed

Graines de céleri. *See* Celery seed

Granny Smith apple, 174

Grape (raisin), 185–186

Grapefruit (pamplemousse), 175

Grapes and berries, 182–187. *See also specific types*

Gratiner. *See* Broiling; Browning

Green globe artichoke, 159

Green onions, 95

Green pepper, 207

Green tripe, 327

Grill cook (grillardin), 25–26

Grilling (griller), 425–427

Gros bonnet. *See* Kitchen chef/manager

Groseilles. *See* red currant

Ground game (gibiers à poil), 330–331. *See also specific types*

Guacamole, 101

Guatemalan avocado, 101–102

Guide Culinaire, Le (Escoffier), 5, 17

Guinea fowl (pintade), 329–330

Gull eggs, 244

H

Habiller. *See* Trimming

Hacher, 54–56

Haddock (aiglefin), 261

Half-and-half, 360

Half-blood orange, 181

Halibut (flétan), 276–277

Hard cooked eggs, 251

Hare (lièvre), 330

Head cabbage, 83

Heavy whipping cream, 360

Heirloom plants, 113

Herbes de Provence, 214

Herbs and spices, 194–214. *See also specific types*

High temperature, short time (HTST) pasteurization, 357

Hogget, 312

Hollandaise sauce (sauce hollandaise), 237–238

Holstein cows, 355

Homard. *See* Lobster

Homogenization, 356, 357

Honeycomb tripe, 327

Honeydew (miellée), 188

Horse crab, 291

HTST (high temperature, short time) pasteurization, 357

Huîtres. *See* Oysters

Human evolution, 157

Humid environment, 423

Humidity, in cooking methods, 423

Humpback bass, 270

Humpbacks, 268

Humpies, 268

Hygiene, 29–30, 31–33

I

Ice-cream maker (glacier), 28

Iceberg lettuce (laitue iceberg), 117

Imperial star artichoke, 159

Indian "holy" basil, 195

Indirect concentration, 421

Ingredient list (bon d'économat), 35–36

Intern (stagiaire), 20

International chefs, 18–19

Iodized salt, 210

Irish potato blight, 139

Italian meringue (meringue Italienne), 414, 415–416

Italian parsley, 206

Italian tomato, 114

J

Jackets, 29

Jamaican jerk seasoning, 214

Japanese black forest mushroom (shitake), 122

Japanese blue crab, 292

Japanese plum, 193

Julienne, 57–61, 116, 124

Junior cook (commis), 27

Juniper berry (baie de Genièvre), 201–202

Jus, 425

Jus de veau lié, 227

K

Kaiser pears, 173–174

Key lime, 178

Kidneys (rognons), 322–323

Kipper, 272

Kitchen brigade, 16–29

Kitchen careers. *See* Careers in the kitchen

Kitchen chef/manager (chef de cuisine, gros bonnet), 17, 21–22

Knife cuts, classic. *See* Vegetable cuts, classic

Knife kit (trousse de couteaux), 31

Knives, 30

Kokanee salmon, 268

Kosher salt, 210

L

La Varenne, François Pierre de, 6
Lactose intolerance, 355
Ladyfinger (biscuit cuillère), 399–402
Laitue. *See* Leaf lettuce
Laitue iceberg. *See* Iceberg lettuce
Lamb, 312. *See also* Mutton
    boning leg of lamb for roasting, 313–315
    defined, 312
    North American cuts, 310–316
    tying leg of lamb for roasting, 311
Lamb's lettuce (mâche), 118
Langouste. *See* Spiny lobster
Langoustine, 295
Langue. *See* Tongue
Larder, 431
Lardons, 307–308
Large cranberry, 185
Leaf lettuce (laitue), 118
Leafy greens, 117–120. *See also specific types*
Leek (poireau)
    about, 92
    bouquet garni, 92–93
    cuts, classic, 61, 70, 72, 94
    julienne, 61
    paysanne, 70
    sifflet, 72
Leg of lamb
    boning for roasting, 313–315
    tying for roasting, 311
Légumes, 134
Légumier. *See* Vegetable cook
Lemon (citron), 176–177
Lemon sole (limande), 281–282
Lettuce, 117, 118, 119–120. *See also specific types*
Liaisons. *See* Thickening agents
Lièvre. *See* Hare
Light cream, 360
Light whipping cream, 360
Limanda ferruginea, 281
Limande. *See* Lemon sole
Lime (citron vert), 178
Lining pastry (pâte à foncer), 365
Liquid eggs, 243
Liver (foie), 326
Livre de Cuisine, Le (Gouffé), 9–10
Lobster (homard), 294–295
Loganberry (múroise), 186
Longtail tuna, 275
Lotte. *See* Monkfish
Loup de mer. *See* Sea bass
Lustrer, 426
Luter, 430

M

Mace (macis), 202
Macédoine, 62
Mâche. *See* Lamb's lettuce

Macintosh apple, 174
Macis. *See* Mace
Maïs. *See* Corn
Maillard, Louis Camille, 421
Maillard reaction, 421
Mandarin (mandarine), 179–180
Mange tout. *See* Snow pea
Mangrove crab, 293
Maraschino cherry, 190
Marcassin, 331
Margarine, 361
Marine fish, 254
Marjoram (marjolaine), 202–203
Marmiton. *See* Pot and pan washer
Martin, Patrick, 4–5
Maryse. *See* Rubber spatula
Masquage, 408–409
Massialot, François, 6
Matignon, 427, 428
Mayonnaise, 235–236
Mealy potatoes, 142
Meats, 304–320. *See also specific types*
    braising, 433–434, 435
    denerving, 305–306
    European cuts, 317–320
    North American cuts, 304–316
    nutrition chart, 345
Melon, 187–189. *See also specific types*
Melon d'eau (watermelon), 188
Mendel, Gregor, 134
Mendelian inheritance, 134
Menon, 9
Menthe. *See* Mint
Menu, 35–37
Meringue. *See also* Crèmes, meringues, and other finishings
Meringue, 414, 415–416
Meringue Italienne. *See* Italian meringue
Merlan. *See* Whiting
Mesclun greens (mesclun), 118
Meunière, 286–288, 431
Mexican avocado, 101
Microstomus kitt, 282
Microwave cooking, 441
Miellée. *See* Honeydew
Mignonnette, 42, 144
Milk, 355–358
    fat content, 357
    homogenization, 356, 357
    liquid/drinking, 355–356
    pasteurization, 356
    sources, 355
    types, 356, 357–358
Milk-fed lamb, 312
Milk powder, 358
Millefeuille glaçage, 416–417
Mint (menthe), 203
Mirepoix, 63–65, 422
Mixed cooking methods, 422
Mobile work area, 34–35

Moëlle. *See* Bone marrow

Molecular cuisine, 11

Mollusks, 298–303. *See also specific types*

Monkfish (lotte), 261

Morel mushroom (morilles), 121–122

Morello cherry, 190

Morilles. *See* Morel mushroom

Moro blood orange, 181

Morue. *See* Cod; Salt cod

Mother sauces (sauces mères), 227–235

Mouillage, 429

Mouiller, 429

Moules. *See* Mussels

Mousseline de poisson, 349–350

Mouton. *See* Mutton

Mud crab, 293

Mullet (rouget), 262

Mûre. *See* Blackberry

Mûre de Boysen. *See* Boysenberry

Mûroise. *See* Loganberry

Mushrooms (champignons), 121–133

  about, 121

  brunoise, 125

  canneler (left handed), 132–133

  canneler (right handed), 130–131

  cuts, 75

  destemming, 126

  dried, 133

  émincer, 123

  évider, 127

  julienne, 124

  peeling, 123

  quartering, 129

  turning, 128

  varieties, 121–122

Mussels (moules), 299

Mustard, 292

Mustard seed (graine de moutarde), 203–204

Mutton (mouton), 312, 316. *See also* Lamb

Myrtille. *See* Bilberry

N

Nantaise sauce (sauce nantaise), 240–241

Navel orange, 181

Navets. *See* Turnips

Neckerchief (tour de cou), 29

Nectarine (brugnon), 191

Noix de muscade. *See* Nutmeg

Northern bluefin tuna, 274

Northern cranberry, 185

Nouveau Cuisinier Royal et Bourgeois, Le (Massialot), 6–8

Nouvelle cuisine, 11, 14

Nutmeg (noix de muscade), 204–205

O

Oakleaf (feuille de chêne), 118

Oeufs au plat, 245

Oeufs frits. *See* Deep-fried eggs

Oeufs pochés. *See* Poached eggs

Offal, 320–327. *See also specific types*

Offshore hake, 261

Oie. *See* Goose

Oignons. *See* Onions

Omega-3 enhanced eggs, 244

Omelettes, 248–250

Oncorhynchus, 272

Onions (oignons)

  about, 95

  browned, 215

  ciseler, 49

  concasser, 97

  cuts, classic, 49, 64, 71, 98

  émincer, 53

  mirepoix, 64

  peeling, 95–96

  rouelle, 71

  winter predictions and, 99

Orange

  about, 178–179

  bitter/sour varieties, 179–180

  sweet varieties, 180–181

  uses, 175

Orange douce. *See* Persian orange

Orange sanguine. *See* Blood orange

Oregano (origan), 205

Organic eggs, 244

Organoleptic properties, 420

Origan. *See* Oregano

Oseille. *See* Sorrel

Ostrich eggs, 244

Oyster mushroom (pleurotte), 122

Oysters (huîtres), 299–300

P

Pacific bluefin tuna, 275

Pacific salmon, 267

Paille, 42, 143

Palourdes. *See* Clams

Pamplemousse. *See* Grapefruit

Pan roasting (poêler), 427–429

Panade, 348, 350

Panier. *See* Basket

Pantry supervisor (garde manger), 24

Pants (trousers), 29

Paprika, 205–206

Paring knife (couteau d'office), 30

Parisienne, 66–67

Parophrys vetulus, 282

Parsley (persil), 54–55, 206

  hacher, 54–55

Partridge (perdrix), 329

Pascal celery, 170

Pasta dough (pâte à pâtes), 398–399

Pastèque. *See* Watermelon

Pasteurization, 356

Pastry brush (pinceau), 31

Pastry cook (pâtissier), 28

Pastry cream (crème pâtissière), 412–413

Pastry doughs, 364

Patagonian toothfish, 270–271

Pâte, as term, 364

Pâte à beignet. *See* Fritter batter

Pâte à brioche. *See* Brioche pastry

Pâte à choux. *See* Choux pastry

Pâte à crêpe. *See* Crêpe batter

Pâte à croissant. *See* Croissant pastry

Pâte à foncer. *See* Lining pastry

Pâte à pâtes. *See* Pasta dough

Pâte à savarin. *See* Savarin pastry

Pâte brisée. *See* Shortcrust pastry

Pâte feuilletée. *See* Puff pastry

Pâte levée. *See* Risen dough

Pâte sablée. *See* Shortbread pastry

Pâte sucrée. *See* Sweet shortcrust pastry

Pâtes de base. *See* Doughs, basic

Pâtissier. *See* Pastry cook

Pâtisson. *See* Pattypan squash

Pâton, 364

Pattypan squash (pâtisson), 109

Paysanne, 68–70

Peach (pêche), 192

Pearl onions, 95

Pears (poire), 173–174

Peas (pois), 134–135

Pêche. *See* Peach

Peeling

    cuts, classic, 100

    garlic, 90

    mushrooms, 123

    onions, 95–96

    potatoes, 140

    shallots, 99

Pepper (poivre), 207

Peppermint, 203

Peppers

    bâtonnet, 44

    bell, 102–103

    brunoise, 46

    chili, 102

Perdreaux, 329

Perdrix. *See* Partridge

Persian lime, 178

Persian orange (orange douce), 181

Persil. *See* Parsley

Persillé cheeses. *See* Blue-veined cheeses

Personal hygiene and appearance, 31–32

Petits pois, 134

Pheasant (faisan), 328

Pickling, 104

Pieds. *See* Trotters

Pigeon, 329

Pigeonneaux. *See* Squab

Piment de la Jamaïque. *See* Allspice

Pin bass, 270

Pinceau. *See* Pastry brush

Pink salmon, 268

Pintade. *See* Guinea fowl

Pintadeau, 330

Piquer, 431

Plaice (plie), 277–278

Pleurotte. *See* Oyster mushroom

Plie. *See* Plaice

Plongeur. *See* Dishwasher

Plum (prune), 193

Plum tomato, 114

Plumcot, 193

Poached eggs (oeufs pochés), 252–253

Poaching (pocher), 437–438

Pocher à chaud, 438

Pocher à froid, 438

Pocher à l'anglaise, 438

Pods and seeds, 134–135. *See also specific types*

Poêler. *See* Pan roasting

Poêler à l'ancienne, 429

Poêler en casserole, 429

Poêler en cocotte, 429

Poire. *See* Pears

Poireau. *See* Leek

Pois. *See* Peas

Poisson á l'anglaise, 257–259

Poissonier. *See* Fish cook

Poissonière (fish poacher), 437

Poivre. *See* Pepper

Poivrons. *See* Bell peppers

Pomelo (pomélo), 182

Pomme. *See* Apple

Pommes de terre. *See* Potatoes

Pont neuf, 42, 145

Porc. *See* Pork

Porcini mushroom (cèpe), 122

Pork (porc)

    French cuts, 318–319

    lardons, 307–308

    North American cuts, 306–307

    trotters, 327

Pot and pan washer (marmiton), 28

Potager. *See* Soup cook

Potatoes (pommes de terre), 139–156

    about, 139–140

    allumettes, 144

    bouchon, 148

    categories, 140–142

    champignon, 153–154

    cheveux, 142

    cuts, classic, 41, 66–67, 73–74, 155–156

    cutting a block, 41, 141

    fondante, 149–150

    as food source, 141

    frying cuts, 142–146

    Irish potato blight, 139

    mignonnettes, 144

    paille, 143

    parisienne, 66–67

    peeling, 140

Peru, 156
pont neuf, 145
savonettes, 147
soufflée, 151–152
tournés, 73–74
Poulet. *See* Chicken
Poultry (volaille), 216, 331–346. *See also specific types*
Poussin. *See* Cornish game hen
Powdered eggs, 243
Prawns, 295
Présalé. *See* Salt marsh lamb
Preserving (confire), 441
Pressed, cooked cheeses, 363
Pressed, uncooked cheeses, 363
Primal cuts
British, 317
defined, 304
French, 317–320
Processed cheeses, 364
Prune. *See* Plum
Puff pastry (pâte feuilletée), 374–386
about, 374
bande de tarte, 380–381
bouchées et fleurons, 382–383
détrempe, 375–376
tourage, 377–379
vol-au-vent, 384–386
Pumpkin (citrouille), 110

Q

Quadrillage, 425
Quadriller, 425
Quail (caille), 330
Quail eggs, 244, 330
Quatre-épices, 214
Queen crab, 292
Quenelles, 351

R

Radicchio (trévise), 118
Radish (radis), 157
Ragoût, 431, 435
Raisin. *See* Grape
Raisins de Corinthe. *See* Dried currants
Raspberry (framboise), 186
Raw milk, 356
Re de Coquinaria (Apicius), 6
Red cabbage (choux rouge), 87
Red currant (groseilles), 186–187
Red Delicious apple, 174
Red mullet (rouget), 262
Red snapper (vivaneau/rouget), 262–263
Reduction, 226
Regreening, 181
Rennet, 361
Ripening curd (affinage), 362
Ris de veau. *See* Sweetbreads
Risen dough (pâte levée), 364, 387. *See also specific types*

Roast, trimming, 305–306
Roast cook (rôtisseur), 25
Roasters, 333, 344
Roasting fork (fourchette), 30
Roasting (rôtir), 424–425
boning leg of lamb for, 313–315
tying leg of lamb for, 311
Rognons. *See* Kidneys
Roma tomato, 114
Romaine lettuce (romaine), 119
Romarin. *See* Rosemary
Root vegetables, 135–138. *See also specific types*
about, 135–136
bulb vegetables vs., 135
human evolution and, 157
Rose-colored pepper, 207
Rosemary (romarin), 208
Rôtir. *See* Roasting
Rôtisseur. *See* Roast cook
Rouelle, 71
Rouget. *See* Mullet; Red snapper
Round fish, 257–276. *See also specific types*
about, 255
filleting, 264–266
Roundsman (tournant), 24
Roux, 223–224
Royal Gala apple, 174
Rubber spatula (maryse), 31

S

Sabler method, 367–369
Safety, 32, 33–34
Saffron (safran), 208–209
Sage (sauge), 209
Salmo, 272
Salmon (saumon), 263, 267–269
Salmonella, 333
Salt cod (morue), 260
Salt marsh lamb (presalé), 312
Salt (sel), 209–210, 220
Saltwater fish, 254
Salvelinus, 272
Sand crab, 291–292
Sand dab, 278
Sanglier. *See* Wild boar
Sanguinello blood orange, 181
Sanitation, 29–30
Sariette. *See* Savory
Satsuma, 180
Sauce au beurre. *See* Butter sauce
Sauce béarnaise. *See* Béarnaise sauce
Sauce béchamel. *See* Béchamel sauce
Sauce espagnole, 227
Sauce espagnole grasse, 227
Sauce espagnole maigre, 227
Sauce hollandaise. *See* Hollandaise sauce
Sauce maker (saucier), 24
Sauce nantaise. *See* Nantaise sauce

Sauce tomate. *See* Tomato sauce

Sauce velouté. *See* Velouté sauce

Sauces, basic (les sauces), 222–241

emulsified sauces, cold and hot, 235–241

mother sauces, 227–235

thickening agents, 222–226

Sauces emulsifiée, froide et chaude. *See* Emulsified sauces, cold and hot

Sauces mères. *See* Mother sauces

Saucier. *See* Sauce maker; Sauté cook

Sauge. *See* Sage

Saumon. *See* Salmon

Sauté cook (saucier), 24

Sautéing (sauter), 429–431

Sauter. *See* Sautéing

Sauter en ragoût, 431

Savarin pastry (pâte à savarin), 397

Savory (sariette), 210

Savoy cabbage (choux dé Savoie), 87

Scallions, 95

Scallops (St. Jacques), 300–302

Scampi, 295

Scissors (ciseaux), 31

Scrambled eggs (brouillé), 246

Sea bass (bar, loup de mer), 269–271

Sea bream (dorade), 271

Sea salt, 210

Sea trout (truite de mer), 271

Seafood. *See* Fish; Shellfish

Seasoning, timing of, 424

Seeds. *See* Pods and seeds

Sel. *See* Salt

Semi-freestone peach, 192

Serrated knife (couteau à scie), 30

Set custard creams, 405

Seville orange, 179

Shallots (échalote)

about, 99

ciseler, 47–48

émincer, 53

peeling, 99

Shellfish, 291–303. *See also specific types*

about, 254

crustaceans, 291–298

mollusks, 298–303

Shellfish fumet (fumet de crustacés), 221–222

Shelling beans, 135

Shitake mushroom, 122

Shoes, 30

Shoot vegetables, 159–172. *See also specific types*

Shortbread pastry (pâte sablée), 372

Shortcrust pastry (pâte brisée), 365

Shrimp (crevette), 295, 296–298

Side towel (torchon), 30

Sifflet, 72

Slicing knife (couteau émincer), 30

Smoking (fumage/fumaison), 440–441

Snails (escargots), 300

Snow crab, 292

Snow pea (mange tout), 135

Sockeye salmon, 268

Soft cooked eggs, 251

Sole, 278–288

about, 278

filleting, 282–285

lemon, 281–282

meunière, 286–288

skinning, 279–281

Sole filet knife (couteau filet de sole), 30

Sorrel (oseille), 119

Soup cook (potager), 27

Sour cherries, 190, 191

Sour cream, 359–360

Sous chef de cuisine. *See* Deputy kitchen chef

Sous-vide. *See* Vacuum cooking

Southern bluefin tuna, 274

Spaghetti squash (courge spaghetti), 109

Spare hand (tournant), 24

Spatulas, 31

Spatule en bois. *See* Wooden spatula

Spearmint, 203

Spice Islands, 199

Spices. *See* Herbs and spices

Spider crab, 292

Spinach dock, 119

Spinach (épinard), 119

Spiny lobster (langouste), 296

Spoilage vs. fermentation, 359

Spring lamb, 312

Spring onions, 95

Spring salmon, 267

Squab (pigeonneaux), 329

Squash, 109–112

Squid (calamari), 303

Sri Lanka cinnamon, 198

St. Jacques. *See* Scallops

Stagiaire. *See* Intern

Star anise (badianne), 210–211

Starberry, 184

Starch, 226, 251

Starchy potatoes, 142

Station chef (chef de partie), 23

Steam cooking (cuisine à la vapeur), 440

Steel (fusil), 30

Steelhead salmon, 269

Stewing chickens, 333

Stocks, basic (fonds), 215–222

essences, 222

fonds, 215–219

fumets, 220–222

glazes, 222

jus, 222

salt in, 220

Stone fruits, 189–193. *See also specific types*

Strawberry (fraise), 187

Stretched-curd cheeses, 363

Striped mullet, 262

Sucker lamb, 312

Sucs, 424
Summer melon, 187
Summer squash, 109
"Sweet" basil, 195
Sweet cherries, 190
Sweet green peas, 134
Sweet marjoram, 202–203
Sweet potatoes, 143
Sweet shortcrust pastry (pâte sucrée)
  about, 365
  crèmer method, 365–367
  lining tart pan, 370–372
  sabler method, 367–369
Sweetbreads (ris de veau), 321–322
Sweetened condensed milk, 357–358
Swiss meringue, 414

T

Table layout, 10
Tahitian lime, 178
Taillevent, 6
Tangelo, 180
Tangerine, 180
Tarocco blood orange, 181
Tarragon (estragon), 211
Tart pans, lining, 370–372
Teaching chefs, 15–16, 17–18
Temporary work area, 34–35
Terminology, development of, 5
Thai basil, 195
Thickening agents (liaisons), 222–226
This, Hervé, 11
Thon. See Tuna
Thyme (thym), 211–212
T'ikapapa initiative, 156
Tilapia, 288–289, 292
Tirel, Guillaume, 6
Tomalley, 292
Tomate. See Tomato
Tomato sauce (sauce tomate), 231–233
Tomato (tomate)
  about, 113–114
  brunoise, 45
  concasser, 51
  dés, 52
  émondée, 114–115
  julienne, 116
  as vegetable vs. fruit, 78, 101, 113–114
  vidées, 115–116
Tongue (langue), 326
Tools, 30–31
Toques, 29
Torchon. See Side towel
Touch, determining doneness by, 426
Tour de cou. See Neckerchief
Tourage, 377–379
Tournant. See Roundsman; Spare hand
Tournés, 73–76

Trévise. See Radicchio
Triangle, 77
Trimming (habiller)
  chicken, 333–336
  roast, 305–306
Tripe, 327
Trotters (pieds), 327
Trousse de couteaux. See Knife kit
Trout (truite), 272
True berry, 182
True laurel, 195–196
Truite. See Trout
Truite de mer. See Sea trout
Trussing (bridage), 337–339
Trussing needle (aigulle à brider), 30
Tubers, 157
Tuna (thon), 272–275
Turbot, 289–290
Turbotière, 437
Turkey (dinde, dindonneau), 345–346
Turmeric (curcuma), 212
Turnips (navets), 157–158

U

Ultra-high temperature (UHT) pasteurization, 357
Uniform, chef's, 29–30

V

Vacuum cooking (sous-vide), 439
Valencia orange (Valence), 181
Vanilla (vanille), 213
Variety meats. See Offal
Veal (veau)
  brown stocks, 215–216
  French cuts, 319–320
  North American cuts, 308–309
  sweetbreads, 321–322
  trotters, 327
  white stocks, 218
Vegetable cook (légumier), 27
Vegetable cuts, classic (coupe de légume classique)
  bâtonnet, 42–44
  brunoise, 44–46
  brunoisette, 47
  chiffonade, 47
  ciseler, 47–50
  concasser, 51
  cutting a block, 40–41
  dés, 52
  émincer, 53
  garlic, 50, 56
  hacher, 54–56
  julienne, 57–61
  macédoine, 62
  mirepoix, 63–65
  parisienne, 66–67
  paysanne, 68–70
  peeling, 100

rouelle, 71
shallot, 47–48, 53
sifflet, 72
tournés, 73–76
triangle, 77
Vegetable peeler (économe), 31
Vegetable stock (fonds de légumes), 219
Vegetables, 79–172. *See also specific vegetables*
  braising, 433, 434
  brassicas, 79–89
  bulbs, 90–100
  fruit, 101–116
  leafy greens, 117–120
  mushrooms, 121–133
  pods and seeds, 134–135
  roots, 135–138
  shoots, 159–172
  as term, 78, 79, 113–114
Vegetarian eggs, 244
Velouté sauce (sauce velouté), 227–229
Venison (chevreuil, cerf, biche), 331
Viandier, Le (Taillevent), 6
Vinaigrette, 237
Vivaneau. *See* Red snapper
Vol-au-vent, 384–386
Volaille. *See* Poultry

W

Ware potatoes, 142
Wash-rind cheeses, 363
Watercress (cresson), 119
Watermelon (pastèque), 188
West Indian avocado, 102
Wet aging, of beef, 304
Whipped cream (crème Chantilly), 409–410
Whipping cream, 360
White asparagus, 167
White braising (braisage à blanc), 433–434, 435

White button mushroom (champignon de Paris), 122
White cabbage (choux blanc), 82–83, 87
White mustard, 204
White pepper, 207
White poultry stocks (fonds blanc de volaille), 218
White sea bass, 270
White stock (fonds blanc), 217–219
White veal stocks (fonds blanc de veau), 218
White weakfish, 270
Whiting (merlan), 275–276
Whortleberry, 183
Wild boar (sanglier), 330–331
Williams' Bon Chrétien pears, 173
Winged game (gibiers à plumes), 328–330. *See also specific types*
Winter melon, 187
Winter squash, 109
Wolves teeth (dents de loup), 176–177
Wooden spatula (spatule en bois), 31
Work area preparation, 34–35

Y

Yams, 143
Yearling lamb, 312
Yeast-risen dough, 364, 387
Yellow onions, 95
Yellow tail flounder, 281
Yellowfin tuna, 273
Yogurt, 358–359

Z

Zucchini (courgette)
  about, 110
  bâtonnet, 43
  canneler émincer, 110–111
  cuts, classic, 43, 59–60, 76, 77, 112
  julienne, 59–60
  tonnelet, 111
  tournés, 76
  triangle, 77